The First World War

The First World War

Edited by

JERE CLEMENS KING

A volume
in
DOCUMENTARY HISTORY
of
WESTERN CIVILIZATION

WALKER AND COMPANY

New York

First published in the United States of America
in 1972 by the Walker Publishing Company, Inc.

Published simultaneously in Canada by Fitzhenry &
Whiteside, Limited, Toronto.

Printed in the United States of America.

Volumes in this series are published in association
with Harper & Row, Publishers, Inc., from
whom paperback editions are available in Harper
Torchbooks.

Contents

Chronology of the First World War
adapted from
Ploetz's Epitome of History

1914

June 28. Assassination of Archduke Franz Ferdinand and the Duchess of Hohenberg at Sarajevo, Bosnia, by Bosnian student. Austria suspects Serbia of aiding and abetting plot.

July 6. Kaiser gives Austria free hand in Serbian affair and promises German aid.

July 23. Austrian ultimatum (48 hours) to Serbia delivered at 6 P.M. immediately after Poincaré leaves Saint Petersburg.

July 25. Serbia concedes all of Austria's demands except direct interference in Serbian government action. Austrian ambassador states Serbian reply unsatisfactory and leaves Belgrade.

July 26. Russia declares "premobilization" period. Russia declares she will mobilize on Austrian frontier if Austria crosses Serbian frontier.

July 28. Austria declares war on Serbia and hostilities commence, after Germany and Austria refuse England's invitation to a conference.

July 29. Ultimatum to Belgium dispatched from Berlin. German ambassador demands that Russia cease military preparations. Kaiser and tsar exchange telegrams in a final effort for peace.

July 30. Austria and Russia order general mobilization.

July 31. First day of the Russian general mobilization. Germany declares imminent-danger-of-war situation. (*Kriegsgefahrzustand*). German ultimatum to France.

Sazonov engages to stop Russia's military preparations if Austria respects Serbian sovereignty. Formula refused by Germany.

Aug. 1. Germany formally declares war on Russia, and troops are ordered mobilized.

France mobilizes.

Aug. 3. Germany declares war on France.

German troops enter Belgium.

Italy proclaims her neutrality.

Aug. 4. England's ultimatum to Germany demanding the latter's attitude respecting Belgian neutrality.

War declared by England on Germany.

President Wilson proclaims the neutrality of the United States.

Aug. 7. Germans occupy Liège although the forts still hold out.

Source: Adapted from *Manual of Universal History* (Boston: Houghton Mifflin Company), pp. 709–743. Reprinted by permission of the publisher.

Aug. 23. Japan in state of war with Germany. British army engaged at Mons.

Aug. 25. Louvain partially destroyed by the Germans.

Aug. 27. Russians defeated by Hindenburg at Tannenberg.

Aug. 30. Germans capture Amiens.

Sept. 2. Allies hold the line of the Seine, the Marne, and the Meuse above Verdun.

Austrians defeated with heavy losses by Russians at Lemberg.

Sept. 3. Troops of the Allies assume the offensive, the Germans approaching the valley of the Marne.

Sept. 5. Pact of London concluded by England, France, and Russia, each agreeing not to conclude separate peace.

Sept. 6. Battle of the Marne begins.

Sept. 12. Allies advance against German intrenchments on the Aisne.

Sept. 19. Allies move to turn the German right flank, the latter making vigorous counterattacks. "Race to the Sea" begins.

Oct. 21. Allies maintain lines in southern Belgium.

Oct. 29. Turkish warships bombard Russian ports on the Black Sea.

Nov. 1. German squadron victorious in naval battle with British off the coast of Chile.

Nov. 14. Sir George Buchanan informs Sazonov that Russia may have Constantinople and the Straits.

Dec. 8. Four German cruisers sunk by British fleet off Falkland Islands.

Dec. 13. Austro-German counteroffensive in Galicia begins.

Dec. 15. Serbians reoccupy Belgrade.

Dec. 29. President Wilson protests against detention of American ships in search for contraband.

1915

Feb. 2. Great Britain places all goods on contraband list.

Feb. 4. Germany proclaims the waters around Great Britain, including the whole English Channel, a war zone after Feb. 18.

Feb. 10. United States warns Great Britain and Germany not to abuse flag nor to attack American ships.

Feb. 18. Germans begin submarine "blockade" by sinking British collier without warning.

Mar. 2. Great Britain declares virtual blockade of German coast.

Mar. 4. Russia hands a memorandum to France and Great Britain claiming Constantinople, the western coast of the Bosphorus, and the Dardanelles.

Mar. 12. Great Britain and France assent to the Russian annexation of Constantinople, etc. Russia to recognize French and British interests in Asia Minor; Constantinople to be made a free port; the Straits open to merchant ships; England to occupy the larger part of the "neutral" zone in Persia, etc.

Apr. 11. German ambassador calls upon American people to stop export of arms to Allies.

Apr. 26. Allies land armies at the Dardanelles.
Great Britain, Russia, France, and Italy sign a secret treaty in London. Italy to receive the Trentino, South Tyrol, Trieste, Istria, Gorizia, Gradisca, Saseno, the Dodecanese Islands; potential territory or concessions in Adalia, Eritrea, Somaliland, and Libya. Italy to begin hostilities within a month.

May 7. British liner *Lusitania* sunk by German submarine off Kinsale, Ireland, 1,396 persons, including about 100 Americans, being lost.

May 13. President Wilson sends stern note to Germany demanding reparation for loss of American lives on the *Lusitania* and insisting that submarine attacks on merchant vessels carrying noncombatants stop at once.

May 23. Italy declares war on Austria.

June 22. Austro-German forces occupy Lemberg, Russian army having abandoned Galician capital.

Aug. 4. British reply to American protest against blockade received. It upholds the blockade as strictly within international law, but is willing to submit disputed cases of seizure to arbitration. Germans assail Warsaw's outer forts.

Sept. 1. Germany agrees to sink no more liners without warning.

Oct. 2. Agreement between Bulgaria and the Central Powers. Bulgaria to enter the war on the 15th.

Oct. 6. French and British troops landed at Salonika, Greece. Greek king dismisses Premier Venizelos. Forms coalition cabinet.

Oct. 7. Austro-German invasion of Serbia begins.

Oct. 10. Bulgarians invade Serbia.

Dec. 4. Greece grants Allies right to use Macedonia for military purposes.

Dec. 5. Bulgarians take Monastir.

Dec. 7. Anglo-French army in the Balkans retires toward its base in Salonika.

Dec. 20. British withdraw Anzac army, estimated at 100,000 men, from Gallipoli.

1916

Jan. 6. British Parliament votes in favor of compulsory military service bill.

Feb. 21. Germans begin new attack against Verdun.

Mar. 24. French steamer *Sussex* torpedoed with Americans on board.

Apr. 10. German general offensive begins on 13-mile front, from Hill 304 to Fort Douaumont, Verdun.

Apr. 26. France and England conclude secret agreement with Russia, relative to Asiatic Turkey. England to obtain southern Mesopotamia, with Baghdad, and two ports in Syria. France to obtain Syria, the Adana vilayet, and western Kurdistan. Russia to obtain Trebizond, Erzerum, Bitlis, Van, and territory in southern Kurdistan. An Arab state or confederation of states to be formed. Palestine to be subject to a special regime.

Apr. 29. General Townshend surrenders Kut-el-Amarna to the Turks.

May 4. Germany in note to the United States maintains that the use of the submarine in self-defense cannot be abandoned.

May 9–16. Secret Anglo-French (Sykes-Picot) treaty relative to Turkey. Both Powers "are prepared to accord recognition and protection to an independent Arab or a Confederation of Arab States"; England to obtain the ports of Haifa and Acre and rights elsewhere; France "is authorized to establish such administration . . . as they desire . . . after agreement with the (contemplated) State or Confederation of Arab States."

May 14. Austrian offensive in Trentino begins.

May 30. Great naval battle in the North Sea off the west coast of Jutland, between British and Germans.

June 6. Fort Vaux, Verdun, occupied by the Germans.

July 1. Allies begin infantry attack in the Battle of the Somme.

Aug. 8. Agreement between Rumania and the Allies giving Rumania the Banat, Transylvania, and Bukowina up to the Pruth.

Aug. 9. Italian forces cross the Isonzo River and occupy Gorizia.

Aug. 18. Great Britain, France, Russia, Italy and Rumania sign treaty. Rumania to begin war within ten days; the Russian and the Allied Salonika army to assist Rumania, who would receive the territory agreed upon on the 8th.

Aug. 27. Italy declares war on Germany as from Aug. 28. Rumania declares war on Austria and invades Transylvania.

Sept. 3. Bulgarian and German troops invade the Dobrudja district of Rumania.

Sept. 15. British break third German line north of the Somme. Tanks used for the first time in battle.

Nov. 23. The Greek provisional government under Venizelos declares war on Germany and Bulgaria.

Dec. 6. Bucharest captured by Germans.

Dec. 18. President Wilson invites the belligerents to announce the terms on which peace might be concluded.

Dec. 26. Germany replies to Wilson's note suggesting that direct discussion between the belligerents in some neutral country seemed the best road to peace. No terms stated.

1917

Jan. 10. Statement of the Allied war aims: the restoration of Belgium, Serbia, and Montenegro; the evacuation of invaded territories in France, Russia and Rumania; the restitution of "provinces formerly torn from the Allies by force"; the liberation of Italians, Slavs, etc.; the "turning out of Europe of the Ottoman Empire"; the reorganization of Europe, guaranteed by a "stable regime and based at once on respect for nationalities and the right of full security and liberty of economic development," etc.

Jan. 22. President Wilson in address to the Senate outlines a program for a "peace without victory."

Jan. 29. German peace terms are sent for the private information of President Wilson: Restitution to France of the part of Alsace occupied by her; the acquisition of a strategical and economic frontier zone separating Germany and Poland from Russia; the restitution of colonial conquests, securing to Germany colonial territory compatible with her population and economic interests; the restoration of occupied France, subject to certain strategic and economic modifications and financial compensation; renunciation of economic obstacles to normal commerce; compensation for German undertakings and civilians damaged by the war; economic and financial salvaging of territory invaded by both sides; and the placing of the freedom of the sea on a secure foundation.

Jan. 31. Germany declares unrestricted submarine warfare in zones surrounding the coasts of the Entente Powers, to begin Feb. 1.

Feb. 3. The United States severs diplomatic relations with Germany.

Feb. 26. President Wilson signs the order for arming merchantmen.

Mar. 1. Interception and publication by British naval intelligence of notorious "Zimmerman Telegram," Germany's note to Mexico proposing a German-Mexican alliance and German support for reconquest by Mexico of lost territory in Texas, New Mexico, and Arizona. Mexico to persuade Japan to change sides in the war. Strong reaction in the United States.

Mar. 11. Secret agreement between France and Russia. Russia to support French demands for Alsace-Lorraine, and the left bank of the Rhine to be constituted a neutral state. In return, France "recognizes Russia's complete liberty in establishing her Western Frontiers."

Mar. 12. Russian Revolution begins; provisional government is formed.

Apr. 2. President Wilson reads war message to Congress and asks for an army of 500,000.

Apr. 6. President Wilson signs resolution declaring a state of war.

Apr. 19-21. Saint Jean de Maurienne Agreement between Great Britain, France, and Italy. Italy gives her assent to the Franco-British agreement of May 9-16. Italy is given concessions in the ports of Alexandretta, Haifa, and Acre. The Anglo-French agreement relative to the Arabian peninsula and the Red Sea is considered "equally applicable to Italy," etc.

May 10. Socialist conference opens at Stockholm.

May 19. Russian provisional government repudiates a separate peace.

July 1. Russians resume offensive in Galicia.

July 17. French retake nearly all Verdun positions previously lost.

July 19. German successes in Galicia. Russian regiments mutiny and abandon their positions.

July 22. Extensive Russian retreat and insubordination of troops. Lvov resigns as premier and is succeeded by Kerensky.

Aug. 2. Brusilov succeeded by Kornilov as commander in chief of Russian armies.

Aug. 19. Italians launch attack from the Isonzo to the sea and carry the entire Austrian first line from Piave to the sea.

Sept. 8. Kerensky dismisses Kornilov, who marches on Petrograd.

Sept. 11. The Russian Council of Workmen's and Soldiers' Deputies votes to support Kerensky and orders the arrest of Kornilov's generals.

Sept. 13. General Kornilov's counterrevolutionary army surrenders.

Oct. 4. British under Haig win victory at Pasachendaele Ridge, near Ypres.

Oct. 22. Kerensky attacked in Petrograd Soviet; Trotsky demands peace.

Oct. 24. Germans re-enforce Austrians on the Isonzo front and defeat Italians northeast of Gorizia, piercing the Italian boundary.

Oct. 29. The Italian Isonzo front collapses and Germans reach outposts before Udine.

Nov. 4. Austro-Germans cross the Tagliamento River in Italy.

Nov. 7. Bolsheviks, with the assistance of the garrison, seize Petrograd, depose Kerensky, and declare for peace.

Nov. 10. The Bolshevik government of Russia makes Vladimir I. Lenin premier and Leon Trotsky minister of foreign affairs.

Nov. 15. Georges Clemenceau made premier of French republic. Bolsheviks defeat government troops near Petrograd. Moscow in hands of the rebels. Kerensky a fugitive.

Nov. 18. Italians stop the Austro-German advance on the Piave.

Nov. 19. Bolsheviks issue offer for immediate armistice for the purpose of discussing a democratic peace.

Dec. 15. Formal armistice between Russia and the Central Powers is signed at Brest-Litovsk.

1918

Jan. 8. President Wilson's address to Congress outlines an American peace program enumerating the "fourteen points."

Jan. 26. Ukraine declares her complete independence.

Feb. 9. Ukraine signs a peace treaty with the Central Powers at Brest-Litovsk.

Feb. 10. Russian government declares the war at an end and orders demobilization.

Feb. 18. Germany resumes hostilities against Russia and moves toward Petrograd.

Mar. 3. Treaty of Brest-Litovsk concluded by the Bolsheviks and the Central Powers.

Mar. 5. Rumania and the Central Powers sign preliminary peace treaty.

Mar. 21. Great German offensive begun from Arras to La Fère along 50 miles of the British and French line.

Mar. 29. French General Ferdinand Foch made commander in chief of the Allied forces in France.

Apr. 4. German offensive renewed near Amiens, but British and French lines hold.

May 27. German offensive renewed after pause since Apr. 30. The attack is southward on a 35-mile front in Aisne sector between Soissons and Reims.

    Chemin des Dames captured.

May 28. American troops in their first important attack capture Cantigny in Picardy.

June 11. In counterattack by French and Americans the marines advance their positions in Belleau Wood, make gains at Château-Thierry, and cross the Marne.

June 15. Austrian armies begin an offensive in Italy on a 97-mile front from Asiago plateau along the Piave to the Adriatic.

June 23. Austrians begin a hurried retreat across the Piave.

July 18. The great offensive of the Allies and the Americans begins. French and American troops attack the western side of the Aisne-Marne salient from Fontenoy to Château-Thierry.

Aug. 3. United States government announces its plan for co-operation with the Allies in aiding the Czecho-Slovak troops in Siberia in their struggle against the Bolsheviks and in guarding the northern ports of Russia from the Germans.

Aug. 11. Organization announced of the first American field army in France under the direct command of General Pershing.

Aug. 15. Secretary of War Baker announces that American toops from the Philippines have landed at Vladivostok to co-operate with Allied forces under Japanese General Otani.

Sept. 3. United States government recognizes the Czecho-Slovaks as associates in the war against Germany and Austria-Hungary and their National Council with headquarters at Washington as a *de facto* government.

Sept. 6. French and British make gains on a 90-mile front, taking Ham and Chauny.

Sept. 12. American army in France carries out its first great offensive, demolishing the Saint Mihiel salient.

Sept. 29. Bulgaria surrenders.

Oct. 1. French troops enter Saint Quentin. British and Arabs occupy Damascus.

Oct. 6. Germany and Austria address pleas for armistice to President Wilson.

Oct. 14. Turkey appeals to President Wilson for armistice.

Oct. 17. British enter Lille and Douai; Germans abandon Ostend.

Oct. 24. Italian army, aided by British and French, opens attack on Austrians between the Brenta and Piave rivers.

Oct. 30. Revolt in Vienna.

    Hungarian republic proclaimed.

    Turkey accepts the conditions imposed by the Allies and signs the armistice.

Nov. 1. Serbians re-enter Belgrade.

Nov. 3–5. Mutiny spreads in German fleet and naval bases, beginning at Kiel.

Nov. 4. Austria-Hungary withdraws from the war.

Nov. 8. German plenipotentiaries receive armistice proposals from Foch at Senlis.

Nov. 9. Chancellor Maximilian von Baden announces abdication of the kaiser and the crown prince and appointment of Friedrich Ebert, vice-president of the Socialist Democratic party, as chancellor pending creation of a "constitutional German national assembly."

Nov. 10. Kaiser William flees to Holland.

A Polish republic is formed at Cracow.

Nov. 11. Armistice signed at Senlis at 5 A.M.; hostilities to cease at 11 A.M. The terms include: Immediate evacuation of invaded countries; repatriation to begin at once of inhabitants of Belgium, France, Alsace-Lorraine, and Luxemburg; surrender of specified war material; evacuation of countries on left bank of Rhine and their occupation by Allied and American garrisons; repatriation of prisoners of war; German troops in territory formerly belonging to Austria-Hungary, Rumania, and Turkey to be withdrawn at once; German troops in Russia to be withdrawn within a period to be decided upon by the Allies; renunciation of the treaties of Bucharest and Brest-Litovsk; immediate cessation of all hostilities at sea.

Introduction

The First World War was not so much a conflagration as a fire storm in which many separate, smouldering issues blazed up and quickly converged into a holocaust of unprecedented intensity and extent. For better or worse (and it seemed to be largely for worse), modern technology had so closely articulated the twentieth-century world that disputes among various nations and peoples which once would have remained localized now spread with dismaying ease.

History was replete with bloody wars, but never before had there been one like this. It was estimated that in the Taiping Rebellion which scourged China between 1850 and 1864 twenty million people lost their lives, but the carnage was restricted to one nation. Between 1914 and 1918 nearly nine million soldiers and thirteen million civilians died in a war fought primarily in Europe, but which spread ultimately to twenty-eight countries. It was waged on all the oceans, in the Near East, and on a small scale in Africa as well as in China. War was fast becoming too dangerous an instrument of policy for a shrinking globe.

There is a consensus among historians that the causes of the war were deep seated and complex. Most agree that no simplistic explanation suffices for such a catastrophe. A dissenter to this viewpoint is the *enfant terrible* of British historians, A. J. P. Taylor, who contended: "Men are reluctant to believe that great events have small causes. Therefore, once the Great War started, they were convinced it must be the outcome of profound forces. It is hard to discover these when we examine the details. Nowhere was there conscious determination to provoke a war. Statesmen miscalculated. They used the instruments of bluff and threat which had proved effective on previous occasion. This time things went wrong." No historian would dispute that "things went wrong" this time, but most historians seem more convinced than Professor Taylor that war was an ever lurking *probability* in the world order of 1914 which was characterized by international anarchy, imperialism cum economic rivalry, repressed nationalism, and militarism.

According to a school of thought expressed by Bertrand Russell in *Freedom Versus Organization,* international anarchy was the root cause of the war. A paradoxical situation prevailed in 1914 in which several score sovereign nations were intricately organized in their own internal structures, yet were grossly deficient in connections of international organization. The tenuous ties of postal, cable, and copyright agreements existing in 1914 hardly provided the necessary checkrein for the caprices of international anarchy. The Permanent Court of International Arbitration which had been established at The Hague in 1899 could exercise jurisdiction over disputes only if the disputants agreed to arbitration. There was no semblance of a League of Nations or a United Nations organization to serve even as a forum for debate. It is true that the system of alliances constricted the otherwise free play of sovereignty of the signatory nations to the extent of a *casus foederis;* but while the counterbalancing of the Triple Alliance of Germany, Austria, and Italy by the Triple Entente of Britain, France, and Russia preserved, for a time, a precarious equilibrium in Europe (the fulcrum of the world's balance of power), once a *casus belli* was alleged the resulting war spread with predictable speed. It has been argued that the system of alliances was in itself a major cause of the war, but this is a dubious contention. As long as there existed the equilibrium provided by the alliances, general war was averted. It was only after the alliance system had been undermined by Italy's virtual desertion of its Austrian and German allies after 1902, by Russia's loss of the war with Japan, and by Austria's progressive weakness due to its disaffected minorities, that Vienna and Berlin resorted to war.

The Marxists (and many others) contend that imperialism and its correlative, economic rivalry, were the basic causes of the war. According to this school of thought, colonies were supposed to lengthen the lifespan of moribund capitalism by providing profitable overseas markets and cheap sources of raw materials and labor, and by furnishing a "safety valve" for excess population which might otherwise have turned revolutionary if left to the resources of the metropolis. Germany was often cited as a classic example. The recently industrialized nation was depicted as a capitalistic parvenu casting about for a means of acquiring status as a world power—"a place in the sun." In addition to striving for European primacy through its maturing economy and its powerful army and expanding navy, the Kaiser's government wanted to overcome the handicap of late entry into the scramble for overseas colonies by creating a German Central Africa which would connect German Southwest Africa with German East Africa. The Moroccan crises of 1904–5 and 1911 were caused by the clash of rival German and French imperialistic and commercial interests, and the resultant war scares demonstrated how precarious the peace was. By the beginning of the twentieth century Germany had become a formidable rival of Great Britain for the markets of Latin America, Africa, the Near East, and Asia. But Germany and Britain were also one another's best customers, a paradox offsetting some of the impact of rivalry. In 1898 the Deutsche Bank of Berlin provided the initial capital for construction of a railway to connect Berlin with Baghdad. This project created alarm not only in British business circles but also in the Admiralty and War Office. There was concern over the prospective outflanking of Britain's "life line to India" which ran through the eastern Mediterranean. The tsarist government was also apprehensive about the construction of the railway, for it portended Russia's being further bottled up in the Black Sea by a German-dominated Turkey. Lenin observed that "imperialism ran along the railroads," referring to the Russian-controlled Manchurian rail line, the German-controlled Berlin-to-Baghdad line, and Cecil Rhodes's proposed Cape-to-Cairo line. By 1914 British and French capitalists were allowed to participate in the construction of the railroad across Anatolia, but for more than a decade mere reference to the Berlin-to-Baghdad railway had rung alarm bells in Paris, London, and Saint Petersburg.

France wanted to recover its "sacred lost provinces," Alsace-Lorraine, with their rich iron ore deposits which would be of great value to French industry. But German industrialists considered Lorraine ore to be equally vital to the Ruhr's metallurgy, and they regarded France's *revanche* as a patent revival of French imperialism. Russia, in search of warm-water ports and sea outlets to expand its export trade and to enable it to become an important naval power, had coveted the Turkish Straits ever since Moscow became the "Third Rome" following the Ottoman conquest of Constantinople in 1453. The doctrine of Pan-Slavism, according to which Russsia was supposed to be the "protector" of all the lesser Slavs—Poles, Czechs, Slovaks, Ruthenians, Serbs, Croats, and Bulgarians—was regarded by the Germans and Austrians as a transparent rationalization of Russian imperialistic designs. When

Austria was excluded from the Italian peninsula in the Austro-Prussian War of 1866, the Hapsburg government sought compensation by a policy of *Drang nach Suden*—a drive to the south through the Balkan peninsula. Austria occupied Bosnia and Herzegovina in 1878, and began pressing for a rail link with the port of Salonika. Again Lenin's dictum that "imperialism ran along the railroads" seemed applicable. Austria's imperialism was on a collision course, not only with Pan-Slavism, but also with land-locked Serbia's objectives of obtaining a port on the Adriatic, and uniting in a kingdom of Yugoslavia those Serbs, Croats, and Slovenes who were alienated subjects of the Hapsburgs. Italy was known to be hankering for *Italia irredenta*, the Italian-speaking border lands under Hapsburg rule. Japan, not content with its recent prize of Korea, was looking for more imperial territory and, once the war broke out, it seized the German naval base at Kiaochow on the Shantung peninsula and German-held islands in the Pacific, such as the Marshalls.

But the phrase, "once the war broke out," is of crucial importance as regards the *causation* of the war, for it points up the fallacy of reasoning *post hoc, ergo propter hoc*. In 1914 there was overwhelming evidence of a drift toward imperialism. And the war itself produced tempting opportunities which revealed latent imperialistic appetites as if through massive Freudian slips. Imperialistic greed was widely shared, but this did not mean that all the nations which became belligerents were equally guilty of seeking a *casus belli* as a pretext for glutting their expansionist appetites. Some were more desirous of being "tempted" than others. During the war Germany's imperialistic voracity was displayed to the world in the rapacious treaties of Brest-Litovsk and Bucharest. That the Allies also succumbed to the lure of imperialism was revealed in the notorious wartime secret treaties which were made public by the Bolsheviks in December, 1917. On March 4, 1915, Russia submitted to its allies, Britain and France, claims to Constantinople, the shores of the Bosphorus, and the Dardanelles, Thrace to the Enos-Midia line, and the islands in the Sea of Marmora, with Imbros and Tenedos. On March 12, Sir Edward Grey, British foreign secretary, approved Russia's claims "subject to the war being carried on and brought to a successful conclusion and to the desiderata of Great Britain and France in the Ottoman Empire and elsewhere being realized." France wanted Russia to agree to the "internationalization" of the Straits, but after encountering Russia's opposition, Foreign Minister Théophile Delcassé acquiesced in Russia's claims on April 10. A second secret pact, the Treaty of London, was signed April 26, 1915, by Britain, Russia, France, and Italy. It enticed Italy from its initial neutrality by promises of the Trentino, South Tyrol, Trieste, Istria, Gorizia, Gradisca, Saseno, and the Dodecanese Islands, as well as potential territory at Adalia, and, on the borders of Eritrea, Somaliland and Libya. This promise was easy for the Allies to make, for it would be primarily at Austria's expense. Austria was naturally reluctant to offer its own territory as an inducement to Italy to honor the Triple Alliance by entering the war on the side of the Central Powers, albeit a year late. Another secret treaty, known as the Sykes-Picot Agreement, was signed by Britain and France on May 16, 1916. It was to be at Turkey's expense. Britain and France agreed to grant "recognition and protection to an independent Arab State or a Confederation of Arab States." France was to obtain Syria, Lebanon, Cilicia, and Mosul, while Britain was to receive Mesopotamia and northern Palestine. The rest of Palestine was to be under an international regime. A fourth secret treaty was signed by France and Russia on March 12, 1917, just before the Russian Revolution. Russia recognized France's claim to Alsace-Lorraine and the Saar valley. Russia agreed further that France could separate from Germany the left bank of the Rhine and constitute there an autonomous and neutral state, to be occupied by French troops until Germany had fulfilled all the obligations to be set forth in a peace treaty. As a *quid pro quo*, France reaffirmed Russia's claims upon Constantinople and the Straits, and its "complete liberty in establishing its western frontiers."

It should be emphasized that proof of comparable imperialistic cupidity brought to light during the war *did not mean equal responsibility for starting the war*. Moreover, Allied imperialistic greed, to a greater extent than Germany's, was susceptible to being curbed, as indeed it was largely checked, partly through America's belated entry into the war professedly "to make the world safe for democracy," and through Bolshevik demands for a peace "without annexations or indemnities." This objective, to a considerable degree, was actually achieved. Whereas in 1914 there were one hundred million Europeans who thought of themselves as "minorities," after the much-debated Treaty of Versailles was signed there were only twenty-five million. But in Africa, Asia Minor, Asia, and in the Pacific, former German and Turkish colonial subjects merely changed masters under the fiction of the colonies becoming postwar "mandates" of Britain, France, and Japan. Most of the French and all of the British territorial acquisitions won by the war were in the underdeveloped regions of Africa, the Near East, or in the Pacific. Germany, by contrast, sought colonial gains, not only in Africa, but also in Europe itself at the expense of Russia, Belgium, and France. Consequently, a German victory would have greatly exacerbated the minorities problem, and moreover it would have shattered the balance of power, for Europe would have been under the hegemony of a single state; whereas an Allied victory guaranteed the continuation of a balance of power, for the Treaty of Versailles provided a polycentered Europe instead of a continent under the ascendancy of one power. Paris of the twentieth century, for example, could not have dominated the continent as a victorious Berlin would have done.

Repressed nationalism is usually cited as one of the underlying causes of the war. When considered in connection with the immediate or the releasing cause of the war—the assassination of Austrian Archduke Franz Ferdinand—it was perhaps the most *decisive* factor. Ambiguity arises from the fact that one nation's "repressed nationalism" is likely to be construed as "imperialistic designs" by a neighboring state. Germany's yearnings for "a place in the sun" may have been regarded as "repressed nationalism" by the Germans, but from Paris it looked suspiciously like imperialistic strivings. France's *revanche* was, in French eyes, merely a recognition of the "repressed nationalism" of the unfortunate inhabitants of Reichsland (as the Germans called the conquered provinces), but viewed from Berlin, it was renewed evidence of the age-old French imperialistic will-to-power. The disaffected Slavic subjects of the Hapsburgs—the Poles, Czechs, Slovaks, Ruthenians, Serbs, Croats, and Slovenes—may have been seething with what they (as well as the Russian and Serbian governments) regarded as repressed nationalism, but viewed from Vienna, Budapest, and Berlin, it was evidence of Pan-Slavic or Greater Serbian agitation or meddlesomeness in another nation's internal affairs.

The South Slavs or Yugoslavs—Serbs, Croats, and Slovenes—were divided between the independent kingdom of Serbia and the Hapsburg monarchy. After 1903, when King Peter of the Austrophobe and Russophile Karageorgevich dynasty succeeded King Alexander Obrenovich following a brutal palace assassination carried out by army officers, Serbian policy became aggressively anti-Austrian. The new dynasty wanted Serbia to perform the same unifying role for the Yugoslavs which in the nineteenth century Prussia had performed for the Germans and Piedmont for the

Italians. Serbia would be the anvil upon which Yugoslav unification would be hammered out by King Peter's resolute policies. Relations between Belgrade and Vienna steadily worsened. In 1906 Austria began a prolonged tariff war against Serbia by closing its frontiers to agricultural exports from Serbia on the pretext that its pork was infected with "swine fever." Landlocked Serbia was more determined than ever, not only to "liberate" its fellow South Slavs, but to obtain a seaport on the Adriatic coast of Albania to end its dependence upon the Austro-Hungarian railway system for its export trade.

In October, 1908, when Austria suddenly announced the annexation of Bosnia and Herzegovina (provinces largely inhabited by Serbs, and still nominally under Turkish suzerainty), Serbian chagrin reached new heights. Some Serbian hotheads clamored for war against Austria then and there, but the Serbian government was sufficiently restrained to ask for compensations by being ceded the Sanjak, which would have linked Serbia with Montenegro and thus with an Adriatic port. Austria refused any territorial concessions to Serbia. Russian Foreign Minister Isvolsky strongly supported Serbia during the Bosnian crisis, for he considered himself as already having been duped by Austrian Foreign Minister Aerenthal who, at a meeting at Buchlau in September, 1908, had led him to believe that the Turkish Straits could be opened to Russian warships in return for Russian acquiescence in the forthcoming annexation of Bosnia and Herzegovina. But before Isvolsky could win approval for the Buchlau agreement from the other signatories of the Treaty of Berlin of 1878, the Austrian foreign minister had perfidiously exploded a bombshell—the annexation of Bosnia-Herzegovina as an accomplished fact. Serbia insisted that the question of the provinces was one of general European interest. In January, 1909, Serbian Foreign Minister Milovanovic warned Austria not to drive Serbia too far. Austria thereupon mobilized, which provoked Russia to offer Serbia its support. When Germany rallied to Austria's side by issuing an ultimatum, Russia had second thoughts and urged Serbia to yield and recognize the annexation. General war was thereby averted at the cost of Slavic pride. Nearly all factions in Serbian politics henceforth regarded a conflict with Austria-Hungary as all but inevitable.

In the First Balkan War of 1912–13, Serbia was stripped of its conquest of the Adriatic port of Durazzo by Austria, which insisted upon the creation of an autonomous Albania. Serbia was outraged at having to surrender its prize. In the Second Balkan

War, Serbia was frustrated again by Austria, for Albania was now converted into an ostensibly independent state under the Teutonic rule of Prince William of Wied. These repeated rebuffs to Serbia lent encouragement to such secret societies as the Yugoslav Club, the Mlada Bosna (Young Bosnia), the Narodna Odbrana (the People's Defense), and the Black Hand. The Black Hand had been organized in Belgrade in May, 1911, by young army officers who were bent upon uniting the South Slavs with Serbia. During the two Balkan wars this Pan-Serbian society influenced Serbian governmental policy, but the Black Hand clashed with Prime Minister Pasich when he established civilian rule in the Macedonian territories won from the Turks. The Black Hand was directed by Colonel ("Apis") Dimitrievich, who began training young Bosnians in terrorist activity in preparation for the day of South Slav "liberation." These fanatics, abetted by the Mlada Bosna, were the ones who plotted the assassination of Franz Ferdinand, but they were not members of the Serbian government. Without the explosiveness of Yugoslav repressed nationalism, the First World War might well have been averted, as other crises had been by-passed or resolved. For as A. J. P. Taylor observed, no war is *inevitable* until it happens. But repressed nationalism was, if not a time bomb, at least a land mine ready to detonate at the slightest pressure.

Militarism, a condition in which military technicians or specialists exercise, usurp, or unduly influence the policy-making functions of government usually performed by civilians, is given as one of the basic reasons for the war. Militarism is generally found in states which exalt martial prowess, live in expectation of fighting, and regard war as the ultimately decisive means by which nations fulfill their destiny. Traces of militarism were discernible in varying degrees in at least half a dozen European countries. In France of the Dreyfus affair, the professional military tried to place the army's "honor" above justice, which all but disrupted the social order. Insular Britain had kept its soldiers on a tight leash ever since its seventeenth-century experience with Cromwell's military dictatorship, but in the person of First Sea Lord Sir John Fisher, Britain had its naval counterpart of Austria's Conrad von Hötzendorf, for Fisher constantly urged a "preventive war" against the growing German fleet. Few of the British took Fisher's rodomontade seriously, but *navalism* remained at least a potential menace. In Austria the chief of staff, Field Marshal Conrad von Hötzendorf, on a score of occasions had advocated a "preventive war" against Italy, a nominal ally, but Conrad's bull-headed aggressiveness was far more dangerous when directed against Serbia, the putative enemy. In the First Balkan War crisis of 1912–13, when Austria-Hungary mobilized to prevent Serbia from acquiring a port on the Adriatic, Conrad clamored for a preventive war against Serbia. Conrad's German counterpart, General Helmuth von Moltke, advocated restraint at that juncture, although he explained that he was convinced that "a European war is bound to come sooner or later, and then it will, in the last resort, be a struggle between Teuton and Slav. It is the duty of all states who uphold the banner of German spiritual culture to prepare for this conflict. But the attack must come from the Slavs." Moltke played a thoroughly irresponsible role in the crisis of July, 1914. On July 31 the Austrian foreign minister, Count Berchtold, who vied with Conrad in pressing for a punitive war against Serbia over the assassination of Franz Ferdinand, was dismayed to learn that German Chancellor Bethmann-Hollweg had undergone a belated change of heart and now cautioned restraint upon learning that England's neutrality was doubtful. Conrad thereupon showed Berchtold a telegram from Moltke, sent without the German chancellor's knowledge, urging immediate Austrian mobilization against Russia to set in train a general European war. Berchtold exclaimed: "That beats everything! Who then rules in Berlin? The chancellor or the General Staff?" The answer was the General Staff—a stark instance of militarism in its most virulent form.

Nor was Russia free from the taint of militarism, although the Russian generals' influence on policy was due more to their professional incompetence and rigidity than to overweening ambition or insubordination, for the Russian military tradition was one of docile obedience to the Tsar. When Foreign Minister Sazonov learned of the Austrian ultimatum to Serbia on July 24, he was enraged. The following day, July 25, at a meeting of the Council of Ministers, Sazonov asked for the mobilization of the Russian army against Austria as a deterrent to an Austrian invasion of Serbia. Sazonov won consent for decreeing a Period Preparatory to War, a questionable move, for not only did it put Russia in the position of being the first nation to mobilize but it was also technically difficult to carry out. For the unimaginative Russian General Staff had drafted mobilization plans upon the fixed assumption that any war against Austria would automatically incur Germany's belligerence. When Austria began its assault upon Belgrade on July 28, Sazonov wanted the Russian army to mobilize at once on Austria's Galician frontier. But Chief of Staff General Janushkevich, and General Dobrorolski, who was in charge of mobilization, bitterly remonstrated against such partial mobilization. They argued that the railway time tables were not adaptable for half measures, and that any attempt to improvise new time tables for partial mobilization would endanger the execution of the rigidly established plans for general mobilization, should that later prove necessary. The weak-willed Tsar Nicholas II was not swayed by his military technicians until July 29, when he learned that the German ambassador to Russia, Pourtalès, had told Sazonov that even a partial Russian mobilization would compel Germany "to mobilize, and in that case a European war could scarcely be prevented."

The tsar had no intention of abandoning all diplomatic-military efforts to deter Austria, and when he realized that even partial mobilization would incur Germany's active hostility, he yielded to his generals' importunities and reluctantly ordered general mobilization. But the vacillating monarch was seized with foreboding at the thought of "the thousands and thousands of men who will be sent to their deaths," and he impulsively canceled the order of general mobilization just before it was to be sent out. Meanwhile he telegraphed his cousin, the German kaiser, to propose submitting the Austro-Serbian controversy to The Hague Court of International Arbitration. The kaiser's notation on the tsar's telegram was "Nonsense!"

On the morning of July 30 General Janushkevich, feeling assured of Sazonov's support, telephoned the tsar and insistently urged him to order general mobilization once again. Nicholas demurred, but he did agree to a conference with Sazonov that afternoon. Disappointed over Germany's refusal even to consider arbitration, the tsar acquiesced in the demands for general mobilization. Sazonov thereupon rushed to a distant telephone and informed General Janushkevich of the tsar's latest change of mind. He concluded the conversation with the words, "Now you can smash your telephone. Give your orders, General—and then disappear for the rest of the day." The Russian military—firmly tied to their railway time tables—thus had the decisive word in Saint Petersburg over a war which Austria had already set in motion by its attack upon Serbia.

It was Serbian militarism which provided Austria with what it claimed to be its *casus belli*. The chief plotters of Archduke Franz Ferdinand's assassination were Serbian army officers, the archconspirator being "Apis," Colonel Dragutin Dimitrievich, the head of the intelligence service of the General Staff, one of the regicides of King Alexander Obrenovich in 1903, a friend of King Peter, and a political enemy of Prime Minister Pasich. The murder of the Hapsburg heir apparent was first proposed by members of the conspiratorial society, the Mlada Bosna, who hated Franz Ferdinand for his enlightened advocacy of "Trialism," a policy of refashioning the Dual Monarchy into a Triple Monarchy with autonomy for the Slavs. This sensible solution to Austria's minorities problem, if ever carried out, would have alleviated much of the alienation of the Serbs, Slovenes, and Croats under Hapsburg rule, and would thereby have diminished their desire to join the kingdom of Serbia to comprise a Yugoslavia. To preclude such a frustration of the Yugoslav dream, the Mlada Bosna society consulted with the Black Hand, whose members were largely army officers who were disgruntled with Pasich's Macedonian policy. The Black Hand leaders, Colonel Dimitrievich and his aide Major Voya Tankosich, managed to suborn six fanatical youths, born in Bosnia but Austrian subjects, to attempt to assassinate Franz Ferdinand. A. J. P. Taylor contends that the real motive of Dimitrievich in doing this was to gain power in Belgrade rather than pursue nationalist ambitions in Bosnia. "He was aiming at Pasich, not at Franz Ferdinand. Dimitrievich wanted a scandal, not a murder." According to this novel interpretation, Colonel Dimitrievich never seriously expected the callow "schoolboys" to succeed in killing the archduke. Rather he assumed that their bungled attempt would enrage Austria and embarrass Pasich, who would either have to repudiate the conspiracy (which would ruin the prime minister with the Serb nationalists) or else support the conspiracy which would make him the mere tool of the Black Hand society and of "Apis."

Whatever his true motive, Colonel Dimitrievich, assisted by Major Tankosich, obtained revolvers and hand grenades from a Serbian arsenal and gave them to the half dozen young "café revolutionaries" who had agreed to carry out the plot.

In May, 1914, Franz Ferdinand had announced his intention of reviewing the army maneuvers in the Bosnian capital of Sarajevo on June 28, which was the anniversary of his marriage in 1900 to his morganatic wife Sophie Chotek. He ignored the notorious fact that June 28 was also Saint Vitus' Day, and in the South Slavic world that meant the "day of national mourning," for on June 28, 1389, the Serbs had been subjugated by the Turks in the Battle of Kossovo. That particular date for the archduke's review of the

Austrian army in sullen and disaffected Bosnia would undoubtedly be construed by the South Slavs as a dangerous provocation. But Franz Ferdinand wanted only to have honors rendered to his beloved wife who, in Vienna, had suffered constant rebuffs as a mere countess at the Hapsburg court. When the archduke acted in his military capacity as inspector-general of the Austro-Hungarian army, full honors were automatically accorded his wife as well as himself. The army was in charge of security during the inspector-general's trip, but it disdained considering even the possibility of serious trouble in a region under its control. Security in Sarajevo was consequently lax, with only one hundred and twenty police assigned to guard the route.

The Pasich government was placed in a quandary when it learned of the archduke's intended trip. Even more disturbing was its discovery of the general outline of the Black Hand's plot. A. J. P. Taylor contends that Pasich had "government agents in the Black Hand just as there were members of the Black Hand in government service. One of them tipped Pasich off." Ljuba Jovanovich, minister of education in the Pasich cabinet, revealed in an article published in 1925 that the Serbian government learned of the plot and discussed it in May or early June. Pasich seems to have assumed that if he arrested the conspirators in Belgrade he "would play Dimitrievich's game," as Taylor expressed it. He therefore decided to send a general warning of the risk of Franz Ferdinand's trip to Leon von Bilinski, the Austro-Hungarian minister of finance, who was also administrator of Bosnia. But Bilinski did not take the warning seriously enough even to pass it on to Franz Ferdinand, or to Emperor Franz Joseph, or to Foreign Minister Berchtold. Pasich also took the precaution of ordering the Serbian frontier officers to intercept any likely conspirators who tried to cross the Bosnian border. Unfortunately the Serbian frontier officers at the point of crossing happened to be members of the Black Hand, and they ignored the orders. The conspirators reached Sarajevo without hindrance on June 3 and were welcomed by a Bosnian teacher, Danilo Ilich, who had been instructed to help them with the details of the plot. Meanwhile, Colonel Dimitrievich had learned of Pasich's interception orders to the frontier officers, and he had second thoughts about the feasibility of his plot. "Apis" belatedly tried to have his contact man with the conspirators in Sarajevo countermand the planned assassination, but the fanatical nineteen-year-old student Gavrilo Princip was determined to prove that *he*, at least, was a resolute Bosnian patriot who would not flinch at the last moment.

Of the six would-be assassins only two made actual attempts on June 28 to kill the archduke, the others being prevented by excitement, fear, the press of spectators, or pity for Sophie Chotek. As the archduke's car was being driven along the Appel Quay beside the river Miljacka, en route to Sarajevo's town hall, one conspirator, a nineteen-year-old printer named Nedjeljko Cabrinovich, threw a bomb at Franz Ferdinand, who managed to deflect it by raising his hand. The bomb exploded behind the archduke's car, wounding an aide of General Potiorek, the governor of Bosnia. Cabrinovich was arrested at once, and the dauntless Franz Ferdinand proceeded to the town hall. Following an incongruous address of welcome by the mayor, the archduke's party set forth by an unscheduled route to visit Sarajevo's museum. The chauffeur took a wrong turn, and after being corrected by General Potiorek, started to back up. At that moment the second conspirator, Gavrilo Princip, emerged from a café and shot at Franz Ferdinand and his wife from a distance of less than six feet, hitting them both. Franz Ferdinand cried out to his wife: "Sophie, Sophie. Don't die. Live for the children." The archduke and his wife died almost at once.

Had Austria *immediately* invaded Serbia in "punishment for the crime of Sarajevo," a shocked and indignant world might have condoned it. But monumental inefficiency and slowness were attributes which the Hapsburg Empire could never overcome. It required at least two weeks for the Austrian army to mobilize, and within a month most people had forgotten the crime. Vienna regarded it as axiomatic that the Serbian government had instigated the murders, but it was thought necessary to prove it first. An official of the Ballhausplatz, Friedrich von Wiesner, was ordered to investigate the plot. Foreign Minister Berchtold and Chief of Staff Conrad von Hötzendorf agreed on June 29 that this time the Pan-Serbian menace would have to be crushed once and for all. The Hungarian premier, Count Stephen Tisza, proved to be surprisingly cautious by insisting first on guarantees of diplomatic support from Rumania and Bulgaria to isolate Serbia before venturing upon a punitive campaign against Belgrade which might easily involve Russia, although no alliance bound Petersburg to Belgrade. Tisza as well as others had doubts about adding still more disaffected Slavs to what was already the Hapsburg Empire's largest ethnic group, yet a war without annexation seemed pointless.

To reassure the advocates of caution, Berchtold turned to Germany for a binding promise of support for any initiative which Austria might take. Even before he was asked by Vienna, the German kaiser had already expressed his convictions as to the proper course to be followed. On July 4, he noted in the margin of a despatch from his ambassador in Vienna, Tschirschky, who had been counseling moderation: "Tschirschky will be so good as to drop this nonsense. We must finish with the Serbs, quickly." On July 5, a special emissary from Vienna, Count Alexander von Hoyos, delivered to the Austro-Hungarian ambassador in Berlin, Szögyény, two documents. The first, prepared by Tisza, stressed the advantage which could be derived from the Serbian crisis by attaching Bulgaria to the Triple Alliance. The second note, in Franz Joseph's handwriting, proposed "eliminating Serbia" as a power factor in the Balkans as the only means of preventing the Dual Monarchy from being swallowed up in the "Pan-Slav flood." Szögyény gave the documents to the kaiser the same day at a lunch at the Neues Palais in Potsdam. The kaiser at first maintained a correct attitude by explaining that he would have to consult his chancellor, Bethmann-Hollweg, before offering Austria advice. But William II was not one to remain reticent for long, and after dining he said to Szögyény: "The attitude of Russia would be hostile in every respect, but [he] had been expecting that for years, and even if war should occur between Austria-Hungary and Russia, [Austria] might be assured that Germany would side with [her], with [Germany's] traditional loyalty to the Alliance. Besides . . . Russia would be totally unprepared for war, and would certainly think twice before issuing a call to arms." The kaiser even went so far as to tell Szögyény that if Vienna decided on military action against Serbia, the Austro-Hungarian army should march at once. The kaiser had thereby given Austria the famous (and eventually fatal) "Blank Check" of unqualified German support of any Austrian initiative. But, as the kaiser acknowledged, it was constitutionally necessary for the chancellor to give his approval to the commitment for it to become effective.

As William had assumed, Bethmann-Hollweg readily agreed with the "Blank Check" when the kaiser spoke with him about it at Potsdam on the same afternoon of July 5. The kaiser then summoned several of his military and naval officials to confirm the preparedness of the armed forces if Germany's "Blank Check" should be cashed. War Minister von Falkenhayn, Adjutant General von Plessen, Head of the Military Cabinet von Lyncker, Admiral von Capelle representing Tirpitz, and Captain Zenker, head of the tactical division of the Navy Staff, all came to Potsdam on the evening of July 5 and the early morning of July 6. The kaiser raised the question of "preparatory measures for war . . . to cover every case" before he departed for his publicized North Sea cruise. Falkenhayn gave "curt" assurance of the army's complete readiness. The kaiser then departed for his cruise "in order not to alarm world opinion." To underscore his conviction of the urgent need of immediate Austrian action against Serbia, the kaiser had his ambassador, Tschirschky, inform Austrian Foreign Minister Berchtold on July 8 that he wanted it "stated most emphatically that Berlin expected the Monarchy to act against Serbia, and that Germany would not understand it if . . . the present opportunity were allowed to go by . . . without a blow struck." The following day, July 9, the German Navy Staff warned the units of the fleet, including the Asiatic squadron, that war between Serbia and Austria was "possible." "It is not impossible that the Triple Alliance will be involved." Germany had thus willingly accepted the calculated risk of a general war in its determination to help Austria shore up its prestige by whatever immediate diplomatic or military measures Vienna thought necessary.

But even the "Blank Check" did not immediately allay the misgivings of Tisza. On July 8 he expressed the view at a ministerial council meeting that an Austrian attack on Serbia would lead to "intervention by Russia and consequently world war." To complicate matters for Vienna's militants, on July 13 Friedrich von Wiesner, who had been conducting the inquest into the responsibility for Franz Ferdinand's murder, wired back from Sarajevo the results of his preliminary investigation: "There is nothing to indicate, or even to give rise to the suspicion, that the Serbian government knew about the plot, its preparation, or the procurement of arms. On the contrary, there are indications that this is impossible." Future disclosures would modify this verdict considerably, but this evidence came after the war had already started.

But, with or without detailed evidence of Serbian guilt, Berchtold, Conrad, and Austrian Prime Minister Stürgkh were determined to humiliate Serbia. And by emphasizing Germany's insistence upon strong action, they were able to win over the hesitant Tisza. By July 14 Tschirschky reported to Berlin that Tisza, theretofore the one Austrian governmental opponent of war with Serbia, was now ready to agree to an Austrian ultimatum to

Belgrade "which would almost certainly be rejected and should result in war."

The Austrian ministry set to work, supposedly in secrecy, preparing its intentionally unacceptable ultimatum. A rumor about it reached the Russian foreign minister, Sazonov, who warned the German ambassador, Pourtalès, on July 21, that if Austria-Hungary "was absolutely determined to disturb the peace, [she] ought not to forget that in that event she would *have to reckon with Europe*. Russia could not look indifferently on at a move at Belgrade which aimed at the humiliation of Serbia." On the same day, the Austrian ambassador to Saint Petersburg, Szápáry, received a guarded warning from the visiting president of the French republic, Raymond Poincaré, who said to him at a diplomatic reception: "With a little good will, this Serbian business is easy to settle. But it can just as easily become acute. Serbia has some very warm friends in the Russian people. And Russia has an ally, France." So Germany and Austria could not complain that they had not been forewarned that Russia and France would support Serbia. But unfortunately for peace, the kaiser, Chancellor Bethmann-Hollweg, Secretary of State Jagow, and General Moltke were all so firmly convinced of Germany's short-run military superiority over Russia that they believed that the time had come to force the issue of Teuton versus Slav. As Jagow expressed it in a letter of July 18 to German ambassador to London, Lichnowsky: ". . . Russia is not ready to strike at present. Nor will France or England be anxious for war at the present time. . . . Russia will be prepared to fight in a few years. Then she will crush us by the number of her soldiers; then she will have built her Baltic Sea fleet and her strategic railroads. Our group, in the meantime, will have become weaker right along." Delay in casting the die would thus be to the detriment of the Central Powers. Russia would either back down ignominiously, or fight and be defeated—such was the conviction of the German and Austrian policy makers.

The Austrian government, notwithstanding Germany's promptings, deliberated for eighteen days before finally submitting to Serbia its ultimatum with demands which, as Hoyos acknowledged to German Chargé d'Affaires Stolberg, "were really of such a nature that no nation that still possessed self-respect and dignity could possibly accept them. . . ." German Secretary of State Jagow was given the text of the ultimatum on the evening of July 22. He proposed to Austrian Foreign Minister Berchtold that the note's delivery to Belgrade should be put back an hour to 6 P.M.,

July 23, to allow ample time for departure by ship from Saint Petersburg of the French visitors, President Poincaré and Premier Viviani, who would thereby be hampered in coordinating French and Russian reaction to the ultimatum.

The note charged that the Serbian government had tolerated anti-Austrian propaganda. The plot, it asserted, had been planned in Belgrade with the complicity of Serbian army officers and government officials. To put an end to such activities, Vienna demanded that Belgrade disavow all anti-Austrian propaganda; express its regrets for the crime; suppress anti-Austrian propaganda, and dismiss all anti-Austrian propagandists; dissolve the Narodna Odbrana (which Vienna confused with the Black Hand); arrest Major Tankosich and "a certain Milan Ciganovich" (who had conveyed the murder weapons from Tankosich to the assassins); punish the Serbian customs officers who had allowed the murderers to cross the frontier into Bosnia; permit Austrian police and members of the Austrian judiciary to take part in the search for the culprits and the suppression of anti-Austrian subversive activity; finally, reply to these demands within forty-eight hours —by 6 P.M., July 25.

When Prince Lichnowsky, the German ambassador to London, showed a copy of the Austrian ultimatum to Sir Edward Grey, the British foreign secretary exclaimed that the note "exceeded anything he had ever seen of the sort before. Any nation that accepted conditions like that would really cease to count as an independent nation." Grey proposed that the four major powers not directly involved—Britain, France, Germany, and Italy—should mediate between Russia and Austria. Grey indicated that Britain "did not wish to mix" in an Austro-Serbian quarrel, but "an Austro-Russian strife meant, in the circumstances, a world war. . . ." He implied British acquiescence in a strictly localized war, if that were possible.

The Serbian government responded to the Austrian ultimatum a few minutes before the expiration of the time limit of 6 P.M., July 25. Belgrade agreed to nearly all of Vienna's demands. It condemned anti-Austrian propaganda, and promised to introduce into the Skupshtina a press law for the punishment of any publication which engaged in such propaganda. It agreed to suppress the Narodna Odbrana "and every other society which may be directing its efforts against Austria-Hungary." Serbia promised "to open an enquiry against all such persons as are, or eventually may be implicated in the plot of 28 June." It demurred over the demand of

allowing Austrian policemen and judges to enter Serbia to participate in the search and trial of the culprits, but it offered to "admit
such collaboration as agrees with the principle of international
law . . . and with good neighborly relations." Assurance was
given that Major Tankosich had already been arrested, and a
search was being made for Ciganovich. The adroit Serbian reply
concluded by proposing that if Austria was "not satisfied with this
reply," the question of the responsibility for the Sarajevo crime
could be submitted to the decision of the International Tribunal
of The Hague, or to the Great Powers which took part in the
settlement of the Bosnian Crisis of 1909.

When the Serbian reply was given to Baron Giesl, the Austrian
ambassador glanced at it and asked for his passports, since the reply was not an unconditional acceptance of every demand. The
following day, July 26, German Ambassador Tschirschky met with
Berchtold and General Conrad von Hötzendorf, the Austrian
chief of staff. Conrad explained that because of the difficult problems of mobilization, he wanted the Austrian declaration of war
against Serbia postponed until August 12. But Ambassador
Tschirschky "warmly supported" the importunity of "the Berlin
authorities" who thought "the utmost rapidity in military operations to be necessary in order to avoid as far as possible the danger of the intervention of a third party." Tschirschky, who had
originally advocated moderation toward Serbia, was only following the hard line which the kaiser had been insisting upon for
weeks. But the mercurial William returned unexpectedly from his
Scandinavian cruise early on July 28 and read the Serbian reply.
According to Professor Imanuel Geiss, "He was quite taken aback
and all his belligerence was suddenly gone." William commented
with delight: "A brilliant performance. . . . This is more than one
could have expected! A great moral victory for Vienna; but with
it every reason for war drops away, and Giesl might have remained
quietly in Belgrade. On the strength of this I should never have
ordered mobilization!" The kaiser dashed off a note to Jagow, his
secretary of state, instructing him to urge Vienna to be conciliatory. He indicated that a military occupation of Belgrade by
Austrian forces would provide an adequate hostage to guarantee
the carrying out of Serbian promises. He apparently entertained
the improbable notion that Serbia would actually agree to surrender its capital without fighting.

William may have turned comparatively pacific for the nonce,
but slower to such conversion was Chancellor Bethmann-Hollweg

who, according to Professor Fritz Fischer, "deliberately deceived" the kaiser by delaying to communicate with Tschirschky until after he had received news of the Austrian declaration of war. Moreover, the chancellor, in his telegram, did not even allude to the kaiser's recent *volte-face* with regard to the removal of "every reason for war" by the Serbian reply. To the contrary, the chancellor instructed Tschirschky: "You will have to avoid very carefully giving rise to the impression that we wish to hold Austria back." Despite the kaiser's last minute vacillation, the German policy continued on its set course of encouraging Austria to make war upon Serbia.

When Sir Edward Grey spoke with Lichnowsky on July 27, he had changed his mind about even the possibility of an Austro-Serbian conflict remaining localized. He attributed Serbia's compliance with nearly all the Austrian demands "to the pressure exerted from Saint Petersburg." He warned that if Austria should "proceed even to the occupation of Belgrade . . . it would then be absolutely evident that Austria was only seeking an excuse for crushing Serbia. . . . It was plain that Russia could not regard such action with equanimity, and would have to accept it as a direct challenge. The result would be the most frightful war that Europe had ever seen. . . ." Grey's prescience was soon borne out by events.

Austria, in its sluggish fashion, plodded ahead with its declaration of war on Belgrade on July 28, and the next day, even before it could mobilize its army, it began a sporadic shelling of the city which ignited the powder train which soon engulfed Europe in flames. Russia, as determined as ever upon a course of deterrence, reacted to the declaration of war by ordering mobilization against Austria alone on July 28, to become effective the next day. But when Pourtalès, the German ambassador to Russia, warned Sazonov on the evening of July 29 that even such partial Russian mobilization "would force" Germany to mobilize, the tsar acceded to his generals' demands for full mobilization, although he soon countermanded the order. Upon learning from his telegraphic exchange with the kaiser that Germany had rejected out of hand his proposal to submit the Austro-Serbian dispute to The Hague Tribunal, Nicholas agreed a second time to full mobilization, to take effect on July 31.

Meanwhile, on July 30 Bethmann-Hollweg, who had been preoccupied with finding a way "to *represent* Russia as the guilty party" and to secure British neutrality, was shaken to learn from

Lichnowsky that Sir Edward Grey had definitely refused to promise British neutrality in return for a German pledge not to acquire
French metropolitan territory but only colonial; to respect Dutch
neutrality and integrity; and as regards Belgium, to respect its
integrity "after the conclusion of the war." Germany would not
promise to respect Belgian neutrality, for that would have precluded the execution of the Schlieffen Plan. Perceiving at the
twenty-third hour that Britain would not accept such terms for its
neutrality, Bethmann-Hollweg belatedly veered about and fell into
line with the kaiser's latest position by wiring Tschirschky on the
evening of July 30 that as regards British attempts to mediate in
Paris and Saint Petersburg: ". . . We stand, in case Austria refuses
all mediation, before a conflagration in which England will be
against us; Italy and Rumania to all appearances will not go with
us, and we two shall be opposed to four Great Powers. On Germany, thanks to England's opposition, the principal burden of the
fight would fall. Austria's political prestige, the honor of her arms,
as well as her just claims against Serbia, could all be amply satisfied
by the occupation of Belgrade or of other places. She would be
strengthening her status in the Balkans as well as in relation to
Russia by the humiliation of Serbia. Under these circumstances we
must urgently and impressively suggest to the consideration of the
Vienna cabinet the acceptance of mediation on the above mentioned honorable conditions. The responsibility for the consequences that would otherwise follow would be an uncommonly
heavy one both for Austria and for us."

Professor Fritz Fischer observed in his book, *Germany's Aims in
the First World War*, that the discovery that Britain would not
accept Germany's terms for neutrality produced on Bethmann-
Hollweg "temporary hesitations and retreats; on the Emperor it
was the opposite." On July 30 William read Lichnowsky's report,
sent the previous day to Jagow, in which Sir Edward Grey was
quoted as saying that Britain "could stand aside as long as the
conflict remained confined to Austria and Russia. But if we and
France should be involved . . . it would not be practicable to
stand aside and wait for any length of time. If war breaks out, it
will be the greatest catastrophe the world has ever seen." Fully
aware that the Schlieffen plan did envisage just such a German
attack upon France, the kaiser reacted violently in his jottings on
the margin of Lichnowsky's cablegram. He called England a
"mean crew of shopkeepers," and Edward Grey a "common cur"
who had made "a threat combined with a bluff, in order to separate

us from Austria and to prevent us from mobilizing, and to shift the responsibility for the war. . . . England *alone* bears the responsibility for peace and war, not we any longer!"

General Moltke, the German chief of staff, upon learning of Russia's partial mobilization on July 30, began pressing Bethmann-Hollweg for immediate German mobilization. The chancellor, however, wanted the full support of the German people, and he was especially apprehensive about the attitude of the peace-minded Social Democrats, who comprised Germany's largest party. According to Imanuel Geiss, "he was anxious to allow the blame for the imminent continental war to fall upon Russia," not only to win Social Democratic support, but also because he hoped "that Britain might still after all remain neutral." Bethmann-Hollweg wanted to wait for Vienna's reply to the "halt in Belgrade" proposal before agreeing to German mobilization. But impatient General Moltke, in a classic example of military usurpation of the policy maker's role, acted behind the chancellor's back by telegraphing Conrad directly: "Stand firm against Russian mobilization. Austria-Hungary must be preserved, mobilize at once against Russia. Germany will mobilize. Compel Italy to do her duty as an ally by compensation." The following day, July 31, Conrad showed Moltke's telegram to Berchtold, who laughingly exclaimed: "That beats everything! Who then rules in Berlin? The chancellor or the General Staff?" A. J. P. Taylor says that the answer was "no one," but H. R. Trevor Roper contends that "the answer was, the General Staff."

The weight of evidence is on Trevor Roper's side. On the evening of July 30, General Moltke and War Minister General Falkenhayn committed Bethmann-Hollweg and Jagow to the promise of a decision to mobilize by noon, July 31. Five minutes before this deadline, word was received from Pourtalès that Russian general mobilization would go into effect that same day, July 31. Imanuel Geiss asserts that "the alibi for German mobilization had finally been provided and Bethmann-Hollweg could make the pronouncement." The kaiser immediately signed a decree proclaiming "the situation of imminent danger of war." That same evening "enquiries" with the effect of ultimata were sent to Saint Petersburg and Paris, and the German Foreign Office began drafting its declarations of war upon Russia and France. Saint Petersburg was warned: ". . . German mobilization must follow in case Russia does not suspend every war measure against Austria-Hungary and ourselves within twelve hours and make us a distinct declaration to

that effect." The deadline was to be noon, August 1. In the ultimatum to France, German Ambassador von Schoen informed Premier Viviani of the demand just made upon the French military
ally, Russia. The German note added the warning: "Mobilization
will inevitably mean war. Did France intend to remain neutral in a
Russian-German war?" Paris was to answer within eighteen hours.
Von Schoen did not actually carry out his additional instructions
to demand a German occupation of Toul and Verdun if France
agreed to neutrality, for the French reply on August 1 was a
guarded one: "France would act in accordance with her interests."
Meanwhile, the French government ordered general mobilization
for August 1, although French troops were to be drawn up at least
ten kilometers inside the Franco-German border to impress upon
Britain France's "defensive" posture.

After receiving a negative reply to the ultimatum to Saint
Petersburg, Germany declared war on Russia on August 1. The
fuse of the alliance commitments and the strategic plans was lit
and now sputtered along its ramified course. To implement the
Schlieffen Plan, which called for knocking out France before
turning with full force upon Russia, the German army invaded
neutral Luxemburg on August 2. On the same day von Below
Saleske, the German minister in Brussels, was told to deliver to the
Belgian government an ultimatum which General Moltke had
drafted as far back as July 26 and which had been sent to Below on
July 29. To justify invading Belgium to execute the Schlieffen
Plan, the German government claimed to be "in receipt of reliable
information relating to the proposed advance of French armed
forces along the Meuse route Givet-Namur." The ultimatum demanded the right of entry of German forces into Belgium "to
anticipate such hostile attack." If, within twelve hours, Belgium
yielded, Germany would restore Belgian independence after the
war with indemnification for damages caused by German troops.
If Belgium declined to suspend its neutrality (guaranteed in the
Treaty of London, 1839, Prussia being one of the signatories),
Germany, in obedience to the "dictate of self-preservation," would
have to treat Belgium as an enemy. The undaunted Belgian government replied at once that "the intentions attributed to France
by Germany are in contradiction to the formal declarations made
to us on August 1, in the name of the French government." If
Belgian neutrality were violated by France, Belgium would resist
as it would any other invader. Imanuel Geiss states that the allegations of French plans of invasion of Germany via Belgium

"from the very beginning . . . were a complete fabrication." Germany began its meticulously prepared invasion of Belgium early on August 4 with an attack on Liège.

The German violation of Belgian neutrality could be justified in world opinion only if it could be presented as a counterstroke against French "aggression." This impression Germany attempted to convey in its declaration of war upon France which Ambassador von Schoen delivered to Premier Viviani on August 3. The declaration stated: "The German administrative and military authorities have established a certain number of flagrantly hostile acts committed on German territory by French military aviators. Several of these have openly violated the neutrality of Belgium by flying over the territory of that country; one has attempted to destroy buildings near Wesel; others have been seen in the district of the Eiffel; one has thrown bombs on the railway near Carlsruhe and Nuremberg. . . . In the presence of these acts of aggression the German Empire considers itself in a state of war with France. . . ." Von Schoen himself later admitted that these allegations were the "product of highly overwrought imaginations."

The Belgian invasion brought Britain into the war alongside France, although London had not been tied by a military alliance to Paris. Lichnowsky reported from London on August 4: "The news that reached here yesterday concerning the invasion of Belgium by German troops brought about a complete reversal of public opinion, to our disadvantage." Lichnowsky noted that apart from some Laborites, the overwhelming majority of members of Parliament approved Sir Edward Grey's speech on British policy. Encouraged by this broad support, Grey, in the early afternoon of August 4, sent an ultimatum to Berlin demanding assurance by midnight that Germany would respect Belgian neutrality. British Ambassador Goschen had a "very painful" conversation with Bethmann-Hollweg, who expressed indignation over Britain's willingness to go to war "just for the sake of the neutrality of Belgium." The chancellor referred to the Treaty of London of 1839, guaranteeing Belgian neutrality, as a "scrap of paper." Germany, he said, must refuse to comply with the British ultimatum on the grounds that "necessity knows no law!"

It was only on August 6 that Austria, while lackadaisically pursuing its campaign against Serbia, got around to a belated declaration of war against Russia, notwithstanding Vienna's contention that it was Russia, by its mobilization, which had been threatening Austria-Hungary as well as Germany. The nexus of belligerency now led to Montenegro's joining Serbia August 7 in a state of war against Austria; on August 9 both declared war on Germany. On August 13, France and England proclaimed a state of war with Austria-Hungary. Japan acknowledged a *casus foederis* under the Anglo-Japanese Alliance of 1902 and joined the Entente Powers on August 23. The Central Powers lured Turkey into belligerency by inducing it to bombard Russian Black Sea ports on October 29. Italy was enticed from its neutrality by the Entente Powers on May 23, 1915. Bulgaria declared war on Serbia on October 14, 1915. On March 9, 1916, Germany declared war on Portugal, which had seized several German ships. Rumania was drawn into the war against the Central Powers on August 27, 1916. Greece was maneuvered by the Allies into hostilities against Bulgaria and Germany on November 23, 1916. On April 6, 1917, America declared war upon Germany. Thus the conflagration spread, eventually involving twenty-eight nations, although most of them—China, Cuba, Siam, Liberia, Brazil, and Haiti, for example—became only nominal belligerents.

Controversy over "war guilt" has continued intermittently down to the present day. From the Austrian point of view, the Russian-supported Serbian government, which was alleged to be privy to the assassination plot, was ultimately responsible for the war. Bethmann-Hollweg stated Germany's case in an address to the Reichstag: "Outwardly responsible are the men in Russia who planned and carried into effect the general mobilization of the Russian Army. But in reality and truth the British Government is responsible. The London Cabinet could have made war impossible if they had unequivocally told Petersburg that England was not willing to let a continental war of the Great Powers result from the Austro-Hungarian conflict with Serbia. Such words would have compelled France to use all her energy to keep Russia away from every warlike measure. Then our good offices and mediation between Vienna and Petersburg would have been successful and there would have been no war!" The Allied position on war guilt was set forth in Article 231 of the Treaty of Versailles which stated: ". . . Germany accepts the responsibility of Germany and her allies for causing all the loss and damage to which the Allies and Associated Governments and their nationals have been subjected as a consequence of the war imposed upon them by the aggression of Germany and her allies." The recent book of Fritz Fischer, *Germany's Aims in the First World War,* and the work of Imanuel Geiss, *July 1914: Selected Documents,* swing full circle back to the war guilt assertion of the Treaty of Versailles. Imanuel Geiss contends that ". . . it was Germany who in the last analysis had made war against Serbia possible and thereby introduced the decisive element which made a peaceful solution virtually impossible." While not minimizing Germany's grave complicity, it must nevertheless be said that if Austria had so desired, it could have finally said no to all of Germany's promptings for a war against Serbia which incurred foreseen risks of spreading. Germany may have been the chief instigator, but Austria bears the major responsibility for being the first nation to begin hostilities. To repeat A. J. P. Taylor's dictum, "No war is inevitable until it occurs."

The First World War had enormous consequences for Europe and the rest of the world. In prewar Europe there were only three republics. The war destroyed the Hohenzollern, Hapsburg, and Romanov dynasties and the Ottoman Empire. With the end of hostilities, republics sprouted in Germany, Austria, Russia, Finland, Estonia, Latvia, Lithuania, Poland, Czechoslovakia, Turkey, and, ephemerally, in Hungary. But the germinating seeds of Wilsonian democracy had only shallow roots in most of these states. Bolshevik "democracy" soon became farcical to all but the fanatics and mystics who professed to believe that the "dictatorship of the proletariat" was the infallible determinant of the peoples' will. The German Social Democrats tried for more than a decade to sustain life in the sickly Weimar Republic, but German democracy could not cope with the impact of the World Depression, nor successfully reject Hitler's proffered nostrum of military socialism and the warfare state as the cure for mass unemployment. Within a few years Poland, Estonia, Latvia, Lithuania, and Turkey fell under dictatorial rule, and Hungary reverted to the status of a monarchy with Admiral Nicholas Horthy as regent in name but autocrat in fact. The monarchies of Yugoslavia, Bulgaria, and Rumania were ruled by royal dictators. By October, 1922, the king of Italy was eclipsed by the demagogue Benito Mussolini, who became a dictator by leading "a counterrevolution against a revolution that never really took place," which is the essential feature of fascism. In 1933 Austria became a fascist state under Engelbert Dollfuss. Czechoslovakia was the only "succession state" in which liberal democracy took deep root, and it managed to survive until the "Munich betrayal" of 1938.

The First World War's staggering casualty total of twenty-two million dead—military and civilian—and the twenty-one million wounded represented the cruelest scourge that Europe had suffered since the Black Death. Worse still, the military casualties were selective since the able bodied were the ones singled out for combat and death. The European officer corps, made up largely of members of the privileged, aristocratic class, was decimated. Most of the Russian aristocracy were either slaughtered during the international war or civil war, or became pauperized, or were forced into exile. The postwar republics ended court life for surviving aristocrats, and the nobility's economic base was restricted or destroyed by the land reforms carried out in Eastern Europe.

The war had a leveling effect upon customs and manners. Women, "the world's largest minority group," were enfranchised at last in Sweden, Denmark, Britain, Germany, Russia, Austria, Hungary, Poland, and Czechoslovakia as well as in America and Canada. Some of the grossest extremes of wealth and poverty were narrowed by the planned economies, the taxes, and the *modus operandi* of the welfare state which came in the wake of wartime rationing and economic controls. This was especially true in Britain and Austria. But the power of the state had been vastly increased by wartime exigencies, and that power became a monstrous, totalitarian growth in postwar communism and fascism.

Nineteenth-century optimism and belief in almost automatic progress scarcely survived the war in Europe. Paradoxically, it was in communist Russia, the Eurasian colossus which had been most frightfully ravaged by the war and the ensuing civil conflict, that there was kindled a fanatical hope in a luminous future which existing reality seemed to belie to those who were not "true believers." The successful retention of power by the Russian Bolsheviks, and the messianic mission undertaken by the Third International and the various national communist parties, depressed and frightened the bourgeois and aristocratic classes of Italy, Germany, Austria, Spain, and the Eastern European states, making them a receptive prey to one form or another of fascism which was invariably fobbed off as a "bulwark against Bolshevism."

The other belligerent which emerged from the war with at least a residue of optimism was remote, unscathed America. It was not likely that a nation which had suffered relatively so few casualties, and which had so notoriously battened upon a war boom, would be plunged into hopeless pessimism by the war. This is not to say that America was not disillusioned by the peace, for indeed it was.

German-Americans, Hungarian-Americans, and Italo-Americans
were outraged by the peace terms affecting their lands of origin.
The tribal syndrome still operated. Many idealists thought that
Wilson had made shameless compromises with the Allies. Conservatives and nationalists were repelled by the Wilsonian internationalism embodied in the League of Nations. So, rich and
powerful America, convinced of its invincibility and its basic vir-
tue, turned inward upon itself and seemed intent upon becoming
the hermit nation of the twentieth century.

It was a false dawn of internationalism which appeared over
Geneva, for the League of Nations soon proved to be only the
palest glimmer of world government. The wartime experiences of
belligerents whose trade had been cut off by land fighting or naval
blockade engendered the conviction that self-sufficiency was the
prerequisite of survival in event of another war. With America in
the vanguard, European states began vying with one another to
see whose tariff barriers and import restrictions could be made
the most impenetrable, thereby preparing the way for the World
Depression of 1929, mass unemployment, military socialism, and
Hitler's campaign for *Lebensraum*.

The war weakened the world's center, Europe, and conversely
strengthened (at least relatively) the periphery—North and South
America, Eurasian Russia, Asia, and Africa. Another world war
would accentuate this trend by making America and Russia
emerge as superstates. The Wilsonian—and, in theory at least, the
Bolshevik—concepts of self-determination of peoples may have
conferred self-rule (or misrule) upon seventy-five million Europeans who had not previously enjoyed it, but the hypocritical system of "mandates" framed at the Versailles Conference brought
no such nationalistic satisfaction to the former German and Turkish colonials who had merely exchanged masters. Hundreds of
thousands of colonials had fought in Europe's war—mostly on
the Allied side—and the rankling memory provided a catalyst
which would destroy almost the entire European colonial system
after another bloodletting in the Second World War.

To document fully a war of the scope, magnitude, complexity,
and duration of the First World War would be impossible in a
volume of this restricted size. All that could be attempted was to
select documents which focused upon important facets of the conduct of operations on land, sea, and in the air; upon the attitudes
toward the war among the troops themselves, the intellectuals

and poets, and the women at home; finally, upon some crucial diplomatic issues such as America's entry into the war, Russia's abandonment of the war, and the disputes over the Treaty of Versailles. Such is the intent of this volume.

PART I

Martial Glory:
The Conduct of Operations

---

1. Land Warfare

1. The Schlieffen Plan

THE GERMAN strategy of fighting a two-front war by first defeating France with a massive thrust through neutral Belgium, and then finishing off torpid Russia, was devised by Count Alfred von Schlieffen, chief of the Great General Staff from 1891 to 1905. His celebrated plan, nullified so dramatically in the Battle of the Marne, became a myth invested with diabolical cunning and cynicism in Allied eyes, and with a masterly comprehension of the art of war in German opinion.

The French diplomat Maurice Paléologue revealed that in April, 1904, an early version of the Schlieffen Plan was betrayed to French military intelligence by a German General Staff officer turned spy. A few months later the British government was informed of the plan by French Ambassador Paul Cambon. Although in possession of this indispensable disclosure of the future enemy's intention, the French Deuxième Bureau was so blinded by its excessive devotion to "logic" that it could not believe that the Germans would knowingly risk British hostility, as well as French, by invading Belgium. The precise text of the Schlieffen Plan, in its final form of the draft of December, 1905, was known only by the German Supreme Command until 1953, when the eminent German scholar Professor Gerhard Ritter was allowed to examine Schlieffen's papers, which were among a mass of military documents captured by the Americans in the Second World War and removed to Washington. Professor Ritter, in his book *The Schlieffen Plan: Critique of a Myth*, has revealed how overrated the plan was, either as demonic cunning or as superhuman insight into the conduct of war.

Schlieffen's predecessors as chief of staff, the elder Moltke, Helmuth Karl von and Count Alfred Waldersee, had differing conceptions of waging a two-front war against France and Russia. Moltke envisaged a campaign which would begin with a holding operation against France while a frontal assault would be made upon Russia, after which France would be brought down in a final offensive. The more aggressive Waldersee accepted Moltke's strategy, but, full of fire and brimstone, he wanted to execute it as soon as possible by a preventive war against Russia which Bismarck refused to countenance.

Schlieffen, upon succeeding Waldersee in 1891, reversed the time table and the major objectives of the strategy. He was convinced that France's fortified strong points, which Séré de Rivieres had set at intervals between Switzerland and southern Belgium, could be outflanked through the simple expedient of violating Belgium's neutrality. France could be defeated by a direct thrust from Aachen through Liège, Namur, Saint Quentin to Paris. The intent was not merely to hamstring but to annihilate the French forces, which Schlieffen thought possible by putting to use Europe's densest network of communication in Belgium and northeastern France. The Russian armies would probably prove much more elusive, since they had one-sixth of the earth's surface as their refuge for withdrawal.

Schlieffen's Plan went through some evolutions before crystallizing in draft of December, 1905. At first Schlieffen thought of invading southern Belgium, but to broaden his field of maneuver and to enlarge the circumference of his wheeling operation, he pushed northward the path of penetration until by 1905 he chose southern Holland as the main avenue of invasion to avoid having the German thrust blunted on the Belgian forts of Liège and Namur. With the Low Countries passed and France invaded, the German right wing would then cross the Seine northwest of Paris to prevent its being outflanked from the capital, and to facilitate snaring any French armies which might try to escape to the south of Paris.

The British expert, Captain B. H. Liddell Hart, in his foreword to Ritter's book, points out that Schlieffen was audaciously committing nearly seven-eights of the German attacking forces to the wheeling operation while only an eighth would be left in southwest Germany to hold off a French offensive aimed at crossing the Rhine. This was a "conception of Napoleonic boldness," but, as Liddell Hart comments, feasible as it may have been in Napoleon's day, it was hardly so in 1914. For the German invaders, advancing on foot and with horse-drawn artillery and convoys, would be rounding "the circumference of the circle, [while] the French would be able to switch troops by rail across the chord of the circle." Moreover, the French would have time for demolishing bridges and rail tracks in the path of the invasion. Only mechanized forces and air forces (which Germany so abundantly utilized during the Second World War) could have provided the Germans with the necessary mobility and speed to cancel the French advantage in the use of their railways.

Schlieffen wanted to offset the loss of superiority in speed by an increase in the number of the invaders, and this he hoped to do by reducing the effectives who had been designated for the eastern front and for the defense of southwest Germany, and by using reservists in the spearhead of invasion. This made the success of the plan precarious. Moreover, the invasion of neutral Belgium and Holland (the latter proposal not actually followed in 1914) would increase the number of Germany's enemies, for to the armies of the Low Countries and France would very likely be added those of Britain, drawn in by historical reflex.

By 1905 Schlieffen seems to have realized that these "political factors" might prejudice the chances of success, but he was the embodiment of the narrow-minded technician who left politics to the politicians, even if the political factors negated the merit of his strategy. Strategy cannot be conceived in a political vacuum, and no great strategist would ignore relevant political considerations even if the responsibility for formulating policy lay outside his sphere.

Schlieffen's successor, the younger Moltke, Helmuth Johannes von, has been unfairly taxed with the bungling of the master's plan. But the younger Moltke had the common sense to reduce Germany's future enemies by at least one when he decided against invading Holland as well as Belgium. Moreover, the notorious alteration of the sacrosanct plan by Kluck's decision to veer southeast of Paris instead of crossing the Seine northwest of the capital, was contemplated by no less than the master himself. For Schlieffen saw that he would not have enough forces for so wide a sweep. Again, Moltke's stationing of a number of the newly created corps on the German left wing, thereby weakening the spearhead, was intended by Schlieffen himself, as his papers have recently revealed. In the light of the belatedly available Schlieffen documents, the "master," as Gerhard Ritter discloses, enjoyed an exaggerated reputation for greatness in the art of war.

GERHARD RITTER,
THE SCHLIEFFEN PLAN: CRITIQUE OF A MYTH

TEXT OF THE MEMORANDUM

War against France   Berlin, December 1905
In a war against Germany, France will probably at first restrict herself to defence, particularly as long as she cannot count on effective Russian support.* With this in view she has long pre-

Source: From *The Schlieffen Plan: Critique of a Myth* (London, Oswald Wolff Ltd., 1958), pp. 134–148, 161–167. Reprinted by permission of the publisher.

* *Marginal note by General von Moltke:*
France's offensive or defensive attitude will essentially depend on the *casus belli*. If Germany causes the war, France will probably be on the defensive. If, however, the war is desired and caused by France, she is most likely to conduct it offensively. If France wants to re-conquer the lost provinces, she has to invade them, i.e. take the offensive. I do not consider it altogether certain

pared a position which is for the greater part permanent, of which
the great fortresses of Belfort, Epinal, Toul and Verdun are the
main strongpoints. This position can be adequately occupied by
the large French army and presents great difficulties to the attacker.

The attack will not be directed on the great fortresses, whose
conquest requires a great siege apparatus, much time and large
forces, especially as encirclement is impossible and the siege can
only be conducted from one side. The attacker will prefer to advance on the intervening gaps. Two of them (Belfort–Epinal
and Toul–Verdun) are filled with barrier forts, but these are of
no considerable importance. It matters more that the gaps are
already strong natural positions in which sector lies behind sector,
and which, by the great fortresses on their wings, impede their
envelopment by the enemy, while threatening him with the same
fate himself. The greatest promise of success is offered by an attack on the right wing of the Moselle forts (Fort Ballon de
Servance). But we are not sufficiently prepared to overcome the
difficult terrain here. Even when that has been attended to, one
will hardly wish to open a campaign with a siege of "Ballon de
Servance." In a later period of the war, however, the reduction of
this fort may be of importance.

Another promise of success is offered by an attack on Nancy,
which is protected by field-works and is open to easy envelopment
and bombardment. But after the town and the heights beyond
are taken (Forêt de Haye) we are faced with the fortifications of
Toul. Almost the only advantage of an attack on Nancy is that
in order to save the capital of Lorraine the French might perhaps
be induced to come out of their fortresses and accept open battle.
But they would then have their defence lines so close in their rear
that a defeat would not bring them great damage, nor the victor
great success. It would be a repulsed sortie from a fortress, involving besieger and defender in about the same number of casualties
and leaving the situation of both unchanged.

Therefore a frontal attack on the position Belfort–Verdun offers
little promise of success. An envelopment from the south would
have to be preceded by a victorious campaign against Switzerland

that France will remain on the defensive under all circumstances. However,
the frontier fortresses built soon after the war of '70–'71 stress the defensive
idea. But this does not accord with the offensive spirit ever inherent in the
nation, nor with the doctrines and views now prevalent in the French Army.

and by the capture of the Jura forts—time-consuming enterprises during which the French would not remain idle.

Against a northern envelopment the French intend to occupy the Meuse between Verdun and Mézières, but the real resistance, it is said, is not to be offered here but behind the Aisne, roughly between St. Ménehould and Rethel. An intermediate position beyond the Aire seems also to be under consideration. If the German envelopment reaches even further, it will run into a strong mountain position whose strongpoints are the fortresses of Rheims, Laon and La Fère.

The Germans are therefore confronted with the following:

(1) The position Belfort, Epinal, Toul, Verdun with a continuation along the Meuse at Mézières. Screening troops are pushed out to the Vosges, the Meurthe, Nancy and the Côtes Lorraines between Toul and Verdun.
(2) The intermediate position on the Aire.
(3) The position on the Aisne.
(4) The position Rheims–La Fère.

One cannot have great confidence in an attack on all these strong positions. More promising than the frontal attack with an envelopment by the left wing seems to be an attack from the northwest, directed on the flanks at Mézières, Rethel, La Fère, and across the Oise on the rear of the position.

To make this possible, the Franco-Belgian frontier left of the Meuse must be taken, together with the fortified towns of Mézières, Hirson and Maubeuge, three small barrier forts, Lille and Dunkirk; and to reach thus far the neutrality of Luxembourg, Belgium and the Netherlands must be violated.

The violation of Luxembourg neutrality will have no important consequences other than protests. The Netherlands regard England, allied to France, no less as an enemy than does Germany. It will be possible to come to an agreement with them.*

[Belgium will probably offer resistance.] In face of the German advance north of the Meuse, her army, according to plan, will retreat to Antwerp and must be contained there, this might be effected in the north by means of a blockade of the Scheldt which would cut communications with England and the sea. For Liège

---

* *Marginal note by General von Moltke:*
If our diplomacy manages this, it will be a great advantage. We need the Dutch railways. The value of Holland as an ally would be incalculable.

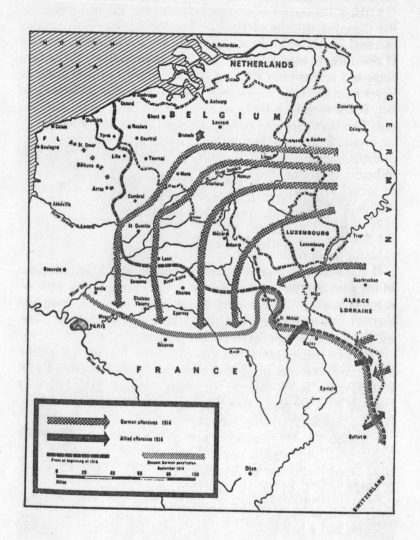

NORTH SEA

NETHERLANDS

River Rhine

GERMANY

Rotterdam

BELGIUM

Ostend Zeebrugge   Antwerp

Ghent   Louvain   Düsseldorf

Dunkirk   Roulers   Brussels   Aachen   Cologne

Calais   Ypres   Courtrai

Boulogne   St Omer   Lille   Tournai

Béthune   Mons   River Sambre   Namur

Arras   Cambrai   Charleroi   Liège

Abbéville   River Somme   Amiens   St Quentin   Mézières   Sedan   LUXEMBOURG   Trier   Luxembourg   River Moselle

Beauvais   Laon   Soissons   River Aisne   Rheims   Verdun   Metz   Saarbrucken   ALSACE LORRAINE

Senlis   Château Thierry   Epernay   St Mihiel   NANCY   Epinal   Belfort

PARIS   Bézanne   River Meuse   FRANCE   River Marne   Dijon

River Seine   River Oise   Mosel   SWITZERLAND

German offensives 1914

Allied offensives 1914

Front at beginning of 1914

Deepest German penetration September 1914

0   20   40   60   80   100
Miles

and Namur, which are intended to have only a weak garrison, observation will suffice. It will be possible to take the citadel of Huy, or to neutralise it.

Making a covered advance against Antwerp, Liège and Namur, the Germans will find a fortified frontier, but not a frontier as thoroughly and extensively fortified as that opposite Germany.* If the French wish to defend it, they will be obliged to move corps and armies from the original front and replace them by reserves from the rear, for instance by the corps on the Alpine frontier. But it is to be hoped that they will not be fully successful in this. Therefore they may perhaps give up the attempt to man such an over-extended line and instead take the offensive against the threatening invasion with all the troops they can scrape together. Whether they attack or defend, it is not unlikely that battle will be joined near the frontier Mézières–Dunkirk; and the Germans' task is to muster the greatest possible strength for this battle. Even if it should not take place and the French remain behind the Aisne, a strong German right wing will still be of the greatest value for the operations to come.

If one wishes to make an attack from the rear on the left flanks of the French positions at Mézières, Rethel, La Fère and beyond, it seems expedient to advance exclusively on the left of the Meuse through Belgium, to wheel left beyond Namur and then to deploy for the attack. But one would lack roads for a march on such a narrow front, and even more so railways with which to bring up one's forces. The railway system obliges the German army to deploy mainly on the line Metz–Wesel. Here twenty-three army corps, twelve and a half Reserve corps and eight cavalry divisions are to be assembled, in order shortly afterwards to wheel left against the line Verdun–Dunkirk. During this, the Reserve corps of the northern wing will cover the right flank, particularly against Antwerp, and the Reserve corps of the southern wing the left flank, against an enemy advance left of the Moselle from the line Toul–Verdun. [Accordingly the attack will not be directed exclusively on the flanks, but also on the left part of the front.]

Three and a half army corps, one and a half Reserve corps and

---

* *Marginal note by General von Moltke:*

Liège and Namur are of no importance in themselves. They may be weakly garrisoned, but they are strong places. They block the Meuse railway, whose use during the war cannot therefore be counted upon. It is of the greatest importance to take at least Liège at an early stage, in order to have the railway in one's hands.

three cavalry divisions remain left of the Moselle. To begin with they will attack Nancy, in order to attract as many enemy as possible on themselves and away from the reinforcement of the northern front; later they will co-operate in covering the left flank, or in reinforcing the right.

The strongpoint for covering the left flank will be Metz. Not the Metz of today, nor the enlarged Metz envisaged in the latest projects, but a Metz fortified largely by field-works. Its size will be determined in general by the courses of the Moselle, Saar and Nied; it will be given a strong garrison and Landwehr troops, as well as numerous pieces of heavy artillery, and will be enabled to draw upon itself a considerable part of the enemy's forces.

If possible, the German Army will win its battle by an envelopment with the right wing. This will therefore be made as strong as possible. For this purpose eight army corps and five cavalry divisions will cross the Meuse by five routes below Liège and advance in the direction of Brussels–Namur; a ninth army corps (XVIIIth) will join them after crossing the Meuse above Liège. The last must also neutralise the citadel of Huy, within whose range it is obliged to cross the Meuse.

The nine army corps will be followed by seven Reserve corps, whose main part is intended for the investment of Antwerp while the remainder initially give further cover to the right flank.

Apart from this, there is a further possible reinforcement in the form of two of the army corps remaining on the left bank of the Moselle. They can be brought up by railway (German and Belgian) as soon as the lines are cleared and put into service. These could bring the decision.

Six army corps and one cavalry division, followed by one Reserve division, will be marched against the Meuse sector Mézières–Namur. When they have crossed the river, between fifteen and seventeen army corps will have linked up left of the Meuse.

Eight army corps and two cavalry divisions will advance on the Meuse front Mézières–Verdun. Five Reserve corps [leaning on Metz] will undertake the cover [of the left flank].

Ten Landwehr brigades will follow them north of the Meuse, six south; six will be in the war garrison of Metz, three and a half will be on the Upper Rhine and one in Lower Alsace.

It can be assumed that the German deployment takes place undisturbed. At the most it might become necessary to de-train the Reserve corps of the far left wing farther back instead of, as hitherto planned, on or beyond the Saar above Saarbrücken. It will also be possible to start the advance of the whole army left of the Moselle according to plan. But whether the French army [left of the Meuse, or right of it, or on both banks] will come to meet us or whether it will await our attack—and if so, where—is quite uncertain. But in any case it is important that north of the Meuse the defile between Brussels and Namur is passed *before* a clash with the enemy, so that beyond it the deployment of the nine army corps can develop without interruption. It is therefore essential to accelerate the advance of the German right wing as much as possible. Since there must be a left wheel, the advance of the rest of the army must slow down progressively towards the left.

The German armies advancing right of the Meuse must daily be prepared for a clash with the enemy still on this side of the river. At all times it must be possible to form a front at least strong enough to fight off the enemy, even if he is superior. This will be rendered more difficult by the fortresses of Longwy and Montmédy, which must be taken or at least neutralised; by the wooded mountains which run across the country south of the Semois, and by the extensive woodlands north of this river. The army commanders must be constantly on the alert and distribute the marching routes appropriately. This will be made easier by the fact that the daily marching distances need only be short. The force will only fulfil its task, if it is trained to move and fight in woods and mountainous country.

Having broken through the French fortress belt left of the Meuse, whether after a victorious battle on Belgian territory, or a successful attack on the fortified position, or without meeting serious resistance, the Germans will turn, according to plan, against the left flanks of the French positions at Mézières, Rethel and La Fère. [The forward Meuse position Mézières–Verdun is likely to be evacuated early. Similarly, in the positions on the Aisne and between Rheims and La Fère the French will not wait passively for the attack on their left flanks.] Either they will seek a new position or they will make a counterattack. The latter would suit us better. Once the two corps have been brought up from right of the Moselle the Germans will have united their forces as far as the prevailing circumstances allow. They will march as a closed formation. Their left wing is covered as far as possible, their right wing is strong. The French [who will have had first to assemble their corps] are unlikely to have their whole army in such good order. The position into which they will have been forced by the enemy's envelopment through Belgium will have prompted them to make precipitate moves and more or less unjustified detachments. When the Belgian and French fortresses on the northern frontier and the unfavourable terrain of the Ardennes have been overcome, the Germans' situation must be regarded as the more favourable. Their situation becomes less favourable if the French await the enemy attack in a position or behind a river-line.

It would not be impossible for an army beaten in southern Belgium or northern France to halt behind the Somme, which is connected with the Oise by a canal at La Fère, and there offer renewed resistance. This would lead to a march of the German right wing on Amiens [or even on] Abbeville.

But this is not very likely. Because of the German advance on the Meuse-sector Verdun–Mézières and [further west] beyond Hirson, the French will be pinned to their positions behind the Aisne and between Rheims and La Fère. [These positions are not tenable, however, if from the direction Lille–Maubeuge the Germans march directly on the left flank and rear. The French must cover this flank, or else retreat behind the Marne or the Seine. They will only take the latter course with misgivings. They will hardly decide to give up northern France without a stiff fight. Unless, therefore, they save their honour by a counter-offensive, they will probably prefer to form a defensive flank behind the Oise between La Fère and Paris rather than surrender a great, rich territory, their fine fortresses, and the northern front of Paris. It can hardly be said that it is impossible to take up a position behind the Oise. Since the main position Belfort–Verdun need only remain weakly occupied, the available forces will be enough to defend the Aisne and the Oise. The position behind the Oise may not be very strong in front, but on the left it rests on the colossal fortress of Paris. Even if it is mastered in front, even if the defender retreats behind the Marne or Seine, the victor must still submit to the necessity of investing Paris, first on the northern front and then on other fronts, and is obliged with considerably weakened forces to continue the attack against a more numerous enemy. To dislodge the latter from his new position, he will by-pass the left flank resting on Paris and will thus again have to use strong forces for the investment of the western and southern front of the gigantic fortress.

One thing is clear. Unless the French do us the favour of attacking, we shall be obliged to advance against the Aisne, the Rheims–La Fère position and the Oise, and we shall be forced, no matter whether our enemies hold the Aisne–Oise position or retreat behind the Marne or the Seine, etc., to follow them with part of our army, and with another part to envelop Paris on the south and invest the fortress. We shall therefore be well advised to prepare in good time for a crossing of the Seine below its junction with the Oise and for the investment of Paris, initially on the western and southern front. Make these preparations how we may, we shall reach the conclusion that we are too weak to continue operations in this direction.] We shall find the experience of all earlier conquerors confirmed, that a war of aggression calls for much strength and also consumes much, that this strength dwindles constantly as the defender's increases, and all this particularly so in a country which bristles with fortresses.

The Active corps must be kept intact for the battle and not used for duties in the lines of communication area, siege-work, or the investing of fortresses.

When the Germans reach the Oise, their lines of communication area will extend on the right to the coast and to the Seine below Paris. In front it will be bounded by the Oise and the Aisne as far as the Meuse below Verdun. The course of its boundary from there to the Rhine depends on what progress the French may have made on the right of the Moselle. The lines of communication area will comprise Luxembourg, Belgium, part of the Netherlands and Northern France. In this wide area numerous fortresses must be besieged, invested or kept under observation. Left of the Moselle, the available seven and a half Reserve corps and sixteen Landwehr brigades will be used for this purpose, except for [at the most] two and a half Reserve corps and two Landwehr brigades which are urgently needed [to reinforce the front and] cover the flank and the rear of the main army. (Under no circumstances is it possible to leave an army at Dunkirk, Calais, Boulogne, etc., as cover against an English landing. Should the English land and advance, the Germans will halt, defend themselves if necessary, detach an adequate number of corps, defeat the English and continue the operation against the French.)

It is calculated:

For the investment of Antwerp five Reserve corps (perhaps not enough)

For the observation of

Liège	2 Landwehr brigades.
Namur	2 Landwehr brigades.
Maubeuge	2 Landwehr brigades.
Lille	3 Landwehr brigades.
Dunkirk	3 Landwehr brigades.
Mézières Givet Hirson	1 Landwehr brigade.
Longwy Montmédy	1 Landwehr brigade.

But the railways necessary to supply the army must also be guarded; the great cities and the populous industrial provinces of Belgium and north-western France must be occupied. The whole area must offer the army a secure base. For this the Landsturm must be used. Should there be legal obstacles, the law must be changed immediately on the commencement of mobilisation.

Still greater forces must be raised. We have as many Reserve battalions as infantry regiments. From these and the available reservists, and if need be from the Landwehr as well, fourth battalions must be formed as in 1866; and from these and Ersatz batteries, again as in 1866, divisions and army corps must be formed. Eight army corps can be created in this way. We shall not wait until the need becomes painfully obvious, until operations are forced to a standstill, before undertaking these re-formations, but do it immediately after the mobilisation of the other troops.

Therefore we must make the Landsturm mobile so that it may occupy the whole lines of communication area from Belfort to Maastricht etc., [we must pull out the Landwehr remaining in the fortresses,] and in addition to this we must form at least eight army corps. That is the very least we are bound to do. We have invented conscription and the *Volk in Waffen* and proved to other nations the necessity of introducing these institutions. But having brought our sworn enemies to the point of increasing their armies out of all measure, we have relaxed our own efforts. We continue to boast of the density of our population, of the great manpower at our disposal; but these masses are not trained or armed to the full number of able-bodied men they could yield. [The fact that France with a population of 39 million provides 995 battalions for the field army, while Germany with 56 million produces only 971, speaks for itself.]

The eight army corps are most needed on or behind the right wing. How many can be transported there depends on the capacity of the railways. Those which cannot be brought up on the left of the Meuse and Sambre through Belgium and Northern France must be brought south of Liège–Namur to the Meuse between Verdun and Mézières. If this is not entirely possible either, the rest can be used as required at Metz and right of the Moselle.

One must be able to count on there being available for the advance on the position Aisne–Oise–Paris etc.

Army corps	25
Reserved corps	2½
Newly formed corps	6
	33½ corps

Of these, more than one-third are needed for the envelopment of Paris: seven army corps for the envelopment proper, and six new corps for the investing of Paris on the [western and] southern front. . . .

[If the enemy stands his ground, the attack will take place] on the whole line, but particularly on La Fère, which is invested from two sides; after a success it will be continued against Laon and Rheims, which is open towards the West. [All along the line the corps will] try, as in siege-warfare, to come to grips with the enemy from position to position, day and night, advancing, digging in, advancing [again,* digging in again, etc., using every means of modern science to dislodge the enemy behind his cover. The attack must never be allowed to come to a standstill as happened in the war in the Far East.

France must be regarded as a great fortress. Of the outer *enciente* the sector Belfort–Verdun is almost impregnable, but the sector Mézières–Maubeuge–Lille–Dunkirk is only fortified in

---

* The operations will not necessarily take the course outlined here. The French are capable of repeated counter-offensives. By so doing they will ease the Germans' task. The latter can then make use of the principle "strategic offensive–tactical defensive," particularly at those points were they obliged to give their fronts great width in order to continue the offensive the more vigorously elsewhere, especially on their right wing.

It is also possible that instead of clinging to their positions, the French will retreat to the south in good time. But it is not unlikely that the positions on the Franco-Belgian frontier, before the Aisne, on the Oise, perhaps even on the Somme, will play a certain part and mark the subsequent phases of the campaign.

parts and at the moment almost unoccupied. Here we must try to break into the fortress. When we have succeeded, a second *enceinte*, or at least part of it, will become apparent, i.e. that adjoining Verdun: the position behind the Aisne to Rheims and La Fère. This section of *enciente* can be outflanked from the south, however. The architect of the fortress counted on a German attack from the south of the Meuse–Sambre, but not from north of this river line. Now it will probably be too late to make good this deficiency by extending the fortified line Rheims–La Fère via Péronne along the Somme. The defender can counter the threatened outflanking by an offensive round the left wing of the position at La Fère. It is to be hoped that this counter-attack, which may be accompanied by an advance from the whole front Verdun–La Fère, will fail. The defeated defender can then try to hold the Oise between La Fère and Paris. The defensibility of this river line is open to doubt. If the doubt is well founded, or the French refrain from defending the Oise and allow the Germans to cross the river in strength, the second *enciente* Verdun–La Fère can no longer be held. La Fère, Laon and Rheims, which is open to the west, the whole hill position designed against an attack from the north-east, will be taken, and the Aisne position will have to be evacuated. With this, the Meuse forts between Verdun and Toul, which can offer only insignificant resistance to an attack from the west, will be exposed. Verdun and Toul will become isolated fortresses. The whole French fortress system directed against Germany will threaten to collapse. It is therefore not impossible that in spite of all the shortcomings of the position, the French may try to hold the Oise, and that they may be able to offer successful resistance. In this event we must march round the south of Paris. The same is true if the French give up the Oise and Aisne and retreat behind the Marne, Seine, etc. If they are allowed to go on in that direction, the war will be endless. By attacks on their left flank we must try at all costs to drive the French eastward against their Moselle fortresses, against the Jura and Switzerland. The French army must be annihilated.

It is essential [to the progress of the whole of the operations] to form a strong right wing, to win the battles with its help, to pursue the enemy relentlessly with this strong wing, forcing him to retreat again and again.*

* To force him against his own fortresses or against the Jura and to encircle him. The enemy must not be allowed to slip away to the south to conduct an endless war there. He must be annihilated.

If the right wing is to be made very strong, this can only be at the expense of the left, on which therefore it will probably fall to fight against superior forces.

If success is to be achieved, the right wing must make very great exertions. But the roads to be used are on the whole very good. Quartering, too, should be satisfactory in many localities, unless the right wing corps are forced to march in such close order that even the densest population is not enough [to provide quartering].

On the other hand there can hardly be a shortage of provisions. The rich lands of Belgium and northern France can furnish much, and if they lack anything they will produce it—under suitable pressure—from outside.

The increased strain on Belgium's resources will perhaps decide her to refrain from all hostilities, hand over her fortresses and secure in exchange all the advantages of a disinterested third party in a fight between two adversaries.

On the outbreak of war, three army corps, one Reserve corps and three cavalry divisions right of the Moselle will attack Nancy. Whether this attack succeeds, depends essentially on (whether) the French confine themselves to defence here, or whether, true to their principle, they advance for a counter-attack. If they take the latter course, the main object of the attack on Nancy, namely, to tie down as great a force as possible on the French eastern front, will be achieved. The more troops the French employ for the counter-attack, the better for the Germans. But the latter must not allow themselves to be engaged in prolonged actions, but must realise that their task is to draw as many enemy troops as possible after them and to hold them down with the help of the enlarged Metz. The army cut off on the right of the Moselle can hardly be in any danger; on the other hand it would be damaging to the [German] main army if the army right of the Moselle possessed numerical superiority. The tendency must be to tie down the maximum number of French with a minimum of German forces.

If the French do not counter-attack, two army corps must be despatched to Belgium as soon as possible for the outermost wing of the German army. Everything depends on being strong on this wing. Only when twenty-five army corps have been made available left of the Moselle for this battle, for which one cannot be too strong, can one await the result with a calm conscience.

The small forces which remain right of the Moselle, i.e.

1 army corps
1 Reserve corps
30th Reserve division (Strasbourg)
possibly 2 new corps
Landwehr brigades on the Upper Rhine and from Metz, if
    this is not attacked
59th Landwehr brigade (Lower Alsace)
6 Jäger battalions in the Vosges

must as far as possible be reinforced. The fortress garrisons still offer material for new formations. Also the South German Landsturm can be used to cover the country left of the Rhine, to mask Belfort, etc. A new army must be formed with the task of advancing on the Moselle between Belfort and Nancy, while the five Reserve corps of the left wing and two Landwehr brigades invest Verdun and attack the Côtes Lorraines.

When in the course of deployment the French learn that the Germans are assembling on the Lower Rhine and on the Dutch and Belgian frontiers, they will have no doubt as to the enemy's intention of marching on Paris; they will be wary of advancing with either their entire forces or their main forces between Strasbourg and Metz, and particularly of invading Germany across the Upper Rhine. That would be a case of the garrison leaving the fortress just when the siege was about to begin. Should they do one or the other nevertheless, [it can only be welcome to the Germans. Their task will be made easier. The best thing would be for the French to choose the route through Switzerland to invade southern Germany. This would be a means of acquiring a much-needed ally who would draw part of the enemy force upon himself.]

It will be advisable for the Germans [in all these cases] to change their operational plans as little as possible. But the Lower Moselle between Trier and Coblenz must be covered, and the sector between the Moselle and the Meuse must be blocked level with Diedenhofen. The German army will try to reach the general line Coblenz–La Fère with reserves on the right wing. The right bank of the Rhine from Coblenz upwards will be occupied from the rear. The attack will be made with the right wing.

[If the French cross the Upper Rhine, resistance will be offered in the Black Forest. The troops will be brought up from the rear and assembled on the Main and Iller.]

If the Germans persevere in their operations they can be sure that the French will hastily turn back, and this not north, but south of Metz, in the direction whence the greatest danger threatens. The Germans must therefore be as strong as possible on their right wing, because here the decisive battle is to be expected.

Graf Schlieffen

SCHLIEFFEN'S ADDITIONAL MEMORANDUM
OF FEBRUARY 1906

As a supplement to his deployment plan of December 1905, Schlieffen composed a further memorandum in February 1906, i.e. after his retirement, in which he discussed the measures to be taken if the English intervened in a Franco–German war with 100,000 men or more. It is to be assumed that this memorandum, too, was handed on to his successor Moltke.

If in a Franco–German war the English plan to land a force of 100,000 men or more in Antwerp, they can hardly do so in the first days of mobilisation. No matter how well they prepare the assembly of their three army corps, their army organisation and defence system present so many difficulties that their sudden appearance within the great Belgian fortress is almost inconceivable. But even if they should land at a relatively early stage and issue from the fortress against the Germans, they would find the enemy in occupation of the few roads which lead from Antwerp across the peat bogs of northern Belgium and the southern Netherlands to the northern and eastern front. If they choose the southern front between the Nethe and Dyle as the starting-point of their attacks, they will come up against the eight German army corps which have crossed the Meuse below Liège.

As the German advance proceeds, one fortress front after another will be sealed off. Any attempt by the Anglo–Belgians to repel the investing corps will be frustrated by the support the latter receive from the advancing German army. Until the left wing-corps has completed the investment left of the Scheldt, a number of German army corps will remain available to intervene in any battle.

Most of the country facing the Anglo–Belgian forces is not suitable for sallies. They must work their way out of defiles in order to deploy. The sectors of the fortress zone which favour a sally will be reduced in number if the Belgians carry out their inundation schemes.

If the English plan to advance to the attack from Antwerp, they will be obliged to engage in battles as hopeless as the many sallies made by the French before Metz and Paris. It is necessary, however, that [during the advance on the fortress] the corps intended for the investment should reinforce their position daily [and always be prepared for an attack], getting as close as possible to the enemy's field-works and improving the strength of their positions until they became impregnable. The right and left wings will attempt to get as close as possible to the Scheldt and seal off the [last] seaward escape route of the fortress with batteries and sea-mines.

There is a not unfounded prospect that if the English go to Antwerp, they will be shut up there, together with the Belgians. They will be securely billeted in the fortress, much better than on their island, where they are a serious threat and a standing menace to the Germans.

The investment of Antwerp will be more than a little impeded by the small fortress of Termonde. However, this is neither strong nor in good repair and can be neutralised, at least so far as artillery is concerned, with the help of the heavy artillery of the next corps. After that it will be possible to complete the investment of Antwerp between Termonde and Rupelmonde.

The battle for Antwerp will be rendered more difficult, however, if the French succeed in reaching the line Namur–Antwerp before us and with the English and Belgians prevent us from advancing farther along the left bank of the Meuse. An envelopment with the right wing will then become impossible. The plan must be changed. [Even combined, our enemies can be prevented from advancing north of Namur–Liège. If they want to throw us back, they must also advance right of the Meuse, and in so doing they cannot help exposing their right flank to a German attack.]*

If the French come up at a later stage, the Germans will be faced with the prospect of a battle in two directions, i.e. with one front facing Antwerp and the other facing Hirson–Maubeuge–Lille.

* An attempt must then be made with a strongly echeloned left wing to envelop the enemy on the left and force him against the sea. Admittedly there is then a very serious threat to the German left wing. But a break-through between Maubeuge and Namur may well become possible.

According to their reiterated intentions, the French are going to advance *en masse* and in depth. The dictum of the late Field Marshal will then be borne out that the narrow front is in danger of being enveloped while the broad front [provided precautions are taken against an enemy break-through] offers great promise of success.

The English are also credited with the intention of landing at Esbjerg and not at Antwerp. Sometimes the supposed plan is to appear at a very early stage on the Jutland coast, sometimes it is to delay with the enterprise until the German and French forces are already engaged in battle. Advantage is to be taken of Germany's completely denuded state for a march on Berlin, possibly with the assistance of some French corps.

In the first case, the Germans would not be able to complete their deployment if an English army were to appear in the north while it was still in progress. The corps still in the rear would have to be halted and sent to annihilate the new enemy by their great superiority. The French would have no choice but to come to their ally's aid [i.e. give up their fortresses and positions and take the offensive. With this, we should be faced with all the advantages of which we have convinced ourselves on various occasions in the event of a war left of the Rhine.]*

But should the English wait [with the intended landing] until a favourable moment, they will [hardly find one before the first battle]. If the battle goes in favour of the Germans, the English are likely to abandon their enterprise as hopeless. The battle is therefore of the utmost importance, and it would be a serious mistake if, in expectation of the English, we were to leave behind in some [distant theatre of the future, an army, a corps, or even a division, which might bring the decision against the French.

If the English nevertheless land after we have completed our deployment, be it before or after a battle, we must] collect all the forces still in the country—and they will still be far from negligible—and crush the English invaders.

[The forces remaining behind must be organised, however.]

Graf Schlieffen

* From this the same kind of war would develop in the West which has been discussed repeatedly in war games and on staff rides—a war in which the Germans have the advantage of the situation.

GENERAL OBSERVATIONS ON THE SCHLIEFFEN
PLAN BY H. VON MOLTKE
(*apparently dated 1911*)

*The Schlieffen papers contain a typewritten copy of the follow-
ing minute, which supplements Moltke's marginal notes to the
Schlieffen Plan of 1905. . . . The only clue to the date is the
note at the end, which points to a conspicuously late one.*

Comments on the memorandum by General von Moltke:

It may be safely assumed that the next war will be a war on
two fronts. Of our enemies, France is the most dangerous and can
prepare the most quickly. Accounts must be settled with her
very soon after deployment. Should the defeat of the French be
achieved quickly and decisively, it will also be possible to make
forces available against Russia. I agree with the basic idea of opening the war with a strong offensive against France while initially
remaining on the defensive with weak forces against Russia. If a
quick decision is sought against France, the attack should not be
directed exclusively against the strongly fortified eastern front of
that country. If, as may be expected, the French army remains on
the defensive behind that front, there is no chance of quickly
breaking through; and even a break-through would expose the
German army, or those sections which have made it, to flank attack from two sides. If one wants to meet the enemy in the open,
the fortified frontier-line must be outflanked. This is only possible
by means of an advance through Switzerland or Belgium. The first
would encounter great difficulties and, because of the defence of
the mountain roads, would take a long time. On the other hand a
successful outflanking of the French fortifications would have the
advantage of forcing the French army towards the north. An advance through Belgium would force the French back into their interior. Nevertheless it should be preferred, because there one can
count on quicker progress. We can count on the somewhat inefficient Belgian forces being quickly scattered, unless the Belgian
army should withdraw without a battle to Antwerp, which would
then have to be sealed off.

It is important, of course, that for an advance through Belgium
the right wing should be made as strong as possible. But I cannot agree that the envelopment demands the violation of Dutch
neutrality in addition to Belgian. A hostile Holland at our back
could have disastrous consequences for the advance of the Ger-

man army to the west, particularly if England should use the violation of Belgian neutrality as a pretext for entering the war against us. A neutral Holland secures our rear, because if England declares war on us for violating Belgian neutrality she cannot herself violate Dutch neutrality. She cannot break the very law for whose sake she goes to war.

Furthermore it will be very important to have in Holland a country whose neutrality allows us to have imports and supplies. She must be the windpipe that enables us to breathe.

However awkward it may be, the advance through Belgium must therefore take place without the violation of Dutch territory. This will hardly be possible unless Liège is in our hands. The fortress must therefore be taken at once. I think it possible to take it by a *coup de main*. Its salient forts are so unfavourably sited that they do not overlook the intervening country and cannot dominate it. I have had a reconnaissance made of all roads running through them into the centre of the town, *which has no ramparts*. An advance with several columns is possible without their being observed from the forts. Once our troops have entered the town I believe that the forts will not bombard it but will probably capitulate. Everything depends on meticulous preparation and surprise. The enterprise is only possible if the attack is made at once, before the areas between the forts are fortified. It must therefore be undertaken by standing troops immediately war is declared. The capture of a modern fortress by a *coup de main* would be something unprecedented in military history. But it can succeed and must be attempted, for the possession of Liège is the *sine qua non* of our advance. It is a bold venture whose accomplishment promises a great success. In any case the heaviest artillery must be at hand, so that in case of failure we can take the fortress by storm. I believe the absence of an inner rampart will deliver the fortress into our hands.

On the success of the *coup de main* depends our chance of making the advance through Belgium without infringing Dutch territory. The deployment and disposition of the army must be made accordingly.

(Troops for the *coup de main*, heavy artillery, preparations for mobilisation.)

B [*Berlin?*] 1911   (signed) v. M.

2. The Battle of the Marne

THE ALLIED victory in the Battle of the Marne sealed the fate of the Central Powers, but four years were to elapse before this was fully recognized. The Marne was one of the most decisive battles in history, although it appeared in September, 1914, to be largely the halting of a long Allied retreat rather than the crushing of the Germans, who soon afterward entrenched themselves for a protracted occupation of northeastern France.

The Schlieffen Plan had envisaged invading Belgium north as well as south of the Meuse River, thus by-passing the French fortifications set at intervals along the Franco-German border. The flat land of Flanders presented few natural obstacles to the German invasion, apart from several rivers. It was the original intention of Schlieffen to cross the Seine northwest of Paris and to encircle the capital from that direction. French armies in the vicinity of the capital would be caught in a hammer lock and pressed eastward against the defensive positions to be held by German armies based upon Luxembourg, Metz, and Strasbourg. The French armies stationed along the German frontier would be trying meanwhile to push into Germany, Schlieffen assumed, and they would therefore be struck from behind as well as from the front. Such were the essentials of the plan of Schlieffen, who hoped to surpass the Battle of Cannae in a classic encirclement.

Plan XVII of General Joseph Joffre, the French commander in chief, called for the deployment of five French armies in a lozenge-shaped formation to parry an anticipated attack between Belfort and Mézières. The massive German assault upon Liège might well have furnished Joffre with a clue to the Schlieffen Plan's objective of a flanking maneuver on the far north, but the French commander was obstinately convinced that the Germans did not have sufficient regular troops to extend their battle line all the way from Belfort to the Meuse, and yet be capable of directing their main thrust along both banks of the river. It was inconceivable to Joffre and to his staff, the "Young Turks," that General von Moltke would use reservists (Landwehr and ersatz troops) in actual combat alongside regular units. The French professional military, unlike the German, were contemptuous of reservists, and they could not comprehend that the Germans planned to mass no less than thirty-six corps of regulars and reserves on their extreme right wing to advance along both banks of the Meuse. The Germans were using twice as many troops in the north as French intelligence had estimated.

Under the illusion that the German right wing would pass south of Liège, between the Meuse and the Ardennes, Joseph Joffre stationed the Fifth Army of General Charles Lanrezac between Givet and Charleroi, where it was to be reinforced on its left by the British Expeditionary Force under General Sir John French. Joffre wanted to use these two armies as one tong of a pair of pincers. The other tong was supposed to be the Third Army of General Ruffey and the Fourth Army of General Fernand de Langle de Cary. These latter two armies tried to press into the Ardennes, but were pushed back in the vicinity of Virton-Neufchâteau.

To the northwest, the German First Army under General Alexander von Kluck, and the Second Army of General Karl von Bülow bore down upon Lanrezac's Fifth Army and the British, while the Third German Army of von Hausen advanced from the east. Thirty German divisions were closing upon Lanrezac's thirteen divisions and Sir John French's four. The clairvoyant Lanrezac, sensing the German purpose, hesitated to risk a crossing of the Sambre. The British meanwhile moved up to Mons on August 22. The following day Lanrezac learned of the threat of von Hausen's Third Army on his eastern flank, and he gave orders for an abrupt retreat. This left the British temporarily exposed, for the First Army of von Kluck was northwest of the British Expeditionary Force and in a position to turn its left flank. Sir John French thereupon ordered a retreat on August 24. General Joffre belatedly perceived that the main German thrust, one of crushing strength, was being directed much farther north than his Plan XVII had anticipated.

Since the signing of the Franco-Russian Alliance in 1893, French strategic doctrine had made a fetish of the *offensive à outrance*. Yet Joffre had to break off contact with the enemy and order a vast southward retreat of his entire center and left while trying to retain Verdun as a hinge. The British had to follow suit, unless they chose to exercise their independence of command and withdraw to the coast, where they might have offered merely a potential threat to the German northern flank. Sir John French admitted that such a withdrawal to the west was recommended by some of his subordinate commanders. Fortunately for the Allies, Sir John French was willing to swallow his wrath over the precipitate withdrawal which Lanrezac had made from the Sambre on August 22, which had left both flanks of the British Expeditionary Force exposed, until it too had pulled back. Sir John French wisely agreed to co-ordinate his strategy with that of Joffre.

The French and British commanders now planned to fall back southward to a defensible position such as the Marne River. Joffre meanwhile ordered the formation of a new army of reinforcements. Part of the "Miracle of the Marne" lay in the ability of the French command to conjure up a fresh army at a time when the forces of Lanrezac, Ruffey, and Langle de Cary were being heavily engaged in Flanders, when General Pau was attacking Colmar in Alsace, and General Noel de Castelnau was fighting for Saarbourg in Lorraine—only to be thrown back at Morhange. The availability of reinforcements was attributable in part to the successful diplomacy of French Foreign Minister Théophile Delcassé and French Ambassador Camille Barrère who, in June 1902, had elicited secret assurances from Italian Foreign Minister Prinetti that, as far as Italy was concerned, the Triple Alliance "contained nothing directly or indirectly aggressive toward France." As British General Edward L. Spears expressed it, "Had not Joffre been certain that the Italians would remain neutral he would have been compelled to leave on the Franco-Italian frontier troops without whom the Battle of the Marne could not have been fought."

Sure of France's southeastern frontier, Joffre dissolved the Army of the Alps on August 17, and transferred its six divisions to a newly formed army, the Sixth, along with troops from the army of General Pau in Alsace which were made available as reinforcements. The Sixth Army was assigned to General Michel-Joseph Maunoury and stationed on the extreme left wing of the Anglo-French forces to await a resumption of the offensive.

The Germans, for their part, committed some great blunders which eventually proved fatal for them. Von Moltke diverted seven regular divisions to seal off the Belgian forces in Maubeuge, Givet, and Antwerp when he could easily have used reserves for this purpose. Another mistake was the detachment on August 25 of four divisions besieging Namur which were sent to East Prussia, where they arrived too late to be of use in the Battle of Tannenberg. These mistaken diversions were all made from the right wing, and they seriously impaired the ability to execute Schlieffen's Plan. But then the German command was under the illusion that victory was already theirs after the French defeat at Charleroi. They swept through Namur, Longwy, Montmédy, Soissons, Laon, Reims, and Maubeuge. The invasion was so swift that the German command in Luxembourg lost touch with the advancing armies, and a gap appeared between the Second Army of von Bülow and the First Army of von Kluck, who began veering to the southeast to regain contact. The German advance was too fast for their own good, since their supply convoys could not keep up with the straining front-line troops.

On August 31, General Maunoury notified Joffre that von Kluck's army was veering to the southeast of Paris and thereby exposing its right flank. This fact was also brought to the attention of General Joseph Galliéni, the military governor of Paris, who importuned Joffre for an immediate attack by the Sixth Army upon the German flank. Joffre agreed, and on September 5 Maunoury's army was rushed out of Paris (transported in part by the "taxis of the Marne") to be deployed as a fresh attacking force against von Kluck's vulnerable side. As von Kluck turned to fend off Maunoury, a gap of thirty miles separated his First Army from the Second Army of von Bülow. The French armies on both flanks of the British Expeditionary Force began turning about to prepare for the general counteroffensive ordered for September 6. The British plodded south another day's march, giving von Kluck a feeling of false security as he turned to meet Maunoury's army to the west. When the forces of Sir John French at last wheeled about and began wearily retracing their route from south to north on September 9, von Bülow in turn feared being outflanked, and he ordered a retreat northward, being followed the same day by von Kluck. Within two days the German armies undertook a general retreat towards the Aisne River. Verdun, meanwhile, had resisted the efforts of the Sixth and Seventh German armies to envelop it. The Germans reached the heights of the Aisne and began digging trenches to provide shelter for desperately needed rest. Even before the ensuing "Race to the Sea," the future configuration of four years of trench warfare was thus already staked out.

We publish an account of the Battle of the Marne from one of the most authoritative of sources, *The Personal Memoirs of Joffre*. "Papa Joffre," who was idolized in France for the first year of the war, was born at Rivesaltes in the Pyrénées-Orientales on January 12, 1852, the son of a cooper with eleven children. A knack at mathematics qualified him for engineering studies at the renowned Ecole Polytechnique. His early career was largely colonial, with service in Indochina and Formosa. In 1893 he led a celebrated expedition to Timbuktu, in the Sahara, and subsequently built railways in Sénégal and port facilities at the Diégo-Suarez in Madagascar which brought about his promotion to general at the early age of forty-nine. In 1911 he was made chief of the General Staff, and two years later he presented his ill-starred Plan XVII to the Supreme War Council. Joffre showed admirable nerveless-ness in August, 1914, when the Germans flooded into northeastern France in callous disregard of his cherished plan. Joffre's ability to improvise a new and flexible strategy, and his acquiescence in Galliéni's arguments for a flanking attack against von Kluck's army on the Marne, made possible the great Allied victory. But Joffre's ensuing "nibbling" operations—his ceaseless piecemeal attacks against formi-dable German entrenchments following the "Race to the Sea"—drained away the almost hysterical adulation which he enjoyed in 1914 and 1915, and in December, 1916, Joffre retired with a marshal's baton as his solace. He died in Paris on January 3, 1931.

MARSHAL JOSEPH JOFFRE,
The Personal Memoirs of Joffre:
Field Marshal of the French Army

We . . . drove to Fontainebleau and so to Melun, where we arrived a little before 2 o'clock.

Huguet was waiting for us at British G.H.Q., and he conducted us to the Château of Vaux-le-Pénil. Here we found Sir John French, surrounded by the officers of his staff, notably Generals Murray and Wilson. These two men represented to my eyes the opposing tendencies which existed at British Headquarters: Wilson standing for the action that was favourable to us, Murray for the ideas I feared.

I immediately entered upon my subject. I put my whole soul into the effort to convince the Field Marshal. I told him that the decisive moment had arrived and that we must not let it escape—

Source: From *The Personal Memoirs of Joffre: Field Marshal of the French Army*, translated by Colonel T. Bentley Mott (New York, Harper & Row, 1932), pp. 254–275. Copyright 1932, 1960 by Harper & Row, Publishers, Incorporated. Reprinted by permission of the publisher.

we must go to battle with every man both of us had and free from all reservations.

"So far as regards the French Army," I continued, "my orders are given, and, whatever may happen, I intend to throw my last company into the balance to win a victory and save France. It is in her name that I come to you to ask for British assistance, and I urge it with all the power I have in me. I cannot believe that the British Army will refuse to do its share in this supreme crisis—history would severely judge your absence."

Then, as I finished, carried away by my convictions and the gravity of the moment, I remember bringing down my fist on a table which stood at my elbow, and crying, "Monsieur le Maréchal, the honour of England is at stake!"

Up to this point French had listened imperturbably to the officer who was translating what I said, but now his face suddenly reddened. There ensued a short impressive silence; then, with visible emotion he murmured, "I will do all I possibly can." Not understanding English, I asked Wilson what Sir John had said. He merely replied, "The Field Marshal says 'Yes.'"

I had distinctly felt the emotion which seemed to grip the British Commander-in-Chief; above all, I had remarked the tone of his voice, and I felt, as did all the witnesses to the scene, that these simple words were equivalent to an agreement signed and sworn to.

Tea, which was already prepared, was then served, after which French accompanied me to my car. I left behind with Huguet, Lieutenant-Colonel Serret, in whose energy and sagacity I had great confidence, and proceeded to Châtillon-sur-Seine, where my headquarters had been moved during the day. The officers of the staff were installed in an ancient convent of the Order of Cordeliers, and my own office was in what had formerly been a monk's cell. It was from here that I directed the battle of the Marne and it was in this room that, at half-past seven the next morning, I signed the following order addressed to the troops:

> We are about to engage in a battle on which the fate of our country depends and it is important to remind all ranks that the moment has passed for looking to the rear; all our efforts must be directed to attacking and driving back the enemy. Troops that can advance no farther must, at any price, hold on to the ground they have conquered and die on the spot rather than give way. Under the circumstances which face us, no act of weakness can be tolerated.

On arriving at Châtillon I found a telegram from the Minister of War in reply to the letter I had sent him to announce the imminent resumption of the offensive and to ask him to aid me in bringing Field Marshal French to a decision. M. Millerand informed me that he raised no objections to my plan, and that the Minister of Foreign Affairs was on his way to see the British Ambassador for the purpose of urging him to make representations to his Government in the sense I desired.

As has been seen, however, my visit to Sir John French had, in the meantime, cleared up the situation, and I now knew that I could count upon the co-operation of the British forces in the decisive battle about to be delivered.

There were also awaiting me at Châtillon the reports sent by the various armies; these showed that the prescribed movements had been effected everywhere without difficulty.

THE BATTLE OF THE MARNE

At the moment when the battle on which the fate of the country depended was about to open, the military situation had taken on an aspect infinitely more favourable than anything I could have dared to hope for a few days before.

The French Third, Fourth, Ninth and Fifth Armies, with their right resting on the entrenched camp of Verdun, were deployed along a front of about 125 miles, roughly marked by Sermaize, Vitry-le-François, Sommesous, the Saint-Gond Marshes, Esternay and Courtacon. Thrown forward on their left in an advanced echelon were the British Army and the French Sixth Army; the first south-west of Coulommiers, the second north-west of Meaux, covered on its left by Sordet's Cavalry Corps. The line, in its general aspect, presented the form of a vast pocket, into which five German armies seemed bent upon engulfing themselves. For all the information gathered during the day of September 5th went to show that the enemy was vigorously pursuing his march to the south. His general dispositions appeared to be as follows:

Von Kluck's army (the First) had reached the vicinity of Coulommiers, having left a few elements on the right bank of the Ourcq; these were entrenching themselves facing west.

Von Bülow's army (the Second) had crossed the Marne between Dormans and Epernay on the morning of September 5th. At noon the heads of its columns were reported to be on a line running through Champaubert, Etoges, Bergères, Vertus.

Von Hausen's army (the Third) had been identified only by

its XII Corps, which, on September 4th, was reported to be at
Condé-sur-Marne, between Epernay and Châlons.

The Prince of Württemberg's army (the Fourth) had reached
the line Châlons, Francheville, Bussy-le-Repos, on September 5th.

The Army of the German Crown Prince (the Fifth) was moving southwards on both sides of the Argonne.

In this way the strategic conditions which I had envisaged on
August 25th had at last been realized. The combination of circumstances which obliged me to renounce the manœuvre conceived that day and attempt another has already been described;
and now, thanks to the movements made by the enemy himself,
the manœuvre sketched out on the 25th again offered itself as a
possibility.

But however advantageous the general situation appeared—
above all, now that I could count upon the co-operation of the
British—it can well be conceived that I was none the less beset by
grave preoccupations. For in spite of the assurances which Generals Foch and Franchet d'Esperey had given me, I could not
blind myself to the fact that this offensive, suddenly undertaken
with armies worn out by an exhausting retreat, presented a problem bristling with uncertainties.

. . . I would have preferred to delay the attack until the 7th, in
order to give time to reorganize the troops and get them better in
hand, and I have explained the reasons which impelled me to renounce this brief delay, which would have been so useful to us.
At the same time, I never for a moment had any doubt as to the
response which our soldiers and their officers would make when
asked to do the work I was about to demand of them. All the reports coming in showed that troops and staff were equally astonished at the length of this retreat, whose necessity they could not
account for, and that they asked nothing better than to face about
the attack. In short, thanks to the precaution I had taken a few
days before in warning army commanders of the reasons which
prompted me to continue to fall still farther back, our troops had
preserved the mentality of a force which is manœuvring, instead
of acquiring that of an army already beaten. In addition to this,
reinforcements from the interior had replaced the heavy losses
that had thinned our ranks during the opening days of the
campaign.

I was confident that our men understood me thoroughly when
I told them that the fate of our country now hung in the balance,
and I felt altogether sure that I could count upon their steadiness;

on the other hand, I was no less certain that the enemy's spirits must be at the highest pitch. And yet, in weighing the matter carefully, I was convinced that this very fact presented a greater danger for him than for us; for we could count upon the effect of the surprise which was certain to be produced by a sudden attack coming at the moment when the Germans were convinced that all they now had to do was to sweep up the remnants of our routed armies.

The army corps which had been sent to reinforce the sensitive points in our line of battle were still in course of movement. These were, notably, the XV Corps, destined for the Third Army, the XXI Corps destined for the Fourth Army, and a division of the IX Corps which was intended for the Ninth Army. This fact had its influence in increasing the regret I felt at having been obliged to start the battle on September 6th.

Ever since the 4th, combats had been raging with great violence on the Lorraine front. Here the enemy was seeking to get possession of Nancy, while at the same time, by an action in the Woëvre, he was menacing the rear of the Third Army. On the front of the First Army, he fortunately showed less activity; but as General Dubail had had his effectives considerably reduced, all he could do was to hold on to his positions.

The German attacks began on the afternoon of the 4th, and during the whole of the 5th they continued in the region of Gerbéviller and the Forest of Champenoux. That evening General de Castelnau reported that the enemy's numerical superiority, added to the power and range of his artillery—whose siege batteries had now made their appearance—rendered it improbable that the Second Army would be able to resist for any length of time. "If I am strongly pressed," he wrote, "I can either defend myself as long as possible where I am, or else I can slip away in good time and take up a position first along the Forest of Haye, Saffais, Belchamps and Borville, then fall back to another line and so try to hold out and continue to cover the right flank of the group of armies."

Now, if the manœuvre I was about to undertake was to succeed, I had to be sure that our two armies on the right flank would hold their ground, and it will be seen, as events are related, how grave a source of apprehension the Second Army continued to be for me during the whole Battle of the Marne.

All of our forces, as I wrote to the Minister of War, were now either in line or on the point of arriving. The only unit which remained available was the Second Moroccan Division; one of its brigades (General Cherrier) had just reached France and the other (General Gouraud) would not be able to complete disembarking before September 12th.

From the point of view of reinforcements, the Germans were in an even more precarious situation than ourselves. Their deployment had long since been completed, and our air service reported that there was no sign of any forces following up the advancing armies; this confirmed me in my idea that the enemy could not have any fresh body of troops available. What was even more encouraging, information which I have previously referred to as indicating that important movements of German troops were taking place from west to east across Belgium, gave rise to the hope that the enemy had weakened the forces opposed to us. But we little guessed to what an extent this weakening of his line would be to our advantage—for it was not until later that we learned that the troops the Germans had withdrawn had been taken from their right—precisely the point against which I was preparing to make my strongest effort.

It has often been said that during a modern battle a commander-in-chief, having once put his forces into position and given his initial orders, has nothing further to do; all he can do is to await the results of a contest whose development he is powerless to control.

The Germans had inherited this theory from Marshal von Moltke. History shows that while the victor of Sadowa and Sedan conducted his troops methodically and with painstaking care up to the eve of battle, once the engagement began, he renounced all idea of directing it, and made no effort to impose his decisions during its progress. This method reflected the Marshal's temperament, disliking as he did to direct events which necessarily escaped all predetermination: he, therefore, admitted that the conduct of a battle was the affair of subordinate commanders. The wars in which he had been a chief actor brought no contradiction to this doctrine, von Moltke having had the rare good fortune to meet as adversaries only generals such as Benedek and Bazaine, whose inertia and passivity, one might say, were absolute.

Having observed that the results obtained by this method were excellent, the Germans decided that it was the right one to follow, and they continued to apply it. The younger von Moltke, nephew of the Marshal, and the general who commanded the German armies during the first weeks of the war, was not the sort of man, as far as one can judge, to modify a formula which accorded so well with the irresolution of his nature and which in his secret moments he must have found particularly satisfactory. In fact, documents now available make it perfectly clear that the German High Command, from its headquarters in distant Luxembourg, knew almost nothing of what was happening on the battlefield of the Marne; as a consequence, its action upon army commanders was only spasmodic: it did not keep them informed as to the general situation, its instructions to them were incomplete and arrived too late.

Quite another conception prevailed amongst us in France. We agreed that sudden inspiration had no place in a modern battle; we recognized that the extent of its front, the size of its masses, and the length of time it might last, necessitated a more minute preparation than was the case in battles whose successive phases the commander-in-chief could follow with a spy-glass. Nevertheless, we believed that, in spite of all the difficulties, a battle could and should be directed. However intelligent and energetic the various army commanders might be, each one of them would know only what was happening over a small fraction of the line, and the events taking place in his immediate front would assume an importance to his eyes which would distort their perspective; the commander-in-chief alone could have a general view of the whole battle and assign its true value to each event. Moreover, as new situations would constantly present themselves, no one but the commander of the whole front could give the orders required to meet each one as it arose.

The Battle of the Marne brought out in strong relief the ideas I have just expressed. It began as soon as we had succeeded in concentrating around the German right a mass sufficiently heavy to give us on this part of the strategic field the double advantage of position and numerical superiority. In spite of this situation, if we had tried to apply inflexibly a formula of envelopment at any price—which, moreover, was never my intention—we would have been playing into the enemy's hands. But our forces were sufficiently strong and our system sufficiently flexible to prevent the inevitable reaction of the enemy from catching us unawares. Von Kluck could only ward off the menace which threatened his right by creating between his army and that of von Bülow a breach which continued to widen progressively. In this way, beginning with the second day, the battle of the Marne took on the characteristics of a rupture of the enemy's line, a rupture which the German Commander-in-Chief had neither the time nor the means to avoid.

This conception of how a battle should be conducted, when it is fought under the conditions presented by the wide extension of modern fronts, presupposes not only the existence of a complete unity of doctrine between the commander-in-chief and his subordinates, but also implies that sure and rapid communication between them can be effected through the telegraph and telephone and by means of staff officers, who are, properly speaking, exponents of the very brain and will of the commander-in-chief. The task which fell to these liaison officers was extremely delicate, and they have sometimes been accused of assuming to themselves an authority out of all proportion to their rank. It is possible that errors were committed by these men; it is also likely that they at times became victims of the enmity aroused by pitiless decapitations which the interest of the country had induced me to make.

Be all this as it may, the fact remains that although I was obliged to stay at my headquarters during the whole of this battle,* in order to take the decisions which circumstances at any hour of the day or night might require, I was able, nevertheless, to command a deployment whose right rested on the Vosges and whose left, if we include d'Amade's divisions, extended as far as Rouen.

The courage and tenacity of our men being granted, it was the French system of command which triumphed at the Marne. . . .

In what follows, I shall confine myself to indicating what my personal action was during its various phases.

Maunoury's army was established during the day of September 5th between the Ermenonville Forest and the Marne, from Meaux to Vers. On its right some collisions occurred that day with the enemy, notably at Penchard, Monthyon, and Saint-Soupplets. For September 6th, its objective was the Ourcq, from Lizy to Neufchelles. But it immediately encountered the German IV Reserve Corps, which put up a desperate resistance and was soon after supported by the whole of the II Corps; the latter had been recalled by forced marches from Coulommiers, and now endeavoured to outflank our left around Etavigny. On September 6th

* I forced myself throughout the battle of the Marne and during the delicate phase which followed it (to be precise, from September 5th to the 20th) to remain at my headquarters. I went out of my office only for the purpose of taking a daily walk of a mile or two and eating my meals. I slept at night in the Château de Marmont, which Colonel Maitre had placed at my disposal.

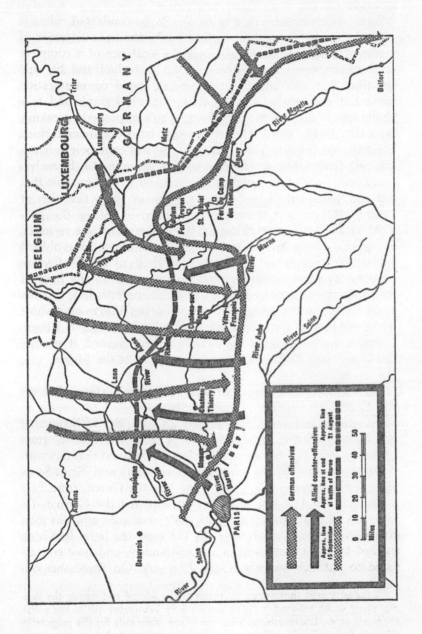

at nightfall, the Sixth Army was halted on the line Chambry-Marcilly-Puisieux-Betz, that is to say, a long way from its first objective. Nevertheless, the earliest results of the entrance into action of this army soon became apparent to my eyes.

The Fifth Army had advanced on the morning of the 6th from the front Sézanne-Villers-Saint-Georges-Courchamps, and towards noon had encountered the enemy. Conneau's Cavalry Corps, to the north of the Jouy forest covered its left and assured its liaison with the British Army. The latter had started that morning, not from the front Changis-Coulommiers, as was indicated for it in General Orders No. 6, but from a line situated 9 miles to the south-east, running from Pézarches to Lagny; by the evening its left had reached the west bank of the Grand Morin without difficulty, while its right, thrown back, lay in the region of Pézarches.

At 11 A.M. on the 7th Franchet d'Esperey reported to me that the German First Army "on the front Esternay-Courtacon was in full retreat towards the north" . . . and that the Fifth Army was pursuing its advance. During the evening, while the X Corps, on its right, was supporting Foch's left division (the 42nd) towards Loizy-au-Bois, its centre and left had reached the line Marsains-Tréof-sil-Moutils, and Conneau's cavalry had arrived at La Ferté-Gaucher. By the close of the day the British Army had attained the line Choisy-Coulommiers-Maisoncelles, without meeting serious resistance.

On the other hand, our Sixth Army attempted in vain to reach the Ourcq; the enemy in front of it continued to receive reenforcements and von Kluck parried all the efforts which Maunoury made to effect an envelopment of his right in the direction of Betz.

On the evening of the 7th the situation of the German armies in front of our left appeared to me to be as follows:

To meet Maunoury's attack, which manifestly had surprised him, von Kluck had constituted on the Ourcq a detachment composed of the IV Reserve Corps, the IV Active Corps and the 4th Cavalry Division, while with the rest of his army, he was fighting, facing the south, against Franchet d'Esperey's left. Between these two main portions of the German First Army, a gap had been produced, opposite the British; this breach was masked by German cavalry forces, large, indeed, but not strong enough to hold up our Allies.

My idea, therefore, was for Franchet d'Esperey with his left to attack that part of the German First Army which faced him; to push the British Army into the gap I have just mentioned (crossing successively the Grand Morin, the Petit Morin and the Marne); and at the same time to accentuate Maunoury's enveloping movement by directing it, no longer upon Château-Thierry but farther north on the right bank of the Ourcq. This was the basis of the instructions I issued to our three armies on the left during the afternoon of September 7th.*

While this was happening on our left, the battle was developing less favourably on our centre and right. The left of Foch's army, strongly supported by Franchet d'Esperey's left, resisted all the assaults of the enemy in the region of Loizy-au-Bois and Mondemont, but its right had been forced to give ground ever since the opening of the battle. Fère-Champenoise had been lost and on the evening of the 8th the line ran through Semoine-Gourgancon-Carroy, which represented a loss of eight miles. This retirement derived additional gravity from the fact that it opened still further the wide interval which separated Foch's right from the Fourth Army's left. As early as the 6th, I had already called General de Langle's attention to the need of keeping strong reserves in rear of his left ready to counter-attack enemy forces which might seek to turn Foch's right, and it was for this purpose that I had placed the XXI Corps at de Langle's disposal. This corps was supposed to arrive in the region of Wassy, Montierender on the 7th.

Unfortunately, ever since the morning of the 7th the Fourth Army had been at grips with the German Fourth Army reinforced by a part of the Third (von Hausen), and by a combination of circumstances for which de Langle was in no way to blame, the left of his army, contrary to anticipations, had become precisely the weakest point of his line. The infantry of the XII Corps, which it had been necessary to send by rail to the region of Chavanges during the preceding days, could as yet put only a few battalions in line to the south of Vitry-le-François; these supported as best they could the corps artillery. Then the main body of the XVII Corps, also much fatigued, had only reached the Aube near Ramerupt and had hardly started its advance east of Mailly.

* In order better to co-ordinate the movements of the Sixth Army, which was now getting farther and farther from the Capital, I sent a telegram on the morning of the 7th to the Military Governor of Paris to inform him that hereafter I would send my orders direct to General Maunoury, a copy being addressed to the Governor. This decision was essential, and, for the purpose of gaining time, I had already been obliged to send orders direct to the Sixth Army—notably General Orders No. 6 of September 4th for the resumption of the general offensive.

What made it all the more difficult for General de Langle to reinforce his left flank during the first days of the battle was the fact that a gap existed (marked by the forest of Trois Fontaines) between his right and Sarrail's left, and the fighting on this wing was extremely severe. Sarrail complained violently of the situation, demanding an energetic action on the part of the II Corps (right of the Fourth Army) against Revigny or Contrisson, while waiting for the XV Corps (sent by the Second Army) to get into line north-west of Bar-le-Duc, between the Saulx and the Ornain.

It was thus that for a moment I was assailed by the fear of seeing the centre of my line broken by a double rupture, one on each wing of the Fourth Army.

Fortunately, nothing of the sort took place. Von Hausen's army, engaged partly against Foch's right and partly against de Langle's left, was unable to penetrate into the 25-mile gap which lay between the two armies, and which was most inadequately masked by our 9th Cavalry Division. Beginning on September 8th the infantry of the now reconstituted XII Corps brought new strength to the front of the Fourth Army, while that same evening the XXI Corps arrived at Sompins, ready to support the left of this army; its entry into action, however, was too late to obtain any tangible results that day.

Turning now to the Third Army, I sent on September 7th, two orders* to General Sarrail. In these I directed him to do all in his power to help the Fourth Army, just as the latter was bending every effort towards supporting the Ninth. Moreover, when evening arrived on September 8th, the XV Corps, after being at first forced back between the Saulx and the Ornain by the enemy's pressure, had finally succeeded in gaining ground, thus assuring the liaison between the Third and Fourth Armies.

But now a new danger arose in front of Sarrail: enemy detachments were marching towards the Meuse in the neighbourhood of Saint-Mihiel, and the fort at Troyon had been vigorously bombarded by the Germans on the evening of the 8th. To parry this threat General Sarrail caused the bridges over the Meuse to be destroyed and had the river guarded by the 7th Cavalry Division.

As a matter of fact the situation of the Third Army had become delicate, largely because its commander considered himself obliged to maintain contact with the fortress of Verdun. At 8

---

* The first at 8.30 A.M. and the second at 4.15 P.M.

P.M. on September 8th I sent him an order authorizing him, if the need arose, to draw back his right so as to assure his communications and thus give greater power to the action of his left wing. In this way I showed Sarrail that I attached more importance to having the Third Army keep in touch with the Fourth than I did to its liaison with Verdun; indeed, in case of necessity, that fortress was quite capable of taking care of itself. To reassure Sarrail and bring some help to his task, I had directed Castelnau, the preceding day, to send the 2nd Cavalry Division on September 8th towards the Woëvre, so as to protect the rear of the Third Army. On the 8th, with the same idea in view, I also approved the despatch by rail to Commercy of a mixed brigade taken from the garrison of Toul.

Although the battle had increased in violence along the whole front and now reached beyond the Meuse and well into the Woëvre, I did not lose sight of the armies which were operating between Nancy and the Vosges. I had already taken very important forces from these armies and I proposed to take more if the situation required it. Nevertheless, I had to make sure that such a step would not compromise their power of resistance; for in that case the enemy would regain the initiative which we had just snatched from him.

I have related at the opening of this chapter that on the evening of September 5th, General de Castelnau had manifested his intention of abandoning the Grand Couronné and Nancy if he could not maintain his army on its positions without compromising its future. On the 6th, at 1.10 P.M., I sent him a telegram informing him that while his intentions, in case he was forced to abandon the Grand Couronné, met with my approval, I considered it preferable that he hold on to his present positions until a decision was obtained in the battle just commenced.

As it turned out, the commander of the Second Army succeeded that day in checking the enemy's attacks and he was even able to assume the offensive. But on the 7th the situation on his front again became threatening, and General de Castelnau, deeply affected by the death of one of his sons and learning that the battalion charged with defending Mount Sainte-Geneviève had abandoned that position, gave orders to his chief of staff, General Anthoine, to have the retreat begun, while at the same time he made ready to inform the civil authorities of Nancy that they must evacuate the town.

The decision was a grave one. This was no moment for giving

the Germans the chance to trumpet to the world that they had
taken Nancy. Moreover, from a strategic point of view, the retreat
of the Second Army would place the First in a serious dilemma.
Either that army would imitate the Second and fall back in liaison
with it, thus abandoning the Franche-Comté and making probable the envelopment of the right flank of our armies, or else it
would continue its resistance, basing itself for that purpose on the
fortified towns of Belfort and Epinal. But this would mean the
rupture of our two right armies, with the additional prospect of
seeing Dubail's army shortly backed up against the Swiss frontier.

Fortunately, before sending out these orders, General Anthoine,
fully appreciating their gravity, telephoned to G.H.Q. to announce
the decision just taken. I immediately had de Castelnau called to
the telephone. I remember this incident all the more exactly as I
very rarely used the telephone myself during the whole campaign.
The General drew a very dark picture of the situation of his army.
There had been serious lapses in one of the corps; whole bodies
of troops had become disbanded. "If I try to hold on where I am,"
he added, "I feel that my army will be lost. We have got to face
the idea of immediately retreating behind the Meurthe."

"Do nothing of the kind," I replied. "Wait twenty-four hours.
You do not know how things are going with the enemy. He is
probably no better off than you are. You must not abandon the
Grand Couronné and I give you formal orders to hold on to your
present positions."

I then gave Major Bel instructions to proceed immediately to
General de Castelnau, confirm the verbal order I had just given
him, delay the execution of the retreat that was in preparation,
and have him hold on in front of Nancy at any cost.

As it turned out, moreover, if Mount Sainte-Geneviève had
been evacuated, it was in no sense due to the enemy's action but
because of a misunderstanding of orders, and the position had
been immediately re-occupied. The German attacks diminished in
violence little by little from this day forward, and on September
11th, abandoning his attempt against Nancy at the very moment
that our victory on the Marne was being concluded, the enemy
marked a considerable retirement in Lorraine; and this was continued during the following days.

During all this period General Dubail had maintained an unshakable confidence, not once did his morale weaken and he never
failed punctually to execute my orders.

We will now return to the armies on the left, which we last saw on the evening of September 7th oriented in the directions I had prescribed for them. On the 8th Maunoury found himself at grips with an enemy who had become still further reinforced during the night and who by a daring manœuvre sought to recover the initiative by attempting to envelop our extreme left.

Fortunately, the IV Corps, which I had previously withdrawn from the Third Army, had begun to detrain at Paris on the 5th, and General Galliéni during the night of the 7th/8th sent one of its divisions (the 7th) to Maunoury. To accelerate its movement and enable the troops to reach the Sixth Army in as fresh a condition as possible, Galliéni made use of every available means of transport—railways, requisitioned motorcars, etc. The other division of the IV Corps (the 8th), the Governor of Paris, in full agreement with Maunoury, thought himself obliged to engage south of the Marne, in order to support closely the movement of the British Army. As a matter of fact, this division was wholly useless in this region, and on the morning of the 8th it was still on the Petit Morin, where it was doing nothing at all. For this reason, about 9 A.M. of that day, I suggested to Maunoury that it would be advantageous to withdraw this division from his right and move it to his left, where there was work for it to do and where it could join the other elements of its corps.

During the morning of this same day, the 8th, I received the distressing news that Maubeuge had fallen the previous day. I had just cited in orders its Governor, General Fournier, for his gallant defence of the place, but the radio did not reach the besieged town until after its surrender. This event came at a bad moment; for it would free at least one army corps, which the Germans could move rapidly to Montdidier or Anizy. Therefore, when I informed Maunoury of this news I directed him to send out Sordet's cavalry to cut the enemy's communications, especially in the direction of Soissons and Compiègne.

At the end of the day, the Sixth Army, far from having succeeded in moving forward, was painfully resisting on its positions, at the same time making ready to refuse its left, which von Kluck was pressing vigorously. Fortunately, the Fifth Army continued its victorious advance. Its right gave a firm point of support to Foch, its centre, overcoming the resistance of the enemy's rearguards, was arriving on the Petit Morin, while its left corps (XVIII) had Marchais-en-Brie.

Between Maunoury and Franchet d'Esperey, the British Army was not advancing as rapidly as I could have wished, although it had already attained appreciable results. On September 7th I had requested the Minister of War to express to Lord Kitchener my warmest thanks for the constant support which the British forces had brought to our armies, and I also sent a personal letter to French to tell him of my gratitude. He answered the same day, thanking me for my message and adding that the situation now presented itself very favourably; he also congratulated me upon the "happy combination" I had just achieved.

All this did not prevent me from being impatient to see the British Army get forward more rapidly. Three times during the day of September 8th I urged upon its commander-in-chief the importance I attached to its action; I insisted upon the need of marching as fast as possible to the assistance of the Sixth Army, which now had to bear the whole brunt of the German First Army's attack; and I expressed the hope that I would see the British emerging on the other bank of the Marne before the day was over. But Sir John replied that German rear-guards had checked him on the Petit Morin; that same evening he had only reached the heights which lay to the north of this river.

When night arrived on the 8th, the situation, on the whole, appeared very promising—very different, indeed, from what a few days before I had thought it possible to anticipate.

All the German attacks between the Vosges and the Meuse had been mastered, in spite of the heavy withdrawals I had made from the First and Second Armies; in the centre, the frontal attacks being conducted by the Fourth and Ninth Armies now gave me a right to hope that the enemy would not succeed in breaking this portion of our front. De Langle's right was at last buttressed by the XV Corps which had just come into action on Sarrail's left. It is true that Foch's right had again yielded ground, a fact which greatly disturbed me; for de Langle was not yet in a position to give him efficient help. But the splendid courage and unshakable confidence of the man at the head of the Ninth Army made me feel certain that the yielding of his line was only a local accident, whose influence upon the engagement as a whole would not be greatly felt.

It is simple justice to do honour here to the exceptional qualities displayed by General Foch during this battle; for throughout its course he gave the full measure of his ability. Admirably assisted by his chief of staff, Colonel Weygand, at no instant did his activity slacken or the inspiration of his morale abate.

On our left wing, the manœuvre I had at first prepared was

now becoming wholly changed in character. General Maunoury
had been obliged to renounce the envelopment of his energetic
adversary; but the latter had only succeeded in parrying our attack against his right by opening between his left and von
Bülow's army a breach into which Franchet d'Esperey's left was
pushing like a wedge, and into which I was making my strongest
efforts to thrust the British. The information sent in by air reconnaissances, and that furnished by identifications secured during
the battle, made me realize the extraordinary possibilities of action which this new situation opened up. Therefore, at 7 P.M., I
sent to the three armies on our left a Special Instruction whose
object was to explain to them the manœuvre I desired to accom-
plish. The following are its most essential passages:*

The combined efforts of the Allied armies composing our left
wing have obliged the German forces to fall back; this they have
done in two distinct groups.

The first group which appears to be composed of the IV Reserve Corps and the II and IV Active Corps, is fighting on the
Ourcq, facing west, against our Sixth Army; it is even trying to
outflank this army on the north.

The other group, comprising the rest of the German First Army
(III and IX Active Corps), and the entire Second and Third
Armies, continues to oppose, facing south, the French Fifth and
Ninth Armies.

The connection between these two groups appears to be maintained solely by several cavalry divisions supported by detachments of all arms; these are opposite the British forces.

It seems essential to crush the German extreme right before
it can be reinforced by troops which will be made available by the
fall of Maubeuge.

I therefore requested:

(a) The Sixth Army to hold in check the enemy forces facing it.

(b) The British Army to cross the Marne between Nogent
l'Artaud and La Ferté-sous-Jouarre and attack the left and rear of
von Kluck's army;

(c) The Fifth Army, while covering with its left the right flank
of the British (aided in this task by Conneau's cavalry), and
also continuing to support with its right the left flank of Foch's
army, which was making ready to assume the offensive, to move

* Special Instruction No. 19.

forward with its main body, faced to the north, and drive the enemy across the Marne.

The first paragraph of this Instruction described the situation in a way which would now be recognized as exact, except in one particular: the III and IV German Corps had been identified during the day's fighting, and the Special Instruction places them as being still facing the Fifth Army; in reality they were already on the move towards the Ourcq front.* The breach opened up between von Kluck and von Bülow was therefore even wider than I had imagined.

The 9th of September seems to have marked the culminating point in the effort made by the enemy to extricate himself from the situation in which he had become involved.

Our Sixth Army succeeded at first in holding on to its positions; in the neighbourhood of Betz the enemy had even marked a slight withdrawal and had evacuated this village. But during the afternoon the German III and IX Corps, debouching from the northeast and from the north, caused the French left to yield and forced it back to the line Chèvreville-Silly-le-Long. Maunoury immediately recalled the 8th Division, as I had directed him to do, and pushed it by a night march towards the left of his army. On my side, I had occupied myself during the morning with the selection of an infantry division to be furnished by the Fifth Army and which I caused to be sent by rail with the utmost speed towards Dommartin-en-Goële. In notifying General Maunoury of the despatch of this division, I explained the attitude I expected him to observe: "While waiting for the arrival of reinforcements intended to enable you to resume the offensive, you must avoid any decisive action, by retiring your left wing, if necessary, in the general direction of the Entrenched Camp of Paris."

However, in spite of the violence of the attacks delivered against him, Maunoury never for a moment lost sight of his mission or gave up the idea of resuming the offensive. This is shown in the telegram he sent me after his left had effected its with-

* The following radio, sent by von Kluck at 6.30 P.M., September 8th, was deciphered a few days later by the Code Section of French G.H.Q.: Today the Army fought a hard engagement against superior enemy forces west of the Ourcq, on the line Antilly (2 miles east of Betz)—Cougis (south of Lizy). The III and IX Corps, sent during the night to the right wing, will make an enveloping attack tomorrow morning. On the Marne, the line Lizy-Nogent l'Artaud will be defended by the II Corps of Cavalry and a reinforced brigade of infantry against attacks coming from the direction of Coulommiers.

drawal: "I will place the 8th Division near Silly-le-Long, and I will then give orders to attack. Heavy losses during the four days' fighting. Morale good. Have sent cavalry well forward."

The stubbornness of the combats delivered by the Sixth Army, the effort demanded of the men, the tenacity and coolness of their chief, secured to us the immense result of making the victorious advance of Sir John French and Franchet d'Esperey comparatively easy. I personally expressed my satisfaction to General Maunoury and to his army, and the Grand Cross of the Legion of Honour marked the high price I placed upon the services just rendered our country by the commander of the Sixth Army.

In the report from which a few lines have just been quoted, Maunoury referred to a new task which had been confided to the Cavalry Corps. This force, composed of three divisions, was admirably placed on our extreme left and it should have done most useful work. Unfortunately, although the war had been going on scarcely a month, Sordet's cavalry had arrived at a most distressing state of exhaustion. The more or less useless raid it had made into Belgium, followed by a retreat which only came to an end to the south-west of Paris, had resulted in enormous wear and tear; but the operations alone were not responsible for ruining this corps—the generals and their staffs had a large share in the matter. It thus came about that on September 7th General Sordet, after having put his corps into action in the vicinity of Betz, decided that night, under pretext that the region where he was operating was short of water, to recall his divisions to Nanteuil-le-Housouin, where they arrived only at midnight. Upon learning of this retirement, General Maunoury ordered Sordet to move again to the front, and in this way the corps, after a rest of barely one hour, had to go all the way back over the same road.

Upon the recommendation of the commander of the Sixth Army, I decided to relieve General Sordet of his command and replace him by General Bridoux who was then commanding the 5th Cavalry Division. I had great esteem for Sordet, and before hostilities broke out he gave evidence of qualities which justified my confidence. Most probably he was a victim of the fact that during the years which preceded the war the cavalry arm had not kept sufficiently abreast of the times. General Bridoux was an officer full of dash and with him at its head the Cavalry Corps would have rendered us the greatest services; but unfortunately he had been in command hardly a day when he was killed. While making a journey one night by motor-car, a mistaken direction caused him and his staff to run into an enemy outpost; General Bridoux was mortally wounded and several of his officers were either killed or wounded at his side. His death was a calamity.

As I had directed him to do on September 8th, General Maunoury tried to push out the Cavalry Corps for the purpose of threatening the right and rear of von Kluck and delay the entry into action of the enemy forces which the fall of Maubeuge had set free; unfortunately the condition of men and horses made it impossible to fulfil this mission. The only thing accomplished was by the division commanded by General Cornulier-Lucinière, which succeeded in creating some confusion in von Kluck's rear and came near capturing (so it seems) the commander of the German First Army and all his staff.

After having been halted in the neighbourhood of La Ferté-sous-Jouarre by a broken bridge, the British Army, on the evening of September 9th, succeeded in gaining a foothold on the north shore of the Marne between La Ferté and Château-Thierry, held by the Fifth Army. This advance menaced the rear of the left wing of von Kluck's army which was now furiously assailing Maunoury.

Franchet d'Esperey's left had continued its forward progress. His XVIII Corps was moving towards Viffort, halfway between the Petit Morin and Château-Thierry. At 2 P.M. I had an order telephoned urging him to push to the Marne: "It is imperative that the XVIII Corps cross the Marne this evening in the vicinity of Château-Thierry, so as to support energetically the British columns." That night, September 9th, this corps did succeed in installing its advanced posts on the northern side of the river. On its left, Conneau's cavalry had also pushed over a brigade. When night arrived the rest of the Fifth Army found itself south of Surmelin, between Condé-en-Brie and Baye. The corps on the right (X), placed at Foch's disposal by Franchet d'Esperey, brought needed relief to the Ninth Army, at that time seriously pressed along its whole front. In his evening report of the day's operations, the commander of the Fifth Army announced himself quite ready to begin an action against the flank of the German forces which were assailing the Ninth Army.

Taken all in all, while the manœuvre which I had prescribed for September 9th in Special Instruction No. 19 had not as yet been fully executed, its development was proceeding satisfactorily.

The retirement of the Sixth Army's left wing was not a serious matter. General Maunoury was cool and confident and he would soon have new forces at his disposal which would permit him to resume his offensive. The British Army and the left of our Fifth were commencing to debouch on the other side of the Marne and, like a wedge, were now penetrating into the space between the German First and Second Armies.

In a new Special Instruction* issued during the evening of the 9th, I announced the results so far obtained and the movements to be effected: the Sixth Army, its right resting on the Ourcq, was to push von Kluck towards the north, whilst the British, supported by the Fifth Army, would march to Clignon and thus complete the separation of von Kluck from the army on his left.

Meantime the frontal engagement continued uninterruptedly. The manœuvre effected by General Foch on September 9th is well known. In response to his request for assistance, Franchet d'Esperey had placed at his complete disposal the X Corps and the 51st Reserve Division. Foch sent the X Corps to the west of Champaubert, between the Petit Morin and Fromentières and relieved the 42nd Division, forming the left of his army, by the 51st Reserve Division. Having thus provided himself with a reserve, he moved the 42nd Division in rear of his centre with orders to make ready to attack in the direction of Fère-Champenoise; then at 4 P.M. he gave orders for his whole line to advance. The II Corps was only able to make a commencement of the movement; the 42nd Division arrived too late to get into action before night fell; the X Corps alone, moving to the north of the Saint-Gond marshes, began to drive the enemy back, while at the same time the 77th Infantry Regiment retook the important point of support constituted by the Château de Mondemont.

In the Fourth Army, the situation likewise improved. The violence of the German attacks on its right and centre weakened visibly; west of the Marne, the entrance into action of the XXI Corps and elements which General de Langle had taken from his two right corps, was destined to render it possible on the following day to make an attack facing north-west, for the purpose of aiding Foch.

In Sarrail's army the fighting went on without the enemy being able to gain any ground; on the left of this army, the XV Corps was moving in close conjunction with de Langle's right. During

* Special Instruction No. 20, September 9, 1914, 8 P.M.

the night of September 9th/10th the Germans launched a violent attack against the front of the VI Corps; this offensive, definitely checked the next morning, marked the end of their efforts against the Third Army.

On the Meuse the enemy vainly continued his attempts. Troyon did not allow itself to be intimidated by the German bombardment, while the screen furnished by the 7th Cavalry Division, the presence of the 2nd Cavalry Division on the right bank near Saint-Mihiel as well as the provisional brigade which Castelnau had sent from Toul towards Commercy, proved sufficient to cover the rear of Sarrail's army.

By the evening of September 9th, therefore, I was justified in considering the situation as favourable: on the left our success had become pronounced while in the centre and on the right the enemy's rush appeared to be definitely checked. But Victory was closer than I had dared to hope for.

On the morning of the 10th, as the Sixth Army moved out to make the attack prescribed in my Instruction of the preceding evening, all of a sudden it felt the enemy's resistance give way and during this day it advanced over nine miles almost without firing a shot.

On its right, the British Army reached Clignon without meeting resistance, and at the close of the day it halted south of the Ourcq, from La Ferté-Milon to Neuilly-Saint-Front.

The Fifth Army was across the Marne from Château-Thierry to Dormans, and General Franchet d'Esperey reported to me that in front of him the enemy's retreat was becoming precipitate, part of his forces moving towards the north, part towards the east.

On the line of the Ninth Army likewise, our success began to be manifest. The general advance which Foch had undertaken to effect the day before was now gaining impetus and all went to show that, here also, the enemy had effected a precipitate retreat during the night. For the evening of the 10th, Foch established his headquarters at Fère-Champenoise which the Prussian Guard had held that very morning.

In front of the Fourth and Third Armies the situation still remained stationary. Instead of de Langle's left being able to work for the benefit of the Ninth Army, as I had hoped would be the case, it was the latter which found itself in a position to aid the army on its right. Opposite Sarrail the enemy's activity lessened still further, and the XV Corps having finished the cleaning up of the forest of Trois Fontaines, now held position abreast of the right corps of the Fourth Army.

What now remained to be done was to follow up the success achieved by our left and centre and at the same time overcome the resistance which continued to hold up our two armies on the right. To this effect I sent out a series of orders on September 10th with the object of giving a fresh impetus to the battle.

To French and Maunoury I made the request that they push straight to the north on each side of the Ourcq; on their extreme left, Bridoux's Cavalry Corps was to endeavour constantly to threaten the enemy's lines of retreat, and on their right the Fifth Army was so to place itself as to be able to act, *facing east,* in the direction of Rheims, against the columns which were retreating before the Ninth Army.*

To General Foch I pointed out that the result of the battle would depend in a large measure on the action of his army against the corps facing our Fourth Army.†

To General de Langle, I urged the necessity of a vigorous advance especially on his left.‡

To General Sarrail I telegraphed that I only expected him to hold fast where he stood.§

In addition to this, I made every effort to threaten the two flanks of the retreating enemy—his right, by sending a radio message to General Coutanceau, Military Governor of Verdun, to attack with all his forces any enemy convoys which crossed the Meuse north of Verdun, and his left, by pushing General d'Amade's Territorial Divisions to the region of Beauvais.||

I also telegraphed the First Army to entrain the XII Corps at Epinal and send it to the north of Paris; for my whole attention was now concentrated upon the necessity of preventing the enemy from recovering himself, and to ensure this I desired to reinforce still further General Maunoury's army, which I considered to be the principal factor in our manœuvre.

That evening I had the certainty of victory, although I was as yet unable to measure its full extent. I reported to the Minister of War the first results, namely, on my left, the enemy in full retreat

* Special Instruction No. 21 of September 10th, afternoon.
† Special Order of September 10th, morning.
‡ Special Order of September 10th, 10 A.M.
§ Special Order of September 10th, 10.10 A.M.
|| Special Order of September 9th.

having already yielded more than 37 miles; his centre weakening in front of Foch; his left, while not yet beaten, at the end of their resistance.

On September 11th, our victory became confirmed along the whole of the line. The Sixth Army had reached the front Pierrefond-Chandun; the British were crossing the upper Ourcq; Franchet d'Esperey, driving before him the weak rear-guards of the enemy, had pushed the heads of his columns south of the Vesle between Chéry and Ville-en-Tardenois; his right corps, the X, which had so powerfully contributed to Foch's success, was moving from Vertus towards Epernay, while the Ninth Army itself was on the Marne between Sarry and Tours. The Fourth Army also was now advancing. Its left, during the night, had reached the Marne below Vitry, its right, the Colonial Corps, occupied the bridges over the Saulx and the II Corps those over the Ornain, in close touch with the left of the Third Army, which itself was in the act of crossing the last-named river. The remainder of Sarrail's army was not making any headway, but at the close of the day a report from his staff stated that an "impressive calm" reigned along the whole of their front.*

That afternoon I telegraphed as follows to the Minister of War: "The Battle of the Marne is an incontestable victory for us."

3. The Eastern Front

TSARIST RUSSIA was perhaps the most "defeated" participant in the First World War. It is true that the Central Powers emerged from the war on the losing side, and the Serbian army was forced entirely out of its homeland, re-entering Serbia eventually by the back door of Salonika. But the most demoralized, mauled, and decimated army was the Russian, which, paradoxically, within several years of the Armistice of November 11, 1918, was to be resuscitated by the Soviet government and metamorphosed into the formidable Red Army—probably communism's greatest single achievement.

In August, 1914, the mobilization of Russia's horde of muzhiks was

---

* I must confess that this report from the Third Army, which, if I remember correctly, was telephoned personally by Colonel Leboucq, chief of staff of this army, caused me the greatest astonishment and excited my liveliest displeasure. At a moment when the enemy showed clearly that he considered himself beaten along the whole line, here was the Third Army, perfectly placed for clinching the victory, satisfied with merely announcing—through fear of some vaguely suspected trap—that entire calm reigned along its front! I immediately gave orders for this army to commence an energetic pursuit of the enemy.

swifter and more efficient than expected. By the third week of August there were two million Russians under arms. Eight Russian army corps were deployed against five German corps in East Prussia, and eighteen Russian corps against Austria's twelve in Galicia. Paris urged Saint Petersburg to conduct an immediate offensive against the Central Powers to relieve the formidable pressure being exerted against Belgium and northeastern France. Russia was so anxious to comply that Grand Duke Nicholas, the Russian commander in chief, ordered the Russian armies into action before they were fully equipped, and with only slapdash logistical planning.

The Russian strategy was simple. Before an offensive toward Berlin could be undertaken, the Russians had to safeguard from flank attacks their exposed salient in Russian Poland by eliminating the German outpost in East Prussia and the Austrian in Galicia. Rennenkampf and Samsonov were supposed to cut off East Prussia by invading it from east and south and effecting a junction there, but Samsonov's loss of the Battle of Tannenberg dispelled this hope. Hindenburg and Ludendorff rounded up 90,000 Russian prisoners between August 26 and September 1. Samsonov committed suicide, and Rennenkampf's army was pushed eastward beyond the Niemen.

Meanwhile, Russia had to cope with the Austrian threat in Galicia. Austria had made a ludicrously ineffective thrust at its original enemy, Serbia—so weak a blow that the Serbs easily parried it, and within the first month of the war they had expelled the Austrian invaders. The Austrian command under Conrad von Hötzendorf could not ignore the Russian colossus. Conrad wanted to throw Russia off balance by an immediate offensive into Russian Poland, thereby engaging their attention while the Schlieffen Plan was being carried out in France. The Austrian command planned an offensive northeastward into Poland by two armies—that of General Dankl based on Przemysl and Jaroslav, and the army of General von Ost-Auffenberg based on Lemberg. These forces were to be protected by two more Austrian armies on their right, farther to the east. According to the original Austro-German strategy, the German forces in East Prussia were supposed to strike southeast while the Austrians pushed northeast, the two allies pursuing a converging course to cut off Russia's Polish salient. But the German command would not allot troops for this convergence, once the war began. Nevertheless General Dankl crossed the frontier on August 10, defeating the Russians near Lublin, and pressing General Ivanov's forces over the Bug River.

The Russians planned to attack Galicia—not from the north but from the east—using Kiev as the rear base, and Dubno and Luck as the points of departure for their offensive. On September 3, Russian Generals Russky and Brusilov bore down upon Lemberg, investing the city and seizing 100,000 prisoners—mostly pro-Russian Slavic subjects of the Hapsburgs. On September 11, the Austrian command ordered a general retreat almost to Cracow, but the Germans, fresh from their victory of Tannenberg, came to Austria's rescue in late October. Hindenburg massed an army of 700,000 Germans between Thorn and

Lublinitz, and slowly pushed the Russians back toward Warsaw, which was captured on August 4, 1915.

A witness to many of the vast operations on the eastern front was the British military attaché assigned to the Saint Petersburg embassy from 1911 until 1918, Major General Sir Alfred Knox. As compared with the abundance of testimony on the fighting on other fronts, there is a relative paucity of documentary material on tsarist Russia's role in the war. Apart from its inherent merits, Knox's book *With the Russian Army, 1814–1917* thus has a scarcity value. Knox was born October 30, 1870, in Newcastle, county Down, Northern Ireland. He was educated at Saint Columba's College, Dublin, and at the Royal Military College, Sandhurst. He joined the Royal Irish Rifles in 1891, and seven years later was posted to India to serve with the Fifty-eighth Vaughn's Rifles. Knox was aide-de-camp to Viceroy and Governor General Curzon from 1899 to 1904, when he was assigned to the Staff College at Camberley for a year, and then to General Staff service at the War Office. In 1911 he was ordered to Saint Petersburg as military attaché, serving in that capacity until 1918. Upon the war's outbreak in 1914, the British sent Sir John Hanbury-Williams to represent the British army at the Russian General Headquarters. This freed Colonel Knox from duties in Petrograd. Provided with a special permit from Tsar Nicholas II, in command of the Russian language, on terms of friendship with a number of Russian generals, Knox was privileged to go as an observer to any part of the front where operations were in progress. In retirement after the war, General Knox represented Wycombe as a Conservative member of Parliament from 1924 until 1945.

In the excerpts from Knox's diary which we publish, the Russian army command appeared hopeful of victory, despite the defeat at Tannenberg. Brusilov's Third Army advanced 220 versts during the latter half of August, 1914. By mid-September the Austrians had to withdraw behind the San River. By October Russian General Erdeli told Knox that the war would be over in several months, and there would be a New Year celebration in Petrograd.

Knox was a sympathetic observer, for the Russians were lavish in their hospitality. As a conservative English professional soldier who knew Russian, he found it easy to establish rapport with the officers. But his penetrating scrutiny quickly took note of the flaws in the vast army—hints of the ultimate débâcle. As early as September 15, 1914, in the Lines of Communication headquarters in Warsaw, he discerned evidence of filth, disorder, and inefficiency. The remount depot had a "collection of dreadful scarecrows." At Lublin, Knox heard from an English tutor that a Russian corps had bolted at Krasnik and was stopped by Cossack whips. Officers upon arriving at bivouac searched for women, leaving the troops and horses "to shift for themselves." These were ominous portents of what the future held in store for tsarist Russia. On the other hand, Knox was favorably impressed by the accuracy and power of Russian artillery. As yet the fatal shell shortage had not appeared. Nor had the Germans yet made their massive penetration of Russian Poland, offsetting Austrian losses.

By

MAJOR GENERAL SIR ALFRED KNOX,

WITH THE RUSSIAN ARMY, 1914–1917

WITH A CAVALRY DIVISION IN SOUTH-WEST

POLAND, SEPTEMBER–OCTOBER, 1914

On the South-West Front by the beginning of September the Russian armies had wrested the initiative from the Austrian Command.

The Austrians had in the first instance some thirty-six infantry divisions to assist the German seventeen divisions to hold back Russia pending the decision in the Western Theatre. They resolved to strike north at the Russian 4th (Ewarth *vice* Salza) and 5th (Plehve) Armies between the Bug and Vistula. For this purpose they detailed a Northern Group, consisting of, from right to left, the 4th Army (Auffenberg), 1st Army (Dankl), and on the left bank of the Vistula a mixed detachment containing a German Landwehr Corps under General Woyrsch. The strength of this offensive wing was about 350 battalions, 150 squadrons and 150 batteries. To guard its right flank from the attack of the Russian 8th (Brusilov) and 3rd (Ruzski) Armies through Eastern Galicia, they formed a right defensive wing, about 200 battalions, 170 squadrons and 130 batteries strong. This right wing was subdivided into the 2nd Army, which assembled between Stanislau and Stryj under General Kovcss, and the 3rd Army (Von Brudermann), which was intended to cover the approaches to Lemberg from the east.

The Russian 4th and 5th Armies completed their deployment on the 18th and moved south from the general line Novo-Alexandriya-Vladimir-Volinsk on August 19th.

The Austrian orders for the advance of the Northern Group were issued on August 22nd, before the completion of the concentration. The advance was at first successful. The battle of Krasnik ended on the 25th with the retreat of the Russian 4th Army. Auffenberg captured Zamostie on the 27th. By the evening of September 1st, Dankl had penetrated upwards of 100 kilometres into Russian territory, and was within a march of Lyublin, the

Source: From *With the Russian Army, 1914–1917* (London: Hutchinson Publishing Group Ltd., 1921), pp. 95–131. Reprinted by permission of the publisher.

third city in the kingdom of Poland. Auffenberg's Army had made less progress, and was held up for several days by Plehve's 5th Army on the general line Krilov-Dashov-Komarov-Grabovets. At length, on September 1st, Komarov was occupied, Plehve having received orders to retire.

Meanwhile the plan of campaign worked out by Alexyeev, Ivanov's Chief of Staff, commenced to take effect, and the threat to the Austrian communications in Galicia became a very real one. Brusilov, with the Russian 8th Army, had crossed the frontier on a wide front west of Proskurov on August 19th. Two days later Ruzski, with the 3rd Army, crossed astride the Brody-Lemberg railway. The progress of both armies was rapid. From August 17th till September 3rd Brusilov covered 220 versts. On the latter date the 3rd Army took Lemberg and the 8th Army Halicz.

The Austrian Command wavered. The main body of Auffenberg's 4th Army was recalled, and on September 5th it faced south, with its right north of Nemierow and its left east of Rawa Ruska. From this position its right moved still further south to unite with the left of the defeated Austrian right wing in an attempt to withstand the enemy's continued pressure west of Lemberg.

Meanwhile the arrival of the Guard and the XVIIIth Corps on the line Lyublin-Kholm had enabled the Russians to take the offensive against Dankl. On September 5th he was forced to withdraw his right, and Woyrsch's German Landwehr Corps was transferred east to strengthen that flank. Dankl held on for some days, but on the 9th pressure on both flanks forced him to retire.

The counter-attacks of the 2nd, 3rd and 4th Armies availed the Austrians nothing against the determined and continued pressure of Plehve, Ruzski and Brusilov. At midday on September 11th the Austrian Command resolved to withdraw its armies to refit behind the San.

The Russian campaign on the South-West Front had opened brilliantly, but the success was not decisive. The officer who was in charge of operations in the Staff of the Front at this time stated months later that the original Russian plan had been by a simultaneous advance to the south up both banks of the Vistula and in a westerly direction south of Lemberg to cut off the Austrian army from both Krakau and the Carpathians. In his opinion the 9th Russian Army should have been sent due south from Ivangorod, instead of its strength being employed in frontal attacks between Lyublin and Kholm.

During the five days I spent in Petrograd—from the evening of

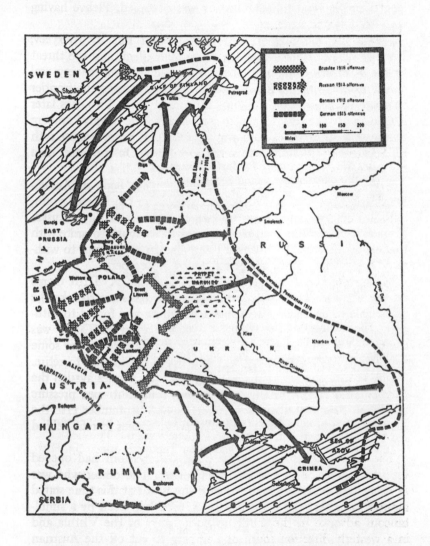

the 7th till the morning of September 13th—the Russian General
Staff professed to be perturbed by reports of transfers from the
Western Theatre. On September 8th it was stated that four corps,
said to have been brought from France, were detraining on the
line Krakau-Chenstokhov; on the 10th that the Russian Military
Attaché had telegraphed from Holland that he calculated only
ten to twelve regular German corps remained in the Western
Theatre. On the same day information was received that the Ger-
mans were detraining a corps at Sambor, south-west of Lemberg.
These reports were all inaccurate.

Tuesday, September 15th, 1914.   WARSAW.
    I arrived at Warsaw 8.30 A.M. Drove to the Hotel Bristol, and
spent the day arranging for further journey.
    At the office of the Commandant of the Lines of Communica-
tion there were, as usual, armed sentries everywhere, annoying
everyone and exercising no discrimination as to who should be allowed to go in and who not. The whole place was in an indescribable state of filth; everyone appeared to be waiting and little
progress seemed to be made with work. However, by making a
row I attracted sufficient attention to induce a clerk who could
read to go through my letter. I was sent to the stable with an
ensign, a nice fellow, who spoke a little English, to see my horses.
The mare has rheumatism. The veterinary surgeon says she will
be able to march in a week, but I doubt it.
    There is a little of everything at the "Base Étape." It comprises
a remount depot—I saw a collection of dreadful scarecrows; also
poor Samsonov's horses, including the black that I remember
walked so fast in Turkistan last year. There were people selling
hay. A non-commissioned officer had come from Lyublin direct to
get horses for his battery, and refused—I perfectly agreed with
him—to take any of those he saw. There were numbers of de-
serters and of convalescents waiting to be sent on to their units.
All seemed content to wait. I heard there were one hundred German female prisoners who had been captured armed in East
Prussia and many other German prisoners. One wagon-load of
thirty-five that arrived on Saturday from Mlava was to go to Minsk
to be shot. They had been brought with only two Russian guards
in the wagon. They murdered one by ripping up his stomach with
a penknife and beat and threw the other out of the train. Luckily
the man thrown out was not killed, and was able to creep to a
station and warn the authorities. Altogether, I would prefer other
jobs to that of Commandant Étapes at Warsaw. Apparently the
unfortunate individual deals with the lines of communication in
every direction.

    I saw two pessimistic Englishmen, both of whom were more or
less convinced that Warsaw is in immediate danger because it is

being fortified and wire entanglements are being put up. I told them that St. Petersburg is also being fortified!

Wednesday, September 16th, 1914. LYUBLIN.

The Russian army is crossing the lower San unopposed. Ruzski, having reached Moseiska, is within a march east of Przemysl.

I met an English tutor who had seen something of operations in the Lyublin Government. He is full of tales of misconduct of troops—that one corps bolted for miles from Krasnik and was only stopped by Cossacks, who used their whips freely—that officers immediately they arrive at the bivouac look about for women and leave horses and men to shift for themselves. The XVIIIth Corps has gone up the Vistula.

I left Warsaw by train at 4 P.M. without my horses, and arrived at Lyublin at 11 P.M., to find that the staff of the 9th Army had left at 4 P.M. for Ivangorod and Ostrovets. It would be much better to drive there, but the Station Commandant, after telephoning to the Commandant Town, advised me to go back to Ivangorod to-morrow to apply to the Commandant Étapes, who would send me by the "organised" route—probably up the Vistula. Meanwhile it was necessary to sleep somewhere, so after waiting an hour for a cab, and none coming, we started to walk the two miles to the town. We picked up a cab halfway, and drove in succession to seven hotels, starting at a palace like the Ritz and ending with a Jewish hovel. None of them had a corner to spare, and most of the rooms had three to six occupants. We drove back to the station and the Commandant Station *most* kindly turned out of his railway compartment to let me sleep there. I felt a brute, and wished I had put up in the refreshment room. It is the getting up in the morning one dreads, with no chance of a wash.

Heavy rain.

Thursday, September 17th, 1914. IVANGOROD.

I waited at Lyublin till 11 A.M. for a train to carry me back to Ivangorod. The captain in command of the station at Lyublin, with his two assistants, a staff captain and an ensign, were kindness itself. They do their work efficiently. I noticed while in the office at the station how everyone who came in was attended to sympathetically and rapidly without red tape, and yet the general accompaniments of the office showed no signs of order. Good temper and unbounded patience seemed to make everything work.

I was given a coupé to myself to return to Ivangorod, and gave seats to two ladies who were dressed in black, and a lieutenant in the horse artillery battery of the Guard from Warsaw. The elder lady had lost her son in the Preobrajenskis in the recent battle at Krasnik. The younger one, who was very pretty and who spoke English well, had come down to Lyublin to nurse her husband through an attack of typhoid. They told me of the death of young

Bibikov, who belonged to the Lancers of Warsaw and was killed in a charge by the Independent Guard Cavalry Brigade against infantry in a wood. Mannerheim, his General, kissed the dead boy and said he would like to be in his place. Mannerheim is blamed for squandering lives. Poor Bibikov won all the prizes at the Concours Hippique at Vienna three years ago. I remember I saw his father and mother dining with the boy at a restaurant the night he returned to Warsaw. The little lady told me to-day that the funeral service had been held in a huge stable, part of which was occupied with horses, and she found this fitting in the case of a boy like Bibikov, who was so devoted to the animals.

The horse gunner told me of a remarkable piece of work by the 16th Narva Hussars. The Guard Rifle Brigade, which had three regiments in occupation of a position, was badly in need of help. The 16th charged the enemy's trenches at 10 P.M.!

I had some conversation with the colonel in charge of the advanced depot which the Guard Co-operative Society maintains for the convenience of the officers and men of the Guard Corps. The society has seven wagons on a siding at Lyublin, three or four at Ivangorod. We took four on with us by the train in which we left for Ostrovets. The wagons are given at half-freight by Government. One can buy almost anything: boots, Sam Browne belts, chocolate, etc. They also sell brandy to officers, but there is absolutely no drinking to excess; as officers say: "The war is too serious for that."

The Russians lost many men at Krasnik, where the Austrians had semi-permanently fortified a position. The enemy fired through loopholes and the Russians were forced to attack without fire preparation. The Russian artillery fire is wonderfully accurate, and as the enemy never has time to get the range to Russian covered positions, the Russian losses in gunners have been extraordinarily small. The cavalry on this front has not suffered much and the infantry has borne the brunt.

Probably as many as 40,000 wounded, including Austrians, were brought into Lyublin. They were carried many miles over bad roads in country carts. Three bad cases were carried in a cart, and more often than not only two men were still alive when they arrived. I gather that the advanced hospital is the regimental hospital, then the field hospital. Then at the railhead, as a rule, is the collecting-point (*Sborni-Punkt*), whence cases are sent to local hospitals (*Myestnie*) in school-houses, etc., or sent to the interior in trains if judged fit to travel.

The 9th Army is south of Sandomir on the right bank of the Vistula, with its chief supply base in Ivangorod. Each corps has a separate line of communications and organisation. Yesterday 40,000 puds were sent by train to Ostrovets, 6,000 on a steamer up the Vistula, and 16,000 by road up the right bank of the river. The Russians have four steamers, each with a capacity of 6,000 puds. The ordinary military train takes 45,000 puds, just enough for an army corps for a day, including forage, etc., etc.

At Lyublin I saw the 56th Supply Transport Battalion (country carts), which had just arrived from Bobruisk, and was met by an order to detrain and carry bread seventy-four versts, as the men at the front were said to be starving.

On leaving Warsaw I noticed that one of the arches of the northern footbridge had been prepared for demolition, and on the right bank of the Vistula there were emplacements ready prepared for a field battery, and pointed towards Warsaw. Similarly at Ivangorod there were recently-constructed trenches.

While we were dining at the hotel at Ivangorod, twenty young, recently-appointed subalterns came in. They had been two years at artillery schools and had got their commissions early on account of the war. They were going to the 9th Army to be appointed to batteries. The poor boys were all as keen as mustard, and told me that their one fear was lest they might be employed till the end of the war against the Austrians and never have a dash at the Prussians. I said to the Colonel: "They think they will be field-marshals." He said: "No, it's the St. George's Cross that they dream of, but war thirsts for the young. In the Pavlovski regiment, out of eleven recently joined, four have been killed and seven wounded." The boys were soon scribbling letters home.

We left Ivangorod by train at 10 P.M.

Friday, September 18th, 1914. SANDOMIR.
I arrived at Ostrovets at 9 A.M. in a downpour, and drove in a motor, starting at midday, via Ojarov and Zavikhost to Sandomir, where we arrived at five. My servant Maxim, the orderly Ivan, and my one remaining horse did not reach Sandomir till 10 P.M. The police-inspector found me a nice, clean room in this very dirty town, which is crowded with troops.

The Russians have a mass of cavalry on the Austrian front. A Cossack officer told me that they had thirty-four second- and third-category Don Cossack regiments, and fifteen Orenburg Cossack regiments alone, to say nothing of Kuban, Terek, Ural, etc. I saw a squadron of Ural Cossacks in Sandomir—big, red-bearded, wild-looking men, nearly all with a waterproof coat over their military great-coat. I don't wonder that the Austrians are frightened by them.

The men generally that I have seen here are not so worn-looking as those with poor Samsonov were.

Sandomir was taken on Monday, the 14th, the Tula regiment losing heavily. The town had been occupied for two and a half weeks by the Austrians. My hostess, who talked a little French, told me that she had had Hungarians and Cossacks and every kind of person in the house.

There was fighting going on near by to-day and the sky was lit up to the south-west by burning villages at night.

Saturday, September 19th, 1914.   SANDOMIR.
I had a good sleep in a comfortable bed, and Madame P. gave us tea before we started to motor to Army Headquarters at Zolbnev, twelve versts south-east of Sandomir.

She told me that her husband had insisted on her leaving for her sister's house when Sandomir was occupied by the Austrians. On the day the Russians re-took the town the Germans seized seventeen of the oldest men and carried them off. Her husband, an apothecary of fifty-six, was one of them, the excuse being that a shot had been fired from a group of houses in which his stood. She is now in despair, for she can hear nothing of him, and, indeed, is unlikely to do for months to come.

We found the staff of the 9th Army in a villa surrounded by pretty gardens. The house was oldish, perhaps dating from the seventeenth century. The furniture was a lot of it good Empire. General Gulevich, the Chief of Staff, took me into a little room apart to talk, and sat down on a chair which collapsed with him and deposited him on the floor with his feet in the air. It may have been a good armchair a hundred years ago, but was not a weight-carrier. I showed my credentials. Gulevich explained that General Lechitski dreaded having me, as he could not speak either English or French. He came in to see me and actually understood my Russian!

The general situation was explained to me. Ruzski and Brusilov are still pressing the Austrians west. Plehve and Ewarth are pushing them south, and will probably take Jaroslav. Lechitski is making ground to the south and south-west. It appears that the Austrians have retreated west from Baranow, which was occupied by the Russians yesterday, and are preparing to defend seriously the line of the River Wistoka.

A raid by five cavalry divisions is to be attempted under General Novikov with the idea of cutting the Austrian communications with Krakau and forcing them to retire. I asked and obtained permission to go with this force.

I spoke for some time with the Polish lady, and she tried to find out what I thought of the Russian army, remarking that it had evidently made wonderful progress since the Japanese war. She showed me the place where two howitzer shells from the Russian guns had burst, one of them making a hole five feet deep within ten yards of her house. She and her husband had spent two nights and a day in the cellar. Her two sons are fighting in the Austrian army and she has not had any news from them since the war commenced. What an unhappy people the Poles are! I hope one result of the war will be to produce a united people under Russia's protection. The idea of the possibility of such shell-craters in our garden in Ulster makes one willing to pay any income tax for an overwhelming army.

We drove further south to Rozwadow to see large quantities of supplies that had been captured from the Austrians. I had an excellent meal of shchi* and black bread—probably all the stuff I will have to eat for a week or so!

Little Durnovo, on his way from General Headquarters to join Lechitski's 9th Army, brought me greetings from the Grand Duke and news that "a second British Army has landed at Ostend and is moving in conjunction with the Belgians against the German lines of communication."

Colonel S., of the Administrative Staff of the 9th Army, with whom I have spent the last few days, is a glorious snorer. Each snore ends with a regular ring. I lay awake imagining how his nostrils must shake and tingle. You could hear him at Vladivostok! He tries to work hard in the day, but gives me the impression of talking too much. However, he is a kind-hearted soul. He was astonished that I shaved every day, and still more so when I told him that many people in England shaved twice a day.

Sunday, September 20th, 1914. KLIMONTOV.
A pouring wet day and not a pleasant start for the raid. General Erdeli, who is in command of the 14th Division, and his A.D.C., Prince Cantacuzene, called for me at 9.30 A.M. We drove through a sea of mud to Klimontov, the Headquarters of the 14th Cavalry Division, for the night. The division arrived about 3 P.M., having marched from Tarnobzeg, south of the Vistula, at 8 A.M. The 8th Division passed through Sandomir moving northwest last night.

General Novikov's corps will be 140 squadrons strong, comprising the 5th, 8th, 14th and two Don Cossack divisions, a Turkistan Cossack brigade and four sotnias of Frontier Guard.

There seems some doubt regarding our "task." It is said that the heavy rain has flooded the Vistula and the possible crossing-places are carefully guarded. The possibility of a turning movement west instead of east of Krakau is canvassed.

We got almost a comfortable dinner, including tea, for forty kopeks (tenpence)! The population of the town is almost entirely Jewish. I found a Jew who had been at Toronto and talked broad "American." "He liked the country and liked the people"!

I saw Novikov yesterday for the first time. He was walking up and down a long room in the Château at Zolbnev discussing plans with his Chief of Staff, Colonel Dreyer. A young officer pointed him out as the foremost cavalry leader of the Russian army. Out-

---

* Cabbage soup.

wardly he appeared merely a tall, handsome man of the type of British cavalry officer.

Erdeli I had met before at St. Petersburg. He is of a more brainy and subtle type. He commenced his serve in the Hussars of the Guard, in which he served with the Emperor. He commanded the Dragoons of the Guard, and at the beginning of the war was General Quartermaster of the St. Petersburg Military District, in which capacity he was appointed to the 9th Army. He is only forty-four.

The division has had a rough time since mobilisation. It has had many skirmishes with Germans and Austrians between Radom and Ivangorod. The doctor says it is "tired," but horses and men look fit and hard.

Monday, September 21st, 1914.   STOPNITSA.

Rode forty-three versts (thirty miles) with the division, from Klimontov *via* Bogoriya to Stopnitsa.

On the march we had two squadrons in front, one furnishing patrols and the other an advance party. The four remaining squadrons of the leading regiment, with a battery, followed us.

The officers of the staff of the division are: Chief of Staff, Colonel Westphalen, who is aged forty-nine and looks more, as he has just recovered from a serious illness.

Captain of General Staff, Sapojnikov, a very capable officer with plenty of initiative.

Two officers attached to the General Staff. One of these was at the Academy when war broke out.

An officer in charge of administration.

A Commandant of the Staff, who is also in charge of the "flying post."

An officer interpreter.

Liaison officers from neighbouring divisions.

An officer and five men from each of the four regiments of the division. These "battle patrols" are sent out immediately before an action when the enemy is only five versts off, with the special task of bringing exact information regarding his distribution and strength.

An officer and two men from each regiment and the artillery of the division as orderlies.

Important messages are sent by the officers and ordinary ones by the men.

We arrived at 6 P.M. at a Polish landowner's house. The hostess, a nice old lady with a comforting admiration for England, was anxious to see me. She doubts the fulfilment of Russia's promises to Poland. She told me that the Russian Government had seized all the balances in the municipal funds and in the private banks, most of which had been sent by Polish emigrants from America. The officials are getting no salaries and the pensioners receive no pensions!

I occupied a room with Cantacuzene last night, and had a very disturbed time. The General Staff Captain only brought orders from the Corps Staff at 2 A.M.; then there was much consultation while the divisional orders were being written in the General's room next door. Then the telephone which connects the divisional staff with the four regiments went continuously the whole night in the room on the other side. Heaven only knows what they had to talk about!

To-night the 5th Division is on our left on the Vistula and the 8th on our right. Our patrols are going as far as the Vistula. The enemy has a bridgehead south-east by south at a distance of about twenty-five versts from Stopnitsa.

Tuesday, September 22nd, 1914.   STOPNITSA.

The Divisional Commander and his two General Staff Officers returned at 1 A.M. from a conference with the Corps Commander. They left again at 10 A.M. with battle patrols and orderlies to carry out a short reconnaissance towards the Vistula.

The Austrians beyond the river are thought to be only Landwehr. A cannonade was audible all morning from a southeasterly direction.

The position of our forces now (morning of 22nd) is:

14th Cavalry Division.—Billets in neighbourhood of Stopnitsa. Patrols to line Korchin-Brjesko (on Vistula).

5th Cavalry Division.—Billets, Korchin. To move 23rd, north-west to Myekhov.

8th Cavalry Division.—Billets, Solets, north-east of Stopnitsa.

Turkistan Cossack Brigade.—Billets, Busk. Moving 23rd, north-west to Naglovitse.

The 14th, 5th and 8th Divisions have been detailed for the southern raid. The 4th and 5th Don Cossacks will protect their right rear.

Till the 4th and 7th Don Cossack Divisions have come up, the task of reconnoitring west will fall to the Turkistan Brigade and the 5th Division. The former will have headquarters at Naglovitse (north-west of Andreev) and will reconnoitre towards the line Lansberg-Sosnitse; the latter will continue the reconnaissance line from Sosnitse by Bendin to Krakau, a front of upwards of three hundred miles for thirty-six squadrons.

The Austrians have burnt the wooden bridge temporarily erected north of Szczucin, and fired to-day on our patrols from the southern bank of the Vistula.

On receipt of corps or army orders, Captain Shapojnikov calls up the orderly officers and dictates the divisional orders, which are then carried by the officers to units. The hour of start only is communicated to units or brigades by telephone. Orders are never written before an engagement against cavalry.

Officers in charge of patrols receive detailed instructions on the area to be reconnoitred and the subjects on which a report is required. It also laid down where and when they shall send in periodical reports. The three squadrons of the 14th Division sent out yesterday morning were to deploy on the front Korchin-Pinchov and wheel to the left to the Vistula on the line Korchin-Brjesko.

Officers ascribe the unwillingness of the Austrian cavalry to meet the Russian cavalry to the absence in the former of the lance. Every trooper in the Russian cavalry would now carry a lance if he were allowed. The German lance is a few inches shorter, a discovery which much pleased the Russians. The Russian cavalry practically follows the same tactics in reconnaissance as the German cavalry is *supposed* to; it rides to kill any hostile patrol it meets. German Uhlans carried pennons in West Poland at the beginning of the war, but these were soon discarded. The Austrian carbine is poor. The 14th Division say they have not yet had a man wounded by it.

The divisional medical officer tells me he has two sons and a daughter. He and his children are Lutherans. One son is married to an Orthodox girl and the other to a Catholic; the girl is married to a Mohammedan.

Wednesday, September 23rd, 1914.   ZLOTA.

We got up at 6.30 A.M. and left at 8 A.M., after saying goodbye to and thanking our hosts of the last two days. We rode in a cold wind over the most dreadful roads I have ever seen, even in Russia, to Vislitza, and then wheeled left (south) in two columns and came into action against some 200 "Sokols," or Polish partisans—not a very exciting affair!

We got to a comfortable house at Zlota at 9.45. We had been practically fourteen hours out. Luckily Maxim had made me some sandwiches, for which I was heartily thankful. The Russians are far too kind-hearted. We lost our way several times on our return journey, and if I had had anything to do with it, I should certainly have seized one of the local inhabitants and have made him come with me to show me the way.

Officers carry their maps generally in their hats. The maps are never mounted. The two-verst map, which is not on sale, seems good. The ten-verst is inaccurate and indistinct.

The supply of the two-verst map was not always sufficient, and some officers used the three-versts—a poor map with hashured hill features.

Officers in command of "battle patrols" were found repeatedly to be without maps of the district in which their task lay. The excuse was, of course, that such maps had been left in the second-line transport.

Each regiment of the 14th Division has received 203 riding remounts since the war began. These were furnished by the reserve squadron. About ninety of them were the annual batch of remounts due a few months later. Others had been prepared for the six new cavalry regiments which it was proposed to raise this year. Most of these animals have been little trained, and they are so soft that many of them have fallen out of the ranks already. Apart from this, sick horses are every day replaced during the march by changing them for fit ones requisitioned on receipts from the civilian owners.

The divisional doctor showed me the return of killed and wounded for the last month—August 13th to September 13th—in which the division had been continuously employed on essentially legitimate cavalry duties. Officers: killed 0, wounded 7. Rank and file: killed 32, wounded 130. This out of a total of 5,200.

Two Jews were discussing the war. One said: "Our side will win," and the other agreed. Someone asked which side was "ours," and both said: "Why, the side that will win."

In our skirmish with the Sokols this evening we burned the Charkov Manor House, a fine old château. Its owner, young Count Palovski, and his agent were brought in a country cart to where we stood. I was sorry for the boy, who looked a cultured gentleman and rather a contrast to some of those crowding round him, but it was clear that he had harboured the Sokols till our arrival, and local evidence marked him out as their chief organiser. His elder brother is an Austrian subject and an officer in an Austrian cavalry regiment. Another brother served as a short-time volunteer in the very regiment that he was captured by to-day. They have estates in Lithuania and a palace at Krakau. The youth bore himself well and without bombast, looking round every now and again at his burning home. He was driven off under escort to Busk. He had doubtless remained in his home in the hope that it might be spared.

The application of the lava formation I saw to-day did not impress me. A squadron simply advanced in open order and when fired upon retired. It roughly located the enemy's trenches and had no casualties because it was opposed to irregulars. The tactics of the day seemed feeble. As we had previous information that we would only be opposed by 200 Sokols, we might have allowed one brigade to march straight to bivouac. If the other brigade had sent forward one regiment in lava formation, it would have quickly found the enemy's flanks and forced him to retire from his trenches and cut him up when retiring.

The orders for the march which were issued on the previous evening indicated the rayon of the bivouac. Verbal orders issued at midday allotted the brigades to villages. The orders for the outposts were written rapidly by Captain Shapojnikov while the "battle" was in progress.

I had a very comfortable night at Count Veselovski's, an excellent supper and actually a bath in the morning.

Thursday, September 24th, 1914.   ZLOTA.
Captain Shapojnikov left at 3 P.M. with a squadron and an officer of the Pontoon Brigade to reconnoitre at Brjesko. It was reported that an Austrian battalion is there and is either destroying or building a bridge. In the latter case we may expect a hostile offensive here, but this, I think, is unlikely. I still hope we will cross, so as to weaken resistance to the 9th Army and hasten its advance on Krakau.

We heard to-day that Plehve has taken Jaroslav and so Przemysl is cut off from direct railway communication with Krakau.

I am very sorry for the Poles. These poor people don't know whether to stay or to try to get away. If armed Sokols come they say they are powerless to resist them and the Russian troops hold them responsible. At tea to-day the old lady of the house asked me who a very young officer at the table was, and shuddered when I told her he was a Cossack. She said that ten days ago at his estate in the neighbourhood her brother had fallen down dead from heart disease while giving a shawl to a Cossack who asked for a disguise. In 1863 her grandfather and father had taken part in the Partisan movement. Their house was surrounded and both men wounded. Her grandmother, an old lady of eighty, was shot dead by a Cossack. I hope the settlement will bring this much-tried nation relief. Our hostess told me that she only heard at 5 P.M. yesterday that her house was to be "invaded." It is hard lines, but this cannot be helped. The poor woman is horrified at the mud the orderlies carry in on their boots, but, after all, there is no mat to clean them on!

She complained to-day bitterly of the theft of apples by the men from a Jew who had bought the contents of her orchards. She told the Commandant of the Staff, but I fancy nothing will come of it. The officers do not seem to understand that this spoils discipline.

Friday, September 25th, 1914.   WOODMAN'S HUT
                                   FIVE KILOMETRES SOUTH OF PINCHOV.
We started at 9 A.M., after saying good-bye. Rode south to Dobyeslavitse. Glorious day. "The Blood-thirsty Cornet" (as we had christened a young officer, who was always thirsting for the blood of the Boche) rode on an Irish horse, a "hunter," that he had bought from our host for Rs.400 and was at once willing to sell for Rs.750. He got no offers over Rs.300, as the horse was evidently a confirmed "puller."

We lunched in the house of a Polish landowner who had some fine old engravings. At lunch the General received information from the Corps that the Germans are advancing in two large groups based on Chenstokhov and Bendin, and that further north they have occupied Novoradomsk. We are ordered to move north in the direction of Pinchov, and have to abandon the idea of crossing the Vistula, which was to have been carried out to-night. Our task will be now to delay the German advance on Warsaw till an army in rear concentrates. We had marched twenty-five versts in the morning, and started at 3.30 P.M. to march thirty-five more in exactly the opposite direction.

The division moved in three parallel columns, a brigade on either flank and the transport in the centre. We rode in advance of the left brigade. At 8 P.M. shots were fired by men of a German patrol on a connecting file of our advanced guard. We were all halted in a hollow at the time. The General ordered a squadron forward, and it streamed out in lava formation. Soon the Blood-thirsty Cornet returned to tell us that a German trooper had been wounded and captured. He carried his sword and helmet in triumph. He said he could not speak very well, as he had been wounded by a lance in the mouth!

An officer's patrol came in to say that the 8th Division was in action against infantry near Myekhov. We will move north to-morrow with the Turkistan Brigade on the right and north of it, the Caucasion Cavalry Division under General Charpentier.

We reached a farmhouse at 11 P.M., but there is little chance of seeing our transport to-night.

Rotmeister Nikolaev, who was marching by the centre road with the pack transport, stumbled on to the top of the German patrol to-day. He did not hesitate, but galloped straight at it, packhorses and all. He accounted for nine Germans. It was fine evidence of the cavalry spirit, for if he had hesitated for a moment the patrol would probably have turned the tables on him, or at any rate would have got away. All the wounded and killed in the skirmish were by the lance. The Captain in command got a horrid wound in the mouth, knocking his teeth out. He lay all night on a sofa of the dining-room of the house we occupied and glared at us. The second officer was killed, and we altogether killed or captured twenty-three men out of twenty-six in the patrol.

The Commander's diary showed that he had seen us march south in the morning. He did not reckon on us returning so quickly. The roads here are sunken and conceal troop movements.

The young lieutenant who acts as interpreter was quite efficient in extracting information from a captured German N.C.O. His method is to tell the man that if he tells lies we are in a position to disprove them, and that he will be at once shot; otherwise he will be sent back as a prisoner of war to Central Russia and will have a good time. He then asks if the man has a wife and children, when his eyes are bound to fill with tears, and he is "brought to the proper frame of mind." It was an unforgettable scene, the room crowded with officers, a single flickering candle, and the prisoners.

Only N.C.O.'s and a few of the men are questioned separately

and their answers are compared. Officers are not questioned, the
Russian theory being that the officer is a man of honour and must
not be insulted by being pressed to give information against his
own country.

The wounded N.C.O. stated that the patrol had been despatched two days previously from one hour west of Myekhov. It
belonged to the Guard Dragoon Regiment. The collecting-point
for reports was a village fifteen versts south-west of our present
billet, and this point was occupied by infantry.

Saturday, September 26th, 1914.   Yasenn, Six Versts.
                                    South-East of Andreev.

Maxim arrived at the workman's hut with the transport about
3 a.m. I slept about three hours. Left at 9 a.m. and rode through
Pinchov.

Pinchov is the peace station of the 14th Uhlans, one of the
regiments of the Division. I rode into the town with Staff Rotmeister Plotnikov, the Commander of the battle patrol furnished
by that regiment, and he was delighted to be once more in
familiar surroundings. He said it made a curious impression to
ride in war through a wood where he had so often gathered
mushrooms with his wife. He got me cigarettes through a friendly
Jew and a meal in the town.

We rode on, crossing the Nida at Motkovitse to Yasenn, south-
east of Andreev, where we stopped in a small country house inhabited by a bevy of women. Their drawing-room is full of
flowers; it will look different to-morrow morning. They can only
give us four rooms, and we are eighteen officers.

A German patrol was sighted by one of our flank patrols as
we crossed the Nida, but got away, though we sent two squadrons
after it—a pity, for this may spoil the impression of yesterday.

The Corps Staff estimates the German strength on the front
Chenstokhov-Bendin at an army corps only, composed of reserve
units of the Guard and the IVth Corps. If we can destroy their
cavalry and so "blind them," as Shapojnikov says, we should have
some fun.

Yesterday Loginov, with the Turkistan Cossack Brigade reconnoitring on too wide a front, was pushed back from Konetspol,
and later, it is believed, from Vloshchova. The 8th Division is
believed to be near Vodzislav and the 5th near Myekhov, but
their commanders are without much energy. One of the Don
Cossack divisions arrives by forced marches to-morrow at Kyeltsi
to assist Loginov; the other will probably go on to the extreme
left. Our *rôle* is to delay. The Nida, with its marshy valley, seems
the natural line.

Maxim, my civilian servant, asked me to recommend him for
a St. George's Cross on account of the skirmish yesterday. As he
was on a cart with the centre column, and was unarmed, I asked
him what he had done. He said: "I yelled 'Hurrah!'"

Fine morning, but cloudy afternoon. Frost last night.

Sunday, September 27th, 1914.   YASENN, SOUTH-EAST OF
ANDREEV.

The enemy's infantry is generally on a radius of thirty-five-
versts from Andreev from right to left west of Vloshchova-
Shchekotsini-Jarnovets-Myekhov. A column of his cavalry which
was trying to get through to Andreev was thrown back by two
of our squadrons last night.

The Turkistan Brigade has re-taken Vloshchova. The 5th Don
Cossack Division arrives at Kyeltsi to-day. The 14th Division is to
go to Andreev; the 8th Division to Vodzislav; the 5th to Skalb-
myerj; the 4th Don Cossack Division *may* arrive at Busk to-day,
but it is doubtful. Agent's information received at 10 A.M. states
that two infantry regiments are advancing on Naglovitse; the bulk
of the Germans seem to be moving south-east towards Myekhov,
i.e., probably against the flank of the 9th Army. They have this
year's recruits in the ranks. The 4th Army is retiring to Ivangorod.
Meanwhile we have only a brigade of the 79th Division at Ivangorod and another brigade of the same division is retiring north
along the Vistula. The Staff of the Cavalry Corps moves to Motkovitse on the river Nida south-east of Andreev to-day. Three railway bridges north-east and west and south-west of Andreev were
destroyed this morning.

While I was writing the above a cannonade started north-west
of Andreev, accompanied by machine-gun fire. We said good-bye
to our hostess and her six daughters, who looked quite terrified.
They had no idea till they heard the firing that the Prussians were
anywhere near. I hope their nice garden and place escapes in the
fighting that will probably take place to-morrow. I am particularly
sorry for them, as the father—the only male of the establishment—
is practically an imbecile. The old lady said she would like to
leave, but she could not get her money from the bank, so had to
cling to her little place, where she could be always certain of a
livelihood by selling the apples from her orchards. There is a long
score to pay against Germany.

We rode about a mile towards Andreev and remained there for
the day. The German guns fired deliberately at the Catholic
church in Andreev and set it on fire. Then first one and then the
other of our batteries came into action and the Germans ceased
fire. An officer of Hussars told me that the fighting had started
with an attack by a company of cyclists and two squadrons of
cavalry on his piquet (a troop strong), and he had been forced to
retire. We got bread and cheese at a farmhouse at 2 P.M., then
rode back to our hosts of the night before to dine at 6 P.M. Then
we rode on to Motkovitse, the estate of M. Gurski, who has mi-
grated to Warsaw while the war lasts. The General, Cantacuzene
and I put up in the drawing-room—I on a glorious sofa. The Corps
Staff is here as well, but the house is a splendid one, with room
for all of us. To-morrow should be an interesting day. It was
interesting to-day, but fog prevented us from seeing properly.

Monday, September 28th, 1914.   KHMYELNIK.

A comfortable night on the sofa in M. Gurski's house at Motkovitse. A good breakfast and start at 6 A.M. We rode north-west
towards Andreev through the outpost line of the night before,
which was five versts from the Staff Headquarters and covered an
arc of twelve versts. We advanced to "bite" the enemy, as the
C.R.A. expressed it. In general the arrangement was: 1st Brigade
right of the *chaussée* and 2nd Brigade left, with the Frontier
Guard in the centre.

I had my first experience of the moral effect of gunfire. The
enemy gunners were evidently attracted by the target offered by
the Staff with orderlies and horses on the *chaussée,* and opened
fire with shrapnel. We had a hot time for five minutes. This was
our surprise; we had one ready for the enemy. He was withdrawing north-east by the *chaussée* to Kyeltsi, when one of our batteries opened fire from a covered position on our right. We could
see through our glasses the disorder in his column. Presently his
guns came into action against our battery, and it seemed as if
nothing could live under his fire. However, it eventually withdrew with a loss of only three wounded! Our other battery came
into action on the right of the road without much effect. There
was a short pause while the enemy no doubt detailed a column to
move against us, for he obviously could not continue his proces-
sional march along the *chaussée* to Kyeltsi and Radom with an
enemy force of unknown strength on his right flank. Suddenly we
heard rifle-fire on the *chaussée* from the direction of Andreev. It
developed with extraordinary rapidity all along our short front.
A Frontier Guard orderly galloped up to ask for leave to retire as
his squadron was in a dangerous position. Erdeli told him not to
be excited but to go back and hold on. We went back to the main
position of the day, where the eight guns were brought into position north-west of the edge of a thick wood, covered by a scattered
line of dismounted cavalrymen about two hundred yards in advance. The calmness of the Russians is wonderful. I saw the gunners actually asleep behind their shields two minutes before fire
was opened. When, ten minutes later, the enemy's guns had got
the range, the place became "unhealthy." Few shells reached us
two hundred yards further at the other side of the wood, but the
din was appalling. When the battery retired a captain of the
Frontier Guard galloped up to say that one of the gun teams had
been destroyed. He took men back to help, and presently a gun
came slowly down the road drawn by two horses, one of which
was badly wounded. A group of men carried a dead comrade.
The batteries had remained in action till the enemy's guns were
within 1,500 yards. Casualties were again trifling. The eight guns
lost one man killed and six wounded, and six horses killed and
twelve wounded.

This was the second and the main position of the day. We then
trotted back four versts through Motkovitse and over the Nida,

where two bridges were prepared with straw and explosives for destruction. A line of men had been told to hold on to the approach to Motkovitse till all that were in front had gone through.

Opposite to the entrance to the house we slept in last night at Motkovitse a Jew was hanging from a tree by the roadside. His cap was on his head, and as we trotted rapidly past in the drifting rain I did not see the rope, and was astonished to see a Jew who did not salute. As I looked again I saw that his feet were some inches from the ground. He had been slung up by the Corps Staff for espionage.

The enemy's cyclists arrived too late to prevent the destruction of the bridge. We had prepared long lines of dismounted men to dispute the passage of the river, but the enemy had probably had enough, and a few gun and rifle shots ended the day.

We stopped at Kai to write orders for the halt, and then rode the twelve versts to Khmyelnik at a walk. Our outpost line is on the edge of a wood about five versts west of Khmyelnik.

The net results of our action to-day is that the enemy, whose strength is estimated at one brigade of infantry, one regiment of cavalry and two six-gun batteries of artillery, was prevented from marching to Kyeltsi, as he evidently wished, and was drawn into a combat with us in which he covered only twelve versts from Andreev to Motkovitse instead of the normal twenty versts' march. He will have to repair the bridges at Motkovitse or else return to Andreev, as a preliminary to a move north-east or south-east to find another crossing for his guns.

We have lost about sixty men killed, wounded and missing. The bulk of them are Frontier Guard, one sotnia of which was left behind in the first position after the German infantry advance. It is said that they were destroyed by machine-gun fire. At any rate, their horse-holders came back without them. The German losses must be as great, for our guns got into their advancing columns. On the other hand, our rifle-fire can have caused him little damage, for our lines had to commence retirement when his firing-line was over 1,000 yards off. The terrain was particularly difficult for cavalry, for the woods were too thick to ride through comfortably with the lance.

Erdeli was coolness itself, receiving reports and directing the action with the utmost calm. The German infantry advanced resolutely and the artillery shooting was good.

General situation: The 8th Cavalry Division is said to be east of Pinchov and the 5th at Busk. No news from Kyeltsi. The Corps Staff is here at Khmyelnik. Our task is "to delay the enemy's advance till October 1st, when the 4th Army will be ready," but on what line, it is not known.

We got a good dinner at Khmyelnik and slept comfortably. The weather throughout the day was awful—strong wind and many showers.

Tuesday, September 29th, 1914.   PRIEST'S HOUSE,
                                                  OTSYESENKI.

We started at nine and rode north-west to Petrokovitse, where
we awaited result of reconnaissance. We had heard that the
enemy had moved his outposts and five companies of infantry
over the Nida late last night, and that he had repaired the bridges
by morning. They must have been very slackly blown up!

Three reports received between 12.30 and 1 P.M. confirmed
the fact that the enemy was continuing his advance on Khmyelnik. We rode east in two columns to Otsyesenki, completing a
march of forty versts in all on awful roads. We arrived at Otsyesenki at 8.30 P.M., and it was a pleasant surprise to find our
baggage arrived and things ready for us at the priest's house. We
won't, however, get dinner till 11 P.M.

No news from Kyeltsi, but it seems probable that the Turkistan
Brigade and the 5th Don Cossack Division have retired from
there.

The 8th Division had left three squadrons, two guns and two
machine-guns to hold the passage at Pinchov, but this was forced
by the enemy's infantry at 11.30 last night. The 8th Division is at
Gnoino, south-east of Khmyelnik, and the 5th is in the neighbourhood of Stopnitsa.

It looks as if we would come out between Ostrovets and
Opatov.

Last night while we were at dinner a Cossack officer brought in
three prisoners. His patrol of eleven men had killed two and
taken three. He announced the fact by saying that he had had a
slight unpleasantness. This was said quite naturally, without the
slightest straining for effect. A piquet to-day took two prisoners
and killed one other man in a German patrol. The Russians are
extraordinarily good to their prisoners, giving away tea and bread
that they are in want of themselves.

Khmyelnik is now occupied by the outposts of the German
column from Andreev.

Wednesday, September 30th, 1914.   PRIEST'S HOUSE,
                                                      LAGOV.

We rested this morning and only resumed our retreat at 3 P.M.,
the priest blessing us as we left.

We rode through beautiful scenery to Lagov, due east (nine
versts only).

The 8th Division has moved north to Rakov and the 5th Division is at and east of Stopnitsa.

I understood that we are to continue to move generally in a
north-easterly direction. The Corps Staff is at Stashov.

A Cossack squadron commander returned to-night from a two-
days' reconnaissance, which he had carried out between two of
the advancing columns. He ran very great risk, but has returned

through a miracle, with the loss of two men only. He looks like a benevolent professor instead of a wild Cossack, and he has a stomach and wears spectacles. On one occasion, in a village at midnight, he stumbled through the German outposts and came on a house in which a number of them were fast asleep. He did nothing, as he "did not know his way back." The information he brought amounts to nothing, for he saw no shoulder-straps. This class of officer spoils good men. Erdeli spoke some "winged words."

Thursday, October 1st, 1914. FARMHOUSE, ZVOLYA-SARNYA.

Slept comfortably at the priest's house at Lagov. His sanitary arrangements are respectable, which is wonderful in Poland.

The Germans are in three groups: the northern at Kyeltsi, the centre at Khmyelnik, the right about Busk. The 4th Don Cossack Division is north-east of Kyeltsi, the Turkistan Brigade with the 5th Don Cossack Division is east of Kyeltsi, the 14th Cavalry Division is at Lagov, the 8th is at Rakov, the 5th at Stashov; the Corps Staff is moving to-day north-east to Ivaniska.

The Germans have the XIth and XXth active Corps and the Guard Reserve Corps.

We started at 2 P.M. and rode fifteen versts north-east to Zvolya-Sarnya by a pretty mountain road. The General examined the ground, selecting a position to delay a column that is reported to be advancing from Kyeltsi in this direction. We put up at a small farmhouse.

The division is armed with eight Maxims of the new (lighter) type. They are used in pairs, *e.g.*, two generally go with the advanced guard or rearguard.

The strength of the cavalry regiment is 44 officers and 996 men; of the squadron, 147 men.

Generally three reconnoitring squadrons are out at a time. Each is given a strip of country, say eight to ten versts wide. The squadron moves, say thirty versts, and sends out three patrols, one of which is generally commanded by an officer and the other two by N.C.O.'s. The patrols may move another ten versts, so the whole squadron searches to a distance of forty versts if not held up. Special officers' patrols are sent out to search sections between the reconnoitring squadrons. "Close reconnaissance" is carried out at the direction of the brigade commanders to a distance of fifteen versts.

Friday, October 2nd, 1914. PRIEST'S HOUSE, VASNEV.

We started at 6.15 on a dreadful morning—cold wind and torrents of rain—to ride west to Novaya Slunya, where we had been ordered by the corps commander to delay the enemy as he debouched from the hills. The 1st Brigade took up a position in readiness on the right of the Opatov-Novaya Slunya road facing west, and the 2nd Brigade a similar position on the left. Both batteries deployed in a field on the ground on the right of the road, some four hundred yards apart.

Erdeli and his staff rode to a hut on the left flank some 400 yards in advance of the batteries. A farmhouse on the extreme left was occupied by a dismounted squadron of Cossacks, who were told to hold on "as long as they could." I asked an officer what this meant in the case of dismounted cavalry as opposed to infantry, and he said that it meant that they should go before the horseholders were in danger, and that was generally before the enemy's infantry reached 1,000 yards' range.

The ground, as we occupied it in the early morning, was hopeless for our purposes. With artillery that cannot fire at a much shorter range than 3,000 yards no ground was visible to more than 1,000 yards, owing to the fog. There is a feeling among officers that their attempts to delay infantry advances are futile. The dismounted cavalry hardly waits to exchange shots and the action resolves itself into an artillery duel, in which our eight guns are opposed to superior strength. The position we would have had to occupy to-day was bad, for all the ground over which the enemy was expected to advance commanded that by which we should eventually have had to retreat.

It cleared at twelve and we waited till at length a report came through that the column whose coming we awaited had turned off south towards Opatov. At 4.15 we received a message (with no time noted on it) that a column of all arms was entering Khibitse, due north of where we were, and with a road to Vasnev, where we had arranged to sleep. We moved off at once and took up a flanking position to oppose the advance of this column, sending out battle patrols to ascertain whether the enemy had stopped for the night at Khibitse, or was moving on. Two officers in command of reconnoitring parties reported that the enemy had entered Khibitse, but were cursed by the General because they had not waited to see whether he moved on, and if so by what roads.

Finally it was decided that we should spend the night at Vasnev, six miles from the enemy's infantry, and the transport, which had been sent east, was called back. We put up at the house of the priest, who entertained us with the best he had, and we had a scratch meal of ham, bread, butter and wine. The kindness of the Russians is wonderful. They are always anxious that I should have all I can possibly require before they think of themselves.

The cottage we spent the day in belonged to an old man of eighty-five, who had forgotten how many children he had had— seven or eight. He was a good type of the sturdy, sober Polish peasant.

To-morrow we should get behind our infantry. I hope they are ready to wake up the Germans.

Saturday, October 3rd, 1914.   COUNTRY HOUSE AT YANOV
                                   (NORTH-EAST OF OSTROVETS).
The retreat is continued, the 8th Division is ordered back from Rudniki, where it spent last night, to Syenno, but probably will not reach it; the 5th Division from Midlov to Ostrovets, but will probably spend the night south-east of that. The three Cossack Divisions, 4th and 5th Don and the Ural (Kaufmann) have moved north and west to the left flank of the enemy's Kyeltsi group, there being a wide interval between the left of the Kyeltsi group and the right of the German group further north.

We slept quietly, though our outposts must have been in touch with the German outposts at Khibitse. We started at 8.30 A.M. and occupied a strong position east of Vasnev.

The Germans soon appeared and moved in thick columns down the opposite slope to occupy Vasnev. They fired a single shot, which fell short. Our left battery fired for a considerable time, but all the shots were short, and the Germans did not reply. It is as well that they did not, for the whole east side of the long village in which we were was crowded with horses and men in which the first shell would have created a panic.

No men were actually extended in the firing-line. We moved off at twelve, when Vasnev had been already occupied by the enemy, and an hour after we had received a message (despatched 10.20) that Kunov was occupied by infantry, cavalry and cyclists and that the latter were moving towards Ostrovets, our line of retreat. We rode rapidly through Ostrovets, for the enemy's cyclists had been sighted very near the town. Clear of the town, we stopped while the general dictated orders for the bivouac at Yanov, twenty-three versts north-east of Ostrovets. The road lay through woods for the most part of the way. It was pleasant riding, but the depth of the sand made our C.R.A.'s heart bleed for his horses.

At Yanov we put up at a pleasant country house that was well known to the 14th Division in its wanderings last month.

The two Don Cossack divisions have been taken from the corps, and the corps (5th, 8th, 14th Cavalry Divisions) is to move north-east to Ivangorod and then to Warsaw, where it will take part in the operations towards the west.

It was rather a blow to hear that the 4th Army is only crossing at Nova Alexandriya and Yuzefov. The 9th Army's crossing has been delayed by the destruction of bridges, one at Sandomir by fire-ships sent down by the Austrians and the others at Zavikhost and Annopol by flood. Still, it is said that the 4th and 9th Armies will both be across by the 6th. It will be a very near thing if they are in time. In any case, if they do not cross they will certainly be able to stop the enemy on the Vistula. The Guard Rifle Brigade and the Independent Guard Cavalry Brigade are at Opatov.

Everyone is very confident that the war will be over in two months. Erdeli said as we rode along to-day, that we would see the New Year in in Petrograd.

We heard to-day that the Commander-in-Chief sent his thanks for the action near Andreev, and the battery commander, who was wounded, has been awarded the gold sword.

The Russian horse-rations are as follows:

Peace	–	10¾ lbs. oats,	10¾ lbs. hay,	4 lbs. straw
War	–	14¾ ” ”	15 ” ”	4 ” ”

Barley is only given when no oats are available.

I had some conversation with Shapojnikov about Intelligence. The District Staff is in peace mainly responsible for the collection of intelligence, but the General Staff of each cavalry division in peace also works at it. The 14th Cavalry Division with head-quarters at Chenstokhov had an agent for German work and another for Austrian. One agent, who is still working, is a Polish reservist and drives about in a cart. He received Rs.100 for his first task and now gets Rs.40 to Rs.50 for each trip. He was most valuable against the Austrians, but finds work more difficult against the Germans. Before the attack on Sandomir he brought exact information of the units and number of guns in the garrison. He changes his disguise continually. Yet S— never trusts him entirely and only tells him approximately where the division may be on a certain date.

Poor Colonel Westphalen, the Chief of Staff, naturally feels his position, as his junior, Shapojnikov, is consulted continually by the General and he never.

We picked up to-day a band of 200 Don Cossacks who had been trying for nine days to join the 4th Don Cossack Division. They are chiefly young men who had been excused service previously on account of family reasons.

There are at present four reconnoitring squadrons out. Two of them have been out for five days. Generally three reconnoitring squadrons have a single collecting pivot for information and this is connected by "Flying Post," laid by the division, with divisional headquarters (a distance of about twenty versts). The headquarters of each squadron connects by its own "Flying Post" with the collecting pivot. Headquarters of squadrons are at about ten to twelve versts from the collecting pivot. The squadron in turn sends out two reconnoitring patrols. Each squadron remains out "till further orders," and these orders are sent by "Flying Post." There has been no possibility of communicating with two of the squadrons mentioned above for three days, and they are now "on their own" well in the enemy's rear.

The method of sending out the battle reconnoitring patrols is this. The divisional commander calls out: "Next battle R.P. of 1st (or 2nd) Brigade for duty," explains the task verbally and the officer gallops off calling out: "Follow me the Uhlan (or Hussar or Dragoon or Cossack) Battle R.P." There are two battle R.P.'s for each brigade (one for each regiment) and similarly two orderly parties (one officer and two men) for each brigade (one for each regiment).

Sunday, October 4th, 1914.   FARMHOUSE, SITSINA.

Last night was the second night that I was too tired to wait for supper. It was not ready till 11 and I turned in at 10.30.

At 1 A.M. we were turned out and had to march east in a torrent of rain to Soleika Volya—sixteen versts on the top of the thirty-five we had done in the day. My throat was hurting me and I felt pretty rotten.

We were disturbed owing to the ambitions of a young cornet. This youth, who has been acting for the past year as regimental paymaster, burned, as his friend told me, to gain some special war honour. He heard from local inhabitants that there was a piquet or reconnoitring party of the enemy two versts outside our outpost line and got leave to take a party to attack them. He started with twenty-four men—sixteen troopers and eight Cossacks. He surprised the enemy's piquet of thirty-two men and killed or burned (for he set fire to the enclosure where they slept) twenty-eight and took one prisoner.

As information came in at the same time that the enemy's infantry had come close to us, the General decided to retire. We tumbled out of bed, Cantacuzene remarking that we would remember this against the Germans in the peace negotiations. While we were waiting for our baggage to get ahead, the prisoner, a boy of seventeen, a native of East Prussia, was brought in. He was trembling and, as he said, tired to death. He had only joined five days before and it can be easily imagined the hell he must have lived through in this skirmish.

The scene in the dining-room was striking—this boy standing facing his enemies, a lot of good-natured and sleepy Russians, our host, a handsome, bearded Pole, his son and daughter listening with intense interest to all that was said—the half-light of a flickering lamp, the heavy downpour and rough gusts of wind outside.

At Soleika Volya we lay down for some hours, but it was hard to sleep. I had our host's bed, but there were sixteen officers in his drawing-room on sofas, chairs, mattresses, camp beds and on the floor. We had a scratch meal at 12 noon and started at 2 P.M. marching sixteen versts over the crossing of a tributary of the Vistula by Tseplev to Sitsina. The crossing had not been occupied and we arrived at 7.30 P.M. at a large farmhouse at Sitsina, which the 14th Divisional Staff proceeded to occupy for the sixth time since the war started. The 14th Division *should* and I believe *does* know the ground.

There are apparently only two groups of Russian infantry west of the upper Vistula—the 75th Division at Radom, which is in touch with the 4th and 5th Don Cossacks, the Ural Cossack Divisions and the Turkistan Cossack Brigade, and the Guard Rifle Brigade which was at Opatov.

Yesterday at Skarishev, south-east of Radom, the 5th Don Cossack Division fought a successful action, and it is said that the 75th Division threw back the enemy ten versts. To-night again our outpost line will be in touch with his infantry outposts. Each day it is a different column, as we carry through our flank march to the north. The Germans burnt all the village this morning where their piquet was cut up last night, and as we rode to our quarters to-night there was an enormous fire burning on the bank of the Vistula. It therefore looks as if the northern line of retreat of the 5th and 8th Divisions is cut off. They can, however, always retreat by Sandomir.

The 8th Cavalry Division, which spent last night near Opatov, was told by the Corps Staff to move to Syenno to-day, and the 5th Division from Midlov (south of Opatov) was told to move to Marushev, south-east of Syenno. It would be interesting to know how far these orders were carried out. The Corps Staff itself was fired on in Ostrovets. It sent orders to us *to-day* to hold Yanov, where we spent the first part of last night, to the last. The situation has changed so rapidly owing to the rapid advance of the Germans that the corps has lost all power of co-ordinating movement, and the safety of each division will ultimately depend on the skill of its commander.

Bread is as a rule supplied by Government bakeries, each army corps having its own. In the latter part of September a civilian bakery was organised at Opatov to supply the 9th Army. Black bread from this bakery was sent to the cavalry operating in south-west Poland. On two occasions when it did not turn up, the 14th Divisional Intendant purchased from local Jewish bakers and distributed to the regiments of the division. For five consecutive days the men of the étape company at Sandomir were without bread. On these occasions fifty kopeks are given to each man and he purchases bread *if he can!*

When Government cattle are not available, each squadron or battalion purchases meat locally. Similarly with cabbages. When the regimental supply of tea, sugar and salt is exhausted it is replenished by the Intendance.

The men of the 14th Division were well fed throughout, though they received the meals often at unnecessarily irregular times.

Forage is wherever possible purchased by squadron commanders and paid for in cash.

4. The Battle of Verdun

THE MOST formidable battle of the First World War was Verdun, which lasted from February 21 to December 15, 1916. Alistair Horne, in *The Price of Glory*, writes:

> Of all the battles of the First World War, Verdun was the one in which most Frenchmen had taken part. . . . Something like seven-tenths of the whole French Army . . . passed through Verdun. . . . Though the Somme claimed more dead than Verdun, the proportion of casualties suffered to the numbers engaged was notably higher at Verdun than at any other First World War battle. . . . The combined casualties of both sides reached the staggering total of over 700,000. . . . It is probably no exaggeration to call Verdun the "worst" battle in history. . . .

The French were unprepared for this terrible onslaught, since General Joffre was so bemused by the map that he failed to grasp the German objective in undertaking so titanic an offensive so far from Paris. Toward the end of 1915 the generalissimo thought that far more tempting points of attack would be the valley of the Oise, Reims, or the Champagne. But General Falkenhayn, Moltke's successor as chief of the General Staff, was not attempting a breakthrough at Verdun, or even the conquest of scraps of territory, but rather the bleeding to death of the French army through its predictable determination to defend at any cost a city so richly incrusted with historic associations.

Joffre's confidence in the defensibility of forts had been shaken by the relatively easy German capture of Liège and Namur. As the fighting settled into the long stalemate of trench warfare, Joffre proceeded to strip Verdun of most of its movable guns, which were transported to other sectors. The French controlled both banks of the Meuse for a distance of five or six miles north of the city's girdle of forts, but this buffer zone was not adequately protected by trench networks, dugouts, machine-gun "pill boxes" and the like. General Coutanceau, military governor of Verdun, risked his command by warning the army commission of the Chamber of Deputies of the city's unpreparedness. Colonel Emile Driant, a soldier-deputy with an irreproachable battle record, confirmed Coutanceau's alarm in regard to Verdun's dangerous unreadiness. When Driant's warning (which was kept anonymous) was sent to Joffre by War Minister General Galliéni at the Briand cabinet's request, the generalissimo was infuriated, and loftily replied that as early as October 22, 1915, he had ordered the commanders to strengthen the front and second lines of trenches at Verdun, with fortified zones to be made ready to the rear of these. To "order" defenses was one thing, but to provide the necessary resources and manpower was something else—and this Joffre had not done.

Despite warnings from military intelligence (including information furnished by the British Royal Navy Intelligence) about German preparations for a gigantic offensive, Joffre dawdled over Verdun's defenses until January 24, 1916, when he belatedly sent his chief of staff,

General de Castelnau, to inspect the sector. De Castelnau ordered completion of the just-begun first and second lines of defense on the right bank of the Meuse, with a new intermediary line between the two. Two army corps of urgently needed reinforcements were moved to the Verdun sector on February 12, 1916, the day Prussian Crown Prince Wilhelm was supposed to begin the meticulously planned attack. Fortunately for the French, rain and snow caused a postponement of the offensive until February 21, thus allowing Colonel Driant more time to work on an ingenious chain of independent strongholds and concrete redoubts in the Bois des Caures which, if finished, would have allowed enfilading fire against German infiltration attempts.

Along a front of only a few miles to the east and north of Verdun, the crown prince concentrated 850 cannon and 72 battalions of elite storm troops. The German artillery included new 280-mm guns, as well as large numbers of 210s and 150s. Most terrible for the Verdun defenders were to be the monstrous 420-mm "Big Bertha" mortars, which the Germans had used with such deadly effectiveness in capturing Liège and Namur. To defend Verdun, Joffre had left in place only 270 nondescript guns, most of them short of ammunition, and only 30 battalions of infantry occupying partially completed positions.

The elaborately prepared German assault began at 7:15 on the morning of February 21, nine days behind schedule, with the firing of a 14-inch shell into the impressive Bishop's Palace of Verdun. This shot signaled a volcanic eruption of artillery fire which, according to General Pétain, was intended "to create a 'zone of death' within which no troops could survive."

Not only Joffre but the Briand government had to answer the harrowing question as to whether it was now better to dig in, however belatedly, and to hold on, or to abandon the east bank of the Meuse and much of the city of Verdun and fall back to the much more easily defended west bank, where French casualties would be reduced. On the night of February 24 Prime Minister Aristide Briand made an unexpected visit to Joffre's headquarters at Chantilly to discuss what should be done. Joffre's staff, the Young Turks, argued for abandonment of the Verdun salient and the rectification of the line. But Briand fully comprehended the damage to French morale which the surrender of the city would cause—a blow which would be all the more insupportable when the unheeded warnings as to its unpreparedness leaked out, as would be certain to happen. Briand became so exasperated with the obstinately "technical" arguments of the Young Turks that he finally shouted at them: "If you surrender Verdun, you will be cowards, cowards! And you needn't wait till then to hand in your resignation. If you abandon Verdun, I sack you all on the spot!" Comatose Joffre had not lost his peasant cunning, and he ended the discussion by saying amiably: "The president [of the council] is right. I share his point of view. No falling back on the left bank. We fight to the end!"

Joffre bestirred himself and accepted the advice of Chief of Staff de Castelnau to create a new Army of Verdun from the existing Second and Third armies, and to assign it to the Second Army's former commander, General Henri Philippe Pétain. Few reputations in the twentieth century have suffered such bathos as that of Pétain. Born April 24, 1856, at Cauchy-la-Tour, Pétain was educated at Saint Cyr and at the Ecole de Guerre, teaching at the latter school and holding various staff posts until 1914. In his lectures at the Ecole de Guerre he had the temerity to stress the decisiveness of fire power, a doctrine repugnant to the proponents of the prevailing strategic concept of the *offensive à outrance*. In August, 1914, he was an over-age colonel of fifty-eight stationed at Saint-Omer. He rose quickly after the war's outbreak. In the Battle of the Marne his defensive action at Montceau-les-Provins brought about his promotion from colonel to major general within six weeks. Pétain, the cold, aloof, and conservative bachelor, commanded the Second Army until he was summoned from one of his regular assignations in a Paris hotel and given the new Army of Verdun.

Pétain was apotheosized by right and left for his successful, albeit costly, defense of Verdun, for his equitable rotation of the divisions which had to endure the unprecedented shelling, and for his damping the mutinies in 1917 by improving the lot of the *poilus*. The discovery of the largely undamaged condition of the guns of Forts Douaumont and Vaux, once they had been recaptured from the Germans, led him—and the French nation—to accept all too uncritically the strategy of a static, linear defense. The Maginot line, which Pétain's school of thought foreshadowed, was simply the extension of lesser Forts Douaumont along the entire Franco-German frontier as far as Belgium. With the best of intentions, Pétain had unwittingly contributed to the collapse of France under German tank and air attacks in June, 1940, when Belgium was once more the avenue of invasion. As *Chef de l'Etat* of the Vichy regime, Pétain tried to save defeated France from total disaster by offering his aged person as a buffer—eventually, as a sort of hostage—to the Germans. His one-time protégé De Gaulle commuted to life imprisonment the death sentence for collaboration pronounced upon the marshal in mid-August, 1945. He died at his place of detention on the Ile d'Yeu July 23, 1951. We publish excerpts from his military classic, *Verdun*.

HENRI PHILIPPE PÉTAIN, MARSHAL OF FRANCE,
VERDUN

OPENING OF THE BATTLE. DESCRIPTION OF ITS NATURE

The struggle was carried on with heroic courage, both by the troops and by their leaders. Bombardments by the German heavy artillery, during February 21st and the night of the 21st–22nd, preceded the charge of the shock divisions. Nowhere before, on any front, in any battle, had anything like it been seen. The Germans aimed to create a "zone of death," within which no troops

Source: From *Verdun* translated by Margaret Mac Veagh (New York: The Dial Press Inc., 1930), pp. 58–79, 164–171. Reprinted by permission of the publisher.

could survive. An avalanche of steel and iron, of shrapnel and poisonous gas shells, fell on our woods, ravines, trenches, and shelters, destroying everything, transforming the sector into a charnel field, defiling the air, spreading flames into the heart of the town, damaging even the bridges and Meuse villages as far as Genicourt and Troyon. Heavy explosions shook our forts and wreathed them in smoke. It would be impossible to describe an action of the kind. I believe that it has never been equalled in violence, and it concentrated the devastating fire of more than two million shells in the narrow triangle of land between Brabant-on-Meuse, Ornes, and Verdun.

During the afternoon of the 21st and the morning of the 22nd, after a night in which the artillery had incessantly kept up its infernal pounding, the German troops advanced in small formations, the different waves pushing one another forward, hoping to progress without opposition. Imagine their amazement and their disappointment to see everywhere along their route the French rising from the wreck, exhausted and in tatters to be sure, but still formidable, defending the ruins from every possible point of vantage.

The resistance offered by the chasseurs under Driant, the soldier-politician who wrote The War of To-Morrow and The War of Fortifications, is worthy of special remembrance. In the Caures woods the Fifty-sixth and Fifty-ninth Battalions of chasseurs stood guard, with a few units from the One Hundred and Sixty-fifth Infantry Regiment, about twelve hundred men in all. They were supported by six batteries of 75's and eight heavy batteries. Four regiments of the German Twenty-first Division (the Eightieth, the Ninety-first, the Eighty-seventh, and the Eighty-eighth) attacked them; that is to say, between eight and ten thousand men, supported by seven batteries of 77's and about forty heavy batteries. The preliminary bombardment had absolutely crushed them, most of their shelters had been blown up by exploding shells, and their losses even before they met the enemy were very heavy. In spite of everything, our chasseurs held their positions in the depths of the woods, surrounded and hunted down from every side, for nearly twenty-four-hours. I quote the moving words of Lieutenant Colonel Grasset, who, with a trained historian's knowledge, wrote a detailed account of those days at Verdun, and described this splendid feat of arms:

"Colonel Driant was in a shell-hole, together with Quartermaster Leclère and Chasseur Papin, who did not leave his side. A bullet struck Papin. The Colonel made a temporary bandage for him, shook hands with him, and left the shell-hole by himself, approaching a trench in which Chasseur Lefèvre was waiting for him. But instead of turning to the left to follow the sheltering line of a low summit, as Lieutenant Simon was doing at the same moment, he went directly under fire from machine guns. About ten yards from the trench, a bullet hit him in the forehead and he fell without a word.

"A little later, Sergeant Lautrez, who was crossing the road a hundred yards or so to the south, saw the Colonel lying on the spot where he had been killed. He was no better able to reach him under the hail of bullets than had been Chasseur Lefèvre. Major Renouard was passing very near at the time, making his way due south. He disappeared behind a hilltop, and was never seen again. . . .

"Driant's noble band were all dead. That evening, from the Caures wood, a few handfuls of men emerged and reassembled gradually at Vacherauville. From the Fifty-sixth Battalion there were Captain Vincent, suffering from two wounds but saved for the time to die heroically on another battle field. Captain Hamel, Captain Berveiller, Lieutenant Raux, and Second Lieutenant Grasset, with about sixty Chasseurs. From the Fifty-ninth Battalion there were Lieutenant Simon, Second Lieutenants Leroy and Malavault, and fifty Chasseurs. These were all that survived of twelve hundred soldiers."

The troops of the Thirtieth Corps exhibited astonishing, almost incredible, heroism. Every center of resistance, whether it were a wood, a village, a network of destroyed trenches, or a chaotic group of shell-holes, was used by our units and became the scene of gallant deeds like those of Driant's chasseurs, where all contributed their share to the task of checking the advance of the enemy. The French, officers and enlisted men alike, realized the importance of their duty and fulfilled it with stoical courage. Lost as if in a raging sea, knowing that there was no one to hear their signals of distress, they bent all their energies to staying the tide that was engulfing them, each in his turn, and they chose death or the misery of a prison camp rather than the safety that they might have won by retreat. Our men toiled and suffered more than can possibly be imagined. They did their duty simply, with no ostentation, and in so doing, they reached sublime heights.

Detachments from the two divisions in general reserve approached the front lines, first by motor truck over the Souilly-Verdun road, then on foot in small columns, using all the routes that led to Saint-Michel and Souville from north of the town. But as soon as they came out beyond the Meuse they were caught, held up, and thrown out of order by the bombardment, blocked by the evacuation of the wounded and by supply parties, and numbed by the cold during the long waits necessitated by the sudden over-crowding of all the rear posts. At the appointed meeting places, whence they were to enter the sectors to which they had been assigned, the units moving forward hunted for the leaders of the detachments already under fire and the guides assigned to take them in, while the latter, driven hither and yon by bursting shells and by gas, themselves wandering at random, were often not to be found. So the battalions and companies of the reënforcing troops marched haphazard, making their way due north, advancing amid the smoke and deafening noises of the battle, and suddenly came into contact with the enemy, clinching with him and seeking to check him, for lack of any better means, by throwing themselves in his path. Wherever fate led, they took their stand, cut off both on the right and on the left, without liaison with the artillery, without definite instructions, without trenches to shelter them or to safe-guard their communications.

The Twentieth Corps, hastily despatched from the detraining stations near Bar-le-Duc towards Souilly and Verdun, made its way, also without preliminary reconnaissances, on to the spur of Douaumont, which became the pivotal point of the struggle and the prize at stake. The men, mingling with those of the Thirtieth Corps, stopped up as well as they could the gaps in the lines, until little by little the first lines, though still confused and disorganized, took on a semblance of consistency. From farther away, the First and Thirteenth Corps were brought post-haste by the Marne rail-roads and began to detrain on the 24th and 25th respectively. Our artillery units were hurriedly reënforced by assigning to them the available batteries from the three new army corps, and they began once more to thunder. Their support renewed the courage of the troops and reawakened the hope that their heart-rending sacrifices might not have been made in vain.

On the third day of the fighting, the enemy held our whole group of advanced positions north of Douaumont. Already public opinion in France, obsessed with the idea that ground must be held at all costs, was highly excited. I repeat, however, that such situations as ours are to be expected at the beginning of an engage-ment, and that the French people might have looked on without losing their heads, as did the troops themselves at Verdun accord-ing to the wise counsels of the local commander.

General de Langle de Cary continued to keep track of events with the utmost calm and a practical sense that cannot be too highly praised. He promptly took account of the fact that the enemy's advance on the Côtes-de-Meuse and towards the Verdun-Étain road endangered the situation of our units deployed in the lowlands of the Woëvre. They would soon be threatened from higher ground at short range, taken in the rear, and entirely cut off. Now the positions in the Woëvre had no intrinsic value except as protection to our observation posts on the Heights of the Meuse, and it seemed as if there was no objection to withdrawing as far as the foot of these heights. On February 24th, at eight o'clock in the evening, General de Langle accordingly gave orders to this effect, and the movement was carried out during the day of the 25th without hindrance from the enemy. No sooner was the General Staff informed than it ratified the orders of General de Langle. Nevertheless, General Joffre continued to feel some anxiety concerning the move and made a point of stipulating that it must not give rise to the idea that the retreat might be continued as far as the Meuse. He telegraphed:

> "I approve in advance whatever decisions you may make regarding the withdrawal in the direction of the Heights of the Meuse of the troops stationed in the Woëvre pocket, if you think necessary. You alone can judge of the necessities of the battle. But you must hold the line facing north between the Meuse and the Woëvre with all the strength you can muster. Use the whole of the Twentieth Corps without hesitation."

To make sure that his wishes should be clearly understood by the men entrusted with their execution, the Generalissimo at the same time sent to the general in command of the central group of armies his right hand man, General de Castelnau. The latter reached Avize on February 25th at five o'clock in the morning. At a quarter to six he wrote out the following brief order:

> "The Meuse must be held on the right bank. There can be no question of any other course than of checking the enemy, cost what it may, on that bank."

General de Castelnau then continued on his way to Verdun, in order to draw his conclusions on the spot and to study the conditions under which the Second Army should there be employed. The General Staff was at the moment moving that army towards Bar-le-Duc.

THE LOSS OF FORT DOUAUMONT AND THE ENTRANCE OF THE
SECOND ARMY INTO LINE

As I was available at Noailles with my staff, I thought it extremely probable that I should be assigned to the Verdun front, where the importance of the struggle and the numbers of reënforcements sent would justify the entrance into line of a new army. On my own initiative, I had already sent the head of my intelligence service to obtain precise information concerning the course of events. Consequently I was not in the least surprised on the evening of February 24th to receive orders to send my headquarters Staff immediately on its way to Bar-le-Duc and to report in person to General Joffre on the morning of the 25th.

I arrived in Chantilly at eight o'clock and was immediately admitted to the office of the Commander-in-Chief, whose usual calm manner was unchanged, though the atmosphere of his surroundings was feverish and excited. General Joffre gave me succinctly his impressions of the situation, which seemed to him serious but not alarming. He directed me to hurry to Bar-le-Duc and there be ready to undertake the work that General de Castelnau, who had definite instructions, would explain to me.

In order to be as quick as possible, I went straight to Souilly, a village on the road between Bar-le-Duc and Verdun, where I expected to find General de Castelnau. But the roads were covered with snow and sleet and my motor journey was a long one. I stopped only once, for a short time at Chalons, and yet I did not meet General de Castelnau and General de Langle, who were together at Souilly, until seven o'clock that evening. The reports of the fourth day of the fighting were coming in slowly, and seemed disturbing. To find out the truth immediately, I hurried to Dugny, south of Verdun, where General Herr had his headquarters. Between Souilly and the Meuse I passed the procession of supply trains, making their way towards Verdun, columns of soldiers blocking all the roads, ambulance sections moving southward, and above all, most distressing of sights, the wretched horde of inhabitants seeking refuge outside of the devastated region.

At Dugny a grave piece of news awaited me. The Twentieth Corps had fought bravely all day around the village of Douaumont, but the fort had just fallen into the hands of the enemy by a surprise attack. In it we had lost the best and most modern of our earthworks, the tangible expression of our reasons for confidence, the lofty observation point from which we should have been able

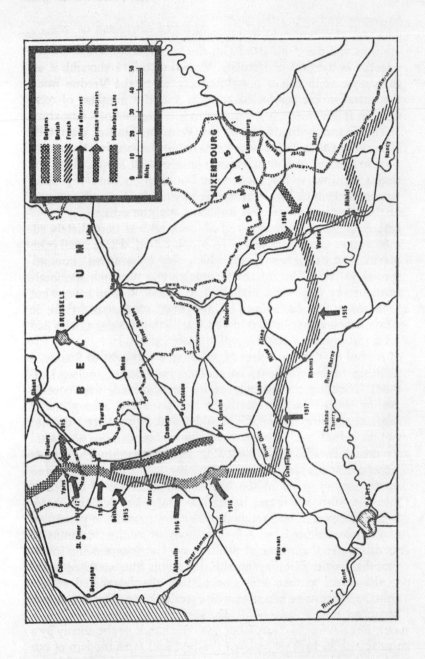

to survey and sweep the ground over which the Germans must advance, and from which the enemy would now be able to spy upon us and direct his attacks on the remotest corners of the consecrated battle field of Verdun. We had at the time no inkling of the causes of this most unfortunate occurrence, but according to the investigation conducted later by General Passaga, the facts were as follows:

The Brandebourg troops of the Prussian Third Corps, under General Lochow, were advancing through the wooded ravines that shut in the fort of Douaumont on both east and west. Our Twentieth Corps, which had entered the line with no knowledge of the terrain, and which had been unable to combine with the remnants of the Thirtieth Corps, was disputing the ground foot by foot as best it could. Relentlessly pushed back and worn out, our men soon found themselves driven to a point behind the great brooding mass of Fort Douaumont, which they believed was held by a special garrison. One of the Brandebourg companies stopped in front of the earthwork, hesitating to attack it, while the leader, Lieutenant Brandis,* stared at the huge mass, covered by the newly fallen snow. Instead of the fear that the sight of so powerful a fortification would normally inspire, this officer felt the spell of a kind of illusion, a loss of balance, an irresistible attraction. Turning to his company, he suddenly shouted "On to Douaumont!" Sensing the attitude of his men, who believed he was leading them to certain death, he had something of a change of heart concerning the impulsive order, but still he was too brave to take it back, and he ran towards the objective. The company, to its own amazement, succeeded in advancing without difficulty, zigzagged across the ravines, slipped into the trenches, clambered up the snowy slopes of the central mound, then climbed down into the inner bowl; and there they found the casements open. They disappeared underground, and encountered a working party of French territorials, who, by the irony of fate, were proceeding to dismantle the pieces of artillery on the parapets. Lieutenant Brandis, hastily counting up the defending forces, could discover as the actual garrison only one battery guard and a handful of gunners assigned to keeping up the service of supply for the turret of 155's.

* The Crown Prince and General Passaga speak of the part played in this affair by Captain Haupt also, but according to General Passaga, to whom I owe the details of this feat of arms, it appears that Lieutenant Brandis was the chief actor.

It must be remembered that Verdun no longer counted as a "stronghold." Its earthworks, included in the whole system of our front-line defences, had no special armament or garrison, but had to be defended at the responsibility of the chiefs of the various sectors, by the troops at their disposition for the battle. Even for Douaumont, in spite of its paramount importance, no provision had been made in time. On February 24th the orders given to the Thirtieth Corps were designed to make sure that it should be specially manned and held, but between the 24th and the 25th, after many conflicts and omissions, responsibility had passed from the Thirtieth Corps to the Twentieth, and the order to occupy the fort had not yet been carried out when the Brandebourg troops came on the scene. Lieutenant Brandis is a hero whom we might well hold up as a model to our young officers. Most other men, even the bravest, would have hesitated before that impressive obstacle, supposedly concealing on its flanks large numbers of defensive weapons primed for action!

I myself carried back to General de Castelnau and General de Langle the news of the fall of the fort. General de Castelnau judged that no time should be lost in "organizing" the command and avoiding further errors like the one that had been committed that day. He had already telephoned to Chantilly in the afternoon to suggest entrusting to me the command of the Verdun fronts on both banks of the Meuse, my mission being to "check the attack being made by the enemy on the northern front of Verdun." General Joffre approved the suggestion.

At eleven o'clock that evening, as soon as I returned to Souilly, General de Castelnau wrote out my commission on a leaf of his pocket notebook, tore it out, and handed it over to me "for immediate execution." So at eleven o'clock I undertook the command of the defence of Verdun, entirely responsible from that moment, but without as yet having any means of action. From an empty room in the town hall I got into telephonic communication with General Balfourier, commanding the forces engaged in the sector under attack.

"Hello! This is General Pétain speaking. I am taking over the command. Inform your troops. Keep up your courage. I know I can depend on you."

"Very well, sir. We shall bear up. You can rely on us, as we rely on you."

Immediately afterwards I called General de Bazelaire, commanding the sectors on the left bank, and I made the same announcement to him, telling him of the particular importance I attached to saving our positions west of the Meuse. He answered as General Balfourier had just done, in a tone of devoted and absolute confidence. From that time on there was no doubt of sympathetic coöperation between the chief and his lieutenants.

A little later, towards midnight, General de Barescut, my Chief of Staff, arrived. I marked in charcoal on a large-scale map, pasted on the wall, the sectors held by the army corps already in the field, and the front still to be occupied; after which I dictated the orders that were to be delivered to every unit the next morning. These were my first measures on taking command at Verdun. . . .

The violent shaking that our front received threatened to crack it at any moment, and the only wise course was to bolster it up. Consequently, I decided that behind the resistance position already mapped out on both banks, a barrage position should be established through Avocourt, Fort de Marre, the northeastern skirts of Verdun and Fort du Rozellier.

It was exceedingly important also to guard against the repetition of such accidents as the desertion of Fort Douaumont on February 25th. Between March 5th and March 10th the chiefs of the sectors were given detailed instructions on this point. Each fort was to have its own commander and a special garrison to be relieved as seldom as possible. It would be supplied for two weeks at a time with food and munitions, and definite orders should be given that no earthwork should be evacuated or surrendered even in case it were completely surrounded and cut off. These measures treated the forts as the chief bulwarks of the system of defence of which they formed the skeleton, and the excellent network of communications that linked them to one another was counted on to facilitate the transmission of orders.

In the matter of artillery, General de Bazelaire, in command of the sector on the left bank, was requested to turn his batteries so that they should face northeast. These, though few in number, were ready-mounted, and could to great advantage sweep with their fire the batteries that the Germans were moving up near their infantry on the right bank. To follow up this measure, I unremittingly urged the activity of the artillery. When the liaison officers of the various army corps, meeting at Souilly for their daily report, began to explain to me in detail the course of the fighting on their several fronts, I never failed to interrupt them with the question: "What have your batteries been doing? We will discuss other points later." At first they were confused in their answers, but my vexation with them communicated echoes of my dominating idea among the various staffs represented, and their reports soon improved to a marked degree. Following the course outlined by me, our artillery began to take the offensive with "bursts of concentrated fire which really constituted independent operations, carefully prepared beforehand, and which, without causing us any losses, inflicted loss on the enemy." Again and again I told them: "The artillery must give the infantry the impression that it is supporting it, and that the enemy's artillery is not overpowering ours."

Nevertheless the army, crowded as it was into a front-line salient, was in danger of being starved out if the bombardments became too intense over its central core and its communication lines. We had to keep the powerful batteries of the enemy sufficiently in awe of us to lessen this risk, but the result could not be definitely achieved without material reënforcements of considerable strength, and the enemy's artillery remained highly superior to our own. In Verdun, house after house was destroyed by shells or burned; the troops and the headquarters companies sustained heavy losses, and the only safe shelters in which to carry on the most important work of insuring the services of supply and communication were the strong underground galleries of the Citadel. All routes leading towards the city and the suburb of Regret, to which came all reënforcements, supplies, and matériel, were under constant bombardment from the enemy's heavy guns and airplanes. . . .

STRUGGLE FOR FORT VAUX, AND ITS PSYCHOLOGICAL EFFECT

Three army corps were . . . hurled against our positions at Fort Vaux during the first part of June, the three being, in order from west to east, the First Bavarian Corps, the Tenth Reserve Corps, and the Fifteenth Corps. All three had a thorough acquaintance with the terrain, where they had been fighting hard for weeks and months. They succeeded, after a terrific bombardment, in gaining a foothold for several groups of assault troops on the superstructure of the fort, and these men then attacked each of our isolated resistance centers in turn. Conditions were more favorable to them than they had been to us a few days earlier at Douaumont, and thanks to the fact that our position at that point formed a salient, they were able to surround the earthwork on three sides. Within a short time our communications with the rear were irremediably endangered. To attempt to hold their position under such circumstances was, on the part of our men, simply a matter of honor. Inspired by this noble ambition, Major Raynal and his heroic comrades in arms refused to yield the fort, and in recognition of their self-sacrifice, General Joffre sent them his congratulations and conferred upon their leader, as a reward, a high rank in the Legion of Honor. There can be no memory more affecting than that of their last stand, when, cut off from us with no hope of assistance, they sent us their final reports.

The following message came to us on the morning of June 4th, by carrier pigeon:

> "We are still holding our position, but are being attacked by gases and smoke of very deadly character. We are in need of immediate relief. Put us into communication with Souville at once for visual signalling. We get no answer from there to our calls. This is our last pigeon!"

Then during the morning of June 5th came this message, relayed by visual signal through Souville:

> "The enemy is working on the west side of the fort to construct a mine in order to blow up the vaults. Direct your artillery fire there quickly."

At eight o'clock came another:

> "We do not hear your artillery. We are being attacked with gas and liquid fire. We are in desperate straits."

Then this one, at nightfall on June 5th:

> "I must be set free this evening, and must have supplies of water immediately. I am coming to the end of my strength. The troops, enlisted men and officers, have done their duty to the last, in every case."

On the 6th came only these few words:

> ". . . you will intervene before we are completely exhausted. Vive la France!"

And finally, on June 7th, at half past three in the morning, these last words, whose meaning we could not make out:

> ". . . must go on."

The French High Command had never for a moment been deaf to these appeals. Counter-attacks, prepared in advance or attempted on the spur of the moment, were launched almost without interruption, but not one of them was able to break through the ring of fire that cut off the fort. As late as June 7th, when the German communiqué reporting the capture of the fort had already been issued, after Major Raynal and his soldiers had already fallen, crushed by shells, suffocated by gas, exhausted by thirst, General Nivelle was despatching to their aid the mixed brigade commanded by Colonel Savy, "on the noblest mission that can be entrusted to French troops, that of succoring comrades in arms who are gallantly doing their duty under tragic conditions." But it was too late! Fort Vaux had fallen, and must wait with Fort Douaumont for better days, before it could resume its place proudly within the French lines. However, the defence of Verdun was in no way endangered by this reverse, and the German Fifth Army failed to win the victory on which it had set its heart, the victory of far reaching effect, which was to extricate the Austro-Hungarians, check the Russians, or dishearten the English.

II. Amphibious Warfare

5. The Dardanelles Campaign

THE ANGLO-FRENCH campaign against the Turkish Straits in 1915 proved to be one of the most controversial undertakings of the war. Upon learning of a request from the commander of the hard-pressed Russian armies, Grand Duke Nicholas, for relief from the Turkish threat to the Russians in the Caucasus, First Lord of the Admiralty Winston Churchill wanted to respond with an amphibious campaign against the Dardanelles, the thirty-eight-mile-long strait separating the Aegean from the Sea of Marmora. Initially, First Sea Lord John Fisher strongly supported this concept. But Field Marshal Herbert Kitchener, the war minister in the Asquith cabinet, thought that troops could not be spared from Flanders, although he was favorably disposed to at least a naval demonstration against the Dardanelles.

The imaginative Winston Churchill regarded a "demonstration" as too timorous, and he proposed broadening the operation into a bold plan for forcing the passage of the Dardanelles and opening a lifeline to munitions-starved Russia. However, the known presence of mines, and of shore batteries of Krupp guns which would be under the fire control of German officers, caused apprehension over the possible fate of the obsolete British warships which would have to operate in confined waters varying from only three-quarters of a mile to four miles in width. Weighing these risks, the British War Council decided on February 16, 1915, to concentrate troops at Lemnos to assist the navy in an attack against the Straits, if such military action should prove necessary. A large force was mustered in Egypt for redeployment under the command of General Sir Ian Hamilton. The French government agreed to provide a small army and four battleships.

To clear the way for the amphibious force which might be needed later, the Anglo-French fleets began a preliminary bombardment of the Straits on February 19. At that time there were only two Turkish divisions at the Dardanelles. Bad weather forced a halt in the shelling until February 25, when small landing parties of marines and sailors went ashore to demolish remaining guns at the entrance to the Straits. But the Turks were now alerted and were able to bring up needed reserves to repel further attacks. The card of surprise had thus already been played by the Anglo-French forces.

By the time the fleet resumed bombardment of the Straits' fortifications on March 18, the Turks had stationed four divisions along the narrow waterway. The naval bombardment of the land fortifications proved relatively ineffective, for despite the large caliber of the guns, the flat trajectory of the shells restricted the damage done to the forts. High trajectory mortars were needed, but they were not part of the naval equipment. Three battleships were sunk by drift mines during this engagement. Debate has continued down to the present as to whether the Straits might have been forced on March 18 by resolute fleet action, even though unaccompanied by an army, if only the Allies had then realized that the Turkish ammunition at the Chanak Narrows forts was all but exhausted. But such was not known at the time, and Admiral Sir John de Robeck decided to turn back and await the accompaniment of a land army. The delay gave the Turks the opportunity to send two more divisions to the Straits, making a total of six. More than a month ensued before General Hamilton's Mediterranean expeditionary force, conveyed by a large armada, arrived at the Dardanelles on April 25.

The landings of the British and Royal Naval divisions and the Anzacs are described from the Central Powers' side by General Liman von Sanders, the German cavalry general who, as inspector general of the Turkish forces, was in charge of the defense of the Dardanelles. Liman von Sanders was born Otto Karl Liman (he acquired the von Sanders in 1913 at the time of his ennoblement) on February 18, 1855, in Schwessin Bei Stolp, Pomerania. He was educated in Posen, Gotha, and at the Friedrich Wilhelm Gymnasium in Berlin. He began his military career in 1874 as an ensign in the Grand Ducal Hessian Foot-guards. He rose through service with the Hessian Dragoon Guards and various staff appointments to the command of the Twenty-second German Division stationed at Kassel. In 1913 Liman von Sanders was sent to Turkey with a German military mission. He was appointed commander of the Turkish First Army, but when Russia and France protested, his appointment was changed to that of marshal and inspector general of the Turkish army. He was undertaking a basic reorganization of the Turkish army at the time of the war's outbreak. In November, 1914, he was given command of Turkish troops in the Caucasus. In March, 1915, as commander of the Turkish Fifth Army, he opposed the Allied attacks on the Dardanelles.

The Turks, under Liman von Sanders' competent direction, so seriously threatened the small Allied beachheads that large British and Dominion reinforcements had to be dispatched, but all to no avail.

First Sea Lord Fisher resigned in May, 1915, because of his irritation over the operation. General Sir Ian Hamilton had wired War Minister Kitchener on March 19 that he believed that battleships alone could not force the Straits. In so doing, Hamilton had by-passed Admiral de Robeck in what was essentially a naval decision, and this irregularity caused great indignation in the Admiralty. By September, 1915, it was clear that massive reinforcements would be needed to clear the Gallipoli peninsula of Turkish resistance before the fleet could reach Constantinople. The British government decided to recall Hamilton and replace him with General Sir Charles Monro. Lord Kitchener visited Gallipoli in November, 1915, and agreed with General Monro in the abandonment of the entire Dardanelles enterprise. Evacuation was completed by January 9, 1916. The ineffectual British and French forces were transferred from Gallipoli to Salonika, where an Allied force (including the rehabilitated Serbian army) under French General Sarrail was attempting to relieve Serbia, which had been overrun by Austro-German and Bulgarian armies.

Sixteen divisions of British Commonwealth and French troops took part in the abortive effort to force the Straits. British Commonwealth casualties were 213,980. A number of old naval ships were lost. The Dardanelles fiasco helped overturn the Asquith government, which was replaced by that of David Lloyd George in December, 1916. Winston Churchill was eclipsed for his role in the Dardanelles campaign. He left England to command for a time an infantry battalion in France. General Sir Ian Hamilton had a prominent part in the disaster because of his overoptimism and faulty planning. The Dardanelles campaign produced only one advantage for the Allies: it diverted large Turkish forces from the Russians, enabling the demoralized tsarist armies to hold out somewhat longer than they might have done otherwise.

And as for General Liman von Sanders, the jealous Turks rewarded the victor of the Straits battle with a sinecure assignment in the interior of the Ottoman Empire, where he vegetated throughout the years 1916–17. At the war's end he was interned at Malta until August, 1919, when he was allowed to return to Germany. The Allies wanted to try him and other German officers as war criminals, but nothing came of it for even General Hamilton, his old foe, rallied to Liman von Sanders' defense in an open letter to the London *Times*.

LIMAN VON SANDERS, GENERAL OF CAVALRY, FIVE YEARS IN TURKEY

. . . The Anglo-French fleet had gradually assembled and found suitable bases in the islands of Lemnos, Imbros and

Source: From *Five Years in Turkey* (Annapolis: United States Naval Institute, 1928), pp. 52–67, 69–74, 76–79, 83, 96–105. Copyright © 1927 by the U.S. Naval Institute. Reprinted by permission.

Tenedos. During the winter flying stations for land planes
and hydroplanes had been erected on the last two islands together
with other military establishments.

The guns of the enemy fleet were at first directed against the old
works and batteries of Seddulbar (Sedd el Bahr) and Kum Kale
which closed the entry to the Dardanelles; the ships with their
modern heavy artillery remaining beyond the range of the older
Turkish guns. The available means in this conflict were too unequal to leave the outcome in doubt. After a few bombardments
the Turkish batteries were silenced and part of the fortifications
destroyed.

Repeated attempts of the enemy to land marines and take Seddulbar (Sedd el Bahr) by surprise were unsuccessful because in
spite of the bombardment small Turkish bodies had remained in
places not reached by the artillery fire and repulsed the landing.

By the end of February Turkish headquarters rather counted on
the enemy fleet breaking through and all sorts of preparations
were made for the Sultan, for his court and the treasury, and for
the military and civil authorities. They were to be taken care of on
the Asiatic side. These precautions were justified. On the other
hand those military preparations, which the Turkish headquarters
had ordered between February 20 and March 1 to meet a successful passage of the allied fleet through the Dardanelles, might have
been fatal.

Had these orders been carried out, the course of the World War
would have been given such a turn in the spring of 1915 that
Germany and Austria would have had to continue the struggle
without Turkey, because these orders exposed the Dardanelles to
a hostile landing!

The orders of February 20 changed the organization of the First
and of the Second Armies, splitting up the units of the First Army
Corps. Furthermore, and that is the essential point, it was ordered
that in case of a successful passage of the hostile fleet, the First
Army was to defend the north coast, the Second Army the south
coast of the straits and of the Sea of Marmara. The line separating
the spheres of the two armies was drawn from the mouth of the
Dardanelles through the Sea of Marmara from west to east as far
as the mouth of the Bosporus in the Black Sea. It did away with
any defense of the exterior coast of the Gallipoli peninsula with its
dominating heights; it did away with the defense of the Asiatic

coast at the mouth of the Dardanelles. It was the feeblest imaginable defensive measure.

I wrote to Enver on February 23 bringing to his attention the incalculable disadvantages of the measures he had ordered. I explained that one Turkish Army was needed for the defense against an Anglo-French landing in the Dardanelles, and another near Constantinople to prevent a Russian landing. That the fronts were west and east, not south and north. On February 25 I received a reply from Enver that he could not concur in my view, without a word of explanation.

On March 1 an order was prepared at Turkish headquarters directing the withdrawal of the Second Army Corps from Adrianople to the lines of Tschataldja, and of the transfer of the Fourth Army Corps from the section Panderma-Balekesri to the Gulf of Ismid. The Second and Fourth Army Corps were the troops nearest to the Dardanelles and the first to be called on in case of a hostile landing on the side of the Dardanelles.

I could not acquiesce in these unfortunate and fatal orders of Enver, and in order to secure a different decision I addressed myself at once on March 1 to the ambassador and to the Chief of the Military Cabinet of H. M. the Emperor.

I am unable to say what was done by these two German authorities to back up my view. Something was done, however, for the execution of these faulty measures was deferred for the present.

In the month of March the action of the allied fleet against the straits of the Dardanelles reached its apex and terminated with the attempt of March 18 to break through.

On March 1 five British battleships with numerous torpedo boats entered the anterior southwestern portion of the strait and engaged the Turkish howitzer batteries on the heights of Erenköj (Eren Keui) and Halil Eli from noon till 6 p.m. . . . .

On March 18 the allied fleet made its great attempt to break through. According to Colonel Wehrle's report sixteen battleships took part; they began at 10.30 a.m. to enter the straits in two echelons, in order to silence the guns of the fortress and the batteries. The artillery battle lasted until 7 p.m.

In spite of the expenditure of enormous amounts of ammunition the hostile fleet accomplished no great results. The damage to the forts and batteries but little diminished their fighting capacity, though their ammunition supply had been reduced. According to the statements of Colonel Djevad Bei, the commander of the fortress, the losses in men did not reach 200.

The enemy suffered serious and weighty losses. Insofar as could be observed by Colonel Wehrle and his subordinates, the *Bouvet*, *Irresistible* and *Ocean* had been sunk and several other battleships were seriously damaged. Several smaller ships, engaged in salvage work, had also been sunk. The fire of Fort Hamidje under Captain Wossidlo was mentioned as particularly effective. It may be assumed that the mine field in Erenköj (Eren Keui) Bay laid at night by the Turkish mine expert, Lieutenant Colonel Geehl, contributed its share to the result.

At any rate the allied fleet had to withdraw and give up the attempt. The 18th of March is and remains a day of honor for the Fortress Dardanelles and for the commander of the straits. The attempt was not renewed by the Entente during the war.

The allies now probably recognized that the road to Constantinople could not be opened by action on the water alone. It was equally clear to me that they would not relinquish such a high prize without further effort. It would not have been in keeping with British tenacity or energy. Hence a large landing had to be counted upon.

As early as March rumors began to circulate of the concentration of a large expeditionary force for that purpose. These reports coming mostly from Athens, Sofia and Bucharest contained many contradictions, which was natural. Once it was 50,000 men, then again 80,000 British troops were being assembled on the Islands of Imbros and Lemnos; another time 50,000 French were named as participants in the expedition. The arrival at the Dardanelles of General Hamilton who was to assume command, and of the French General d'Amade on the cruiser *Provence*, were duly reported. It was known that a landing pier had been constructed in Mudros and that equipment and subsistence were being unloaded there daily. On March 17 four British officers had arrived at Piraeus and bought forty-two large lighters and five tugs for cash.

Now at last, on the 25th of March, Enver decided to form a separate army, the Fifth, for the defense of the Dardanelles. My constantly renewed efforts to bring about such a decision of Turkish headquarters had of late received effective support from the German Embassy and Admiral Souchon; Admiral von Usedom, however, after his experiences in China, would not yet believe in the probability of large landing operations.

Late on the afternoon of March 24 Enver requested me to wait for him in my office. He came soon afterward and asked if I were

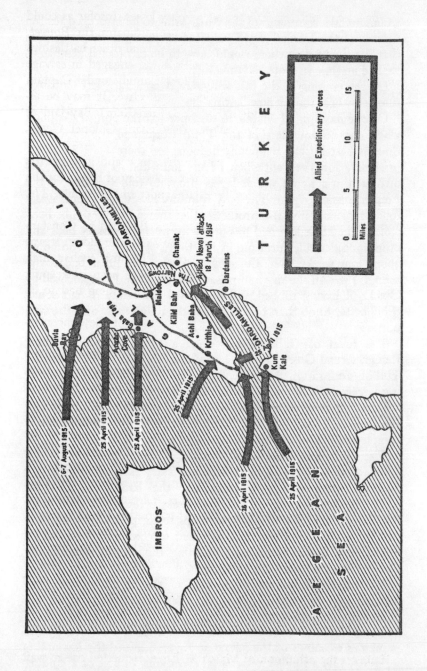

willing to take command of the Fifth Army to be organized for the
defense of the Dardanelles. I assented at once and informed him
that the troops now there would have to be reënforced at once as
we had no time to spare.

On the evening of the following day, March 25, I left Constantinople by boat for my new destination. . . .

On the morning of March 26 we landed at the port of Gallipoli
where the headquarters of the Third Corps had been for some
time, and established temporary headquarters there.

Myself, and the gentlemen of my immediate entourage, were
quartered in a house which I was afterward told was that of the
French consular agent. The only furniture in my two rooms was a
round table and a wall mirror. All other things had no doubt been
stolen. The kaimakan had to borrow for us the necessary beds and
other indispensable furniture in the town. When I left the house
about four weeks later, the greater part of my linen had disappeared. I was all the more surprised later on when I was accused by
Greeks of having robbed and plundered the house. I had something better to do than to carry away the round table and the wall
mirror.

The town of Gallipoli was then a fairly prosperous town,
though several Greek families had previously been expelled by the
Turkish authorities. At the end of the Dardanelles Campaign it
was largely a pile of ruins due to hostile bombardments.

Days full of work ensued since the grouping of the troops and
the guarding of the important stretches of coast had to be changed
completely.

The Fifth Army numbered but five divisions, which were distributed on the European and Asiatic sides as coast guards; the
divisions numbered 9–12 battalions, the battalions 800–1000
men. The British gave me four full weeks before their great landing. They had sent part of their troops to Egypt and perhaps also
to Cyprus. The time was just sufficient to complete the most indispensable arrangements and to bring the 3rd Division under
Colonel Nicolai from Constantinople.

The exterior coasts on both sides of the mouth of the Dardanelles were the first places where a landing might be expected.

The littoral region of the Asiatic coast consisted of fertile undulating hills and large flats with meadow land, traversed by the
numerous windings of the Mendere River. Seaward the lowland is
terminated by a ring of low coastal elevations. In case of a landing
these elevations would be the natural artillery positions of the

enemy whence his guns, in combination with the long range artillery of the fleet, could dominate the open country to the east. The Mendere River and the marshy stretches were not such as to seriously impede an army with modern equipment in spring and summer.

The narrow peninsula of Gallipoli which bounds the straits on the north on the European side, is pronounced mountainous terrain with precipitous ridges, the slopes of which are rent by deep ravines and sharp clefts.

A few low pine woods, a few bushes on the ridges and on the banks of the creeks and coulees, formed the sole natural covering of the generally waste landscape.

The cultivation is dependent on the water supply and limited to the surroundings of the few villages, which are all on low ground. It is only the valleys around the small town of Maidos, the latter lying directly on the straits, that show some higher cultivation. Here are olive and mulberry plantations.

Toward the upper part of the Gulf of Saros (Xeros) the interior of the peninsula contains considerable plains which are open and more fertile.

The important question was where the hostile landing should be expected. On it depended the grouping of the troops, which were rather inconsiderable in comparison with the great extent of the coast.

Technical feasibility for the landing of large bodies of troops existed in many parts of the coast. All could not be occupied. The decision therefore must be made on tactical grounds. . . .

Conformably to the degree of danger I formed three groups. The 5th and 7th Divisions were stationed on the upper Saros (Xeros) Gulf, the 9th and newly organized 19th Division were ordered to the southern part of the peninsula and the 11th Division was stationed on the Asiatic side together with the 3rd Division which soon arrived by boat.

The positions of the five existing divisions up to March 26 had to be altered completely. They had been posted on different principles and distributed along the entire coast, somewhat like the frontier detachments of the good old days. The enemy on landing would have found resistance everywhere, but there were no reserves to check a strong and energetic advance.

I ordered the divisions to hold their troops together and to send only the most indispensable security detachments to the coast within their sectors.

Whatever might be in store, in view of our weak forces, our success depended not on sticking tight, but on the mobility of our three battle groups.

The next step necessary after getting the troops in their new positions—they had grown stiff in their coast guard positions—was to make them as mobile by marches and exercises as we wanted them to be at the decisive moment. To expedite the movements of troops at the proper moment without loss of time, boats were assembled in suitable ports of the straits and the labor battalions were at once set to work constructing direct communications between sectors. So far there was hardly a through road on the peninsula. There were only foot paths and pack trails for the movement of pack animals in single file.

The new positions were taken up by night marches to conceal them from hostile aviators.

The Fifth Army had not a single aeroplane. The few aeroplanes in Tschanak-Kale (Chanak) belonged to the fortress and were barely able to serve its purposes.

In those days the planning of troop exercises called for some caution, because hostile ships were cruising everywhere and firing on any detachment that became visible. Much to our surprise the ships fired even on such single horsemen or pedestrians as they caught sight of.

For the improvement of the field fortifications of the most endangered stretches of the coast all available men were put to work and mostly at night. The available Turkish means of obstruction were as short as were the tools, but we did the best we could. Torpedo heads were used alongside with the regular land mines and the fences of gardens and fields were stripped of their wood and wire. At places particularly suitable for landings barbed wire was stretched under water. . . .

At 5 a.m. of April 25th reports were received in rapid succession at army headquarters of extensive landings of troops made or about to be made. . . .

From the many pale faces among the officers reporting in the early morning it became apparent that although a hostile landing had been expected with certainty, a landing at so many places surprised many and filled them with apprehension. My first feeling was that our arrangements needed no change. That was a great satisfaction! The hostile landing expedition had selected those points which we ourselves considered the most likely landing places and had specially prepared for defense.

It seemed improbable to me that extensive landings would take place at all of these places, but we could not discern at that moment where the enemy was actually seeking the decision.

After alarming the 7th Division in the town of Gallipoli and instructing it to march at once in the direction of Bulair, I rode ahead to the heights of Bulair with my German adjutants.

On the narrow ridge of Bulair where neither tree nor bush impedes view or gives cover, we had a full view of the upper Saros (Xeros) Gulf. About twenty large hostile ships, some war vessels, some transports, could be counted in front of us. Some individual vessels were lying close in under the steep slopes of the coast. Others were farther out in the gulf or were still underway. From the broadsides of the war vessels came an uninterrupted stream of fire and smoke and the entire coast including our ridge was covered with shells and shrapnel. It was an unforgettable picture. Nowhere, however, could we see any debarking of troops from the transports.

After a while Essad Pasha, commanding the Third Army Corps, arrived on our heights and brought some detailed reports. The reports stated that British landing attempts at the south point of the peninsula had so far been repulsed by the 9th Division, but that the enemy was tenaciously bringing up more and more troops. At Kabatepe (Gaba Tepe) things were going well; the enemy had not been able so far to get a footing. But at Ari Burnu the heights along the coast were in the hands of the British, though the 19th Division was on the march to recapture the former. No detailed reports had yet been received from the Asiatic side.

I directed Essad Pasha to find any ship he could and go to Maidos to take command of the southern part of the peninsula.

I myself had to remain for the present at Bulair because it was of the utmost importance that at this point the peninsula be kept open. The troops on the Asiatic side I knew were in the safe hands of Colonel Weber.

This was the beginning of the Dardanelles Campaign which was to last eight and one-half months and which, counting both sides, brought together over three quarters of a million men for battle on the Gallipoli peninsula.

The preparations of the enemy were excellent, their only defect being that they were based on reconnaissances that were too old and that they underestimated the powers of resistance of the Turkish soldier. Hence they failed to bring in the first few days the decisive results which would have converted this grand operation into a decisive and swift military achievement.

According to our estimation the enemy was using 80,000 to 90,000 men in trying for the first success, while the Fifth Army numbered at the most 60,000 men, from which total certain deductions should be made for troops guarding other places. Moreover the superiority of the enemy's artillery was so immense as to defy estimation. His means of transportation seemed almost unlimited. On April 25 the various posts of observation along our coast counted nearly 200 ships—warships and transports. . . .

In the course of April 25 the transports in the Gulf of Saros (Xeros) repeatedly put out boats which sought to approach the coast but retreated under our fire. This action appeared to me to indicate a demonstration. It was noted that the transports were not deep in the water as could be seen on the sides of the ships. The decks of all transports were lined with dense rows of vertical branches so that it could not be seen whether there were troops on board. But the artillery fire of the warships continued without interruption.

In the afternoon the chief of staff sent word from Gallipoli that according to the reports received all enemy attempts to land in Besika (Bashika) Bay had been repulsed, and that perhaps it might be a demonstration.

Soon a telegram came from Essad Pasha from Maidos, that in the southern part of the peninsula at Seddulbar (Sedd el Bahr) and at Eski Hissarlik in Morto Bay there was pressing need of reënforcements; that the enemy had gained a footing there and was constantly being reënforced; that Colonel Sami Bei, commanding the 9th Division, had put his last available troops into the fight. As the impression of a demonstration in the Gulf of Saros (Xeros) was more and more confirmed, I ordered the 7th Division, which I had stopped at the road fork southwest of Bulair, to embark that evening two battalions in the harbor of Gallipoli and despatch them during the night to report to Essad Pasha. At the same time I ordered the 5th Division, which stood in readiness at the eastern edge of the Gulf of Saros, to send at once three battalions to Scharkeui and to get them to Maidos during the night. All such shipments had to be made at night because enemy submarines had gotten through the straits and into the Sea of Marmara. . . .

I have found that quite erroneous ideas existed in Germany where it was frequently maintained in speech and in writing that in the Gallipoli Campaign, which was so important for the outcome of the war, the Turkish Army and Navy took equal parts in the fighting.

The Turko-German fleet took no direct part except that it furnished to the Fifth Army two machine gun detachments with about twenty-four machine guns which were of great benefit. The *Haireddin Barbarossa* and *Tourgout Reis*, the old *Weissenburg* and *Woerth*, assisted in the first few weeks after the landing with indirect fire from the straits against the British landing places and ships near Ari Burnu. The movements of a Turkish torpedo boat in the lower part of the straits during the night of the 12th of May and the, unfortunately very brief, activity of the German submarines will presently be discussed. The *Goeben* and the *Breslau* did not ever throughout the campaign of eight and one-half months, come into the Dardanelles.

The separate German naval detachment under Admiral von Usedom was tied to the works and batteries of the Dardanelles fortress and of the Bosporus and had no direct part in the many battles and engagements of the Fifth Army on the Gallipoli peninsula. The tasks of the special detachment all lay on the interior of the straits, while the big battles were fought on the exterior coasts, except those of the south group which took place on the inner coast. The guns of the fort of In Tepe on the Asiatic shore did valuable work against the landing place and the camps at Seddulbar (Sedd el Bahr), and against the communications leading thence northward, but could do nothing against the battle fronts farther north on account of the distance and the intervening terrain.

A frequent and prolonged bombardment of the coast at Seddulbar (Sedd el Bahr), and of the Bay of Morto from the Asiatic side could not be kept up till autumn on account of lack of ammunition for the guns of the fortress.

I have no doubt that the bombardment from In Tepe frequently proved harassing to the enemy and that he sometimes assigned special ships to bombard these batteries. But all this remained secondary in comparison with the great battles on the peninsula. . . .

The enemy ships protected the landed troops in the fullest sense of the word. We on our side in those days had nothing but field artillery, which was badly needed to repulse the enemy's land attacks and which even then had to economize its ammunition. Their power and range precluded any action against the ships.

Nothing remained but to drive the landed troops back to their ships by night attack. On orders from the Fifth Army Colonel von Sodenstern made the attempt during three nights. Reinforcements now gradually arriving from Constantinople were attached to his force. All three attacks were successfully carried forward during darkness, one of them got close to Seddulbar (Sedd el Bahr), but the purpose could not be accomplished. In each case daybreak brought an overwhelming fire from the ships which compelled the Turks to withdraw to their positions. Only a part of the captured machine guns could be carried off.

Painful as it was for me, I now had to give orders to abstain from further attacks on the Seddulbar (Sedd el Bahr) front and to remain on the defensive. But not an inch of ground was to be yielded as the enemy was not far from Eltschitepe (Achi Baba) ridge, his next great objective. I ordered the Turkish troops of the first line to entrench themselves as close to the enemy as possible. A distance of a few paces between the hostile lines would inhibit the fire from the ships which would now equally endanger the troops of both sides. This was explained to the leaders and to their troops.

Since the Dardanelles Campaign is the only great operation in the World War where a land army had to do steady battle against a hostile army and navy, it must be stated here that the artillery effect of the hostile battleships constituted a support of extraordinary power for the landing army. No heavy land artillery can so easily change position and direct its fire on the enemy's flank and rear as was possible to the guns of the ships. Add to this that the ships' guns could direct their fire as on the firing ground without being under fire themselves, and that observation was assisted by captive balloons and aviators, in both of which the Fifth Army was wholly deficient.

At Ari Burnu we had likewise failed to drive the enemy from the coast. On the 29th of April a strong Turkish attack was driving part of the landed Australians and New Zealanders from the ground they had gained and they were beginning to reembark when reënforcements hurriedly arrived and the arrival of battleships restored the situation. It should be kept in mind that the enemy's base, the Island of Imbros, was not more than twenty kilometers from Ari Burnu where the British maintained ample reserves of troops and ships.

Later the Anzac corps—Australians and New Zealanders— made several strong attacks on the Turkish lines after preparation by the heaviest kind of naval bombardment. They invariably failed with heavy loss.

After the first two weeks of the bloody battles it became imperative to order Essad Pasha to abstain from any extensive attack until further orders, and to defend our positions on the ridges obstinately; to use every bit of favorable ground and every dark night to push our foremost lines to within a few paces of the enemy. In this way we here also deprived the British of the support of the ships' fire against the foremost Turkish trenches.

Thus on both fronts which had remained in the enemy's hands after his great landing, the mobile war gradually assumed the character of a war of position in the first third of May.

The few villages of the peninsula situated in the sectors of the two battle fronts or in their rear, suffered severely from the fire of the British ships. The prosperous port of Maidos went up in flames on April 29 under the fire of the British ships. The first building to become the victim of British naval shells was the large local hospital which was crowded with wounded. In spite of every effort many Turks and some twenty-five wounded British became victims of the conflagration, which spread with irresistible force. Many peaceful inhabitants likewise perished. Men, women and children, who were trying to save their most indispensable possession, had to be removed from their houses under a rain of projectiles. From Kilid Bay they were transferred to the Asiatic side to save their lives. In Maidos, which was not fortified or occupied by staffs or troops, not a single house or wall remained intact.

Similarly other Turkish villages, for instance Kodjadere (Koja Dere), were levelled to the ground, and others like Bulair, Kara Burgas, Jenikeui and the town of Gallipoli, were heavily damaged. With the same moral right with which the reconstruction of the destroyed parts of Belgium and northern France is insisted on, the Turks might ask for the reconstruction of all those places on the peninsula of Gallipoli which were destroyed though they were of no military value.

Similarly to the villages in the interior of the narrow peninsula, Ak Bashi and Kilia, ports of the Fifth Army on the European shore of the Dardanelles, were subjected to heavy indirect fire. They were the debarking ports for most of the food and military supplies.

The bringing up of food to the Fifth Army was especially difficult. The railroad station in Usunköpri (Uzun Kupru) in Thrace was seven marches distant and the means of transport were very limited. In those days the armies in Turkey had no auto trucks and it was with much difficulty that the columns of camels, pack animals and Turkish ox wagons managed to get a few tons to the front. Hence the Fifth Army had to depend for its supplies almost completely on water transport through the Sea of Marmara where British and French submarines tried to close this line. It was fortunate that the submarines could not do it, otherwise the Fifth Army would have died of hunger.

In judging the action of submarines it should be noted that in the narrow and open Sea of Marmara four or five submarines operating at the same time were unable to stop transportation by boat. Several Turkish ships were torpedoed, but the majority came through and reached their destination by steaming at night from etape to etape. Various things came to the debarking stations by sailboat and towed mahones. . . .

Both sides began to construct complete systems of field fortifications in three and more lines, with numerous dugouts and many kilometers of approaches. The tools with which the two sides worked were sadly different. The enemy controlled all the resources of the world and possessed the most modern war material, the poor Turks had few entrenching implements and frequently had to capture the tools for the construction of their field works from the enemy. The wood and iron for the dugouts were collected from the destroyed villages. Not even sand bags could be procured in anywhere nearly sufficient quantity. When a few thousands of them arrived from Constantinople, there was danger of their being used by the troop leaders for patching the ragged uniforms of their men. It was due solely to the stoic calmness of the Anatolian soldier and to his freedom from wants that all these difficulties were overcome.

The officers no longer had the same nerve as the soldier. I received repeated and urgent suggestions from various parties during the ensuing weeks to move the battle front of the south group back to the Eltschitepe (Achi Baba), because the plain south of Kirte (Kritha) afforded no natural positions. After acrimonious discussions I declined all these suggestions as they would have completely broken down my principle of a step by step defense. It was plain that the farther I withdrew to the north, the more troops were required for the defense, because the peninsula broadened out in that direction. Furthermore a line of defense abreast of the Eltschitepe (Achi Baba), visible from every direction, would have offered an excellent target to the overwhelming fire of the naval guns. The events justified me. . . .

We now gradually gathered the impression that the enemy was seeking the decision on the south front at Seddulbar (Sedd el Bahr) as he constantly increased his reënforcements and renewed his severe attacks. At Ariburnu (Ari Burnu) on the other hand there were few combined attacks during the first few weeks and action was somewhat desultory. Small actions succeeded each other day and night, sometimes increasing somewhat, in various places.

In the month of May the Turko-German fleet brought us some temporary relief by its action against enemy war vessels. On the evening of May 13 the Turkish torpedo boat *Muavanet-i-Miliet* under Lieutenant Firle sank the British battleship *Goliath* in the southernmost part of the Dardanelles near Morto Bay by a few torpedo discharges. The attack was so well prepared and so sudden that the Turkish torpedo boat was able to withdraw through the straits without damage.

On the 25th and 27th of May the recently arrived German submarines scored two great successes in that Lieutenant Hersing torpedoed the British battleships *Triumph* and *Majestic* off the outer coast of the peninsula. The enemy now temporarily withdrew the greater part of his battleships to the protected ports of Imbros and Lemnos and during the next few weeks the artillery support of the landed army came chiefly from the destroyers and torpedo boats. At the same time, however, all the effective means of defense against submarines were put in operation by the enemy who had at his disposal every kind of material he wanted. Thereafter the German submarines were unable, during the next seven months of the campaign, to score any success against the hostile fleet, except that they torpedoed a transport.

As early as June 16th I had to telegraph to the naval chief, Admiral Souchon in Constantinople, that the enemy was again using his large transports unhindered in transferring and relieving his troops. On June 20 I telegraphed him that the enemy war vessels had begun the same activity with their artillery as before the success of the submarines. On June 29th I informed him that in a large attack on the preceding day against the right flank of the south front, they had strongly coöperated with their fire and were doing the same on June 29th in the still continuing battle on the south front. The idea expressed in German papers, that the coöperation of the submarines had broken the backbone of the attack against the Fifth Army on the Gallipoli peninsula, was therefore quite erroneous. At home such erroneous statements led to a false estimation of the efficiency of the submarines.

In the very hot summer of 1915 the invariably calm sea and the clear steady air greatly assisted the artillery fire of the hostile fleet and facilitated the direction of artillery fire by means of aeroplanes and captive balloons. The roar of the guns on the coasts of the peninsula never ceased day or night. When the land batteries ceased firing, the ships' guns began, and *vice versa*. In all the attacks the guns on land and on shipboard coöperated.

The only German organization which took a part in the Dardanelles campaign on the Gallipoli peninsula joined the Fifth Army toward the end of June. It was an extemporized German pioneer company whose non-commissioned officers and men had gotten into Turkey as travellers by various routes. This pioneer company with a strength of 200 men was attached to the south group at Seddulbar (Sedd el Bahr). In consequence of the torrid climate and Turkish subsistence to which they were not used and of severe losses in battle, its numbers were soon reduced to forty men. They were now distributed on both fronts to act as foremen. In this capacity they rendered valuable service.

No other German unit reached Gallipoli during this campaign. Individual German officers and non-commissioned officers, the latter mostly from the artillery, were employed at the various headquarters and with the troops of the Fifth Army.

On account of severe losses and the constant battles, part of the Turkish troops on the south front had to be relieved. They were relieved by fresh troops of the Second Turkish Army and the chief of the Second Army, Wehib Pasha, relieved Colonel Weber in command of the south group at Seddulbar (Sedd el Bahr). Wehib Pasha was the younger brother of Essad Pasha who was in command at Ari Burnu. It was a good thing that these closely united brothers were the chiefs of the two battle groups. It eliminated jealousy and lack of coöperation so common among Turkish general officers. In this position Wehib Pasha, an energetic man, proved himself in every way a determined and far seeing leader and this commendation applies equally to the older brother at Ari Burnu, the knightly and valorous Essad Pasha, the celebrated defender of Janina in the Balkan War.

Just as the troops at Seddulbar (Sedd el Bahr) were being relieved by those of the Second Army on July 13, a heavy Anglo-French attack materialized which was repulsed with difficulty and not without the use of the last reserves. It was fortunate for us that the British attacks never lasted more than one day, and were punctuated by pauses of several days. Otherwise it would have been impossible to replenish our artillery ammunition.

During the second half of July rumors were increasing that another great landing was imminent. A report arriving via Salonika on the 16th spoke of the concentration of 50,000 to 60,000 men on the Island of Lemnos alone and gave the number of war and transport vessels assembled there as 140. Other sources named higher figures. The probability of another landing lay above all in the fact that the heavy battles of the past months had not brought the enemy sensibly nearer to his objectives. At that time the English Minister Churchill stated in a much quoted speech that the final success of the landed army was now in prospect. . . .

On the evening of August 6 the new grand operations of the enemy began, during which gradually five fresh British divisions— among them a dismounted cavalry division—were landed on the Gallipoli peninsula between Ari Burnu and the north end of Suvla Bay. At the same time severe attacks were made on the south group at Seddulbar (Sedd el Bahr) and on the left wing of the Ari Burnu group.

Essad Pasha at first believed that the decisive attack was directed against his left wing. But on the evening of the 6th it was discovered that from the beach at Ari Burnu the enemy was moving northward along the coast and that still farther north strong forces were being disembarked at various points. This was the decisive moment.

The first reports were received at the headquarters of the Fifth Army toward 9 p.m. Kiazim Bei, the chief of the general staff, had gone late in the afternoon to Ari Burnu for a conference with Essad Pasha and was unable to return during the next few hours because the entire country in rear of Ari Burnu was under severe fire.

Immediately upon receipt of the foregoing report I telephoned to the 7th and 12th Divisions on the upper Saros (Xeros) Gulf, ordering that they be alarmed and made ready to march at once. About an hour later orders were sent to start both divisions at once in the general direction of Usun-Hisirli east of Anafarta Sagir. Essad Pasha that evening alarmed the 9th Division and ordered it to march northward. . . .

It seems that in the late fall the British authorities were no longer sanguine about a favorable ending of the campaign, as is evidenced by a telegram of Secretary Chamberlain of October 21st to the Viceroy of India in which he says "our situation and our prospects in Gallipoli are very uncertain."

A new landing on Gallipoli was once more announced from Germany on November 1st. It materialized no more than did the passage of the fleet through the Dardanelles announced from Berne on November 24th.

At last in November the long coveted German artillery ammunition reached the Fifth Army. Its arrival increased the hope of a successful ending of the campaign. The Turkish artillery was in excellent training and its firing was good, but with its poor ammunition it could not produce more than limited results. From now on it was different.

The first troops from the Central Powers arrived in Gallipoli November 15 for our active support. It was an excellent Austrian 24-cm. mortar battery which was posted on the left of the Anafarta front and soon opened a very effective fire against the Mastan Tepe. An equally good Austrian 15-cm. howitzer battery, which followed in December, was attached to the south group. No other non-Turkish troops reached Gallipoli before the withdrawal of the British. The total of all Germans employed there, officers, noncommissioned officers and soldiers, had increased to about 500.

Toward the end of November the Fifth Army began to work on a plan for an attack in force. It was planned to pierce part of the Ari Burnu front and the adjoining right wing of the Anafarta front and thus to force back the outer parts of these two fronts. Reënforcements for this purpose from the Second Army were promised by Turkish headquarters. Technical troops for the purpose were to be drawn from Germany. Under instructions from German headquarters Colonel von Berendt, Lieutenant Colonel Klehmet and Major Lothes came to Gallipoli to gather the requisite information and make preparations. The divisions selected for the attack were taken out of the front and practiced for the attack on the instruction works erected behind the front.

The enemy anticipated the execution of the attack by his withdrawal from both the northern fronts. The withdrawal was due in the first place to Lord Kitchener as we learned later. He had in person visited all the fronts of Gallipoli in November and accurately informed himself of the conditions of the present offensive and of its chances if continued. After this inspection he deemed it best to give up the attack and stated that the withdrawal from the peninsula was feasible without great losses. Before this some other British leaders had considered a withdrawal from the peninsula very difficult. The events justified Lord Kitchener.

Since the aim of the Anafarta landing had not been accomplished, there was no prospect for the enemy to carry the attack to a successful ending with the means at hand. During the last few weeks the enemy's progress on all the fronts had been very limited and dearly paid for in blood. All dominating heights were in the hands of the Turks. The best plan probably for the British was to give up the attack. Though the first and innermost reason therefor was the hopelessness of success, there was the reflection that reënforcements would hardly be able to change the course of events after the Central Powers had opened the way to Turkey.

We of course knew nothing of the intended withdrawal and did not learn of it up to the last minute. Its possibility had been considered by the Fifth Army and all leaders had been called on in writing for special watchfulness in that direction. But the very skilful beginning and execution of the withdrawal prevented its being seen from the front line of the Turks.

On the night of the 19/20 December a dense fog covered the peninsula and the coast. The fire along the fronts continued in customary volume till midnight. Then it became a little weaker. The enemy's naval guns were firing from several directions. On the afternoon of the 19th a heavy attack on the south front had been repulsed. During the night the British withdrew from the Ari Burnu and Anafarta fronts.

The events on the side of the Fifth Army were as follows:

Between 1 and 2 in the morning the enemy had exploded a mine in the Ari Burnu front. The Turkish troops, advancing according to instructions to seize the crater, found no resistance.

When the adjoining Turkish companies were feeling their way toward the foremost enemy trenches, there were a few shots and then firing ceased. The trenches were occupied by the Turks. Reports were despatched to the higher commanders. There was some natural delay before they could arrive and give instructions for further action, since no special instructions had been issued for such a case, and the fog prevented vision. Where the way led through the enemy's trench system, there were obstacles to be removed everywhere. In several places mines exploded when stepped on and caused confusion and loss. In this way the rearmost troops of the enemy had gained a good start. The fire of the ships covered the ground traversed by the advancing Turks. Though the road to the coast was short, the descent through the steep rocky hills of the coast in the dark foggy night was troublesome. When the leading troops reached the coast, the enemy had disappeared. The ships at once changed their aim to the beach.

The withdrawal on the Anafarta front was similar except that contradictory reports caused difficulties in the issuing of orders. In several places where the fog was less dense, red lights were visible on the shore and some of the subordinate leaders conjectured another landing.

The first reports that reached me at the headquarters camp at 4 a.m. were written in this dubious style. I at once ordered a general alarm and the turning out of all reserves including the cavalry. Each unit in its own sector was to advance in a direct line to the shore. But orders do not circulate as fast as one hopes, particularly when two languages are involved.

The troops of the Anafarta group encountered minefields which caused much loss. At some points short engagements took place with the rear points of the enemy, as in case of the Turkish 126th Infantry Regiment. Here too the enemy had embarked with hardly any loss. The withdrawal had been prepared with extraordinary care and carried out with great skill. The hostile artillery had been removed except a small number of guns which now fell into our hands. This removal had been possible because all British land batteries lay close to the shore.

One or another artillery commander had noticed that in the last few days some batteries had fired with one gun only or not at all, but no importance was attached to the fact which therefore was not reported to superiors. It had happened several times that the batteries paused one or two days in their firing, particularly when changing positions. On such occasions the fire from the ships became heavier.

Immense stores of all kinds were abandoned by the British on their withdrawal. Between Suvla Bay and Ari Burnu five small steamers and more than sixty boats were abandoned on the beach. We found large quantities of material for dummy rail lines, telephones and obstacles, piles of tools of all kinds, medicine chests, medical supplies and water filters.

A great mass of artillery and infantry ammunition had been abandoned and whole lines of carriages and caissons, hand arms of all kinds, boxes of hand grenades and machine gun barrels. Many stacks of conserves, flour, food and mountains of wood were found. The tent camps had been left standing and sacrificed. This probably served better than anything else to mask the withdrawal. Several hundred horses which could not be embarked were killed and lay in long rows.

How sudden the order for withdrawal must have come to the last troops on the peninsula appears from the fact that in some tents freshly served food stood on the tables. From the written orders found in the camp it appeared that a large part of the troops not in first line had been embarked during the past two nights and carried away. These captured British papers informed us of other interesting matters.

On the Anafarta front we found foot paths lined with white-washed sandbags so as to be visible on a dark night. They had shown the last troops the way of carefully avoiding the minefields.

It should be taken in consideration in the entire withdrawal that the distance from the front lines to the shore was short, varying between one and four and one-half kilometers. Hence the British withdrawal from Gallipoli cannot be compared with the great rearward movements of European fronts, as has been done by some.

The enemy continued to hold the position at Seddulbar (Sedd el Bahr).

On the forenoon of December 20 orders were given by the Fifth Army to bring the best batteries of the abandoned fronts to the south group. In like manner it was ordered that the best grenade throwers, scouts and pioneers be at once put in march to the south group.

There was some possibility that in Seddulbar the enemy wanted to keep a base for further operations. The position there was particularly strong and well protected by the fire of the ships. The authors of this idea spoke of a second Gibraltar supplementary to the Salonika position. No such idea was entertained by the Fifth Army. It was thought possible, however, that the enemy might hang on for some time. That could not be permitted.

Hence a plan of attack on the enemy's position at Seddulbar was at once taken in hand, giving due consideration to the technical troops expected from Germany. An attack was prepared on the entire south front by the four divisions there and eight others to be brought up. No troops had to be taken from the Second Army since on the other fronts our own troops had become available and because only limited troops were needed to guard the coast. Superfluous units were ordered by the Turkish headquarters to march to Thrace.

New Year's Eve 1915/16 I sent to the military attaché in Constantinople a telegram for German headquarters, proposing that after the complete withdrawal of the British from Gallipoli, an army be constituted from our troops and pushed via Demotika and Xanthi against the right flank and rear of the enemy army at Salonika, while German and Bulgarian troops attacked from the front. From our point of view the Salonika Army of the Entente remained a constant reservoir for menacing the Turkish coast and threatened our only land communication with Europe, our sole bridge to the Central Powers. We were aware of course, that there were other considerations for the German headquarters to weigh and that ours was merely a suggestion of Turkish coöperation in an attack on the Salonika front. No reply was received.

During the first days of January 1916 it appeared as though the fire of the land artillery at Seddulbar (Sedd el Bahr) was becoming weaker. But one gun was firing from several batteries, frequently changing its position, while the fire from the ships, including the largest calibers, sometimes grew to great vehemence. The removal of guns was observed from the Asiatic side. The scouting parties which were pushed forward against the hostile front at all hours of evening and night, invariably met with strong resistance. Of the troops designated for the attack, the 12th Division had arrived in rear of the south front. The division was designated to capture a section of trenches projecting northward opposite the extreme Turkish right, from which the British artillery could have flanked the great attack we were planning.

In the midst of these preparations the Turkish headquarters ordered on January 5 that nine divisions of the Fifth Army were to be withdrawn at once and put in march for Thrace. Several of these divisions had been designated for the attack. The situation on the south front had not become sufficiently clear for such a step nor was there any necessity for it, as the complete Second Army stood in Thrace. I explained the situation to Enver by telegraph and requested my discharge from the Turkish Army because his wholly unwarranted order was at the last moment jeopardizing the final result of the Dardanelles Campaign. He withdrew his order by telegraph. Like many other things in Turkey I have never been able to ascertain whether this matter, as was subsequently stated, was a misunderstanding due to another incorrect Turkish translation or whether the orders were actually issued in the form in which they reached me.

On January 7th I ordered the 12th Division to carry out the

attack planned on the extreme Turkish right after two hours of preparation by the heaviest artillery fire and explosion of mines. It met with strong resistance, but was partly successful in that we gained some of the ground at the projecting point.

The Turkish troops on the south were cautioned again and again to watch attentively for any indication of a withdrawal during the night. Bridges were everywhere placed in readiness to enable the artillery to cross the enemy trenches quickly. A field artillery battalion of the 26th Division on the Asiatic side, under the command of Captain Lehmann, was ordered by the Fifth Army to push to the outermost point of land at Kum Kale, where during the night of 8/9 January it bombarded such ground at Seddulbar (Sedd el Bahr) as was within range. In like manner the fortress guns near In Tepe assisted by a heavy fire.

During the night from the 8th to the 9th of January the enemy withdrew from the southern sector. The Turkish troops pursued at once when the fire from the advanced trenches was no longer answered by the enemy. In some places there were bloody conflicts. But all in all the enemy here again was successful in his withdrawal in spite of all our watchfulness. A large part of the troops were not marched the longer way to the place of embarkation at the south point, but had reached the south shores of the peninsula by the shortest routes and were embarked at suitable points in every kind of war and transport vessels, while the last rear guard was still maintaining a heavy fire from the advanced trenches. Fireworks had been used to give the impression of lively firing and the artillery fire came from the ships.

The Turkish divisions reached the coast everywhere long before daybreak. In many places they had been delayed by fields of land mines which caused serious losses. One division had captured nine guns on the way to the coast.

When it became daylight, our artillery sank a loaded transport on the west coast. The hostile torpedo boats in the vicinity opened a heavy fire into the sea near the transport believing that it had been torpedoed by a submarine. Unfortunately none were present at the withdrawal.

The booty at the south group was extraordinary. Wagon parks, automobile parks, mountains of arms, ammunition and entrenching tools were collected. Here too most of the tent camps and barracks had been left standing, in part with all of their equipment. Many hundreds of horses lay in rows, shot or poisoned, but quite a number of horses and mules were captured and turned over to the Turkish artillery. Here as at the other fronts the stacks of flour and subsistence had some acid solution poured over them to render them unfit for our use. In the next few days the hostile ships made vain attempts to set the stacks and the former British tent camps and barracks on fire. It took nearly two years to clean up the grounds. The immense booty of war material was used for other Turkish armies. Many ship loads of conserves, flour and wood were removed to Constantinople. What the ragged and insufficiently nourished Turkish soldiers took away, cannot be estimated. I tried to stop plundering by a dense line of sentinels but the endeavor was in vain. During the ensuing time we saw the Turkish soldiers on the peninsula in the most incredible garments which they had made up from every kind of uniform. They even carried British gas masks for fun.

The tribute of tenacious and steadfast prowess cannot be withheld from the Turkish troops, of whom at the height of the fighting twenty-two divisions stood in the primary and secondary fronts or as reserves, under the command of the Fifth Army. They had held their ground in unnumbered conflicts with a brave enemy who ever renewed his attacks and was supported by the fire of his fleet.

The total loss of the Fifth Army in the Dardanelles Campaign is very high and corresponds to the duration and severity of the fighting. It amounted to about 218,000 men, of whom 66,000 were killed and of the wounded 42,000 were returned to duty. There were Turkish infantry regiments which in this campaign needed and received 5,000 replacements.

The Gallipoli peninsula remained under the command of the Fifth Army, the headquarters being transferred to Lule Burgas in Thrace toward the end of January. Djevad Pasha received the command of the peninsula.

Upon the completion of the Dardanelles Campaign I recommended to Turkish headquarters to place the Dardanelles, the only approach to Constantinople from the sea and a source of apprehension for centuries, on a different basis by constructing a canal west of Bulair. I stated that a second water way from the Sea of Marmara to the Ægean Sea would afford a secure exit to the Turkish fleet, which will always have to be based on Constantinople. The mouth of the Gulf of Saros (Xeros) is thirty kilometers wide and much more difficult to blockade than the narrow exit of the Dardanelles. As against the former, Tenedos was of no

value and Imbros of partial value only. The north shore of the
Gulf of Saros, to which could be brought all the resources of
Thrace, would form one corner pillar after the erection of fortifications and shore batteries. The Asiatic coast of the Dardanelles
could be made into the other pillar. The suggested canal was so
far drawn back from the sea that if the north coast of the peninsula
was properly protected, any hostile influence was precluded.

The economic effect of the construction of this canal for Turkey
in Europe was bound to be considerable. The site was located on
the peninsula where the latter was but five kilometers wide, and
its construction offered no technical difficulties as surveyed and
attested by experts. Perhaps the project will be resumed at some
future time.

In the foregoing I have given a summary of the campaign in the
Dardanelles from the point of view of the commander in chief,
because little is known of the campaign in Germany. A detailed
description of battles must be left to the Turkish general staff.

III. Mountain Warfare

6. The Italian Front

ITALY, WHICH had joined Austria and Germany in 1882 to form the
Triple Alliance, was only a nominal member of that pact after 1902,
when Rome had signed a secret agreement with Paris which assured
the French of Italian abstention in event of a Franco-German war.
Rome's link with Vienna was an unnatural one, for Austria was the
traditional enemy of the Italians, and Italy coveted Hapsburg territories in which Italian was spoken, the border lands of *Italia irredenta*.
There was little surprise when Italy, on August 2, 1914, declared its
neutrality in a war which Rome regarded as being caused by an
Austrian offensive against Serbia.

After some fruitless negotiations undertaken by Vienna, Italy was
eventually enticed from its neutrality by the secret Treaty of London,
which it signed with Britain, France, and Russia on April 26, 1915.
Unlike the Central Powers, the Allies found it easy to promise Italy
booty at Austria's expense—the Trentino, the Alto Adige Valley to
the Brenner Pass, Gorizia, Gradisca, Trieste, the Istrian peninsula,
and North Dalmatia. Thus lured by the prospect of acquiring *Italia
irredenta* as well as by promises of Adalia in Turkey and extensions of
territory in Eritrea, Somaliland, and Libya, Italy declared war on its
former ally Austria on May 23, 1915, such a declaration against Germany being deferred until August 27, 1916. Italy at once put in the
field an army of more than a million men, but the terrain in the

Trentino and along the Isonzo was all to Austria's strategic advantage. In being constantly exposed to flank attack from the Trentino, and in having to fight up the Alpine slopes, the Italians were badly handicapped. This was acknowledged by German General Erich von Falkenhayn, who conceded: "The hopes placed in the defensive strength of the mountainous territory of the Austro-Hungarian and Italian frontier were altogether fulfilled." Moreover, upon outbreak of hostilities, the Italian army had only 112 field guns, 14 siege guns, 70 airplanes, and a munitions shortage. Italy, consequently, did not cut a figure of great martial prowess. But even so, its combat record was much more impressive than under the fascist regime in the Second World War.

A classic description of Italy's mountain warfare is to be found in *The Diary of Gino Speranza: Italy, 1915–1919*, from which we publish an excerpt. Gino Speranza was born in Bridgeport, Connecticut, on April 23, 1872, the son of Professor Carlo Leonardo Speranza, who taught at Yale and later at Columbia. The Speranza family stemmed from highly cultivated bourgeois stock in Verona. Gino Speranza was educated partly in Verona and partly in New York, graduating from City College in 1892, and from New York University Law School in 1894. He was thus steeped in Italian culture and yet was thoroughly Americanized.

Admitted to practice before the state and federal bars and before the United States Supreme Court in 1895, Gino Speranza specialized in cases involving Italian immigrants, who were flooding into America at the end of the century. He was one of the organizers of the Society for the Protection of Italian Immigrants. In 1912 he gave up law practice for a writing career, treating such topics as the Mafia, the outlook of Italian immigrants, and the role of Italian lawyers in New York.

When the war broke out Gino Speranza wrote several articles for the *Nation* on public opinion in neutral Italy. When Italy entered the war in May, 1915, he became a feature correspondent for the *New York Evening Post* and for the *Outlook*, arriving in Italy in August, 1915. Speranza's articles reflected sanity and balance, all the more remarkable when it is recalled that war time censorship would not let him discuss candidly the policy of Sonnino, who viewed the war largely as an opportunity for Italian territorial expansion, ignoring Serbia's aspirations, and Woodrow Wilson's views on the rights of self-determination of peoples. In April, 1917, Gino Speranza became a volunteer worker in the office of the American military attaché in Rome. The American secretary of state, Robert Lansing, soon appointed him attaché of political intelligence, whose chief function was to inform the State Department in regard to Italian public opinion. Speranza traveled all over Italy during the war, recording invaluable observations in his *Diary*. Despite physical weakness he requested special permission to climb Monte Adamello, and he wrote a memorable description of the unique hardships of warfare amidst the soaring peaks and undulating foothills of northeastern Italy.

After the war he concerned himself with immigration problems once more, publishing *Race or Nation* in 1925, in which he advocated halting the tide of immigration, if possible dispersing the alien ghettos in America, and abating "Anglo-Saxon" snobbery and prejudice. Gino Speranza died on July 12, 1927, a polemical figure, a gifted journalist and chronicler.

FLORENCE COLGATE SPERANZA (ED.),
THE DIARY OF GINO SPERANZA: ITALY, 1915–1919

MAY 5 [1916]

The city [Udine] has flowered into a thousand flags. The standards of Italy and England are flying from the staffs on the Piazza and those of all the Allies from the balcony of the Loggia. The porter of the hotel came to hang a flag out of my window. He didn't know why he was hanging it out, he said, but thought he had better follow suit on general principles. Later I learned that the flags are up in honor of the Prince of Wales who is paying a visit to the Italian front.

Lieutenant Domenico Palazzoli has been appointed to take Ambrosini of the *Stampa* of Turin, Cantalupo of the Catholic Trust, Lapido of the *Tribuna* of Montevideo, and me to the Adamello. . . . *The Trip to the Adamello*. On May 6th, at six o'clock in the evening, we left Udine in a very crowded train. Lieutenant Palazzoli of the Fourth Alpini, a tall, sinewy, striking-looking Brescian, as violent as a storm and as refreshing, is a man of means and an occasional journalist. A fervid patriot, he enlisted early in the war as a volunteer. He is a passionate Alpinist. I have actually seen him drink in a deep draught of mountain air as if he were intoxicated by it. Daredevil as he is in a very real sense, he has led many a gallant charge and won the medal for military valor at Pal Piccolo, where he was wounded, but I doubt if he has ever had as difficult a task as that of leading four war correspondents, untrained to mountain climbing, in a determined attempt to make a journalistic Alpine record. Two weeks ago a party of newspaper men from the United States reached an altitude of ten thousand feet; but the South American and Italian journalists in my party were resolved to beat the North American record; and I was equally determined to carry the Stars and Stripes to share in the new achievement.

At Mestre, where we expected to dine, we had a long wait be-

Source: From *The Diary of Gino Speranza: Italy, 1915–1919* (New York: Columbia University Press, 1941), pp. 250–263. Reprinted by permission of the publisher.

cause the restaurant in the station was closed on account of Cadorna's presence. Finally, however, we procured something to eat, and Palazzoli invested in a basket luncheon, a luxurious little affair with a tiny knife and fork, for his orderly, Tomà. It did not, however, stay the boy's appetite forever, and I recollect seeing him fall, like a famished dog, on a crate of hardtack at the Brizio Pass. Tomà, who proved most helpful on our strenuous expedition, is a tall, lithe, fine-featured soldier, as agile as he is enduring. He calls Palazzoli "Paron," and follows him about like a big Newfoundland dog, though Palazzoli leads the boy, fond of him as he is, a hard life.

While waiting in the station at Mestre, Palazzoli told us some tales of his Alpine campaigns. One night, during a nine-hour march up a steep and snowy height on Pal Grande in Carnia, he noticed a man refusing apparently to obey the order to advance; he struck him to enforce his command and found that he was dead! Several soldiers died, and a large percentage of the regimental officers collapsed on this expedition. Up on the great snow heights, Palazzoli told us, the men's skin becomes blackened from exposure—an experience I myself went through during our short stay on the Adamello.

After a sleepless, endless night in a crowded train, we arrived at Brescia at the unearthly hour of 4 A.M. and went to a café to kill time. Finally we boarded a train on the narrow single-track road to Edolo and stretched ourselves out in a compartment to sleep. It was Sunday, and, after resting, I enjoyed watching from the window the day's quiet festivities on the shore of the Lago d'Iseo and in Val Camonica. I saw no signs of war except a trainload of Alpini—and they were singing!

At Edolo we saw some recently captured Austrian prisoners eating their *rancio* with great relish. Edolo is a pleasant, clean, busy town, with some quaint buildings and a fountain capped by a stricken stag on its irregularly shaped piazza. After paying our respects to General Cavaciocchi, a quiet type of soldier in command of Val Camonica, we lunched at the Hotel Derna and then boarded a huge 50 H.P. Fiat camion for the trip to Vezza d' Oglio. It took the grades of the splendid road built in tourniquets by Italian military engineers as smoothly and easily as a roadster. The road, flanked by wooded slopes and backed by snow-topped mountains, was lovely. On top of the substantial cement trenches running through the valley grew a profusion of dainty wild flowers, including forget-me-nots and delightful yellow pansies.

At Vezza d' Oglio we were introduced to Colonel Carlo Giordana, Commander of the Fourth Alpini, a Piedmontese snow-bronzed mountaineer, a man of few words, strenuous, insistent, and impatient with half measures, somewhat hard and brusque for an Italian, but thoroughly convincing. In showing us, on the map of the Adamello region, the progress of the campaign and his plans for the future, the assurance with which he spoke of the objectives he intended to reach would have sounded perhaps like boastfulness in any other man, but, in him, it only bespoke the certainty of their attainment. He is a military man, not at all sentimental about his men, but kind to them, I understand, in many ways, always standing by them to the last ditch if they are unfairly treated. Colonel Giordana was much concerned about our comfort. As a judge of men he saw, no doubt, that unless he reduced the strain of our journey to a minimum, Alpine fighting in high altitudes would not become a newspaper feature.

Leaving the Colonel to follow us, we started in a camion for Temù, a little hamlet facing a great defile in the group of mountains that form the Adamello *massif*.

At one end of Temù lies the village cemetery; it has recently been enlarged to receive the bodies of soldiers brought down on sleds from the glacier battlefields, for the Italians take great pains to bury their dead carefully, even when they have to carry them long distances.

There are about 2,000 mules in Temù, which is the boundary line between modern, mechanical traction and the slow, primitive, but unfailing methods of pack mule and human brawn. Mounted bareback on some splendid looking animals, each led by a soldier, and followed by a pack animal loaded with our rucksacks, we headed for the Rifugio Garibaldi, the Italian Alpine Club's famous mountain shelter. As we wound up a road running through the green pastures of a pleasant valley, past quaint barns and occasional wayside crucifixes simply and effectively carved, Ambrosini stopped to greet a young lieutenant he recognized in a group of men coming down from the mountains. The recognition was mutual, though it lasted on the young man's part but a moment. Temporarily deranged by exposure and hardship, he talked wildly of the cold on the mountains until his companions led him gently away.

In about two hours we reached the first *teleferica*, a device used by the Italians in their mountain warfare, consisting of two sets of steel cables stretching from a base in a valley to a post on a moun-

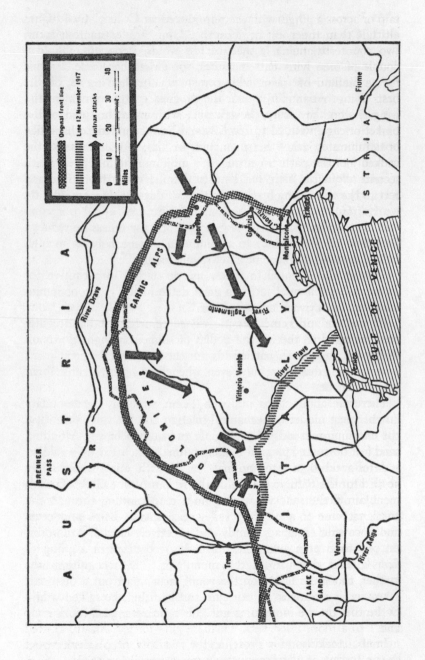

tain or across a gorge, with the terminus generally at a much higher altitude than the point of departure. Over these steel trolleys run two counterbalancing iron baskets, each large enough to hold a couple of men lying flat on its bottom. Once accustomed to this heroic method of travel, one may enjoy mountain scenery at its best, flying over superbly inaccessible spaces like a hawk on the wing. I stood my first ride very well, reclining at one end of the basket or cage, with Lieutenant Palazzoli at the other. A dizzy ride of ten minutes jacked us up some fifteen hundred feet, whence we walked along a path hewn out of a sheer mountain slope, to the second *teleferica*. This hoisted us up an additional two thousand feet to the third, which we found temporarily out of order; so here we confronted our first real Alpine work.

It was twilight. Around us rose peak upon peak, whose snowy tops piercing crowns of soft clouds were delicately tinted by the fading rays of the sun, and out of the thick mist below sprang mountain tops like the grim heads of giants chained to invisible rocks. Ascending with short even step the path that winds and winds in its skyward course was an endless line of soldiers laden with muskets and supplies, and descending were lines of stretcher bearers, carrying the wounded and sick or dragging sleds upon which lay men in the delirium of fever or figures, strangely still, wrapped in great blankets, bound perhaps for the little field of soldiers' crosses at Temù. The approach of darkness and the great silence enveloping the scene added a mystic touch to the phantasmal spectacle of this slender moving line of men who anchor the encampments on peaks and glacier to their base, twelve thousand feet down and two days' journey away.

After a climb of two hours, we reached the Rifugio Garibaldi, at an altitude of 8,258 feet. Around it is set up a little encampment of officers' shacks, barracks, built in the shape of half an egg cut lengthwise to shed the snow, and heaps of supplies, covered and uncovered. It is a scene of buzzing activity, for it is the nearest organized post to the fighting lines on the Adamello. The officers greeted us warmly and invited us to share their mess in the kitchen of the Rifugio, but Colonel Giordana arrived shortly and asked us to dine with him in his shanty. After a very good meal by candlelight we were assigned to our sleeping quarters, Lapido and I to a room filled with Milanese gifts for the Alpini, knitted helmets, stockings, fur coats, and a quantity of blankets under the protection of which we warmly and peacefully reposed.

By six the next morning I had said good-bye to a large Newfoundland pup that had fondly attached himself to me, and was off on the most difficult part of the trip. It was snowing hard! Dressed in a fur coat, white mittens, and black goggles, but stripped of everything possible in the way of luggage, I made my way through the storm with an alpenstock and Tomà's invaluable help. The night before, the Colonel had given orders for a *corvée* to meet us at the Passo di Brizio, with coffee and provisions. The Colonel insists he can furnish supplies to any number of mountain posts, even though a snowstorm or a glacier confronts him, provided he has enough men. He has it all carefully and mathematically worked out, as we could see with our own eyes when we joined that interminable line once more; that line, heroically patient and epically enduring, that daily carries supplies up mountain peaks and across the trail on the glacier, which only within the past few days has been freed from the menace of Austrian guns—that line that must neither break nor linger, for, hard as is the task of these men, there are men beyond the glacier whose tasks are harder. It must not break because it is the line upon' which battalions and battalions of men depend. They must be fed, sheltered, and kept up to fighting scratch; they must be housed, rested, medically cared for, and munitioned. Guns must be mounted on dominating heights and kept in readiness, and all parts of this icebound region must be held in constant and living connection by telephones and signaling devices. Every smallest item, every wheel and pulley of the huge but precarious mechanism erected on it must be carried by hand up precipitous paths, over snow-drifted passes, and across the desert wastes of the glacier.

We met squads of Territorials shoveling snow and debris of avalanches off the path and *corvées* of soldiers, from ten to one hundred men, carrying shells roped on their shoulders, cases of ammunition, or gun parts; boards, windows, doors, casks of nails, or rolls of roofing; bags of bread, condensed milk, chocolate, small kegs of wine, alcohol for cooking, boots, blankets—even smoked glasses!

The storm made the climb very laborious, but the Colonel led us—upward and on! Perhaps it was well that it hid from our view the precipice at the edge of the trail running part of the way along an indentation between two heights, on one of which the Italians have mounted a "149" gun, the highest piece of artillery in the world.

We were very tired when we arrived at the pass, but could not rest in the refuge there because a surgeon was using it to examine sick Alpini. So, we sat for a while on some boards, under the shelter of a wide, conical-shaped tent fastened to the ice, with a number of picturesque-looking men awaiting their turn for medical inspection. Their faces, unshaven, bronzed black by the *tormenta*, were almost distorted from exposure, but their eyes, clear and gentle, grew keen and interested when they heard we were newspaper men come to write of their deeds. They all asked when the war would end. An oldish man uttered the only complaint, if complaint it can be called, that I heard on our long trip, "Fortunate they who died early in the war—they did not have to bear our hardships." Hospitably welcomed at length into the doctor's busy shack, we gathered up our strength, with the aid of hot coffee, for the stretch still ahead of us. A sense of sinful pride cheered us too and gave us a second wind, for now with every step forward we should be leaving the American journalists' record a pace behind, and our arrival at Lobbia Bassa would put a mighty glacier between the new and the old record and raise the correspondents' notch for perpendicular forwardness from 10,227 feet to about 12,000 feet in a country where every foot counts and at a season still considered winter.

Off again!—down some precipitous rocks on the farther side of the pass and on to the glacier! We were ordered to walk close together because the snow was covering the path and even the sticks marking it could scarcely be seen through the haze of that terrible storm, the Alpine *tormenta*, which cut our faces like handfuls of broken glass as we painfully pushed our way forward. The guide took a wrong turn, but, even in the midst of that impenetrable wilderness, the Colonel immediately discovered the error. At first nothing was visible, and all was silent on the vast ocean about us, an ocean without ebb or roar, but, before long, there appeared again out of the mist that slender but interminable line of men, that fantastic but incredibly stout life line, which day after day is thrown from the valleys below over huge mountain tops to the handful of brave men carving out great deeds toward whom we were heading. The Colonel seemed to know just when and where we should encounter this or that *corvée*, for the ascending and descending file of men keeps its daily schedule with almost clocklike precision. Despite the impenetrable white curtain about us, he knew just under what post or *vedetta* we were passing and the exact location of every telephone wire. As a mariner steers his ship on the trackless sea, so does this officer lead battalions of men on altitudes where vegetation ceases and even stout-winged birds dare not come.

Suddenly we saw, through the haze and mist of the storm, close ahead of us, a group of *skiatori* darting noiselessly and phantasmally down a white mountain slope to meet an ascending *corvée*, due at this hour with newspapers and mail as well as the more substantial necessities of life. *Pulcinelli* they are called because of the white rubber blouses and baggy trousers they wear.

Stranger than these was a single *skiatore* whom we could see, though he could not see us. He was trying to find his way, through the mist, up a slope of pathless whiteness. As I gazed at his lonely figure in the silence of those great spaces, I felt as if I were looking through a veil at a stirring spiritual drama, a veil sacredly guarding the final, most intimate vision.

Farther along the trail the mist lifted, and we saw a line of men rounding a height above us, disappearing into some unknown corner of the world, on their way up perhaps to that high peak from which an Italian gun projects shells a distance of nine kilometers into the Val di Genova.

At the end of two hours, as we were drawing near to the encampment of Lobbia Bassa, the storm suddenly ceased, disclosing a scene of sublime beauty. All about us lay an undulating sea of long white billows, billows not breaking noisily like those of a restless ocean, but reposing silently against one another—a sea encircled by huge peaks robed in the ermine of the recent fall of snow. The sublime character of the picture came from its wondrous blending of strength and softness: masses of granite embedded in drifts of snow, inaccessible summits resting olympically against a heavenly blue, ice undissolved through the ages tinted by a touch of sun into the pink of rose petals.

The officers at Lobbia Bassa, which was wrested from the Austrians only a short time ago, greeted us warmly. They are using an Austrian shanty as a mess room, and shacks erected during the last few days as sleeping quarters. Until better shelter can be provided, the soldiers are sleeping in wells gouged out of the glacier and covered with tarpaulin held in place by stacked muskets, or in dugouts hollowed out of the side of the glacier and protected by canvas curtains.

After our party had been fitted out with enormous fur-lined "sentinel boots," Colonel Giordana insisted on my resting awhile in his cabin which had been warmed up by a powerful little stove.

Later I joined my companions in the infirmary, a dugout roofed by a double tent top, with walls and floor of ice sheathed in matting, where, by the light of candles stuck in tin cans, they were scribbling notes of the campaign on the Adamello.

At the beginning of the war, this section of mountainous country near the boundary line, little fitted for a battleground, was militarily almost a No Man's Land, though it was a favorite resort of Alpine climbers from the provinces of Brescia and Bergamo. Last winter these mountaineers patriotically organized the Compagnia Autonoma del Rifugio Garibaldi with the purpose of perfecting themselves in skiing and becoming thoroughly acquainted with the glaciers, peaks, and passes of this Alpine country.

On March 21st, one hundred and fifty Alpini, many of whom belonged to this group, set out from their base at the Rifugio Garibaldi (8,258 feet), at 3 A.M. of a beautiful starry night, skied over the pathless snow to the Passo di Brizio, crossed the glacier without incident, and took a good look into the Austrian Val di Genova. Seeing no signs of the enemy, they returned to the Rifugio Garibaldi about 5 P.M. of the same day. In the evening scouts reported that the Austrians had established posts along the boundary line on the edge of the glacier immediately after the departure of the Italians. The commander of the Alpini decided to attack as soon as he could place mountain guns on certain dominant heights. By the aid of the sheer brawn and muscle of three hundred men he accomplished this feat without loss or injury of any kind. On the evening of April 11th three detachments of *skiatori,* dressed in white and equipped with white-covered muskets and machine guns, started for the Brizio Pass. Overtaken by a terrible *tormenta,* they lost their way, and wandered about during the night, unaware of the location of one another, for no signaling or whistling was allowed. A passing moment of light at daybreak enabled them to meet and re-form. Shortly afterwards the storm ceased, the sun shone brightly, and they saw the Austrians entrenched on a string of snowy mountain slopes about two kilometers away. Lining up in four columns spread in the shape of a fan toward the four heights held by the enemy, they made a quick dash, fired a volley, and sprinted upward. This manoeuvre they repeated again and again, so quickly that, despite the machine gun fire directed against them, they succeeded in reaching and completely disorganizing the enemy. The Austrians surrendered, and the battle resulted in the occupation of all the heights on the edge of the glacier, the capture of fifty prisoners, two machine guns, one hundred rifles, and a large amount of ammunition and

supplies. Incidentally I may say that at the present time one battalion of Alpini has eight machine guns captured from the enemy,
which are being put to excellent use against the former owners.

On returning to the mess room, I found Colonel Giordana
reading by lamplight. After hearing that all the telephone wires
were in working order, he called up every station, picket post, and
artillery battery, far and near, to inquire if food had arrived.
Despite the storm, supplies had reached every point. The telephone was in charge of a young Alpino, an *Americano* from Wy-
oming, who exclaimed, "Gee!" in unmistakable American style
every time an electric shock came over the storm-charged wires.
The Colonel often answered it himself, telephoning orders on
every conceivable subject as if he found it as easy to carry out his
plans on a glacier as in a big city. The acceptance of the situation
as normal gives to this Alpine command its fine character. To
every request, the Colonel had an instant, comprehensive, and
unappealable reply. He required no explanation, he understood
what was needed, and just how much officers and men could endure at this altitude. On receiving a report of an increase in the
number of men suffering from frozen feet, he issued an order for
the men in the trenches to grease their feet twice a day, and announced his intention of holding the officers personally responsible for cases of freezing. The Colonel looked black when an officer
appeared, saluted, and informed him that two Territorials laden
with *rhum* for the encampment had considerably lightened their
burden by consuming some of it on the way up; one, indeed, had
become so hopelessly intoxicated that it had been necessary to
transport him the last lap of the way on a sled. After inflicting a
punishment on these men respectively of fifteen and thirty days
of camp jail, with two hours in chains in the snow every day, "fair
or foul," he explained to me that it was necessary to make an example of these men, for a drunken man is sure to lose his way or
die on the glacier.

Meanwhile the cook, a tall corporal, and his assistant, were preparing dinner with the help of two alcohol stoves upon which
they first melted kettlesful of snow to provide the water they
needed. An excellent dinner it proved to be: antipasto, a splendid
soup, boiled meat, good army bread, cheese, sparkling wine, coffee,
nuts, oranges, and bars of Cailler nut chocolate, as a special treat.

Afterwards, while we sat discussing politics and war with the
well-known Socialist deputy, Leonida Bissolati, sixty years of age,
who is serving as a sergeant of Alpini, a young and inexperienced

sublieutenant came into the shack, saluted Colonel Giordana and asked whether a company of Alpini he had brought up to Lobbia Bassa could rest, for they were so tired that some had even swooned on the trail. The Colonel waxed wrathful and asked him in fine scorn if his men were Pappini or Alpini and ordered him to proceed at once to the trenches, where they were needed. As the young Alpino officer, embarrassed and humiliated, saluted and retired, Sergeant Bissolati rose, stood at attention, and saluted his youthful superior who had been so severely rebuked. It was an impressive little incident, for the gesture of this famous and elderly man seemed more like proffer of sympathy to a lad young enough to be his son than an act of official etiquette.

A quarter moon and stars were shining as I went to bed, turning the vast white expanse into a land of silver enchantment. The silver light had the sharp glint of steel, though it was as soft as a vapor. The sight of the moon and stars, which I recognized as belonging to the plains and valleys of life, gave me a sense of being anchored to the old earth and the old life even in this strange, rich, and phantasmal environment. I slept in a shack with a captain, my fur sleeping bag covered with three blankets and a fur overcoat! Foolishly I took off my boots. An orderly who came very early in the morning to light a small stove found them frozen. He took them away to grease and came back with them shortly, bringing me a cup of hot coffee. Meanwhile the pail of snow he had put on the stove had melted, but my peeling face was too sore to wash.

The Colonel advised us to climb to Lobbia Alta, and see the view from the observatory there. To reach it without being exposed to the enemy's fire, we had to scale three thousand feet of almost sheer, snow-covered rock. On top of the frozen canvas roofs of the picket dugouts we walked to the observation post, built of snow in the form of a pulpit, and looked out upon a magnificent scene on which the sun shone brightly. To our left were the glacier and the Passo di Brizio; below, the Austrian Val di Genova with the enemy's trail emerging out of some evergreens, the only plant life in sight; in the distance, Lares, Monte Fumo, Fargorida, and other peaks recently won by the Italians, and farther away, in a sea of clouds, the Bergamasque Alps. A battery on one of the Austrian summits was shelling an advance gun post of the Italians, and the solemn reverberating bolts of Italian artillery came from a peak above the Passo di Brizio. The Italian guns, mounted on dominating heights, were very active, and the reply of the Austrian guns sounded faint in the great spaces about us.

On our way back to Lobbia Bassa, we passed a detachment of Alpini ranged in double file against a snow bank. Some were being counted and equipped to go to the firing line, and others were singing the "Hymn of the Skiatori":

> Allora squilla il nostro riso
> Come squilla una fanfara.

We had an excellent luncheon with the Colonel at Lobbia Bassa, a vegetable soup, tongue, scrambled eggs, fruit and wine, after which we bade him and his staff good-bye. Under a sunny sky we crossed the silent expanse of the white glacier, with the Passo di Brizio mounting smoothly in the background. Far ahead of us was the ever-moving line of soldiers who looked no bigger than dots.

On reaching the Rifugio Garibaldi, we found Colonel Giordana's shanty, in which we had left some of our belongings, locked and the sergeant in charge of it away. We were all tired, tense, and irritable, and I thought there would be a battle when the captain of the day practically ordered Palazzoli under arrest for breaking into it without permission. Finally our differences were adjusted, and we started off. My heart sank when we arrived at the first *teleferica* and found it still out of repair, for I was now not only carrying a full rucksack, but I had no alpenstock, and my spiked boots were worn smooth. With the help, however, of Tomà and an Alpino making the descent in chamoislike fashion, I reached the intermediate *teleferica* safely. By this and the third *teleferica* we were swung down to the terminus, where some mules awaited us. The sight of the green pastures was very restful, and I enjoyed the ride down the lovely valley of the Oglio, past mountain cataracts, lakes, shrines, wooden houses, and an infinite quantity of wild flowers, pink, blue, and yellow.

At Temù, where Colonel S—— met us with a limousine, the reaction set in and we acted like lunatics, laughing and singing. We consumed, like famished dogs, the Colonel's great spread at Vezza d' Oglio, which was cooked and served by an Alpino and, on learning afterwards at the hotel that separate rooms and real beds had been reserved for us, we showed our pleasure so wildly that the proprietress made a hasty retreat, thinking she had on her hands a houseful of madmen.

The next morning, after a long sleep, I looked out of my window on a superb group of magnificent snowy peaks framed by a semicircle of beautiful green hills. Below were trenches and wire entanglements, with forget-me-nots and wild flowers of all kinds running up to the cannon's mouth.

Tomà came in for instructions and I sent him to wire Florence that I was safe and sound.

We had an excellent lunch with the Colonel and a lieutenant surgeon, a Sicilian, who was going up to Lobbia, though he has never climbed a hill. The Colonel told us that the Swiss border is carefully guarded and that the Italian military code is changed every week.

After luncheon Palazzoli presented me to Cavaliere Martino, Sindaco of Vezza d' Oglio. He showed me the spot where the Garibaldians in 1866 tried to make a stand against the Austrians who held all the heights. They were obliged to retreat, after their commander, Major Castellini, was wounded. The Austrians, however, frightened by a rumor that Garibaldi himself was coming, withdrew later.

The Sindaco says that all of the Italians who emigrate from this section to Australia or America invariably return and settle down, even after an absence of twenty years.

A camion took us from Vezza d' Oglio to Edolo, where we made a stop at the Albergo Derna and played *boccie* while Palazzoli induced the officer in command, by telling him what journalistic heroes we were, to let the camion take us all the way to Brescia. On that heavenly ride of one hundred kilometers we passed many interesting villages and numberless painted crucifixes and wayside shrines, one of which was embowered in a great rosebush. We were all quite wild, enjoying the flowers, the trees, and the fresh country girls who waved at us.

At Lago d' Iseo, Cantalupo and Ambrosini invited Palazzoli, Lapido, and me to dine on the terrace of the Leon d' Oro, overlooking the lake. The townspeople came to look at us, the girls waved, and the children cheered, for our fame had spread. During dinner we had a long discussion which brought out a singular fondness for Germany and some surprising points of view.

MAY 11

After a dreary, tiresome railroad trip we are back in Udine.

IV. Desert Warfare

7. The Arab Revolt

THE YOUNG TURKS, the junta of army officers led by Enver Pasha, Djemal Pasha, and Talaat Bey who seized power in the Ottoman Empire in 1908, greatly offended the Muslim fundamentalists of Arabia by proclaiming the equality of all faiths and other reforms. The Hejaz, in northwestern Arabia where the holy cities of Mecca and Medina were situated, seethed with indignation over the innovators' latitudinarian policies. When Turkey entered the war as an ally of Christian Germany at the end of October, 1914, the resentment of the Arab fundamentalists was heightened. Hussein, the sheriff of Mecca and a scion of the Hashemites (who claimed direct descent from the family of Mohammed), learned of cruel treatment of Syrian Arabs by a Turkish governor, and sent one of his sons to investigate. The young emissary was imprisoned, which provoked Hussein into leading an uprising against the apostates of Constantinople. He proclaimed the independence of Hejaz on June 27, 1916, and dispatched armies under the command of several of his sons to rid the land of heretical Turkish control. Mecca was captured and designated capital of the kingdom of Arabia on October 25, 1916. But the Turks repulsed the wild Arab rush on Medina, and Fakhri Pasha, commanding its Turkish garrison, ordered hideous atrocities perpetrated upon Arab prisoners. Medina was regarded by the Turks as of crucial importance, for if they could keep open their railroad from Damascus to this southern terminus, they might be able to send reinforcements to Fakhri and eventually crush the revolt of the undisciplined Arab armies. Such were the assumptions.

The British saw in the Arab revolt a providential opportunity for striking the Ottoman Empire from its vulnerable southern flank, which might offset the Dardanelles fiasco of the previous year. Sent on a mission from Cairo to the Hejaz in October, 1916, were Ronald Storrs, the scholarly Oriental secretary to the British Agency in Cairo, and Captain T. E. Lawrence, one of the most eccentric, colorful, and "unmilitaristic" leaders of the First World War.

Thomas Edward Lawrence was born August 16, 1888, at Tremadoc, Wales, the son of Sir Thomas R. Chapman, a baronet of Scotch-Irish extraction who had eloped with his daughters' Scottish governess Sara Maden. Biographers make much of the trauma of Lawrence's belated discovery of his illegitimacy, which may have been a factor in shaping him into a bizarre albeit brilliant iconoclast who dreaded women and despised pretension. Mr. and Mrs. Lawrence, as the puritanical yet adulterous parents styled themselves, had five sons, of whom Thomas Edward was the second. The family moved to Oxford in 1896, and young Lawrence enrolled in the Oxford High School, where he soon became known for his astounding erudition. He loved reading and tinkering (especially with motors). History, particularly military history, held a great appeal for him. In 1907 he entered Jesus College, Oxford, and began the study of medieval fortifications. He cycled through France to study its historic castles. In 1909 he traveled to Syria to prepare a thesis on the architecture of crusader castles (which was published posthumously in 1936). He traveled on foot for twelve hundred miles through Syria and Palestine, learning about the Levant the hard way, sleeping on dirt floors with hospitable peasants, eating their fare, and practicing a broken Arabic which he had begun studying at Oxford with a Syrian Protestant missionary. He gained thereby an invaluable first-hand knowledge of the region which he was later to put to use during the Arab revolt. In 1910 he took first-class honors in modern history, and was provided with a traveling endowment by Magdalen College. The distinguished archaeologist D. G. Hogarth let him take part in the expedition which excavated the site of Carchemish. Lawrence not only supervised the diggings but apparently gathered military intelligence data about the Germans, who were constructing the Berlin-to-Baghdad railway which passed by Carchemish. Between 1910 and 1914 Lawrence was repeatedly in and out of Syria. He became fluent in spoken Arabic, but, according to Jean Beraud Villars, he never learned to read or write it.

At the outbreak of the war Lawrence was in England writing a report on an exploration which he and Captain S. F. Newcombe and Sir Leonard Woolley had made on the Turkish side of the Sinai-Egyptian border, ostensibly studying ruins, but in reality gathering information for the War Office in London. Lawrence was commissioned second lieutenant and put to work drawing maps and preparing a guide to the Sinai peninsula. In December, 1914, he was sent to Cairo, where he was attached to the military intelligence staff.

In October, 1916, Lawrence (by now captain) accompanied Ronald Storrs to the Hejaz to establish liaison with the insurgent Sheriff Hussein and his sons. Storrs conferred with son Abdullah about the Arab revolt, while Lawrence was given permission to visit the camp of son Feisal, who commanded an army southwest of Medina. When Lawrence reported his observations to Cairo in November, 1916, he was posted to Feisal's army as British political and liaison officer. His encyclopedic knowledge of the Levant, his comprehension of strategy, his courage and stamina offsetting his small size, all enabled him to galvanize the Arab revolt with a much-needed stimulus. But his role was that of adviser, not commander. He saw the need of harassing the Damascus-Medina railway, and he induced Feisal to move his army north of Medina to conduct hit-and-run attacks upon this lifeline of Turkish reinforcements. Lawrence made his first attack on the railroad in March, 1917. The British command in Cairo had recently sent an Egyptian army to Wejh, a Red Sea port, which had been captured in January, 1917. Lawrence persuaded Feisal to march his army to Wejh and leave the Turkish garrison in Medina to "wither on the vine."

Lawrence described his strategy as follows: "We wanted the enemy to stay in Medina, and in every other harmless place, in the largest numbers. The factor of food would eventually confine him to railways, but he was welcome to the Hejaz railway, and the Trans-Jordan railway, and the Palestine and Damascus and Aleppo railways for the duration of the war, so long as he gave us the other nine hundred and ninety-nine thousandths of the Arab world. . . . Range is more to strategy than force."

This strategy of hit-and-run irregular warfare was the antithesis of the Napoleonic or Foch concept of the mass attack and attempted annihilation, but it admirably suited the highly mobile, brave, and undisciplined Arabs, who could be provisioned by the British from the port of Wejh, while the Turks were suffering from attrition and malnutrition as they tried obstinately to defend their railway strong points. Lawrence's full realization of the possibilities of this "strategy of the indirect approach" proved his genius. In broad outline, this was the flexible strategy which the Senussi tribes had already used against the Italians in Libya, and which Mao Tse Tung was later to use in China, which General Giap and Ho Chi Minh were to follow in Vietnam, and which the FLN insurgents were to use with success in the Aurès mountains of Algeria. Modern air power, however, has restricted such guerrilla strategy to vegetated or mountainous terrain which offers concealment. But the Turks had too few planes, and they were too primitive for far-ranging reconnaissance, or intensive bombing of the Arabs.

In May, 1917, Lawrence and Sheik Aduda Abu Taya led the Huwaitat tribesmen in an expedition of formidable hardship across a great expanse of searing desert northward from Wejh to Aqaba, a small fort on the eastern coast of the Sinai peninsula. The Turks never imagined an attack from the south, and they allowed Aqaba to fall to the Arabs on July 6, 1917. Lawrence was decorated and promoted major for this feat. With Aqaba as a base, Feisal's army could now function as an eastern wing for a British advance from Egypt into southern Palestine. When the British forces under the command of General Sir Edmund Allenby laid siege to Jerusalem in October, 1917, Lawrence proposed an Arab raid on the railway connecting the city with Damascus. Lawrence wanted to cut the railway from Dar'a in the Yarmuk valley, but the raid failed, although a bridge was blown up between Dar'a and Amman. Lawrence was captured and subjected to bestial abuse by the Turks, who failed to recognize him. He managed to escape and took part in the victory parade in Jerusalem in December. A month later he participated in the capture of Tafila, south of the Dead Sea, after Feisal's army had marched up from its base at Aqaba. Lawrence was decorated and promoted lieutenant colonel.

Feisal's Arabs played a supporting role in the classic battle of Megiddo, which was considered by Liddell Hart to be the "strategic masterpiece" of the First World War. At Megiddo, in northern Palestine, in September, 1918, General Allenby brilliantly demonstrated the validity of Napoleon's dictum that "the whole secret of the art of war lies in making oneself master of the communications." Allenby distracted Turkish attention in the summer of 1918 by dummy "preparations" in the Jordan Valley, while he concentrated Australian and Indian cavalry divisions and a French contingent in orange groves in the coastal Plain of Sharon. Turkish communications into Palestine led from the Hejaz railway junction at Dar'a through the valley of Jezreel southward to Jerusalem. On September 17, 1918, Feisal's Arabs, guided by Lawrence, blew up the railway north, south, and west of Dar'a. This temporarily cut off the flow of Turkish supplies, and enabled the Fourth Cavalry Division to force a passage through the valley of Jezreel, while the Australian Mounted and the Fifth Cavalry circled west of the Sea of Galilee and headed for Damascus. The remnant of the Turkish army fled from Dar'a northward toward Damascus, harassed constantly by Feisal's Arabs, and by the Fourth Cavalry Division. Damascus was captured on October 1, 1918.

Colonel Lawrence was deeply troubled over the Sykes-Picot agreement of May, 1916, one of the notorious wartime "secret treaties," which envisaged a virtual partitioning of northern Arab territories between Britain and France under the fiction of spheres of influence. Lawrence regarded this as no less than a betrayal of the Arab cause. He was exhausted by the rigors of desert warfare, and he left Damascus the day after Allenby and Feisal arrived. He returned to England and served on the British delegation to the Versailles Conference, vehemently opposing the cession of Syria and Lebanon to France as a mandate. In disgust with the peace settlement, Lawrence joined the Royal Air Force as a mere mechanic under the name of Ross. When the brilliant eccentric was identified by a newspaper in 1923, he joined the Tank Corps under the name of Shaw, and two years later was allowed back in the Air Force. He died May 19, 1935, as a result of a motorcycle accident. He was in part genius, in part charlatan, and entirely an enigma.

T. E. LAWRENCE,
SEVEN PILLARS OF WISDOM

Just at sunset . . . we went off up our valley, feeling miserably disinclined to go on at all. Darkness gathered as we rode over the first ridge and turned west, for the abandoned pilgrim road, whose ruts would be our best guide. We were stumbling down the irregular hill-side, when the men in front suddenly dashed forward. We followed and found them surrounding a terrified pedlar, with two wives and two donkeys laden with raisins, flour and cloaks. They had been going to Mafrak, the station just behind us. This was awkward; and in the end we told them to camp, and left a

Source: From *Seven Pillars of Wisdom* (Garden City: Doubleday & Company), pp. 419–434. Copyright 1926, 1935 by Doubleday & Company, Inc. Reprinted by permission of Doubleday & Company and Jonathan Cape Ltd.

Sirhani to see they did not stir: he was to release them at dawn, and escape over the line to Abu Sawana.

We went plodding across country in the now absolute dark till we saw the gleam of the white furrows of the pilgrim road. It was the same road along which the Arabs had ridden with me on my first night in Arabia out by Rabegh. Since then in twelve months we had fought up it for some twelve hundred kilometres, past Medina and Hedia, Dizad, Mudowwara and Maan. There remained little to its head in Damascus where our armed pilgrimage should end.

But we were apprehensive of to-night: our nerves had been shaken by the flight of Abd el Kader, the solitary traitor of our experience. Had we calculated fairly we should have known that we had a chance in spite of him: yet a dispassionate judgement lay not in our mood, and we thought half-despairingly how the Arab Revolt would never perform its last stage, but would remain one more example of the caravans which started out ardently for a cloud-goal, and died man by man in the wilderness without the tarnish of achievement.

Some shepherd or other scattered these thoughts by firing his rifle at our caravan, seen by him approaching silently and indistinctly in the dark. He missed widely, but began to cry out in extremity of terror and, as he fled, to pour shot after shot into the brown of us.

Mifleh el Gomaan, who was guiding, swerved violently, and in a blind trot carried our plunging line down a slope, over a breakneck bottom, and round the shoulder of a hill. There we had peaceful unbroken night once more, and swung forward in fair order under the stars. The next alarm was a barking dog on the left, and then a camel unexpectedly loomed up in our track. It was, however, a stray, and riderless. We moved on again.

Mifleh made me ride with him, calling me 'Arab' that my known name might not betray me to strangers in the blackness. We were coming down into a very thick hollow when we smelt ashes, and the dusky figure of a woman leaped from a bush beside the track and rushed shrieking out of sight. She may have been a gipsy, for nothing followed. We came to a hill. At the top was a village which blazed at us while we were yet distant. Mifleh bore off to the right over a broad stretch of plough; we climbed it slowly, with creaking saddles. At the edge of the crest we halted.

Away to the north below our level were some brilliant clusters of lights. These were the flares of Deraa station, lit for army traffic: and we felt something reassuring perhaps, but also a little blatant in this Turkish disregard for us. [It was our revenge to make it their last illumination: Deraa was obscured from the morrow for a whole year until it fell.] In a close group we rode to the left along the summit and down a long valley into the plain of Remthe, from which village an occasional red spark glowed out, in the darkness to the north-west. The going became flat; but it was land half-ploughed, and very soft with a labyrinth of cony-burrows, so that our plunging camels sank fetlock-in and laboured. Nonetheless, we had to put on speed, for the incidents and roughness of the way had made us late. Mifleh urged his reluctant camel into a trot.

I was better mounted than most, on the red camel which had led our procession into Beidha. She was a long, raking beast, with a huge piston-stride very hard to suffer: pounding, yet not fully mechanical because there was courage in the persistent effort which carried her sailing to the head of the line. There, all competitors out-stripped, her ambition died into a solid step, longer than normal by some inches, but like any other animal's, except that it gave a confident feeling of immense reserves in strength and endurance. I rode back down the ranks and told them to press forward faster. The Indians, riding wooden, like horsemen, did their best, as did most of our number; but the ground was so bad that the greatest efforts were not very fruitful, and as hours went on first one and then another rider dropped behind. Thereupon I chose the rear position, with Ali ibn el Hussein who was riding a rare old racing camel. She may have been fourteen years old, but never flagged nor jogged the whole night. With her head low she shuffled along in the quick, hang-kneed Nejd pace which was so easy for the rider. Our speed and camel-sticks made life miserable for the last men and camels.

Soon after nine o'clock we left the plough. The going should have improved: but it began to drizzle, and the rich surface of the land grew slippery. A Sirhani camel fell. Its rider had it up in a moment and trotted forward. One of the Beni Sakhr came down. He also was unhurt, and remounted hastily. Then we found one of Ali's servants standing by his halted camel. Ali hissed him on, and when the fellow mumbled an excuse cut him savagely across the head with his cane. The terrified camel plunged forward, and the slave, snatching at the hinder girth, was able to swing himself into the saddle. Ali pursued him with a rain of blows. Mustafa, my man, an inexperienced rider, fell off twice. Awad, his rank-man, each time caught his halter, and had helped him up before we overtook them.

The rain stopped, and we went faster. Downhill, now. Suddenly Mifleh, rising in his saddle, slashed at the air overhead. A sharp metallic contact from the night showed we were under the telegraph line to Mezerib. Then the gray horizon before us went more distant. We seemed to be riding on the camber of an arc of land, with a growing darkness at each side and in front. There came to our ears a faint sighing, like wind among trees very far away, but continuous and slowly increasing. This must be from the great waterfall below Tell el Shehab, and we pressed forward confidently.

A few minutes later Mifleh pulled up his camel and beat her neck very gently till she sank silently on her knees. He threw himself off, while we reined up beside him on this grassy platform by a tumbled cairn. Before us from a lip of blackness rose very loudly the rushing of the river which had been long dinning our ears. It was the edge of the Yarmuk gorge, and the bridge lay just under us to the right.

We helped down the Indians from their burdened camels, that no sound betray us to listening ears; then mustered, whispering, on the clammy grass. The moon was not yet over Hermon, but the night was only half-dark in the promise of its dawn, with wild rags of tattered clouds driving across a livid sky. I served out the explosives to the fifteen porters, and we started. The Beni Sakhr under Adhub sank into the dark slopes before us to scout the way. The rainstorm had made the steep hill treacherous, and only by driving our bare toes sharply into the soil could we keep a sure foothold. Two or three men fell heavily.

When we were in the stiffest part, where rocks cropped out brokenly from the face, a new noise was added to the roaring water as a train clanked slowly up from Galilee, the flanges of its wheels screaming on the curves and the stream of its engine panting out of the hidden depths of the ravine in white ghostly breaths. The Serahin hung back. Wood drove them after us. Fahad and I leaped to the right, and in the light of the furnace-flame saw open trucks in which were men in khaki, perhaps prisoners going up to Asia Minor.

A little farther; and at last, below our feet, we saw a something blacker in the precipitous blackness of the valley, and at its other end a speck of flickering light. We halted to examine it with glasses. It was the bridge, seen from this height in plan, with a guard-tent pitched under the shadowy village-crested wall of the opposite bank. Everything was quiet, except the river; everything was motionless, except the dancing flame outside the tent.

Wood, who was only to come down if I were hit, got the Indians ready to spray the guard-tent if affairs became general; while Ali, Fahad, Mifleh and the rest of us, with Beni Sakhr and explosive porters, crept on till we found the old construction path to the near abutment. We stole along this in single file, our brown cloaks and soiled clothes blending perfectly with the limestone above us, and the depths below, until we reached the metals just before they curved to the bridge. There the crowd halted, and I crawled on with Fahad.

We reached the naked abutment, and drew ourselves forward on our faces in the shadow of its rails till we could nearly touch the grey skeleton of underhung girders, and see the single sentry leaning against the other abutment, sixty yards across the gulf. Whilst we watched, he began to move slowly up and down, up and down, before his fire, without ever setting foot on the dizzy bridge. I lay staring at him fascinated, as if planless and helpless, while Fahad shuffled back by the abutment wall where it sprang clear of the hillside.

This was no good, for I wanted to attack the girders themselves; so I crept away to bring the gelatine bearers. Before I reached them there was the loud clatter of a dropped rifle and a scrambling fall from up the bank. The sentry started and stared up at the noise. He saw, high up, in the zone of light with which the rising moon slowly made beautiful the gorge, the machine-gunners climbing down to a new position in the receding shadow. He challenged loudly, then lifted his rifle and fired, while yelling the guard out.

Instantly all was complete confusion. The invisible Beni Sakhr, crouched along the narrow path above our heads, blazed back at random. The guard rushed into trenches, and opened rapid fire at our flashes. The Indians, caught moving, could not get their Vickers in action to riddle the tent before it was empty. Firing became general. The volleys of the Turkish rifles, echoing in the narrow place, were doubled by the impact of their bullets against the rocks behind our party. The Serahin porters had learned from my bodyguard that gelatine would go off if hit. So when shots spattered about them they dumped the sacks over the edge and fled. Ali leaped down to Fahad and me, where we stood on the obscure abutment unperceived, but with empty hands, and told us that the explosives were now somewhere in the deep bed of the ravine.

It was hopeless to think of recovering them, with such hell let loose, so we scampered, without accident, up the hill-path through the Turkish fire, breathlessly to the top. There we met the disgusted Wood and the Indians, and told them it was all over. We hastened back to the cairn where the Serahin were scrambling on their camels. We copied them as soon as might be, and trotted off at speed, while the Turks were yet rattling away in the bottom of the valley. Turra, the nearest village, heard the clamour and joined in. Other villages awoke, and lights began to sparkle everywhere across the plain.

Our rush over-ran a party of peasants returning from Deraa. The Serahin, sore at the part they had played (or at what I said in the heat of running away) were looking for trouble, and robbed them bare.

The victims dashed off through the moonlight with their women, raising the ear-piercing Arab call for help. Remthe heard them. Its massed shrieks alarmed every sleeper in the neighbourhood. Their mounted men turned out to charge our flank, while settlements for miles about manned their roofs and fired volleys.

We left the Serahin offenders with their encumbering loot, and drove on in grim silence, keeping together in what order we could, while my trained men did marvellous service helping those who fell, or mounting behind them those whose camels got up too hurt to canter on. The ground was still muddy, and the ploughed strips more laborious than ever; but behind us was the riot, spurring us and our camels to exertion, like a pack hunting us into the refuge of the hills. At length we entered these, and cut through by a better road towards peace, yet riding our jaded animals as hard as we could, for dawn was near. Gradually the noise behind us died away, and the last stragglers fell into place, driven together, as on the advance, by the flail of Ali ibn el Hussein and myself in the rear.

The day broke just as we rode down to the railway, and Wood, Ali and the chiefs, now in front to test the passage, were amused by cutting the telegraph in many places while the procession marched over. We had crossed the line the night before to blow up the bridge at Tell el Shehab, and so cut Palestine off from Damascus, and we were actually cutting the telegraph to Medina after all our pains and risks! Allenby's guns, still shaking the air away there on our right, were bitter recorders of the failure we had been.

The grey dawn drew on with gentleness in it, foreboding the grey drizzle of rain which followed, a drizzle so soft and hopeless that it seemed to mock our broken-footed plodding towards Abu Sawana. At sunset we reached the long water-pool; and there the rejects of our party were curious after the detail of our mistakes. We were fools, all of us equal fools, and so our rage was aimless. Ahmed and Awad had another fight; young Mustafa refused to cook rice; Farraj and Daud knocked him about until he cried; Ali had two of his servants beaten: and none of us or of them cared a little bit. Our minds were sick with failure, and our bodies tired after nearly a hundred strained miles over bad country in bad conditions, between sunset and sunset, without halt or food.

Food was going to be our next preoccupation, and we held a council in the cold driving rain to consider what we might do. For lightness' sake we had carried from Azrak three days' rations, which made us complete until to-night; but we could not go back empty-handed. The Beni Sakhr wanted honour, and the Serahin were too lately disgraced not to clamour for more adventure. We had still a reserve bag of thirty pounds of gelatine, and Ali ibn el Hussein who had heard of the performances below Maan, and was as Arab as any Arab, said, 'Let's blow up a train'. The word was hailed with universal joy, and they looked at me: but I was not able to share their hopes, all at once.

Blowing up trains was an exact science when done deliberately, by a sufficient party, with machine-guns in position. If scrambled at it might become dangerous. The difficulty this time was that the available gunners were Indians; who, though good men fed, were only half-men in cold and hunger. I did not propose to drag them off without rations on an adventure which might take a week. There was no cruelty in starving Arabs; they would not die of a few days' fasting, and would fight as well as ever on empty stomachs; while, if things got too difficult, there were the riding-camels to kill and eat: but the Indians, though Moslems, refused camel-flesh on principle.

I explained these delicacies of diet. Ali at once said that it would be enough for me to blow up the train, leaving him and the Arabs with him to do their best to carry its wreck without machine-gun support. As, in this unsuspecting district, we might well happen on a supply train, with civilians or only a small guard of reservists aboard, I agreed to risk it. The decision having been applauded, we sat down in a cloaked circle, to finish our remaining food in a very late and cold supper (the rain had sodden the fuel and made fire not possible) our hearts somewhat comforted by chance of another effort.

At dawn, with the unfit of the Arabs, the Indians moved away for Azrak, miserably. They had started up country with me in hope of a really military enterprise, and first had seen the muddled bridge, and now were losing their prospective train. It was hard on them; and to soften the blow with honour I asked Wood to accompany them. He agreed, after argument, for their sakes; but it proved a wise move for himself, as a sickness which had been troubling him began to show the early signs of pneumonia.

The balance of us, some sixty men, turned back towards the railway. None of them knew the country, so I led them to Minifir, where, with Zaal, we had made havoc in the spring. The re-curved hill-top was an excellent observation post, camp, grazing ground and way of retreat, and we sat there in our old place till sunset, shivering and staring out over the immense plain which stretched map-like to the clouded peaks of Jebel Druse, with Um el Jemal and her sister-villages like ink-smudges on it through the rain.

In the first dusk we walked down to lay the mine. The rebuilt culvert of kilometre 172 seemed still the fittest place. While we stood by it there came a rumbling, and through the gathering darkness and mist a train suddenly appeared round the northern curve, only two hundred yards away. We scurried under the long arch and heard it roll overhead. This was annoying; but when the course was clear again, we fell to burying the charge. The evening was bitterly cold, with drifts of rain blowing down the valley.

The arch was solid masonry, of four metres span, and stood over a shingle water-bed which took its rise on our hill-top. The winter rains had cut this into a channel four feet deep, narrow and winding, which served us as an admirable approach till within three hundred yards of the line. There the gully widened out and ran straight towards the culvert, open to the sight of anyone upon the rails.

We hid the explosive carefully on the crown of the arch, deeper than usual, beneath a tie, so that the patrols would not feel its jelly softness under their feet. The wires were taken down the bank into the shingle bed of the watercourse, where concealment was quick; and up it as far as they would reach. Unfortunately, this was only sixty yards, for there had been difficulty in Egypt over insulated cable and no more had been available when our expedition started. Sixty yards was plenty for the bridge, but little for a train: however, the ends happened to coincide with a little bush about ten inches high, on the edge of the watercourse, and we buried them beside this very convenient mark. It was impossible to leave them joined up to the exploder in the proper way, since the spot was evident to the permanent-way patrols as they made their rounds.

Owing to the mud the job took longer than usual, and it was very nearly dawn before we finished. I waited under the draughty arch till day broke, wet and dismal, and then I went over the whole area of disturbance, spending another half-hour in effacing its every mark, scattering leaves and dead grass over it, and watering down the broken mud from a shallow rain-pool near. Then they waved to me that the first patrol was coming, and I went up to join the others.

Before I had reached them they came tearing down into their prearranged places, lining the watercourse and spurs each side. A train was coming from the north. Hamud, Feisal's long slave, had the exploder; but before he reached me a short train of closed box-waggons rushed by at speed. The rainstorms on the plain and the thick morning had hidden it from the eyes of our watchman until too late. This second failure saddened us further and Ali began to say that nothing would come right this trip. Such a statement held risk as prelude of the discovery of an evil eye present; so to divert attention, I suggested new watching posts be sent far out, one to the ruins on the north, one to the great cairn of the southern crest.

The rest, having no breakfast, were to pretend not to be hungry. They all enjoyed doing this, and for a while we sat cheerfully in the rain, huddling against one another for warmth behind a breast-work of our streaming camels. The moisture made the animals' hair curl up like a fleece, so that they looked queerly dishevelled. When the rain paused, which it did frequently, a cold moaning wind searched out the unprotected parts of us very thoroughly. After a time we found our wetted shirts clammy and comfortless things. We had nothing to eat, nothing to do and nowhere to sit except on wet rock, wet grass or mud. However, this persistent weather kept reminding me that it would delay Allenby's advance on Jerusalem, and rob him of his great possibility. So large a mis-fortune to our lion was a half-encouragement for the mice. We would be partners into next year.

In the best circumstances, waiting for action was hard. To-day it was beastly. Even enemy patrols stumbled along without care, perfunctorily, against the rain. At last, near noon, in a snatch of fine weather, the watchmen on the south peak flagged their cloaks wildly in signal of a train. We reached our positions in an instant, for we had squatted the late hours on our heels in a streaming ditch near the line, so as not to miss another chance. The Arabs took cover properly. I looked back at their ambush from my firing point, and saw nothing but the grey hill-sides.

I could not hear the train coming, but trusted, and knelt ready for perhaps half an hour, when the suspense became intolerable, and I signalled to know what was up. They sent down to say it was coming very slowly, and was an enormously long train. Our appetites stiffened. The longer it was the more would be the loot. Then came word that it had stopped. It moved again.

Finally, near one o'clock, I heard it panting. The locomotive was evidently defective (all these wood-fired trains were bad), and the heavy load on the up-gradient was proving too much for its capacity. I crouched behind my bush, while it crawled slowly into view past the south cutting, and along the bank above my head towards the culvert. The first ten trucks were open trucks, crowded with troops. However, once again it was too late to choose, so when the engine was squarely over the mine I pushed down the handle of the exploder. Nothing happened. I sawed it up and down four times.

Still nothing happened; and I realized that it had gone out of order, and that I was kneeling on a naked bank, with a Turkish troop train crawling past fifty yards away. The bush, which had seemed a foot high, shrank smaller than a fig-leaf; and I felt myself the most distinct object in the country-side. Behind me was an open valley for two hundred yards to the cover where my Arabs were waiting and wondering what I was at. It was impossible to make a bolt for it, or the Turks would step off the train and finish us. If I sat still, there might be just a hope of my being ignored as a casual Bedouin.

So there I sat, counting for sheer life, while eighteen open trucks, three box-waggons, and three officers' coaches dragged by. The engine panted slower and slower, and I thought every moment that it would break down. The troops took no great notice of me, but the officers were interested, and came out to the little platforms at the ends of their carriages, pointing and staring. I waved back at them, grinning nervously, and feeling an improbable shepherd in my Meccan dress, with its twisted golden circlet about my head. Perhaps the mud-stains, the wet and their ignorance made me accepted. The end of the brake van slowly disappeared into the cutting on the north.

As it went, I jumped up, buried my wires, snatched hold of the wretched exploder, and went like a rabbit uphill into safety. There I took breath and looked back to see that the train had finally stuck. It waited, about five hundred yards beyond the mine, for nearly an hour to get up a head of steam, while an officers' patrol came back and searched, very carefully, the ground where I had been seen sitting. However the wires were properly hidden: they found nothing: the engine plucked up heart again, and away they went.

Mifleh was past tears, thinking I had intentionally let the train through; and when the Serahin had been told the real cause they said 'Bad luck is with us'. Historically they were right; but they meant it for a prophecy, so I made sarcastic reference to their courage at the bridge the week before, hinting that it might be a tribal preference to sit on camel-guard. At once there was uproar, the Serahin attacking me furiously, the Beni Sakhr defending. Ali heard the trouble, and came running.

When we had made it up the original despondency was half forgotten. Ali backed me nobly, though the wretched boy was blue with cold and shivering in an attack of fever. He gasped that their ancestor the Prophet had given to Sherifs the faculty of 'sight', and by it he knew that our luck was turning. This was comfort for them: my first instalment of good fortune came when in the wet, without other tool than my dagger, I got the box of the exploder open and persuaded its electrical gear to work properly once more.

We returned to our vigil by the wires, but nothing happened, and evening drew down with more squalls and beastliness, everybody full of grumbles. There was no train; it was too wet to light a cooking fire; our only potential food was camel. Raw meat did not tempt anyone that night; and so our beasts survived to the morrow.

Ali lay down on his belly, which position lessened the hungerache, trying to sleep off his fever. Khazen, Ali's servant, lent him his cloak for extra covering. For a spell I took Khazen under mine, but soon found it becoming crowded. So I left it to him and went downhill to connect up the exploder. Afterwards I spent the night there alone by the singing telegraph wires, hardly wishing to sleep, so painful was the cold. Nothing came all the long hours, and

dawn, which broke wet, looked even uglier than usual. We were
sick to death of Minifir, of railways, of train watching and wreck-
ing, by now. I climbed up to the main body while the early patrol
searched the railway. Then the day cleared a little. Ali awoke,
much refreshed, and his new spirit cheered us. Hamud, the slave,
produced some sticks which he had kept under his clothes by his
skin all night. They were nearly dry. We shaved down some
blasting gelatine, and with its hot flame got a fire going, while the
Sukhur hurriedly killed a mangy camel, the best spared of our
riding-beasts, and began with entrenching tools to hack it into
handy joints.

Just at that moment the watchman on the north cried a train.
We left the fire and made a breathless race of the six hundred
yards downhill to our old position. Round the bend, whistling its
loudest, came the train, a splendid two-engined thing of twelve
passenger coaches, travelling at top speed on the favouring grade.
I touched off under the first driving wheel of the first locomotive,
and the explosion was terrific. The ground spouted blackly into
my face, and I was sent spinning, to sit up with the shirt torn to
my shoulder and the blood dripping from long, ragged scratches
on my left arm. Between my knees lay the exploder, crushed under
a twisted sheet of sooty iron. In front of me was the scalded and
smoking upper half of a man. When I peered through the dust
and steam of the explosion the whole boiler of the first engine
seemed to be missing.

I dully felt that it was time to get away to support; but when I
moved, learnt that there was a great pain in my right foot, because
of which I could only limp along, with my head swinging from the
shock. Movement began to clear away this confusion, as I hobbled
towards the upper valley, whence the Arabs were now shooting
fast into the crowded coaches. Dizzily I cheered myself by repeating aloud in English 'Oh, I wish this hadn't happened'.

When the enemy began to return our fire, I found myself much
between the two. Ali saw me fall, and thinking that I was hard hit,
ran out, with Turki and about twenty men of his servants and the
Beni Sakhr, to help me. The Turks found their range and got seven
of them in a few seconds. The others, in a rush, were about me—fit
models, after their activity, for a sculptor. Their full white cotton
drawers drawn in, bell-like, round their slender waists and ankles;
their hairless brown bodies; and the love-locks plaited tightly over
each temple in long horns, made them look like Russian dancers.

We scrambled back into cover together, and there, secretly, I felt myself over, to find I had not once been really hurt; though besides the bruises and cuts of the boiler-plate and a broken toe, I had five different bullet-grazes on me (some of them uncomfortably deep) and my clothes ripped to pieces.

From the watercourse we could look about. The explosion had destroyed the arched head of the culvert, and the frame of the first engine was lying beyond it, at the near foot of the embankment, down which it had rolled. The second locomotive had toppled into the gap, and was lying across the ruined tender of the first. Its bed was twisted. I judged them both beyond repair. The second tender had disappeared over the further side; and the first three waggons had telescoped and were smashed in pieces.

The rest of the train was badly derailed, with the listing coaches butted end to end at all angles, zigzagged along the track. One of them was a saloon, decorated with flags. In it had been Mehmed Jemal Pasha, commanding the Eighth Army Corps, hurrying down to defend Jerusalem against Allenby. His chargers had been in the first waggon; his motor-car was on the end of the train, and we shot it up. Of his staff we noticed a fat ecclesiastic, whom we thought to be Assad Shukair, Imam to Ahmed Jemal Pasha, and a notorious pro-Turk pimp. So we blazed at him till he dropped.

It was all long bowls. We could see that our chances of carrying the wreck were slight. There had been some four hundred men on board, and the survivors, now recovered from the shock, were under shelter and shooting hard at us. At the first moment our party on the north spur had closed, and nearly won the game. Mifleh on his mare chased the officers from the saloon into the lower ditch. He was too excited to stop and shoot, and so they got away scatheless. The Arabs following him had turned to pick up some of the rifles and medals littering the ground, and then to drag bags and boxes from the train. If we had had a machine-gun posted to cover the far side, according to my mining practice, not a Turk would have escaped.

Mifleh and Adhub rejoined us on the hill, and asked after Fahad. One of the Serahin told how he had led the first rush, while I lay knocked out beside the exploder, and had been killed near it. They showed his belt and rifle as proof that he was dead and that they had tried to save him. Adhub said not a word, but leaped out of the gully, and raced downhill. We caught our breaths till our lungs hurt us, watching him; but the Turks seemed not to see. A minute later he was dragging a body behind the left-hand bank.

Mifleh went back to his mare, mounted, and took her down

behind a spur. Together they lifted the inert figure on to the
pommel, and returned. A bullet had passed through Fahad's face,
knocking out four teeth, and gashing the tongue. He had fallen
unconscious, but had revived just before Adhub reached him, and
was trying on hands and knees, blinded with blood, to crawl
away. He now recovered poise enough to cling to a saddle. So they
changed him to the first camel they found, and led him off at once.

The Turks, seeing us so quiet, began to advance up the slope.
We let them come half-way, and then poured in volleys which
killed some twenty and drove the others back. The ground about
the train was strewn with dead, and the broken coaches had been
crowded: but they were fighting under eye of their Corps Commander, and undaunted began to work round the spurs to outflank us.

We were now only about forty left, and obviously could do no
good against them. So we ran in batches up the little stream-bed,
turning at each sheltered angle to delay them by pot-shots. Little
Turki much distinguished himself by quick coolness, though his
straight-stocked Turkish cavalry carbine made him so expose his
head that he got four bullets through his head-cloth. Ali was angry
with me for retiring slowly. In reality my raw hurts crippled me,
but to hide from him this real reason I pretended to be easy, interested in and studying the Turks. Such successive rests while I
gained courage for a new run kept him and Turki far behind the
rest.

At last we reached the hill-top. Each man there jumped on the
nearest camel, and made away at full speed eastward into the
desert, for an hour. Then in safety we sorted our animals. The
excellent Rahail, despite the ruling excitement, had brought off
with him, tied to his saddle-girth, a huge haunch of the camel
slaughtered just as the train arrived. He gave us the motive for a
proper halt, five miles farther on, as a little party of four camels
appeared marching in the same direction. It was our companion,
Matar, coming back from his home village to Azrak with loads of
raisins and peasant delicacies.

So we stopped at once, under a large rock in Wadi Dhuleil,
where was a barren fig-tree, and cooked our first meal for three
days. There, also, we bandaged up Fahad, who was sleepy with the
lassitude of his severe hurt. Adhub, seeing this, took one of Matar's
new carpets, and, doubling it across the camel-saddle, stitched the
ends into great pockets. In one they laid Fahad, while Adhub

crawled into the other as makeweight: and the camel was led off southward towards their tribal tents.

The other wounded men were seen to at the same time. Mifleh brought up the youngest lads of the party, and had them spray the wounds with their piss, as a rude antiseptic. Meanwhile we whole ones refreshed ourselves. I bought another mangy camel for extra meat, paid rewards, compensated the relatives of the killed, and gave prize-money, for the sixty or seventy rifles we had taken. It was small booty, but not to be despised. Some Serahin, who had gone into the action without rifles, able only to throw unavailing stones, had now two guns apiece. Next day we moved into Azrak, having a great welcome, and boasting—God forgive us—that we were victors.

V. Sea Warfare

8. Battle of Jutland

THERE WERE few great naval battles in the First World War compared with the number of massive engagements on land. Admirals were far more reluctant than generals to commit their forces to battle unless they were reasonably certain of an advantage over the enemy. A fleet can easily be destroyed in one short, cataclysmic encounter, as the French experienced at the hands of Nelson at Trafalgar in 1805. Winston Churchill appreciated this grave possibility when he said of the commander of the British Grand Fleet, "Jellicoe was the only man on either side who could lose the war in an afternoon."

British naval strategy was more concerned with maintaining sea supremacy—keeping open the vital supply lines to the British Isles—than with defeating the German fleet. Great Britain entered the war with a navy far more powerful than Germany's—with twenty-nine all big-gun capital ships and thirteen building, compared with Germany's eighteen built and nine under construction. The German naval strategic plan was one of attrition—reducing the British preponderance piecemeal by sinking its ships through mines and torpedoes until the two fleets reached more comparable size, when German combativeness could offer a reasonable prospect of success in a confrontation of the two battle fleets. The contrary determination to avoid losses by being lured into German mine fields, or being enticed within target range of U-boats or torpedo boats, reinforced the professional caution of British Admiral John Jellicoe. The consequence of this reciprocal wariness of admirals was that no great sea battles were fought during the first two years of the war. The "fleet in being" concept proved a mutual deterrent.

It is true that there were some spectacular skirmishes such as the escape of the *Goeben* and the *Breslau* from their British pursuers in the Mediterranean, and even engagements of squadrons in the battles of Coronel and the Falkland Islands. But these were all minor actions compared with the single titanic naval battle of the war, the Battle of Jutland. On May 31, 1916, in the North Sea off the coast of the Danish peninsula, the world's two most powerful fleets at last collided, but the blows they exchanged were almost as wild and as glancing as if the antagonists had been playing a grotesque game of blindman's buff. German Admiral Reinhard Scheer did not intend a frontal attack upon the still markedly superior Grand Fleet of Admiral Sir John Jellicoe, but hoped merely to lure it out of its bases by an ostentatious German sortie which might allow German U-boats stationed by preassignment off the British coast to torpedo some of the larger enemy ships. Scheer thought that, at best, he might intercept and destroy a detached British squadron.

To bait the British into action, Vice Admiral Franz Hipper, in command of the First and Second Scouting Groups consisting of five battle cruisers and four light cruisers, was ordered to steam north from Wilhelmshaven to flaunt German presence in the Skagerrak, off the Norwegian coast. This scouting force was to be followed at an interval of fifty miles by Admiral Scheer's High Seas Fleet. It was hoped that the tempting presence of the German fleet so far north of its base would entice out of Rosyth (near Edinburgh) the southern section of the British Grand Fleet—that is, the Battle Cruiser Fleet and the Fifth Battle Squadron commanded by Vice Admiral Sir David Beatty. Scheer hoped to finish off Beatty's force before the bulk of Jellicoe's Grand Fleet had time to sail south from Scapa Flow (in the Orkney Islands) to Beatty's rescue. All units of the German High Seas Fleet were notified of Scheer's battle plan at 3:40 P.M. on May 30 by wireless signals which were intercepted and decoded by British listening stations. The British were thus made aware of the magnitude of the operation of the High Seas Fleet, but they lacked exact knowledge as to its dispositions or destination.

The intercepted German signals were at once relayed to Admiral Jellicoe, who left Scapa Flow with the Grand Fleet at 10:30 P.M.— two and a half hours before Hipper's Scouting Groups left their Jade River base. Simultaneously with Jellicoe's sailing, Admiral Beatty put out from Rosyth with the Battle Cruiser Fleet and the Fifth Battle Squadron, together with the departure of Vice Admiral Sir Martyn Jerram's Second Battle Squadron from Cromarty. Jerram was ordered to rendezvous with Jellicoe by 2 P.M., May 31, some fifty miles off the Norwegian coast. At this same time Beatty's force was expected to be sixty-nine miles south-southeast of the main rendezvous. If the enemy had not been sighted by then, Jellicoe planned to proceed south towards Heligoland Bight, with Beatty accompanying him within sight.

Beatty arrived punctually at his rendezvous point and was turning north toward Jellicoe when one of his light cruisers, the *Galatea*, sighted to the east-southeast the smoke of a small Danish steamer, the *N. J. Fjord*, at the very moment that the *Elbing*, on the western flank of Hipper's Scouting Group, also saw the smoke and approached to investigate. In this way both cruisers flashed the alarm of the enemy's presence, and the *Galatea* fired the first shot of the Battle of Jutland. Had there not been this fortuitous sighting of the Danish steamer's smoke, Hipper's Scouting Groups, trailing unaware behind Beatty, would have conducted Scheer's High Seas Fleet straight into the unsuspected bulk of Jellicoe's Grand Fleet, which was still sixty-five miles to the north of the *Galatea*. This would have brought predictable disaster to Scheer, but, thanks to the *N. J. Fjord*'s smoke, the trap into which he was blundering was sprung prematurely.

Upon receiving the warnings from the *Galatea* and the *Elbing*, both Beatty and Hipper wheeled about and converged upon their respective cruisers, which were already engaged in a gun duel. At 3:20 P.M. the battle cruiser forces of Beatty and Hipper came within sight of one another and began maneuvering into line of battle, which is to say, into columns, to permit broadside fire. Hipper assumed that the British force was stronger than his own, and he turned about on a southeasterly course, hoping to tempt Beatty into the path of the oncoming High Seas Fleet of Admiral Scheer. Beatty sped east-southeast, intending to cut off Hipper and bring his Scouting Groups to action before they could reach Horns Reef, off the Danish coast, where they would have the advantage of air reconnaissance. Beatty had no inkling of the closeness of Scheer's advancing High Seas Fleet. Beatty and Hipper maneuvered into parallel lines, about nine miles apart, steaming southeast and getting into formation for broadsides. Both began shooting at 3:47 P.M. Because of bad light, the British miscalculated the distance, thereby losing the advantage of their guns' superior range over the German guns. This was not the British navy's finest hour. British shells had not been designed for the oblique impact caused by plunging fire at long range, and they burst before penetrating German armor. By contrast, German fire was of astonishing effectiveness. Beatty's column of ships was aligned to the west of Hipper's, and was profiled against the afternoon sky, thus offering a better target to the Germans. Beatty's flagship, the *Lion*, was hit repeatedly, as were the *Princess Royal* and *Tiger*. The *Indefatigable* capsized and sank, and the *Queen Mary* blew up. Then the *Princess Royal* exploded in a cloud of smoke and spray, prompting Admiral Beatty, standing on an exposed bridge of the damaged *Lion*, to observe phlegmatically to his flag captain: "Chatfield, there seems to be something wrong with our bloody ships today." There was indeed something wrong that day with British gunnery and ammunition. And as for the design of the British ships, it was inferior to the German primarily in one respect: the British magazines were not protected against the danger of cordite-flash, and the doors connecting the magazines with the adjacent handling rooms (where charges were stowed in readiness for loading the guns) were generally left open by the crews to expedite gun loading. This made possible cordite-flash explosions set off by turret hits from enemy fire, and five British ships blew up during the Battle of Jutland because of this deficiency.

The Fifth Battle Squadron of Rear Admiral Hugh Evan-Thomas, meanwhile, was moving up astern of Beatty, and its four super-dreadnoughts were able to train their 15-inch guns upon the *Moltke* and the *Von Der Tann* at the tail of Hipper's column, scoring damaging hits. But the defective quality of the British shells caused them to burst prematurely. At 4:35 P.M. Beatty received a message from Commodore W. E. Goodenough's Second Light Cruiser Squadron, two miles in advance of the *Lion*, that the entire German High Seas Fleet had just been sighted to the southeast. Scheer, who had learned at 3:54 P.M. of Hipper's gun duel with British cruisers, had been speeding northwest with a score of battleships to reach the German First Scouting Group. Warned by Goodenough's signal (which was relayed by wireless to Jellicoe), Beatty continued southeast so that he could come within Scheer's range of vision to lure him toward Jellicoe, and then at 4:40 P.M. Beatty reversed course to the north to join Jellicoe, followed by the Fifth Battle Squadron of Evan-Thomas.

Jellicoe was still forty miles to the north of Beatty's battle cruisers. It was of vital importance to Jellicoe to know the exact position at which he could expect to engage Scheer's High Seas Fleet. The twenty-four battleships of the British Grand Fleet were steamnig in six columns abeam of each other until they reached the point for maneuvering into line of battle, which required veering in a 90-degree turn to allow the columns to dovetail into one impressive line which could then fire broadsides at the oncoming enemy, who would be able to reply only with the forward guns of his leading ships. This was what was meant by crossing the enemy's T—the classic stratagem that admirals dream of. But Jellicoe's fateful decision to deploy either to the port (left) or starboard (right) or to converge his wings upon his central column of ships, depended upon his having precise knowledge as to the German battle fleet's formation, position, course, and speed. Yet Commodore Goodenough's signal to Jellicoe had been maddeningly vague as to Scheer's exact whereabouts. In rushing north to join Jellicoe, Beatty had lost touch with Scheer's fleet and even with Hipper's. Beatty sighted Jellicoe at 6 P.M. In the following quarter hour Jellicoe signaled three times to Beatty: "Where is enemy's battle fleet?" Jellicoe described what ensued: "At 6:15 P.M. Rear Admiral Hugh Evan-Thomas, in the *Barham*, commanding the Fifth Battle Squadron, signaled by wireless that the enemy's battle fleet was in sight, bearing south-southeast. The distance was not reported . . . but in view of the low visibility, I concluded it could not be more than five miles. . . . So at 6:16 P.M. a signal was made to form a line of battle on the port wing column, on a course southeast by east. . . ." Jellicoe's decision to turn to port (left) to form the line of battle caused a polemic which has continued intermittently down until today. One can only guess what would have happened had Jellicoe deployed to starboard. But deployment to port had obvious advantages for Jellicoe: it enabled him to cross Scheer's T; it placed the British Grand Fleet to the east of the High Seas Fleet, thereby cutting off its potential line of retreat whether through the Bight of Heligoland or the Skagerrak; it gave the British the advantage of having the German ships to the west, silhouetted against the misty horizon, whereas the British ships could be located chiefly by their gun flashes.

As Jellicoe's last battleship wheeled majestically to port and into line of battle in readiness for broadside fire, the haze lifted partially to reveal the leading ships of Scheer's High Seas Fleet rushing straight into the center of the Grand Fleet's long column—an answer to Jellicoe's prayer. Perceiving the deadly peril into which he had plunged, Scheer successfully executed a maneuver of astounding complexity and risk of collision. Confident that his disciplined subordinates could hold their relative positions and yet slip out of Jellicoe's trap, Scheer at 6:36 P.M. ordered an instant turnabout—a 180-degree "somersault" of all the German ships simultaneously, so that the ships which had been bringing up the rear were now at the head of the High Seas Fleet. The German fleet fired Parthian shots at the British as Scheer raced away to the southwest in a murk made virtually opaque by smoke screens laid down in his rear by his torpedo boats. During the operations leading up to the turn about, two German cruisers, *Lützow* and *Derfflinger*, and the battleship *König*, were subjected to broadside fire from ten British battleships, yet the German ships were so well constructed, their gunnery so accurate, and their crews so disciplined that they withstood the British punishment, and before escaping they blew up yet another battle cruiser, the *Invincible*, besides sinking an armored cruiser, and leaving another ready to founder.

By 6:45 P.M. contact with the Germans had been lost as the High Seas Fleet fled westward in the haze and smoke. The British Grand Fleet was groping about to the east, between Scheer and his home ports, still a deadly menace for all of its surprising ineffectualness in the battle so far. At 6:55 P.M. Scheer ordered another 180-degree turn, this time to the east, with the intention of slipping astern of Jellicoe's fleet before daylight on June 1 would expose him again. But once more Scheer encountered great peril, for he had blundered yet again into the battle line of Jellicoe. Scheer's battle line was now dangerously compressed, and his leading ships were targets for formidable broadsides from the British Grand Fleet. After twenty minutes of this punishment, Scheer made a desperate decision. At 7:13 P.M. he gave the order to his damaged battle cruisers to attack the British battleships in a seemingly suicidal screening operation to allow the German battleships to flee to the west again. Scheer ordered his destroyer flotillas to charge the British battleships. Most of the German torpedoes missed their targets, but Jellicoe, overrating their danger, made the crucial decision to disengage his battle fleet by ordering it to steer southeast at 7:22 P.M. Had Jellicoe audaciously rammed through Scheer's screen of battle cruisers and destroyers and resolutely held contact with the evasive German High Seas Fleet, he might have destroyed most of it. As it turned out, Jellicoe's cautious decision to disengage to safeguard the Grand Fleet from the uncertainties of night action allowed Scheer to skulk in the darkness to the west of him, and then sneak back astern of him, crossing eastward in Jellicoe's wake at 9:06 P.M. The British Admiralty, with incredible negligence, failed to notify Jellicoe of an intercepted radio request of Scheer's for air reconnaissance around the Horns Reef. This message clearly revealed the intended escape route of Scheer, but Jellicoe steamed on to the south in night formation, in sovereign ignorance, until daylight on June 1, when he wheeled about to the north in further search for the High Seas Fleet. But the Germans had already gained the safety of the Horns Reef mine fields.

Who won the Battle of Jutland? The British lost three battle cruisers, three armored cruisers, and eight destroyers—a total of 111,-000 tons. The British sustained 6,784 casualties, of whom 6,097 officers and men were killed. The German fleet lost one battleship, one battle cruiser, four light cruisers, and five destroyers, totaling 62,-000 tons. German personnel losses were 3,058, of whom 2,551 were killed. Jutland was an inconclusive battle, conferring tactical credit upon the Germans, but yielding a strategic advantage to the British, for the German High Seas Fleet stayed safely in port for the remainder of the war. After Jutland the British control of sea communications was challenged only by submarines, and that challenge was unsuccessful when countered by the convoy system. Moreover, German resort to unrestricted submarine warfare triggered America's entry into the war a year later, to the incalculable advantage of the Allies. Yet Jutland, for all its fury and tumult, was certainly no Battle of Trafalgar or Tsushima—no battle of annihilation.

We reprint Admiral Jellicoe's version of the main action as it appeared in his book *The Grand Fleet, 1914–1916*. John Rushworth Jellicoe was born December 5, 1859, at Southampton, the son of a captain of a vessel of the Royal Mail Line. Jellicoe was educated at Rottingdean and entered the navy as a cadet at the age of thirteen, serving on the battleship *Britannia*. His marked proficiency in gunnery brought about his appointment as a junior officer in 1884 at the Portsmouth gunnery school where John Fisher was captain. When Fisher became director of the Naval Ordnance Department, he asked for Jellicoe as an assistant in the task of conversion to big-gun ships. Jellicoe served on several ships, and during the Boxer Rebellion he was a member of a landing party which pushed inland from Taku Bar to Peking. In this action he was badly wounded in the chest. When Admiral Sir John Fisher became First Sea Lord in 1904, Jellicoe served again as his assistant, working on the design of the epoch-making battleship *Dreadnought*. He advanced the techniques of long-range firing. Promoted Rear Admiral, he was appointed Third Sea Lord and Controller in 1908. First Sea Lord Fisher had Jellicoe designated Vice Admiral in command of the Atlantic Fleet in 1910, and Fisher was resolved to have him command the Grand Fleet in event of war.

In August, 1914, Jellicoe was placed in command of the Grand Fleet based at Scapa Flow. Disappointment over his failure to take greater risks in trying to destroy the German High Seas Fleet in the Battle of Jutland did not prevent Jellicoe from returning to the Admiralty as First Sea Lord toward the end of 1916. He did not have great success in coping with the U-boat menace. It was Prime Minister David Lloyd George who insisted upon the convoy system, and Jellicoe's slowness in adopting it provoked Lloyd George into retiring him from the Admiralty in December, 1917. After the war Jellicoe was sent on a mission to the Dominions to advise them in the organization of their navies. For his war services he received the thanks of Parliament, a grant of 50,000 pounds, and the titles of Viscount Jellicoe of Scapa and Viscount Brocas of Southampton. He served as governor of New Zealand from 1920 until 1924, and soon after his return to England he was made an earl. Jellicoe maintained an aloof and dignified silence during the polemic conducted in the press as to whether he had prized the Grand Fleet too highly to subject it to serious risk to win a decisive naval battle. He died on November 20, 1935, and was buried in Saint Paul's Cathedral.

ADMIRAL VISCOUNT JELLICOE OF SCAPA, THE GRAND FLEET, 1914–1916

THE BATTLE FLEET IN ACTION

The "plot" made on the reports received between 5 and 6 P.M. from Commodore Goodenough, of the 2nd Light Cruiser Squadron, and the report at 4.45 P.M. from Sir David Beatty in the *Lion* giving the position of the enemy's Battle Fleet, showed that we, of the Battle Fleet, might meet the High Sea Fleet approximately ahead and that the cruiser line ahead of the Battle Fleet would sight the enemy nearly ahead of the centre. Obviously, however, great reliance could not be placed on the positions given by the ships of the Battle Cruiser Fleet, which had been in action for two hours and frequently altering course. I realised this, but when contact actually took place it was found that the positions given were at least twelve miles in error when compared with the *Iron Duke's* reckoning. The result was that the enemy's Battle Fleet appeared on the starboard bow instead of ahead, as I had expected, and contact also took place earlier than was anticipated. There can be no doubt as to the accuracy of the reckoning on board the *Iron Duke*, as the movements of that ship could be "plotted" with accuracy after leaving Scapa Flow, there being no disturbing elements to deal with.

The first accurate information regarding the position of affairs was contained in a signal from the *Black Prince*, of the 1st Cruiser Squadron (the starboard wing ship of the cruiser screen), which was timed 5.40 P.M., but received by me considerably later, and in which it was reported that battle cruisers were in sight, bearing

Source: From *The Grand Fleet, 1914–1916* (New York: George H. Doran Company, 1919), pp. 341–369. Copyright 1919 by George H. Doran, Inc. Reprinted by permission of Doubleday & Company, Inc. and Curtis Brown Ltd.

south, distant five miles. It was assumed by me that these were our own vessels.

Prior to this, in view of the rapid decrease in visibility, I had directed Captain Dreyer, my Flag-Captain, to cause the range-finder operators to take ranges of ships on bearings in every direction and to report the direction in which the visibility appeared to be the greatest. My object was to ascertain the most favourable bearing in which to engage the enemy should circumstances admit of a choice being exercised. Captain Dreyer reported that the visibility appeared to be best to the southward.

At 5.45 P.M. the *Comus* (Captain Hotham), of the 4th Light Cruiser Squadron, which was stationed three miles ahead of the Battle Fleet, reported heavy gunfire on a southerly bearing, i.e., three points from ahead, and shortly afterwards flashes of gunfire were visible bearing south-south-west although no ships could be seen.

At about 5.50 P.M. I received a wireless signal from Sir Robert Arbuthnot, of the 1st Cruiser Squadron, reporting having sighted ships in action bearing south-south-west and steering north-east. There was, however, no clue as to the identity of these ships. It was in my mind that they might be the opposing battle cruisers.

At 5.55 P.M. a signal was made by me to Admiral Sir Cecil Burney, leading the starboard wing division in the *Marlborough*, inquiring what he could see. The reply was: "Gun flashes and heavy gunfire on the starboard bow." This reply was received at about 6.5 P.M.

The uncertainty which still prevailed as to the position of the enemy's Battle Fleet and its formation caused me to continue in the Battle Fleet on the course south-east by south at a speed of 20 knots, in divisions line ahead disposed abeam to starboard, the *Iron Duke* at 6 P.M. being in Lat. 57.11 N., Long. 5.39 E.

The information so far received had not even been sufficient to justify me in altering the bearing of the guides of columns from the *Iron Duke* preparatory to deployment, and they were still, therefore, on the beam. The destroyers also were still disposed ahead in their screening formation, as it was very desirable to decide on the direction of deployment before stationing them for action.

At 5.56 P.M. Admiral Sir Cecil Burney reported strange vessels in sight bearing south-south-west and steering east, and at 6 P.M. he reported them as British battle cruisers three to four miles distant, the *Lion* being the leading ship.

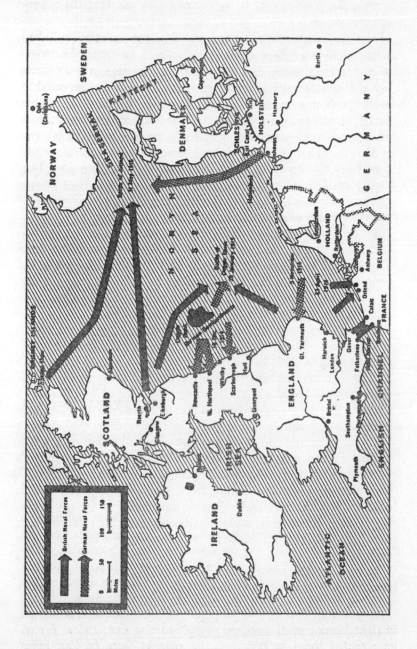

This report was made by searchlight and consequently reached
me shortly after 6 P.M., but as showing the interval that elapses
between the *intention to make a signal* and the actual receipt of it
(even under conditions where the urgency is apparent, no effort is
spared to avoid delay, and the signal staff is efficient), it is to be
noted that whereas the report gave the bearing of our vessels as
south-south-west, notes taken on board the *Colossus* placed our
battle cruisers one point on the starboard bow of that ship, that is,
on a south-south-east bearing and distant two miles at 6.5 P.M.

Shortly after 6 P.M. we sighted strange vessels bearing south-
west from the *Iron Duke* at a distance of about five miles. They
were identified as our battle cruisers, steering east across the bows
of the Battle Fleet. Owing to the mist it was not possible to make
out the number of ships that were following the *Lion*.

At this stage there was still great uncertainty as to the position
of the enemy's Battle Fleet; flashes of gunfire were visible from
ahead round to the starboard beam, and the noise was heavy and
continuous. Our cruisers ahead seemed to be hotly engaged, but
the fact that they were not closing the Battle Fleet indicated to
me that their opponents could hardly be battleships.

In order to take ground to starboard, with a view to clearing up
the situation without altering the formation of the Battle Fleet, a
signal had been made to the Battle Fleet at 6.2 P.M. to alter course
leaders together, the remainder in succession, to south (a turn of
three points). Speed was at the same time reduced to 18 knots to
allow of the ships closing up into station. Immediately afterwards
it became apparent by the sound of the heavy firing that enemy's
heavy ships must be in close proximity, and the *Lion*, which was
sighted at this moment, signalled at 6.6 P.M. that the enemy's
battle cruisers bore south-east. Meanwhile, at about 5.50 P.M., I
had received a wireless report from Commodore Goodenough,
commanding the 2nd Light Cruiser Squadron, to the effect that
the enemy's battle cruisers bore south-west from their Battle Fleet;
in other words, that his Battle Fleet bore north-east from his battle
cruisers.

In view of the report from Sir Cecil Burney that our battle
cruisers were steering east, and observing that Sir David Beatty
reported at 6.6 P.M. that the enemy's battle cruisers bore south-
east, it appeared from Commodore Goodenough's signal that the
enemy's Battle Fleet must be *ahead* of his battle cruisers. On the
other hand, it seemed to me almost incredible that the Battle Fleet
could have passed the battle cruisers. The conflicting reports added

greatly to the perplexity of the situation, and I determined to hold on until matters became clearer.

The conviction was, however, forming in my mind that I should strike the enemy's Battle Fleet on a bearing a little on the starboard bow, and in order to be prepared for deployment I turned the Fleet to a south-east course, leaders together and the remainder in succession, and the destroyer flotillas were directed by signal, at 6.8 P.M., to take up the destroyer position No. 1 for battle. This order disposed them as follows:

6th	5th	4th	3rd	2nd	1st
Div.	Div.	Div.	Div.	Div.	Div.

2 miles   1 flotilla

Marlborough   *Iron Duke*   *King George* V.

3 miles   3 miles

1 flotilla   1 flotilla

There was, however, a very short interval between this signal to the destroyers and the signal for deployment, and consequently the destroyers did not reach their positions before deployment. The subsequent alterations of course to the southward and westward added to their difficulties and delayed them greatly in gaining their stations at the van of the Fleet after deployment. The correct position for the two van flotillas on deployment was three miles ahead of the Fleet, but slightly on the engaged bow.

At 6.1 P.M., immediately on sighting the *Lion*, a signal had been made to Sir David Beatty inquiring the position of the enemy's Battle Fleet. This signal was repeated at 6.10 P.M., and at 6.14 P.M. he signalled: "Have sighted the enemy's Battle Fleet bearing south-south-west"; this report gave me the first information on which I could take effective action for deployment.

At 6.15 P.M. Rear-Admiral Hugh Evan-Thomas, in the *Barham*, commanding the 5th Battle Squadron, signalled by wireless that the enemy's Battle Fleet was in sight, bearing south-south-east. The distance was not reported in either case, but in view of the low visibility, I concluded it could not be more than some five miles. Sir Cecil Burney had already reported the 5th Battle

Squadron at 6.7 P.M. as in sight, bearing south-west from the *Marlborough*.

The first definite information received on board the Fleet-Flag-ship of the position of the enemy's Battle Fleet did not, therefore, come in until 6.14 P.M., and the position given placed it thirty degrees before the starboard beam of the *Iron Duke*, or fifty-nine degrees before the starboard beam of the *Marlborough*, and apparently in close proximity. There was no time to lose, as there was evident danger of the starboard wing column of the Battle Fleet being engaged by the whole German Battle Fleet before deployment could be effected. So at 6.16 P.M. a signal was made to the Battle Fleet to form line of battle on the port wing column, on a course south-east by east, it being assumed that the course of the enemy was approximately the same as that of our battle cruisers.

Speed was at the same time reduced to 14 knots to admit of our battle cruisers passing ahead of the Battle Fleet, as there was danger of the fire of the Battle Fleet being blanketed by them.

During the short interval, crowded with events, that had elapsed since the first flashes and sound of gunfire had been noted on board the *Iron Duke*, the question of most urgent importance before me had been the direction and manner of deployment.

As the evidence accumulated that the enemy's Battle Fleet was on our starboard side, but on a bearing well before the beam of the *Iron Duke*, the point for decision was whether to form line of battle on the starboard or on the port wing column. My first and natural impulse was to form on the starboard wing column in order to bring the Fleet into action at the earliest possible moment, but it became increasingly apparent, both from the sound of gunfire and the reports from the *Lion* and the *Barham*, that the High Sea Fleet was in such close proximity and on such a bearing as to create obvious disadvantages in such a movement. I assumed that the German destroyers would be ahead of their Battle Fleet, and it was clear that, owing to the mist, the operations of destroyers attacking from a commanding position in the van would be much facilitated; it would be suicidal to place the Battle Fleet in a position where it might be open to attack by destroyers during such a deployment, as such an event would throw the Fleet into confusion at a critical moment.

The further points that occurred to me were, that if the German ships were as close as seemed probable, there was considerable danger of the 1st Battle Squadron, and especially the *Marlbor-*

ough's Division, being severely handled by the concentrated fire of the High Sea Fleet before the remaining divisions could get into line to assist. The 1st Battle Squadron was composed of many of our weakest ships, with only indifferent protection as compared with the German capital ships, and an interval of at least four minutes would elapse between each division coming into line astern of the sixth division and a further interval before the guns could be directed on to the ship selected and their fire become effective after so large a change of course.

The final disadvantage would be that it appeared, from the supposed position of the High Sea Fleet, that the van of the enemy would have a very considerable "overlap" if the deployment took place on the starboard wing division, whereas this would not be the case with deployment on the port wing column. The overlap would necessitate a large turn of the starboard wing division to port to prevent the "T" being crossed, and each successive division coming into line would have to make this turn, in addition to the 8-point turn required to form the line. I therefore decided to deploy on the first, the port wing, division.

The further knowledge which I gained of the actual state of affairs after the action confirmed my view that the course adopted was the best in the circumstances.

The reports from the ships of the starboard wing division show that the range of the van of the enemy's Battle Fleet at the moment of deployment was about 13,000 yards. The fleets were converging rapidly, with the High Sea Fleet holding a position of advantage such as would enable it to engage effectively, first the unsupported starboard division, and subsequently succeeding divisions as they formed up astern. It is to be observed that it would take some twenty minutes to complete the formation of the line of battle.

The German gunnery was always good at the start, and their ships invariably found the range of a target with great rapidity, and it would have been very bad tactics to give them such an initial advantage, not only in regard to gunnery but also in respect of torpedo attack, both from ships and from destroyers.

A subsequent study of the reports and the signals received has admitted of the accompanying plans being drawn up.

The reports on being reviewed fit in very well, and show clearly how great would have been the objections to deploying to starboard. It will be seen that the bearings of the enemy Battle Fleet, as given by the *Lion* and the *Barham* at 6.14 and 6.15 respectively, give a fair "cut," and the bearing on which the *Marlborough* opened fire enables the position of the Battle Fleet to be placed with considerable accuracy.

Assuming that the German Battle Fleet was steaming at 17 knots on an easterly course between 6.14 and 6.31, it will be observed that at the latter time it bore 21 degrees before the starboard beam of the *Iron Duke* at a range of 12,000 yards. The *Iron Duke* actually engaged the leading battleship at this time on a bearing 20 degrees before the starboard beam at a range of 12,000 yards. The accuracy of the "plot" is therefore confirmed, so far as confirmation is possible. It appears certain that between about 6.0 P.M. and 6.16 P.M. the German battle cruisers turned 16 points towards their Battle Fleet, and again turned 16 points to their original course. This is borne out by observations on board the *Warrior*, which ship was being engaged by the *starboard* guns of enemy vessels. The German account also shows such a turn at this period.

Rear-Admiral Evan-Thomas, commanding the 5th Battle Squadron, had sighted the *Marlborough* at 6.6 P.M. and the remainder of the 6th Division of the Battle Fleet a little later. Not seeing any other columns, he concluded that the *Marlborough* was leading the whole line, and decided to take station ahead of that ship. At 6.19 P.M., however, other battleships were sighted, and Admiral Evan-Thomas realised that the Fleet was deploying to port, the 6th Division being the starboard wing column. He then determined to make a large turn of his squadron to port, in order to form astern of the 6th Division, which by this time had also turned to port to form line of battle. During the turn, which was very well executed, the ships of the 5th Battle Squadron were under fire of the enemy's leading battleships, but the shooting was not good, and our vessels received little injury.

Unfortunately, however, the helm of the *Warspite* jammed, and that ship, continuing her turn through sixteen points came under a very heavy fire and received considerable injury. The disabled *Warrior* happened to be in close proximity at this time, and the turn of the *Warspite* had the effect for the moment of diverting attention from the *Warrior*, so that the latter vessel got clear.

The *Warspite* was well extricated by Captain Phillpotts from an unpleasant position and was steered to the northward to make good damages, and eventually, in accordance with directions from Rear-Admiral Evan-Thomas, returned independently to Rosyth, considerably down by the stern owing to damage aft, but otherwise not much injured.

By 6.38 P.M. the remaining ships of the 5th Battle Squadron were in station astern of the *Agincourt* (1st Battle Squadron), the last ship of the line.

At 6.33 P.M., as soon as the battle cruisers had passed clear, the speed of the Battle Fleet was increased to 17 knots, and this speed was subsequently maintained. The reduction of speed to 14 knots during the deployment caused some "bunching" at the rear of the line as the signal did not get through quickly. The reduction had, however, to be maintained until the battle cruisers had formed ahead.

Experience at all Fleet exercises had shown the necessity for keeping a reserve of some three knots of speed in hand in the case of a long line of ships, in order to allow of station being kept in the line under conditions of action, when ships were making alterations of course to throw out enemy's fire, to avoid torpedoes, or when other independent action on the part of single ships, or of divisions of ships, became necessary, as well as to avoid excessive smoke from the funnels; for this reason the Fleet speed during the action was fixed at 17 knots. The experience of the 1st Battle Squadron, in which some ships had at times to steam at 20 knots, is proof of the necessity for this reserve.

At 6.14 P.M. the enemy's salvoes were falling near ships of the 1st Battle Squadron, and the *Marlborough's* Division of the Battle Squadron became engaged with some ships of the enemy's Battle Fleet at 6.17 P.M. immediately after turning for the deployment. At this time fire was opened by the *Marlborough* on a ship stated to be of the "Kaiser" class, at a range of 13,000 yards and on a bearing 20° abaft the starboard beam; this knowledge enables us to deduce the position of the van of the German Battle Fleet at this time.

Our rear ships were now able to make out the enemy's Fleet steering to the eastward, the battle cruisers leading, followed by the Battle Fleet in single line, the order being, four ships of the "König" class in the van, followed by ships of the "Kaiser" and "Heligoland" classes, the rear of the line being invisible. A report that had reached me at 4.48 P.M. from the Commodore of the 2nd Light Cruiser Squadron indicated that ships of the "Kaiser" class were in the van of the Battle Fleet. The order of the Fleet may have been changed subsequent to this report, but there is no doubt that ships of the "König" class led during the Fleet action. The point is not, however, of importance.

At about 6.38 P.M. the 6th Division was in line and our deployment was complete.

Enemy shells had been falling close to the *Colossus* and her 5th Division since 6.18 P.M., and these ships opened fire at 6.30 P.M.; but the conditions of visibility made it difficult to distinguish the enemy's battleships.

At 6.23 P.M. a three-funnelled enemy vessel had passed down the line, on the starboard, or engaged, side of our Fleet, apparently partly disabled. Her identity could not at the time be clearly established, but her German colours were flying and she was in a position for attacking the Battle Fleet by torpedoes; at 6.20 P.M. the *Iron Duke* fired a few turret salvoes at her; she was fired at with turret guns by other vessels and was seen to sink at the rear of the line.

At this time, owing to smoke and mist, it was most difficult to distinguish friend from foe, and quite impossible to form an opinion on board the *Iron Duke*, in her position towards the centre of the line, as to the formation of the enemy's Fleet. The identity of ships in sight on the starboard beam was not even sufficiently clear for me to permit of fire being opened; but at 6.30 P.M. it became certain that our own battle cruisers had drawn ahead of the Battle Fleet and that the vessels then before the beam were battleships of the "König" class. The order was, therefore, given to open fire, and the *Iron Duke* engaged what appeared to be the leading battleship at a range of 12,000 yards on a bearing 20° before the starboard beam; other ships of the 3rd and 4th Divisions (the 4th Battle Squadron) opened fire at about the same time, and the van divisions (2nd Battle Squadron) very shortly afterwards; these latter ships reported engaging enemy battle cruisers as well as battleships. The fire of the *Iron Duke*, which came more directly under my personal observation, was seen to be immediately effective, the third and fourth salvoes fired registering several palpable hits. It appeared as if all the enemy ships at that time in sight from the *Iron Duke* (not more than three or four, owing to smoke and mist) were receiving heavy punishment, and the second battleship was seen to turn out of the line badly on fire, and settling by the stern. A large number of observers in the *Thunderer, Benbow, Barham, Marne, Morning Star* and *Magic* stated afterwards that they saw this ship blow up at 6.50 P.M.

The visibility was very variable and perhaps averaged about

12,000 yards to the southward, though much less on other bearings, but ranges could not at times be obtained from the range-finders of the *Iron Duke* at a greater distance than 9,000 yards, although at 7.15 P.M., in a temporary clear channel through the mist, good ranges of 15,000 yards were obtained of a battleship at which four salvoes were fired by the *Iron Duke* before she was again hidden by smoke and mist. The very baffling light was caused principally by low misty clouds, but partly also by the heavy smoke from the funnels and guns of the opposing Fleets. The direction of the wind was about west-south-west with a force 2, causing the enemy's funnel smoke to drift towards our line, thus further obscuring our view of his Fleet.

The visibility at the rear of the battle line was apparently greater than in the centre at about 7 P.M., and the enemy's fire, which was probably being concentrated on our rear ships, was more accurate at this period, but quite ineffective, only one ship, the *Colossus*, being hit by gunfire, although numerous projectiles were falling near the ships of the 1st and 5th Battle Squadrons.

Whilst observers in ships in the van and centre of the Battle Fleet could see only three or four enemy vessels at any one time, those in the ships of the rear division did occasionally see as many as eight, and were consequently better able to distinguish the formation and movements of the enemy's Battle Fleet. It was not possible, owing to the small number of ships in sight, due to smoke and mist, to distribute the fire of the battleships by signal in the customary manner; the only course to adopt was for the captains to direct the fire of their guns on to any target which they could distinguish.

The course of the Fleet on deployment had been south-east by east, as already stated, but the van had hauled on to south-east without signal shortly after deployment in order to close the enemy, and at 6.50 P.M., as the range was apparently opening, the course was altered by signal to south "by divisions" in order to close the enemy. The *King George* V., leading the van of the Battle Fleet, had just anticipated this signal by turning to south. The alteration was made "by divisions" instead of "in succession" in order that the enemy should be closed more rapidly by the whole Battle Fleet.

This large turn (of four points) "by divisions" involved some small amount of "blanketing" of the rear ships of one division by the leading ships of that next astern, and at one time the *Thunderer* was firing over the bows of the *Iron Duke*, causing some slight inconvenience on the bridge of the latter ship; the "blanketing," however, was unavoidable and the loss of fire involved was inappreciable.

At 6.45 P.M. one or two torpedoes crossed the track of the rear of our battle line, and the *Marlborough* altered course to avoid one. They were apparently fired, at long range, by enemy destroyers, which were barely visible to the ships in rear and quite invisible to those on board the *Iron Duke*. They might, however, have been fired by enemy battleships which were within torpedo range, or by a submarine, the *Revenge* reporting that it was thought that one had been rammed by that ship. The tracks of some of the torpedoes were seen by the observers stationed aloft, and were avoided by very skilful handling of the ships by their captains.

At 6.45 P.M., however, a heavy explosion occurred under the fore bridge of the *Marlborough*, abreast the starboard forward hydraulic engine-room. The ship took up a list of some seven degrees to starboard, but continued in action so effectively that she avoided three more torpedoes shortly afterwards, re-opened fire at 7.3 P.M., and at 7.12 P.M. fired fourteen rapid salvoes at a ship of the "König" class, hitting her so frequently that she was seen to turn out of line.

The signal from Sir Cecil Burney of the damage to his flagship stated that the vessel had been struck by a "mine or torpedo." It was assumed by me that a torpedo had hit the ship, as so many vessels had passed over the same locality without injury from mine. This proved to be the case, the track of this torpedo not having been sufficiently visible to enable Captain Ross to avoid it.

The fact of the tracks of so many of the enemy's torpedoes being visible was a matter of great surprise to me, and I think to other officers. Reports had been prevalent that the Germans had succeeded in producing a torpedo which left little or no track on the surface. The information as to the visibility of the tracks did not reach me until the return of the Fleet to harbour, as although one torpedo was reported by observers on board the destroyer *Oak* to have passed close ahead of the *Iron Duke* at about 7.35 P.M., finishing its run 2,000 yards beyond that ship, and a second was observed by the *Benbow* to pass apparently ahead of the *Iron Duke* at 8.30 P.M., neither of them was seen on board the flagship by the trained look-outs specially stationed for the purpose.

Some ten minutes after the alteration of course to south, a signal was made to the 2nd Battle Squadron to take station ahead of the *Iron Duke* and for the 1st Battle Squadron to form astern. This signal had, however, been already anticipated by the vessels ahead of the *Iron Duke* in accordance with the general battle orders giving discretionary powers to the commanders of squadrons, and the line had been partly reformed before the signal was made.

An incident occurred at about 6.47 P.M. which was an indication of the spirit prevailing in the Fleet, of which it is impossible to speak too highly. The destroyer *Acasta*, which had been badly hit aft during her attack on enemy light cruisers in company with the *Shark* and had her engines disabled, was passed by the Fleet. Her commanding officer, Lieut.-Commander J. O. Barron, signalled the condition of his ship to the *Iron Duke* as that ship passed, leaving the *Acasta* on her starboard or engaged side. The ship's company was observed to be cheering each ship as they passed. It is satisfactory to relate that this destroyer and her gallant ship's company were subsequently brought into Aberdeen, being assisted by the *Nonsuch*.

Shortly after 6.55 P.M. the *Iron Duke* passed the wreck of a ship with the bow and stern standing out of the water, the centre portion apparently resting on the bottom, with the destroyer *Badger* picking up survivors. It was thought at first that this was the remains of a German light cruiser, but inquiry of the *Badger* elicited the lamentable news that the wreck was that of the *Invincible*. It was assumed at the time that she had been sunk either by a mine or by a torpedo, and, in view of the safe passage of other ships in her vicinity, the latter appeared to be the more probable cause of her loss. Subsequent information, however, showed that she was destroyed by gunfire, causing her magazines to explode, as already recorded.

At 7 P.M. Sir David Beatty signalled reporting that the enemy was to the westward.

Our alteration of course to south had, meanwhile, brought the enemy's line into view once more, and between 7.0 and 7.30 P.M. the Battle Fleet was again in action with battleships and also battle cruisers, as they could be distinguished in the haze, which at that period was very baffling. The range varied from as much as 15,000 yards at the van to as little as 8,000 in the rear, this difference in range indicating that the enemy's Fleet was turning to the westward. . . .

In spite of the difficult conditions the fire of many of our battleships was very effective at this period. Some instances may be given. At 7.15 P.M. the *Iron Duke*, as already mentioned, engaged a hostile battleship at 15,000 yards' range and on a bearing 74 degrees from right ahead. At 7.20 she trained her guns on a battle cruiser of "Lutzow" type, abaft the beam, which hid herself by a destroyer smoke screen; at 7.17 P.M. the *King George* V. opened fire on a vessel, taken to be the leading ship in the enemy's line at a range of about 13,000 yards; the *Orion* at a battleship*; the *St. Vincent* was "holding her target (a battleship) effectively till 7.26 P.M., the range being between 10,000 and 9,500 yards"; the *Agincourt* at 7.6 P.M. opened fire at 11,000 yards on one of four battleships that showed clearly out of the mist, and judged that at least four of her salvoes "straddled" the target; the *Revenge* was engaging what were taken to be battle cruisers, obtaining distinct hits on two of them; the *Colossus* from 7.12 to 7.20 P.M. was engaging a ship taken to be a battle cruiser, either the *Derfflinger* or *Lutzow*, at ranges between 10,000 and 8,000 yards, and observed several direct hits, two being on the water line; whilst the *Marlborough*, as already mentioned, "engaged a ship of the 'König' class." Other vessels reported being in effective action during this period. The *Royal Oak*, the ship next astern of the *Iron Duke*, opened fire at 7.15 P.M. on the leading ship of three vessels taken to be battle cruisers, at a range of 14,000 yards; this ship was hit and turned away, and fire was shifted to the second ship which was lost to sight in the mist after a few rounds had been fired. It was difficult to be certain of the class of vessel on which fire was being directed, but one or more of the enemy's battle cruisers had undoubtedly dropped astern by 7 P.M., as a result of the heavy punishment they had received from our battle cruisers and the 5th Battle Squadron, and were engaged by ships of the Battle Fleet.

Both at this period and earlier in the action, the ships of the 1st Battle Squadron were afforded more opportunities for effective fire than the rest of the Battle Fleet, and the fullest use was made of the opportunities. This squadron, under the able command of Sir Cecil Burney, was known by me to be highly efficient, and very strong proof was furnished during the Jutland battle, if proof were needed, that his careful training had borne excellent results. The immunity of the ships of the squadron from the enemy's fire, whilst they were inflicting on his vessels very severe punishment,

* The *Calliope* reported at 7.1 P.M.: "Two enemy battleships, 'König' class, engaged by *Orion's* division, observed to be heavily on fire."

bears very eloquent testimony to the offensive powers of the squadron.

At 7.5 P.M. the whole battle line was turned together three more points to starboard to close the range further; immediately afterwards two ships ahead of the *Iron Duke* reported a submarine a little on the port bow; at 7.10 P.M. a flotilla of enemy destroyers, supported by a cruiser, was observed to be approaching on a bearing S. 50 W. from the *Iron Duke*, and the Fleet was turned back to south in order to turn on to the submarine and bring the ships in line ahead ready, for any required manœuvre. A heavy fire was opened on the destroyers at ranges between 10,000 and 6,500 yards. At the latter range the destroyers turned and passed towards the rear of the line in a heavy smoke screen. One destroyer was seen by several observers to sink from the effects of the gunfire.

At a sufficient interval before it was considered that the torpedoes fired by the destroyers would cross our lines, a signal was made to the Battle Fleet to turn two points to port by subdivisions. Some minutes later a report was made to me by Commander Bellairs (the officer on my Staff especially detailed for this duty and provided with an instrument for giving the necessary information) that this turn was insufficient to clear the torpedoes, as I had held on until the last moment; a further turn of two points was then made for a short time. As a result of this attack and another that followed immediately, some twenty or more torpedoes were observed to cross the track of the Battle Fleet, in spite of our turn, the large majority of them passing the ships of the 1st and 5th Battle Squadrons at the rear of the line. It was fortunate that, owing to the turn away of the Fleet, the torpedoes were apparently near the end of their run, and were consequently not running at high speed. They were all avoided by the very skilful handling of the ships by their captains, to whom the highest credit is due, not only for their skill in avoiding the torpedoes, but for the manner in which the ships, by neighbourly conduct towards each other, prevented risk of collision and kept their station in the line. The captains were most ably assisted by the admirable look-out kept by the organisation that existed for dealing with this danger.

The skill shown could not, however, have prevented several ships from being torpedoed had the range been less and the torpedoes consequently running at a higher speed. Frequent exercises carried out at Scapa Flow showed conclusively that the percentage of torpedoes that would hit ships in a line when fired from de-

stroyers at ranges up to 8,000 yards was comparatively high, even
if the tracks were seen and the ships were manœuvred to avoid
them. One very good reason is that torpedoes are always a considerable but varying distance ahead of the line of bubbles marking their track, making it difficult to judge the position of the
torpedo from its track. Many ships experienced escapes from this
and other attacks; thus the *Hercules* reported that she "turned
away six points to avoid the torpedoes, one of which passed along
the starboard side and 40 yards across the bow, and the other
passed close under the stern"; the *Neptune* reported that "the
tracks of three torpedoes were seen from the foretop, one of which
passed very close and was avoided by the use of the helm"; in the
Agincourt's report, a statement occurred that "at 7.8 P.M. a torpedo just missed astern, it having been reported from aloft and
course altered"; and again, "at 7.38 P.M. tracks of two torpedoes
running parallel were observed approaching; course altered to
avoid torpedoes which passed ahead; and at 8.25 P.M. torpedo
track on starboard side, turned at full speed; torpedo broke surface at about 150 yards on the starboard bow"; the *Revenge* remarked, "at 7.35 P.M. altered course to port to avoid two torpedoes,
one passed about ten yards ahead and the other about twenty
yards astern, and at 7.43 P.M. altered course to avoid torpedoes,
two passing astern"; the *Colossus* stated, "at 7.35 P.M. turned to
port to avoid a torpedo coming from starboard side"; the *Barham*
at this period reported that "at least four torpedoes passed through
the line close to the *Barham*"; the *Collingwood* reported, "torpedo
track was seen 20 degrees abaft the beam and coming straight at
the ship; large helm was put on and the torpedo passed very close
astern; at the same time another was seen to pass about thirty
yards ahead." The captain of the *Collingwood*, in remarking on
the destroyer's attack, added, "the great value of this form of
attack on a line of ships is, to me, an outstanding feature of the
Battle Fleet action."

The first two-point turn was made at 7.23 P.M. and the Fleet
was brought to a south by west course by 7.33 P.M. (that is, to a
course one point to the westward of the course of the Fleet before
the destroyer attack). The total amount by which the range was
opened by the turns was about 1,750 yards.

The 4th Light Cruiser Squadron and the 4th and 11th Flotillas
had been delayed in reaching their action station at the van until
about 7.10 P.M., owing to the turns to the westward made by the
Battle Fleet to close the enemy. In accordance with arrangements

made previously to counter destroyer attacks, these vessels were ordered out to engage the enemy destroyers, which, according to the report of the Commodore Le Mesurier, commanding the 4th Light Cruiser Squadron, were steering towards the head of the division led by the *King George V.*, the van ship of the Battle Fleet. Although not very well placed for the first attack for the reason given above, they were in a very favourable position to counter the second destroyer attack, which took place at 7.25 P.M. The enemy's flotilla was sighted bearing 30 degrees before the starboard beam of the *Iron Duke* at a range of 9,000 yards and was heavily engaged by the light forces and the 4th, 1st, and 5th Battle Squadrons. During this attack three enemy destroyers were reported as sunk by the fire of the battleships, light cruisers and destroyers; one of them, bearing a Commodore's pendant, being sunk at 7.50 P.M. by a division of the 12th Flotilla, consisting of the *Obedient, Marvel, Mindful* and *Onslaught,* which attacked them near the rear of our battle line. The *Southampton* and *Dublin,* of the 2nd Light Cruiser Squadron, attacked and sank a second destroyer at this period. At least six torpedoes were observed to pass ahead of, or through the track of, the 4th Light Cruiser Squadron during their attack on the German flotilla.

The destroyer attacks were combined with a retiring movement on the part of the enemy's Battle Fleet, the movement being covered with the aid of a heavy smoke screen. Although this retirement was not visible from the *Iron Duke* owing to the smoke and mist, and was, therefore, not known to me until after the action, it was clearly seen from the rear of our line, as is indicated by the following citations:

> The Captain of the *Valiant* stated in his report: "At 7.23 P.M. enemy's Battle Fleet now altered course together away from us and broke off the action, sending out a low cloud of smoke which effectually covered their retreat and obscured them from further view."
>
> The Captain of the *Malaya* reported, referring to this period: "This was the last of the enemy seen in daylight, owing to their Battle Fleet having turned away."
>
> Sir Cecil Burney stated in regard to this period: "As the destroyer attack developed, the enemy's Battle Fleet in sight were observed to turn at least eight points until their sterns were towards our line. They ceased fire, declined further action, and disappeared into the mist."
>
> The Captain of the *St. Vincent* said: "The target was held closely until 7.26 P.M. (32 minutes in all), when the enemy had turned eight or ten points away, disappearing into the mist and

with a smoke screen made by destroyers to cover them as well."

Rear-Admiral Evan-Thomas remarked: "After joining the Battle Fleet the 5th Battle Squadron conformed to the movements of the Commander-in-Chief, engaging the rear ships of the enemy's battle line, until they turned away and went out of sight, all ships apparently covering themselves with artificial smoke."

The Captain of the *Revenge* recorded: "A flotilla of destroyers passed through the line and made a most efficient smoke screen. At this period the enemy's fleet turned eight points to starboard and rapidly drew out of sight."

In the German account of the action at this stage, it is stated, in more than one passage, that the British Fleet during this action between the Battle Fleets was to the northward of the High Seas Fleet. This is correct of the earlier stages. The account refers to the attacks on our line by the German destroyer flotillas, and states finally that in the last attack the destroyers did not sight the heavy ships, but only light cruisers and destroyers to the north-eastward. The accuracy of this statement is doubtful, since the destroyers were clearly in sight from our heavy ships. But the account then proceeds to state that "the German Commander-in-Chief turns his battle line to a southerly and south-westerly course *on which the enemy was last seen,* but he is no longer to be found."

This is illuminating. It is first stated that our ships bore north and north-east from the enemy and then that the enemy turned to south and south-west, that is, *directly away from the British Fleet.* Thus the fact that the German Fleet turned directly away is confirmed by Germans.

No report of this movement of the German Fleet reached me, and at first it was thought that his temporary disappearance was due to the thickening mist, especially as firing could be heard from the battleships in rear, but at 7.14 P.M., the enemy Battle Fleet being no longer in sight from the *Iron Duke,* course was altered "by divisions" three points more to starboard (namely, to south-west) to close the enemy, and single line ahead was again formed on the *Iron Duke* on that course.

At this period the rear of our battle line was still in action at intervals with one or two ships of the enemy's fleet, which were probably some that had dropped astern partially disabled, but by 7.55 P.M. fire had practically ceased.

At about 7.40 P.M. I received a report from Sir David Beatty stating that the enemy bore north-west by west from the *Lion,* distant 10 to 11 miles, and that the *Lion's* course was south-west. Although the battle cruisers were not in sight from the *Iron Duke,*

I assumed the *Lion* to be five or six miles ahead of the van of the Battle Fleet, but it appeared later from a report received in reply to directions signalled by me at 8.10 P.M. to the *King George* V. to follow the battle cruisers, that they were not in sight from that ship either.

At this time the enemy's Battle Fleet seems to have become divided, for whilst Sir David Beatty reported the presence of battleships north-west by west from the *Lion*, other enemy battleships were observed to the westward (that is, on the starboard bow of the *Iron Duke*), and the course of the Fleet was at once altered "by divisions" to west in order to close the enemy; this alteration was made at 7.59 P.M.

It will be observed that all the large alterations of course of the Battle Fleet during the engagement were made "by divisions" instead of "in succession from the van, or together." The reason was that in this way the whole Fleet could be brought closer to the enemy with far greater rapidity, and in a more ordered formation, than if the movement had been carried out by the line "in succession."

The objection to altering by turning all ships together was the inevitable confusion that would have ensued as the result of such a manœuvre carried out with a very large Fleet under action conditions in misty weather, particularly if the ships were thus kept on a line of bearing for a long period.

The battleships sighted at 7.29 P.M. opened fire on the ship of the 4th Light Cruiser Squadron, which had moved out to starboard of the battle line to engage a flotilla of enemy destroyers which were steering to attack the Battle Fleet. The *Calliope*, the flagship of Commodore Le Mesurier, was hit by a heavy shell and received some damage, but retained her fighting efficiency, and fired a torpedo at the leading battleship at a range of 6,500 yards; an explosion was noticed on board a ship of the "Kaiser" class by the *Calliope*.[*] The ships sighted turned away and touch could not be regained, although sounds of gunfire could be heard from ahead at 8.25 P.M., probably from our battle cruisers, which obtained touch with and engaged some of the enemy's ships very effectively between 8.22 and 8.25 P.M. The *Falmouth* was the last ship of the Battle Cruiser Fleet to be in touch with the enemy,

---

[*] All our battle cruisers felt this heavy explosion which was clearly concussion under water, and may have been caused by the *Calliope's* torpedo obtaining a hit.

at 8.38 P.M.; the ships then in sight turned eight points together away from the *Falmouth*.

At 8.30 P.M. the light was failing and the Fleet was turned "by divisions" to a south-west course, thus reforming single line again.

During the proceedings of the Battle Fleet described above, the battle cruisers were in action ahead as mentioned in Sir David Beatty's report. . . .

At first, touch with the enemy was lost owing to the large alterations of course carried out by the High Sea Fleet, but it was regained at 7.12 P.M., the battle cruisers opening fire at 7.14 P.M., though only for two and a half minutes, and increasing speed to 22 knots. At this period the battle cruisers were steering south-west by south to south-west, and this course took them from the port to the starboard bow of the Battle Fleet by 7.12 P.M. The movements of our battle cruisers, which were at this time between four and five miles ahead of the van of the Battle Fleet, could not be distinguished, owing, partly, to the funnel and cordite smoke from the battle cruisers themselves, but even more to the funnel smoke from the numerous cruisers, light cruisers and destroyers which were attempting to gain their positions ahead of the van.

The movements of the enemy's fleet could not be distinguished from our Battle Fleet owing again to their own funnel and cordite smoke, and, also, to the smoke screens which ships and destroyers were making to conceal their movements.

It will be realised that these conditions, which particularly affected the Battle Fleet, did not apply to the same extent to our ships ahead of our Battle Fleet. They had little but the smoke of the enemy's leading ships to obscure the view. Farther to the rear, the Battle Fleet had the smoke of all our craft ahead of it as well as that of the enemy's long line of ships.

Conditions which were perhaps difficult ahead of the Battle Fleet were very much accentuated in the Battle Fleet. Vice-Admiral Sir Martyn Jerram, in his report, remarked on this point: "As leading ship, in addition to the hazy atmosphere, I was much hampered by what I imagine must have been cordite fumes from the battle cruisers after they had passed up, and from other cruisers engaged on the bow, also by funnel gases from small craft ahead, and for a considerable time by dense smoke from the *Duke of Edinburgh*, which was unable to draw clear."

The general position at 6.45 P.M. and again at 7.15 P.M. is shown in plans 8 and 9.

At 7.10 P.M., according to remarks from the *Minotaur*, flagship of Rear-Admiral W. L. Heath, commanding the 2nd Cruiser Squadron, the position as seen from that ship was as follows: "The 2nd Cruiser Squadron was in single line ahead three to four miles on the port side of the *King George* V., gaining on her slightly, but with all the destroyers and light craft between her and the *King George* V. The battle cruisers were about four miles distant on the starboard bow of the *Minotaur*; owing to their higher speed, the battle cruisers rapidly increased their distance from the Battle Fleet to some eight miles."*

At 7.5 P.M. according to a report from the *Shannon*, of the 2nd Cruiser Squadron, the *Shannon's* course was S. 10 W., "the 2nd Cruiser Squadron endeavouring to take station on the engaged bow of the Battle Fleet; the Battle Fleet still engaged, the battle cruisers not engaged and turned slightly to port." And again at 7.22 P.M. a report says: "The *Duke of Edinburgh* had now taken station astern of the *Shannon*, the battle cruisers were engaged and had wheeled to starboard. Leading ships of the 2nd Cruiser Squadron were starting to cross the bows of the Battle Fleet from port to starboard. Battle cruisers firing intermittently, light cruisers making their way through the destroyer flotillas to attack the enemy light cruisers." Rear-Admiral Heath stated: "At 7.11 P.M. I proceeded with the squadron at 20 knots to take up station astern of the Battle Cruiser Fleet, which was then engaged with the enemy." He added: "One salvo fell short on the starboard bow of the *Minotaur* and some others in close proximity"; and later says, "even when the salvo referred to in the preceding paragraph fell, no more than the flashes of the enemy's guns could be seen."

Further remarks from the *Shannon*, at a later stage, were: "At 8 P.M. Battle Fleet altered course to starboard to close the enemy, and by 8.15 was lost to sight, bearing about north by east."

"At 8.15 P.M. Battle Fleet, out of sight from *Shannon*, was heard to be in action."

"At 8.30 P.M. the visibility of grey ships was about 9,000 yards." "At 8.45 P.M. *King George* V. again sighted, bearing north-north-east. Visibility had again improved, and her range was estimated at about 10,000 yards. Conformed to her course S. 75 W. to close enemy."

At 7.20 P.M. the ships engaged by our battle cruisers turned away and were lost to sight. They were located for a moment at

* Judged by reports from other cruisers the positions here described should be timed at about 6.50 to 7 P.M., and the diagrams show this accordingly.

8.20 P.M. with the aid of the 1st and 3rd Light Cruiser Squadrons, and, although they disappeared again at once, they were once more located and effectively engaged between 8.22 and 8.28 P.M. at about 10,000 yards range. They turned away once more and were finally lost to sight by the 3rd Light Cruiser Squadron (the last ships to keep in touch) at 8.38 P.M., steaming to the westward.

This was the last opportunity which the battle cruisers had of putting the finishing touch upon a fine afternoon's work. They had, under the very able and gallant leadership of Sir David Beatty, assisted by the splendid squadron so well commanded by Admiral Evan-Thomas, gone far to crush out of existence the opposing Battle Cruiser Squadron.

It will be seen from the above account that our battle cruisers experienced great difficulty in locating and holding the enemy after 7.20 P.M., even when far ahead of the Battle Fleet, with its small craft, and therefore in a position of freedom from the smoke of our own vessels and the enemy's line. After this time, 7.20 P.M., the battle cruisers were only engaged for some six minutes. The enemy turned away on each occasion when he was located and showed no disposition to fight.

The visibility by this time had become very bad; the light was failing, and it became necessary to decide on the disposition for the night.

VI. Air Warfare

9. The Red Battle Flyer

A NEW dimension was added to combat during the First World War when, for the first time on a large scale, it was projected from the accustomed battlefields on land and sea into the air. At the outbreak of the war Germany had a first-line strength of 232 airplanes; Britain had 50 naval airplanes and seaplanes and 63 military aircraft; France had 120 military airplanes; and Germany had 8 military Zeppelins while Britain had 6 such airships and France 5.

When hostilities began aircraft served largely for reconnaissance, but by 1918 they had evolved into a weapon of long-range attack. In August, 1914, four squadrons of the Royal Flying Corps were attached to the British Expeditionary Force, and their airplanes were flown over to France. It was air reconnaissance which detected the German turning movement from Louvain. And French Lieutenant Watteau, an aviator of the Paris garrison, made the crucial discovery on an observation flight on the morning of September 3 that General von Kluck was unexpectedly deviating from his previous line of march and was veering away from Paris in a southeasterly direction toward the Marne. This item of intelligence, when brought to the attention of General Galliéni and General Joffre, enabled the French to make their flanking attack upon the German First Army which culminated in the decisive Allied victory at the Marne. In the "Race to the Sea" which followed, reconnaissance aircraft of the British Royal Flying Corps and the Royal Naval Air Service helped prevent the Channel ports from falling into German possession. Systematic aerial reconnaissance had all but ruled out strategic surprise in military operations.

Winston Churchill, First Lord of the Admiralty, was one of the first to appreciate the possibilities of long-range air attack. After German air raids on Liège forts by a Zeppelin, Churchill endorsed the idea of an aerial counterattack. On October 9, 1914, Flight Lieutenant R. L. G. Marix, in a Sopwith Tabloid plane, took off from Antwerp shortly before the city's capture by the Germans, and flew across neutral Holland to Düsseldorf, where Marix scored a direct hit on a Zeppelin hangar with two 20-pound bombs which he dropped by hand from the open cockpit. The Z-9 was totally destroyed. Encouraged by this exploit, the British shipped four of their Avro airplanes from a factory in Manchester to Belfort. On November 21, 1914, the planes were flown on a 250-mile round-trip mission to bomb the Zeppelin works at Friedrichshafen, on Lake Constance. Little damage was done in the air raid, but the potentialities of long-range strategic air strikes were already demonstrated.

Following the immobilization of the western front into trench warfare, air reconnaissance became virtually the only means of obtaining accurate information about enemy positions and formations. Cavalry, scouts, and pickets were henceforth almost as obsolete as medieval knights when confronted by barbed wire and machine guns. The development of the Thornton-Pickard camera and its use in aerial photography greatly increased the accuracy of artillery spotting. The British Royal Flying Corps was especially resourceful in advancing reconnaissance tactics. The Germans responded with determined attempts to interfere with Allied observation aircraft. There ensued air combat in which planes fought one another. This contest produced the fighter plane in which the Germans gained the advantage in 1915.

But aerial combat was still in a ludicrously primitive stage during the first year of the war. The German General Staff issued hand grenades and pistols to its pilots. The German flyers soon displayed a knack at lobbing their hand grenades at Allied planes flying beneath them, and taking potshots at their antagonists with their revolvers. The Allied pilots retaliated with the same amateurish tactics, which the Germans countered by steep-banking. The strafing of ground troops was an Allied invention, British Captain A. A. B. Thomson of Number 16 Squadron initiating it in 1915 by flying his plane a few feet above German trenches while he shot at their infantry with his revolver.

The Germans achieved a great break-through in air fighting by perfecting a fixed machine gun which could shoot forward through an airplane's propeller. The French ace Roland Garros improvised a crude deflector of bullets from a machine gun which he attached to the nacelle of his Morane-Saulnier monoplane. The deflector consisted of triangular steel plates which he fitted to each blade of the propeller. Needless to say, there was an inescapable risk of ricochet. When the daredevil Garros was shot down behind German lines, his monoplane and deflector were examined by the Dutch airplane designer in German employment, Anthony Fokker. Within several days the ingenious Fokker had improved upon Garros' dangerous contraption by attaching "a small knob to the propeller which struck a cam as it revolved. This cam was hooked up with the hammer of the machine gun which automatically loaded itself. Thus, as . . . the propeller . . . revolved . . . the gun shot between the blades." The Germans soon had an effective flying machine gun mounted on their maneuverable Fokker monoplane. The pilot aimed the gun by aiming his airplane.

Until the French and British could match the deadly Fokker fighter plane, they had to resort to formation flying and the safety of numbers. British Air Vice Marshal J. E. Johnson explained that "the pilots found that they had to fight for information and there began a crude form of duelling in the air. These early air fighters flew and fought alone, but they soon discovered that a lone pilot could not guard his own tail and they began to hunt in pairs. Pairs grew into sections of four or five machines, sections into squadrons, and squadrons into wings of sometimes fifty machines. So team fighting was developed, and great daylight air battles took place. Scouts were also used for night fighting, and for bombing and strafing."

In this way there emerged from a ground war of anonymous hordes the flamboyant aces whose names became widely known during the last years of the war. France idolized René Fonck, Georges Guynemer, and Charles Nungesser, while Germany lavished its adulation upon Baron Manfred von Richthofen, Oswalk Boelcke, Max Immelmann, and Herman Göring. Aces Edward Mannock and Albert Ball were lionized by Britain, William A. Bishop by Canada, and Francesco Baracca by Italy. America in time produced Edward V. Rickenbacker and Frank Luke. Less prominent were Zeppelin pilots, the chief of whom was Ernst A. Lehmann.

The Allies were goaded into developing fighter planes equal to the Fokker monoplane in performance. The need of effective fighters was made all the more urgent by the ease with which German pilots shot down French and British kite balloons, which were invaluable for artillery observation but which were extremely vulnerable to an airplane's machine-gun fire. They required fighter-plane protection. By 1916 the British had developed the small, single-seater "pusher" plane, the de Havilland 2, with a pair of machine guns mounted at the very front of its fuselage, and capable of firing either directly forward or in a forward arc. The French produced the single-seater Nieuport fighter plane with a 110-horsepower engine, which was able to cope with the Fokker. The Germans tried to regain air superiority by developing the flying circus under the command of General von Hoeppner. A circus was a mobile group of German aces who fought in tightly disciplined formations. The first circus, led by the celebrated Oswald Boelcke, fought against a British bombing formation in September, 1916, shooting down six of the fourteen British aircraft. With the improved Fokker D as well as the two-gun Albatross and the powerful Halberstadt fighter planes, Boelcke's squadron, Jasta 2, became the best-known of the German *Jagdstaffeln*, or "hunting packs." During the fall of 1916 Boelcke and his pupils (one of whom was von Richthofen) easily dominated the skies over the German lines.

But Allied aircraft were also beginning to be equipped with machine-gun synchronizers by the end of 1916. And Major General Hugh Trenchard succeeded in detaching his Royal Flying Corps fighter planes from the army units to which they had originally been assigned. Trenchard established the principle of freeing fighter aircraft from observation and ground support missions, allowing them to concentrate on the contest for air supremacy. Allied dominance was gained during the summer of 1917 through the introduction of greatly improved fighters—the two-seater Bristol Brisfits, and de Havilland D.H. 4s, as well as the single-seater Sopwith Camels and the Spads. General Trenchard maintained a continuous air offensive with the new machines. British pilots flew from dawn to dusk over the battle zone between the German front lines and their line of barrage balloons ten thousand feet to the rear.

Robbed thereby of their previous ascendancy over the battlefield, the Germans shifted to long-range bombing raids on Britain. On June 13, 1917, fourteen Gotha bombers raided London, killing 162 residents and wounding 432—the largest number of casualties inflicted on England in a single raid during the war. Bombing missions against towns had been undertaken as early as December 24, 1914, when Dover was bombed by German aircraft. The Hague Convention had outlawed the bombing of undefended towns "by any means whatsoever," but the Convention had not been signed by Germany, France, Russia, Italy, and Japan. Moreover, it was not possible to differentiate in practice between defended and undefended towns. The British bombing raids against Germany in 1914 had been directed against strictly military targets such as Zeppelin hangars or factories. But in January, 1915, Kaiser William II authorized the "area" bombing of London and other British towns. On January 19, 1915, naval Zeppelins bombed villages in Norfolk, killing two civilians. A single German plane raided London on May 26, 1915, killing seven residents and injuring thirty-five. London was bombed five times during 1915, mostly by Zeppelins.

The British countered by ordering a blackout in East Anglia, by placing antiaircraft guns and searchlights around probable targets, and by stationing fighter planes near the coast to intercept the German raiders. The use of incendiary bullets by British pilots made the Zeppelins, buoyed up by hydrogen, exceedingly vulnerable, and Zeppelin attacks against England tapered off from twenty-two in 1916 to seven in 1917 and only four in 1918.

However, German bombing planes took up where their dirigibles left off. By 1916 the Staaken-Riesenflugzeug (or Staaken giant airship) was in large-scale production. The enormous five-engine plane had a wingspread of 138 feet and a fuselage over 75 feet long—larger, in fact, than the American Boeing Flying Fortress of 1942. Its cruising speed was 80 miles per hour, and it could fly from six to seven hours. It was heavily armed against fighter attack, and it had engines which could be serviced in flight by crewmen daring enough to crawl along the wings. Less impressive than the Staaken R. plane was the Gotha bomber, a large, clumsy three-seater biplane.

The British War Office was so disturbed by the Gotha daylight raid upon London on June 13, 1917, that it doubled the number of Royal Flying Corps squadrons to two hundred, and it rushed to completion the de Havilland 9A bomber. This aircraft had a 400-horsepower American-built Liberty engine, and it could fly for almost six hours at a maximum speed of 125 miles per hour. It performed well in France in attacking German billets, supply dumps, and railway junctions. Supplementing the de Havilland was Britain's Handley Page bomber, which had a crew of five, two Rolls-Royce engines, and an armament of five machine guns. It could reach a speed of 98 miles per hour and an altitude of 9,000 feet. The Super-Handley Page, built toward the war's end in 1918, had four engines, a crew of six, and a bomb load of thirty 250-pound bombs.

The year 1917 was marked by steadily increasing air action. The Royal Flying Corps maintained an unremitting offensive with its fighter patrols over the western front to prevent German fighters from interfering with Allied reconnaissance, artillery spotting, and bombing missions. There was debate in Britain over the practicality of a bombing offensive against Germany. Winston Churchill, who exulted over the RAF retaliatory saturation raids against German cities in the Second World War, opposed indiscriminate bombing against German cities in the First World War. As minister of munitions he wrote in a report on October 21, 1917: "It is not reasonable to speak of an air offensive as if it were going to finish the war by itself. It is improbable that any terrorization of the civil population which could be achieved by air attack would compel the government of a great nation to surrender." Churchill's opposition to area bombing was shared by President Woodrow Wilson, who wrote after America's entry into the war: "I desire no sort of participation by the Air Service of the United States in a plan . . . which has as its object promiscuous bombing upon industry, commerce, or populations in enemy countries dissociated from obvious military needs to be served by such action." Churchill and Wilson were undoubtedly correct in their opinion that area bombing would merely sacrifice civilian life without breaking morale, for in 1917 air power was still circumscribed by the relatively small number of bombing planes and by the limited power of bombs which had been enlarged only from the puny 20-pounders of 1914 to 112- and 250-pounders. Even the thousand-plane RAF raids over Germany during the Second World War—saturation attacks with conventional blockbusters and myriads of fire bombs—failed to make Germany capitulate. Quite different, of course, was the case with the atomic bombs dropped upon Hiroshima and Naga-saki in 1945, but *conventional bombing* by itself as a sovereign formula for victory is yet to be demonstrated, as the Americans have been ruefully reminded by their experience in Vietnam.

Churchill's opposition to area bombing did not prevail in 1917 and in 1918. Between October, 1917, and June, 1918, three squadrons of Handley Page, de Havilland, and F.E. 2B bombers carried out fifty-seven raids against the cities of Frankfurt am Main, Coblenz, Köln, Mainz, Stuttgart, Karlsruhe, and Mannheim. The British bombers generally flew in small formations, rarely exceeding a dozen planes, and their bomb loads were relatively light. On April 1, 1918, Lord Trenchard won parliamentary consent to unite the Royal Flying Corps and the Royal Naval Air Service into the independent Royal Air Force. And by May, 1918, the air defenses of London had been made so formidably effective that the Germans shifted their air raids to Paris as their primary target.

During the last year of the war airplanes as well as Zeppelins were used extensively for long-range naval reconnaissance and antisub-marine patrols. The first massive air raid occurred in September, 1918, when forty Handley Pages bombed German factories and air fields in a single operation, a portent of the terrifying, thousand-plane RAF raids over the Ruhr which were to become routine during the Second World War. In October, 1918, Super-Handley Page bombers dropped the first blockbusters weighing 1,650 pounds each, the largest bombs of the war. At the war's end the Royal Air Force had a first line strength of 3,330 planes, the French air force 4,511, and the German air force 2,390. Air warfare was no longer in its infancy, although only about 1,400 Englishmen and 750 Germans had been killed in all the air raids of the war. Within a generation, space, as a safeguard against possible military attack or even annihilation, would be made all the more obsolete by the world-girdling nuclear rocketry capable of sup-planting manned aircraft.

To illustrate the nature of fighting in the new element, we publish a description of air combat by the best-known ace, the Red Baron, Captain Manfred Freiherr von Richthofen, who was credited with destroying eighty enemy planes, the highest score of the war. Richtho-fen was born in Breslau on May 2, 1892. He was the son of a profes-sional soldier serving in the First Regiment of Cuirassiers at the time of Manfred's birth. Richthofen's mother belonged to the family Von Schickfuss und Neudorf, typical Junker landowners who were pas-sionately addicted to hunting and horsemanship. Young Manfred was privately tutored at Kleinburg until he was nine years old, when he left home to attend school at Schweidnitz. At the age of eleven he was enrolled in the cadet corps at Wahlstatt, where he proved to be an indifferent student, excelling only in gymnastics and football. He was never burdened with much intellectual baggage. Nevertheless, he managed to graduate in 1911 and entered the First Regiment of Uhlans, which was garrisoned in Silesia. He loved the life of a cavalry officer, winning the Kaiser Prize for horsemanship in 1913.

At the war's outbreak Lieutenant von Richthofen served briefly on the eastern front, taking part in scouting action in the vicinity of Kieltze. The First Regiment of Uhlans was almost immediately transferred to Luxembourg, and thence to Belgium and France. When Richthofen was assigned to dispatch-bearer duties in the Verdun sector, he chafed at the immobility of trench warfare, but found some relief from his frustrations by hunting wild pigs in the forest of La Chaussée. Being restless by nature and a man of action above all, he asked permission of his commanding general to join the German air force, which he was allowed to do in May, 1915.

Richthofen served as an observer during his first five months in the air force. After twenty-five lessons in piloting a plane he made his first solo flight on October 10, 1915, only to crash—an unpromising beginning for the pilot destined to become "the greatest aviator of the war." In March, 1916, he joined the Second Battle Squadron, which was based near Verdun. He flew innumerable missions over the western front (generally in defensive combat behind the German lines, on orders from higher authority) and against Russian forces as well. He commanded a group of daredevil pilots who were styled the Richthofen Circus. With almost childlike naiveté, Richthofen revealed enough about himself in *The Red Battle Flyer* to give one pause. He became the very paragon of the killer. In recounting his air duels with British pilots, he wrote: "My father discriminates between a sportsman and a butcher. The latter shoots for fun. When I have shot down an Englishman my hunting passion is satisfied for a quarter of an hour. If one of them comes down I have the feeling of complete satisfaction. Only much, much later I have overcome my instinct and have become a butcher."

Frederick Oughton, in his book *The Aces*, wrote of the Red Baron: "Richthofen's technique was to improve enormously. They started to say that he flew with his brains, not with the 'innocent courage' of other pilots. . . . Richthofen, the Red Baron, so called because he had his plane painted scarlet to make it easily recognizable by enemy and friend alike, flew with a kind of mathematical certainty. He always moved fast, attacking before the others. . . . He started to kill for the sake of killing and was known to shoot helpless grounded men as they struggled out of the cockpits of their burning machines. He fought like a madman . . . and only when he killed did his face break into smiles. . . . He was now coming to have a morbid curiosity about death. . . . He was always passing a photograph around. It showed a terribly mutilated body, the remains of a pilot."

Richthofen, the killer, who shot down eighty planes within two years, was himself killed when his red Fokker triplane was shot down near Amiens by Canadian Captain Roy Brown of the Royal Flying Corps, who flew a Sopwith Camel in a wild dogfight participated in by thirty German and British fighter planes. Richthofen was buried in a cemetery near Bertangles. The next day, in a chivalrous gesture, a British pilot flew over Richthofen's base at Cappy and dropped a photograph of the Red Baron's funeral and an explanatory note which read:

To the German Flying Corps: Rittmeister Baron Manfred von Richthofen was killed in aërial combat on April 12, 1918. He was buried with full military honors.

From the British Royal Air Force

On November 19, 1925, Richthofen's body was removed to Berlin for a state funeral.

CAPTAIN MANFRED FREIHERR VON RICHTHOFEN, THE RED BATTLE FLYER

BOMBING IN RUSSIA

In June we were suddenly ordered to entrain. No one knew where we were going, but we had an idea and we were not over much surprised when our Commander told us that we were going to Russia. We had traveled through the whole of Germany with our perambulating hotel which consisted of dining and sleeping cars, and arrived at last at Kovel. There we remained in our railway cars. There are many advantages in dwelling in a train. One is always ready to travel on and need not change one's quarters.*

In the heat of the Russian summer a sleeping car is the most horrible instrument of martyrdom imaginable. Therefore, I agreed with some friends of mine, Gerstenberg and Scheele, to take quarters in the forest near by. We erected a tent and lived like gypsies. We had a lovely time.

In Russia our battle squadron did a great deal of bomb throwing. Our occupation consisted of annoying the Russians. We dropped our eggs on their finest railway establishments. One day our whole squadron went out to bomb a very important railway station. The place was called Manjewicze and was situated about twenty miles behind the Front. That was not very far. The Russians had planned an attack and the station was absolutely crammed with colossal trains. Trains stood close to one another. Miles of rails were covered with them. One could easily see that from above. There was an object for bombing that was worth while.

One can become enthusiastic over anything. For a time I was delighted with bomb throwing. It gave me a tremendous pleasure

---

* This is the first reference to the regular "Traveling Circus" idea, in which the whole squadron works as a self-contained unit, with a special train to move its material, stores, spares, and mechanics, from place to place, and also provides living accommodations for the pilots.

to bomb those fellows from above. Frequently I took part in two expeditions on a single day.

On the day mentioned our object was Manjewicze. Everything was ready. The aeroplanes were ready to start. Every pilot tried his motor, for it is a painful thing to be forced to land against one's will on the wrong side of the Front line, especially in Russia. The Russians hated the flyers. If they caught a flying man they would certainly kill him. That is the only risk one ran in Russia for the Russians had no aviators, or practically none. If a Russian flying man turned up he was sure to have bad luck and would be shot down. The anti-aircraft guns used by Russia were sometimes quite good, but they were too few in number. Compared with flying in the West, flying in the East is absolutely a holiday.

The aeroplanes rolled heavily to the starting point. They carried bombs to the very limit of their capacity. Sometimes I dragged three hundred pounds of bombs with a normal C-machine.* Besides, I had with me a very heavy observer who apparently had not suffered in any way from the food scarcity. I had also with me a couple of machine guns. I was never able to make proper use of them in Russia. It is a pity that my collection of trophies contains not a single Russian.

Flying with a heavy machine which is carrying a great dead weight is no fun, especially during the mid-day summer heat in Russia. The barges sway in a very disagreeable manner. Of course, heavily laden though they are, they do not fall down. The 150 h.p. motors prevent it.† At the same time it is no pleasant sensation to carry such a large quantity of explosives and benzine.

At last we get into a quiet atmosphere. Now comes the enjoyment of bombing. It is splendid to be able to fly in a straight line and to have a definite object and definite orders. After having thrown one's bombs one has the feeling that he has achieved something, while frequently, after searching for an enemy to give battle to, one comes home with a sense of failure at not having brought a hostile machine to the ground. Then a man is apt to say to himself, "You have acted stupidly."

* The German C-type machines are the two-seater reconnaissance types. The D-type are the single-seater fighters or "chaser" machines. The G-type are the big three-seater bombers.

† It was 150 horsepower in 1916. By the beginning of 1918 all modern German C-type machines had 260 h.p., and by April, 1918, German biplanes with 500 h.p. in one engine were beginning to appear. In consequence the extreme height (or "ceiling") of a C-type machine had risen from 12,000 feet to 20,000 feet.

It gave me a good deal of pleasure to throw bombs. After a while my observer learned how to fly perpendicularly over the objects to be bombed and to make use of the right moment for laying his egg with the assistance of his aiming telescope.

The run to Manjewicze is very pleasant and I have made it repeatedly. We passed over gigantic forests which were probably inhabited by elks and lynxes. But the villages looked miserable. The only substantial village in the whole neighborhood was Manjewicze. It was surrounded by innumerable tents, and countless barracks had been run up near the railway station. We could not make out the Red Cross.

Another flying squadron had visited the place before us. That could be told by the smoking houses and barracks. They had not done badly. The exit of the station had obviously been blocked by a lucky hit. The engine was still steaming. The engine driver had probably dived into a shelter. On the other side of the station an engine was just coming out. Of course I felt tempted to hit it. We flew towards the engine and dropped a bomb a few hundred yards in front of it. We had the desired result. The engine stopped. We turned and continued throwing bomb after bomb on the station, carefully taking aim through our aiming telescope. We had plenty of time for nobody interfered with us. It is true that an enemy aerodrome was in the neighborhood but there was no trace of hostile pilots. A few anti-aircraft guns were busy, but they shot not in our direction but in another one. We reserved a bomb hoping to make particularly good use of it on our way home.

Suddenly we noticed an enemy flying machine starting from its hangar. The question was whether it would attack us. I did not believe in an attack. It was more likely that the flying man was seeking security in the air, for when bombing machines are about, the air is the safest place.

We went home by roundabout ways and looked for camps. It was particularly amusing to pepper the gentlemen down below with machine guns. Half savage tribes from Asia are even more startled when fired at from above than are cultured Englishmen. It is particularly interesting to shoot at hostile cavalry. An aerial attack upsets them completely. Suddenly the lot of them rush away in all directions of the compass. I should not like to be the Commander of a Squadron of Cossacks which has been fired at with machine guns from aeroplanes.

By and by we could recognize the German lines. We had to dispose of our last bomb and we resolved to make a present of it to a Russian observation balloon, to the only observation balloon they possessed. We could quite comfortably descend to within a few hundred yards of the ground in order to attack it. At first the Russians began to haul it in very rapidly. When the bomb had been dropped the hauling stopped. I did not believe that I had hit it. I rather imagined that the Russians had left their chief in the air and had run away. At last we reached our front and our trenches and were surprised to find when we got home that we had been shot at from below. At least one of the planes had a hole in it.

Another time and in the same neighborhood we were ordered to meet an attack of the Russians who intended to cross the river Stokhod. We came to the danger spot laden with bombs and carrying a large number of cartridges for our machine guns. On arrival at the Stokhod, we were surprised to see that hostile cavalry was already crossing. They were passing over a single bridge. Immediately it was clear to us that one might do a tremendous lot of harm to the enemy by hitting the bridge.

Dense masses of men were crossing. We went as low as possible and could clearly see the hostile cavalry crossing by way of the bridge with great rapidity. The first bomb fell near the bridge. The second and third followed immediately. They created a tremendous disorder. The bridge had not been hit. Nevertheless traffic across it had completely ceased. Men and animals were rushing away in all directions. We had thrown only three bombs but the success had been excellent. Besides, a whole squadron of aeroplanes was following us. Lastly, we could do other things. My observer fired energetically into the crowd down below with his machine gun and we enjoyed it tremendously. Of course, I cannot say what real success we had. The Russians have not told us. Still I imagined that I alone had caused the Russian attack to fail. Perhaps the official account of the Russian War Office will give me details after the war. . . .

MY FIRST ENGLISH VICTIM
(17TH SEPTEMBER, 1915)

We were all at the butts trying our machine guns. On the previous day we had received our new aeroplanes and the next morning Boelcke was to fly with us. We were all beginners. None of us had had a success so far. Consequently everything that Boelcke told us was to us gospel truth. Every day, during the last few days, he had, as he said, shot one or two Englishmen for breakfast.

The next morning, the seventeenth of September, was a gloriously fine day. It was therefore only to be expected that the English would be very active. Before we started Boelcke repeated to us his instructions and for the first time we flew as a squadron commanded by the great man whom we followed blindly.

We had just arrived at the Front when we recognized a hostile flying squadron that was proceeding in the direction of Cambrai. Boelcke was of course the first to see it, for he saw a great deal more than ordinary mortals. Soon we understood the position and every one of us strove to follow Boelcke closely. It was clear to all of us that we should pass our first examination under the eyes of our beloved leader.

Slowly we approached the hostile squadron. It could not escape us. We had intercepted it, for we were between the Front and our opponents. If they wished to go back they had to pass us. We counted the hostile machines. They were seven in number. We were only five. All the Englishmen flew large bomb-carrying two-seaters. In a few seconds the dance would begin.

Boelcke had come very near the first English machine but he did not yet shoot. I followed. Close to me were my comrades. The Englishman nearest to me was traveling in a large boat painted with dark colors. I did not reflect very long but took my aim and shot. He also fired and so did I, and both of us missed our aim. A struggle began and the great point for me was to get to the rear of the fellow because I could only shoot forward with my gun. He was differently placed for his machine gun was movable. It could fire in all directions.

Apparently he was no beginner, for he knew exactly that his last hour had arrived at the moment when I got at the back of him. At that time I had not yet the conviction "He must fall!" which I have now on such occasions, but on the contrary, I was curious to see whether he would fall. There is a great difference between the two feelings. When one has shot down one's first, second or third opponent, then one begins to find out how the trick is done.

My Englishman twisted and turned, going criss-cross. I did not think for a moment that the hostile squadron contained other Englishmen who conceivably might come to the aid of their comrade. I was animated by a single thought: "The man in front of me must come down, whatever happens." At last a favorable moment arrived. My opponent had apparently lost sight of me. Instead of twisting and turning he flew straight along. In a fraction of a second I was at his back with my excellent machine. I gave a

short series of shots with my machine gun. I had gone so close
that I was afraid I might dash into the Englishman. Suddenly, I
nearly yelled with joy for the propeller of the enemy machine had
stopped turning. I had shot his engine to pieces; the enemy was
compelled to land, for it was impossible for him to reach his own
lines. The English machine was curiously swinging to and fro.
Probably something had happened to the pilot. The observer was
no longer visible. His machine gun was apparently deserted. Obviously I had hit the observer and he had fallen from his seat.

The Englishman landed close to the flying ground of one of our
squadrons. I was so excited that I landed also and my eagerness
was so great that I nearly smashed up my machine. The English
flying machine and my own stood close together. I rushed to the
English machine and saw that a lot of soldiers were running towards my enemy. When I arrived I discovered that my assumption
had been correct. I had shot the engine to pieces and both the
pilot and observer were severely wounded. The observer died at
once and the pilot while being transported to the nearest dressing
station. I honored the fallen enemy by placing a stone on his
beautiful grave.

When I came home Boelcke and my other comrades were already at breakfast. They were surprised that I had not turned up.
I reported proudly that I had shot down an Englishman. All were
full of joy for I was not the only victor. As usual, Boelcke had shot
down an opponent for breakfast and every one of the other men
also had downed an enemy for the first time.

I would mention that since that time no English squadron ven-
tured as far as Cambrai as long as Boelcke's squadron was
there. . . .

English and French Flying. (*February*, 1917)

I was trying to compete with Boelcke's squadron. Every evening we compared our bags. However, Boelcke's pupils are smart
rascals. I cannot get ahead of them. The utmost one can do is to
draw level with them. The Boelcke section has an advantage over
my squadron of one hundred aeroplanes downed. I must not allow
them to retain it. Everything depends on whether we have for
opponents those French tricksters or those daring rascals, the English. I prefer the English. Frequently their daring can only be described as stupidity. In their eyes it may be pluck and daring.

The great thing in air fighting is that the decisive factor does
not lie in trick flying but solely in the personal ability and energy
of the aviator. A flying man may be able to loop and do all the

stunts imaginable and yet he may not succeed in shooting down a single enemy. In my opinion the aggressive spirit is everything and that spirit is very strong in us Germans. Hence we shall always retain the domination of the air.

The French have a different character. They like to put traps and to attack their opponents unawares. That cannot easily be done in the air. Only a beginner can be caught and one cannot set traps because an aeroplane cannot hide itself. The invisible aeroplane has not yet been discovered. Sometimes, however, the Gaelic blood asserts itself. The Frenchmen will then attack. But the French attacking spirit is like bottled lemonade. It lacks tenacity.

The Englishmen, on the other hand, one notices that they are of Germanic blood. Sportsmen easily take to flying, and Englishmen see in flying nothing but a sport. They take a perfect delight in looping the loop, flying on their back, and indulging in other stunts for the benefit of our soldiers in the trenches. All these tricks may impress people who attend a Sports Meeting, but the public at the battle-front is not as appreciative of these things. It demands higher qualifications than trick flying. Therefore, the blood of English pilots will have to flow in streams.

PART II

The War's Misery:
Attitudes Toward the War

VII. Trench Life

IN THE trenches of the western front millions of ordinary men—British, Germans, French, and Belgians—endured nearly four years of perhaps the most sustained misery in recorded history. If the war's occurrence could be viewed as evidence of the limitation of reason, then the ability of that hapless creature Everyman to withstand its protracted horrors and discomforts without going stark mad confirms Dostoevski's observation that "Man is an animal that can become accustomed to anything."

One of the most acidly realistic accounts of the daily routine in the trenches of Flanders appears in *Goodbye to All That,* the autobiography of Robert Graves, the poet, novelist, and scholar. Born in Wimbledon on July 26, 1895, Graves was a headstrong youth who disdained formal study although his omnivorous reading enabled him to attend the public school, Charterhouse, and to win an "exhibition" to Saint John's College, Oxford, which he chose not to accept, preferring to enlist in the Royal Welch Fusiliers. Wounded in 1918, he was sent to recuperate in Oxford where he led a Bohemian life, but eventually received a university degree and became a prolific writer. He published verse, erudite historical novels (*I, Claudius, Claudius the God, Count Belisarius*), critical works and satires. In 1961 he left his home on the island of Majorca to serve for a year as a professor of poetry at Oxford.

In our excerpt from *Goodbye to All That,* Graves vividly describes his arrival at the front at Auchy. The relative coziness of the officers' dugouts was in contrast to the dismal holes in which the enlisted men slept. But all alike shared the constant dangers. All hoped for the "lucky wound"—best obtained on night patrol in no man's land—which might secure the fortunate casualty's release from more fighting. Nonetheless, Graves was proud of the fighting efficiency of his outfit, the Second Royal Welch. The prejudices and antipathies of the combat troops bore out Napoleon's dictum, "All coalition armies are enemies at heart." No love was lost by the British upon their French and Belgian allies, and vice versa. The troops tended to discount propaganda stories; they respected the enemy's fighting qualities; they despised religion in general and chaplains in particular (except for Roman Catholic chaplains who were enjoined to be at the front to give extreme unction to the dying); and they regarded patriotism as a sentiment fit only for civilians. The front was a vast underworld with a philosophy at variance with civilian attitudes.

The spirit of stoical detachment and granite-like endurance in Grave's writing is absent from the war poetry of an equally heroic author who also served in the British army, Siegfried Sassoon. Born September 8, 1886, to a wealthy London family of Sephardic extraction, Sassoon grew up in an atmosphere of maternal affection, affluence, and love of the arts. This precocious youth volunteered as a second lieutenant in France and won the Military Cross for feats of courage which bordered suspiciously upon the suicidal, earning for him the sobriquet "Mad Jack." In Sassoon's war poems there is a despairing note of dutiful resignation to the endless nightmare of trench warfare which is often punctuated by savage outbursts against the fatuous incomprehension of the civilian "patriots" who follow the war vicariously from the remote safety of their homes. When Sassoon was gravely wounded by a sniper's bullet in 1917 and was sent back to England for recovery, he publicized his revulsion against the war by refusing to perform further military service and by dramatically throwing his Military Cross into the Mersey River. The British army discreetly sent him to a sanatorium, and then to the relatively quiet sector of Palestine. But true to his nature of heroic extremes, Sassoon arranged to be sent back to France, where he was wounded again. After the war he wrote for newspapers, campaigned for the Labor Party, and published his *Collected War Poems* and a trilogy, *The Memoirs of George Sherston*. He embraced Roman Catholicism several years before his death on September 1, 1967.

Lyrical despair and compassionate irony are the distinctive characteristics of the war poems of Wilfred Owen. In unforgettable vignettes of only a few lines of verse, Owen was able to crystallize all the terror, pain, misery, and numbing sorrow of warfare. Unlike Graves and Sassoon, Owen had few advantages of birth, wealth, or formal education. Born March 18, 1893, to an impecunious but literate Victorian family of Oswestry, Shropshire, Owen had to make the most of his bleak prospects of attending Birkenhead Institute and Shrewsbury Technical School. But encouraged by his parents' example, he read diligently and selectively. He learned at first hand how abrasive rural poverty could be when he served as a lay assistant to the vicar of Dunsden, Oxfordshire. When the war broke out Owen was working as a private tutor to the sons of a Catholic family in Bordeaux. Wilfred Owen was late in being seized with war fever, returning to England only in September, 1915. A year later he was posted to France, where he served with the Lancashire Fusiliers, winning the Military Cross for bravery. He was released from the inferno of the trenches on November 4, 1918, a scant week before the Armistice, when he was killed in action trying to get his men across the Sambre Canal.

It was all too easy for a citizen of one of the Allied nations to regard the kaiser's troops as either supermen or robots. The German war machine that penetrated Belgium and northern France seemed too formidably efficient to have been the product of merely human contrivance. But obviously it was composed of mortals who found the war quite as trying as did the French, British, or Belgians. The dangers, the pain, the discomforts, the disgusting corpse-rats, the haunting proximity of the unburied dead on the battlefield were as gruesomely omnipresent for the Germans as for the Allies. And the Germans appeared even more convinced than the Allies of the "sacredness" of their cause. Nowhere is this more evident than in the *German Students' War Letters*, selected and translated by A. F. Wedd from a larger collection published in German by Professor Philipp Witkop of Freiburg-im-Baden. As Wedd points out in the introduction of his book, "The writers of these letters . . . are all young University men, studying for every variety of profession—philosophy, theology, medicine, law, engineering, and so on. Thoughtful, poetic, romantic, religious youths for the most part, they hate war in itself and shrink from the bloodshed, the dirt, the terror and the privations; yet to not one of them is there ever any question of where their duty lies. The Fatherland has need of its sons, and as a matter of course they must answer the call."

We publish selections from these letters which reflect the German reaction to life and death in the trenches of the western front. The reader will experience even keener poignancy when he realizes that all the authors of some hundreds of letters selected by Wedd were killed in action or died of wounds, most of them in the first two years of the war. Had they endured four years of the war, more of their patriotism would probably have evaporated.

ROBERT GRAVES,
GOODBYE TO ALL THAT

The troop-train consisted of forty-seven coaches and took twenty-five hours to arrive at Béthune, the rail-head. We went via St. Omer. It was about nine o'clock in the evening and we were hungry, cold and dirty. We had expected a short journey and so allowed our baggage to be put in a locked van. We played nap to keep our minds off the discomfort and I lost sixty francs, which was over two pounds at the existing rate of exchange. On the platform at Béthune a little man in filthy khaki, wearing the Welsh cap-badge, came up with a friendly touch of the cap most unlike

Source: From *Goodbye to All That* (London: Jonathan Cape Ltd.), pp. 130–142, 174–177, 232–243. Copyright © 1957 by Robert Graves. Reprinted by permission of Collins-Knowlton-Wing, Inc. and A. P. Watt & Son.

a salute. He was to be our guide to the battalion, which was in the Cambrin trenches about ten kilometers away. He asked us to collect the draft of forty men we had with us and follow him. We marched through the unlit suburbs of the town. We were all intensely excited at the noise and flashes of the guns in the distance. The men of the draft had none of them been out before, except the sergeant in charge. They began singing. Instead of the usual music-hall songs they sang Welsh hymns, each man taking a part. The Welsh always sang when they were a bit frightened and pretending that they were not; it kept them steady. They never sang out of tune.

We marched towards the flashes and could soon see the flare-lights curving over the trenches in the distance. The noise of the guns grew louder and louder. Then we were among the batteries. From behind us on the left of the road a salvo of four shells came suddenly over our heads. The battery was only about two hundred yards away. This broke up *Aberystwyth* in the middle of a verse and set us off our balance for a few seconds; the column of fours tangled up. The shells went hissing away eastward; we could see the red flash and hear the hollow bang where they landed in German territory. The men picked up their step again and began chaffing. A lance-corporal dictated a letter home: 'Dear auntie, this leaves me in the pink. We are at present wading in blood up to our necks. Send me fags and a lifebelt. This war is a booger. Love and kisses.'

The roadside cottages were now showing more and more signs of dilapidation. A German shell came over and then whoo—oo—oooooOOO—bump—CRASH! twenty yards away from the party. We threw ourselves flat on our faces. Presently we heard a curious singing noise in the air, and then flop! flop! little pieces of shell-casing came buzzing down all around. 'They calls them the musical instruments,' said the sergeant. 'Damn them,' said Frank Jones-Bateman, who had a cut in his hand from a jagged little piece, 'the devils have started on me early.' 'Aye, they'll have a lot of fun with you before they're done, sir,' grinned the sergeant. Another shell came over. Every one threw himself down again, but it burst two hundred yards behind us. Only Sergeant Jones had remained on his feet and laughed at us. 'You're wasting yourselves, lads,' he said to the draft. 'Listen by the noise they make coming where they're going to burst.'

At Cambrin village, which was about a mile from the front trenches, we were taken into a ruined house. It had been a chemist's shop and the coloured glass lights were still in the window. It was the billet of the Welsh company quarter-master-sergeants. Here we were issued with gas-respirators and field dressings. This was the first respirator issued in France. It was a gauze-pad filled with chemically-treated cotton waste, to be tied across the mouth and nose. It seems it was useless against German gas. I never put it to the test. A week or two later came the 'smoke-helmet,' a greasy grey-felt bag with a talc window to look through, but no mouthpiece. This also was probably ineffective against gas. The talc was always cracking and there were leaks where it was stitched into the helmet.

These were early days of trench-warfare, the days of the jam-tin bomb and the gas-pipe trench-mortar. It was before Lewis or Stokes guns, steel helmets, telescopic rifle-sights, gas-shells, pill-boxes, tanks, trench-raids, or any of the later improvements of trench-warfare.

After a meal of bread, bacon, rum and bitter stewed tea sickly with sugar, we went up through the broken trees to the east of the village and up a long trench to battalion headquarters. The trench was cut through red clay. I had a torch with me which I kept flashed on the ground. Hundreds of field mice and frogs were in the trench. They had fallen in and had no way out. The light dazzled them and we could not help treading on them. So I put the torch back in my pocket. We had no picture of what the trenches would be like, and were not far off the state of mind in which one young soldier joined us a week or two later. He called out very excitedly to old Burford who was cooking up a bit of stew in a dixie, apart from the others: 'Hi, mate, where's the battle? I want to do my bit.'

The trench was wet and slippery. The guide was giving hoarse directions all the time. 'Hole right.' 'Wire high.' 'Wire low.' 'Deep place here, sir.' 'Wire low.' I had never been told about the field telephone wires. They were fastened by staples to the side of the trench, and when it rained the staples were always falling out and the wire falling down and tripping people up. If it sagged too much one stretched it across the top of the trench to the other side to correct the sag, and then it would catch one's head. The holes were the sump-pits used for draining the trenches. We were now under rifle-fire. I always found rifle-fire more trying than shell-fire. The gunner was usually, I knew, firing not at people but at map-references—cross-roads, likely artillery positions, houses that suggested billets for troops, and so on. Even when an observation

officer in an aeroplane or captive balloon or on a church spire was
directing the gun-fire it seemed unaimed, somehow. But a rifle
bullet even when fired blindly always had the effect of seeming
aimed. And we could hear a shell coming and take some sort of
cover, but the rifle bullet gave no warning. So though we learned
not to duck to a rifle bullet, because once it was heard it must
have missed, it gave us a worse feeling of danger. Rifle bullets in
the open went hissing into the grass without much noise, but
when we were in a trench the bullets, going over the hollow, made
a tremendous crack. Bullets often struck the barbed wire in front
of the trenches, which turned them and sent them spinning in a
head-over-heels motion—ping! rockety-ockety-ockety-ockety into
the woods behind.

Battalion headquarters was a dug-out in the reserve line about
a quarter of a mile from the front companies. The colonel, a
twice-wounded regular, shook hands with us and offered us the
whisky bottle. He said that we were welcome, and hoped that we
would soon grow to like the regiment as much as our own. It was
a cosy dug-out for so early a stage of trench-warfare. (This sector
had only recently been taken over from the French, who knew
how to make themselves comfortable. It had been a territorial
division of men in the forties who had a local armistice with the
Germans opposite; there was no firing and apparently even civilian
traffic through the lines.) There was an ornamental lamp, a clean
cloth, and polished silver on the table. The colonel, adjutant,
doctor, second-in-command, and signalling officer were at dinner.
It was civilized cooking, with fresh meat and vegetables. Pictures
were pasted on the walls, which were well papered; there were
beds with spring mattresses, a gramophone, easy chairs. It was
hard to reconcile this with accounts I had read of troops standing
waist-deep in mud and gnawing a biscuit while shells burst all
around. We were posted to our companies. I went to C Company.
'Captain Dunn is your company commander,' said the adjutant.
'The soundest officer in the battalion. By the way, remind him
that I want that list of D.C.M. recommendations for the last show
sent in at once, but not more than two names, or else they won't
give us any. Four is about the ration for the battalion in a dud
show.'

Our guide took us up to the front line. We passed a group of
men huddled over a brazier. They were wearing waterproof capes,
for it had now started to rain, and cap-comforters, because the
weather was cold. They were little men, daubed with mud, and

they were talking quietly together in Welsh. Although they could see we were officers, they did not jump to their feet and salute. I thought that this was a convention of the trenches, and indeed I knew that it was laid down somewhere in the military textbooks that the courtesy of the salute was to be dispensed with in battle. But I was wrong; it was just slackness. We overtook a fatigue-party struggling up the trench loaded with timber lengths and bundles of sandbags, cursing plaintively as they slipped into sump-holes and entangled their burdens in the telephone wire. Fatigue-parties were always encumbered by their rifles and equipment, which it was a crime ever to have out of reach. When we had squeezed past this party we had to stand aside to let a stretcher-case past. 'Who's the poor bastard, Dai?' the guide asked the leading stretcher-bearer. 'Sergeant Gallagher,' Dai answered. 'He thought he saw a Fritz in No Man's Land near our wire, so the silly b——r takes one of them new issue percussion bombs and shoots it at 'im. Silly b——r aims too low, it hits the top of the parapet and bursts back. Deoul! man, it breaks his silly f——ing jaw and blows a great lump from his silly f——ing face, whatever. Poor silly b——r! Not worth sweating to get him back! He's put paid to, whatever.' The wounded man had a sandbag over his face. He was dead when they got him back to the dressing-station. I was tired out by the time I got to company headquarters. I was carrying a pack-valise like the men, and my belt was hung with all the usual furnishings—revolver, field-glasses, compass, whisky-flask, wire-cutters, periscope, and a lot more. A Christmas-tree that was called. (These were the days in which officers went out to France with swords and had them sharpened by the armourer before sailing. But I had been advised to leave my sword back in the billet where we had tea; I never saw it again or bothered about it.) I was hot and sweaty; my hands were sticky with the clay from the side of the trench. C Company headquarters was a two-roomed timber-built shelter in the side of a trench connecting the front and support lines. Here were tablecloth and lamp again, whisky-bottle and glasses, shelves with books and magazines, a framed picture of General Joffre, a large mirror, and bunks in the next room. I reported to the company commander.

I had expected him to be a middle-aged man with a breastful of medals, with whom I would have to be formal; but Dunn was actually two months younger than myself. He was one of the fellowship of 'only survivors.' Captain Miller of the Black Watch in the same division was another. Miller had only escaped from the Rue du Bois massacre by swimming down a flooded trench. He has carried on his surviving trade ever since. Only survivors have great reputations. Miller used to be pointed at in the streets when the battalion was back in reserve billets. 'See that fellow. That's Jock Miller. Out from the start and hasn't got it yet.' Dunn had not let the war affect his morale at all. He greeted me very easily with: 'Well, what's the news from England? Oh sorry, first I must introduce you. This is Walker—clever chap, comes from Cambridge and fancies himself as an athlete. This is Jenkins, one of those patriotic chaps who chucked up his job to come here. This is Price, who only joined us yesterday, but we like him; he brought some damn good whisky with him. Well, how long is the war going to last and who's winning? We don't know a thing out here. And what's all this talk about war-babies? Price pretends he knows nothing about them.' I told them about the war and asked them about the trenches.

'About trenches,' said Dunn. 'Well, we don't know as much about trenches as the French do and not near as much as Fritz does. We can't expect Fritz to help, but the French might do something. They are greedy; they won't let us have the benefit of their inventions. What wouldn't we give for parachute-lights and their aerial torpedoes! But there's no connection between the two armies except when there's a battle on, and then we generally let each other down.

'When I was out here first, all that we did in the trenches was to paddle about in water and use our rifles. We didn't think of them as places to live in, they were just temporary inconveniences. Now we work all the time we are here, not only for safety but for health. Night and day. First, the fire-steps, then building traverses, improving the communication trenches, and so on; lastly, on our personal comfort—shelters and dug-outs. There was a territorial battalion that used to relieve us. They were hopeless. They used to sit down in the trench and say: "Oh my God, this is the limit." They'd pull out pencil and paper and write home about it. Did no work on the traverses or on fire positions. Consequence—they lost half their men from frost-bite and rheumatism, and one day the Germans broke in and scuppered a lot more of them. They allowed the work we'd done in the trench to go to ruin and left the whole place like a sewage-farm for us to take over again. We were sick as muck. We reported them several times to brigade headquarters, but they never got any better. Slack officers, of course. Well, they got smashed, as I say, and were sent away to the

line-of-communication troops. Now we work with the First South
Wales Borderers. They're all right. Awful chaps those territorial
swine. Usen't to trouble about latrines at all; left food about and
that encouraged rats; never filled a sandbag. I only once saw a
job of work that they did. That was a steel loop-hole they put in.
But they put it facing square to the front and quite unmasked,
so they had two men killed at it—absolute death-trap. About our
chaps. They're all right, but not as right as they ought to be. The
survivors of the show ten days ago are feeling pretty low, and the
big new draft doesn't know anything yet.'

'Listen,' said Walker, 'there's too much firing going on. The
men have got the wind up over something. Waste of ammunition,
and if Fritz knows we're jumpy he'll give us an extra bad time.
I'll go up and stop them.'

Dunn went on. 'These Welshmen are peculiar. They won't
stand being shouted at. They'll do anything if you explain the
reason for it. They will do and die, but they have to know their
reason why. The best way to make them behave is not to give
them too much time to think. Work them off their feet. They are
good workmen. Officers must work too, not only direct the work.
Our time-table is like this. Breakfast at eight o'clock in the morning, clean trenches and inspect rifles, work all morning, lunch at
twelve, work again from one till about six, when the men feed
again. "Stand-to" at dusk for about an hour, work all night,
"stand-to" for an hour before dawn. That's the general pro-
gramme. Then there's sentry duty. The men do two-hour sentry
spells, then work two hours, then sleep two hours. At night sentries are doubled, so our working parties are smaller. We officers
are on duty all day and divide up the night in three-hourly
watches.' He looked at his wrist watch. 'I say,' he said, 'that
carrying-party must have got the R.E. stuff by now. Time we all
got to work. Look here, Graves, you lie down and have a doss on
that bunk. I want you to take the watch before "stand-to." I'll
wake you up and show you round. Where the hell's my revolver?
I don't like to go out without that. Hello, Walker, what was
wrong?'

Walker laughed. 'A chap from the new draft. He had never
fired his musketry course at Cardiff, and to-night he fired ball for
the first time. It seemed to go to his head. He'd had a brother
killed up at Ypres and he said he was going to avenge him. So he
blazed off all his own ammunition at nothing, and two bandoliers
out of the ammunition-box besides. They call him the Human

Maxim now. His foresight's misty with heat. Corporal Parry should have stopped him; but he was just leaning up against the traverse and shrieking with laughter. I gave them both a good cursing. Some other new chaps started blazing away, too. Fritz retaliated with machine-guns and whizz-bangs. No casualties. I don't know why. It's all quiet now. Everybody ready?'

They went out and I rolled up in my blanket and fell asleep. Dunn woke me about one o'clock. 'Your watch,' he said. I jumped out of the bunk with a rustle of straw; my feet were sore and clammy in my boots. I was cold, too. 'Here's the rocket-pistol and a few flares. Not a bad night. It's stopped raining. Put your equipment on over your raincoat or you won't be able to get at your revolver. Got a torch? Good. About this flare business. Don't use the pistol too much. We haven't many flares, and if there's an attack we will want as many as we can get. But use it if you think that there is something doing. Fritz is always sending up flare lights, he's got as many as he wants.'

He showed me round the line. The battalion frontage was about eight hundred yards. Each company held two hundred of these with two platoons in the front line and two platoons in the support line about a hundred yards back. Dunn introduced me to the platoon sergeants, more particularly to Sergeant Eastmond of the platoon to which I was posted. He asked Sergeant Eastmond to give me any information that I wanted, then went back to sleep, telling me to wake him up at once if anything was wrong. I was left in charge of the line. Sergeant Eastmond was busy with a working-party, so I went round by myself. The men of the working-party, who were building up the traverses with sandbags (a traverse, I learned, was a safety-buttress in the trench), looked curiously at me. They were filling sandbags with earth, piling them up bricklayer fashion, with headers and stretchers alternating, then patting them flat with spades. The sentries stood on the fire-step at the corners of the traverses, stamping their feet and blowing on their fingers. Every now and then they peered over the top for a few seconds. Two parties, each of an N.C.O. and two men, were out in the company listening-posts, connected with the front trench by a sap about fifty yards long. The German front line was about three hundred yards beyond them. From berths hollowed in the sides of the trench and curtained with sandbags came the grunt of sleeping men.

I jumped up on the fire-step beside the sentry and cautiously raising my head stared over the parapet. I could see nothing except the wooden pickets supporting our protecting barbed-wire entanglement and a dark patch or two of bushes beyond. The darkness seemed to move and shake about as I looked at it; the bushes started travelling, singly at first, then both together. The pickets were doing the same. I was glad of the sentry beside me; his name, he told me, was Beaumont. 'They're quiet to-night, sir,' he said, 'a relief going on; I think so, surely.' I said: 'It's funny how those bushes seem to move.' 'Aye, they do play queer tricks. Is this your first spell in trenches, sir?' A German flare shot up, broke into bright flame, dropped slowly and went hissing into the grass just behind our trench, showing up the bushes and pickets. Instinctively I moved. 'It's bad to do that, sir,' he said, as a rifle bullet cracked and seemed to pass right between us. 'Keep still, sir, and they can't spot you. Not but what a flare is a bad thing to have fall on you. I've seen them burn a hole in a man.'

I spent the rest of my watch in acquainting myself with the geography of the trench-section, finding how easy it was to get lost among *culs de sac* and disused alleys. Twice I overshot the company frontage and wandered among the Munsters on the left. Once I tripped and fell with a splash into deep mud. At last my watch was ended with the first signs of dawn. I passed the word along the line for the company to stand-to arms. The N.C.O.'s whispered hoarsely into the dug-outs: 'Stand-to, stand-to,' and out the men tumbled with their rifles in their hands. As I went towards company headquarters to wake the officers I saw a man lying on his face in a machine-gun shelter. I stopped and said: 'Stand-to, there.' I flashed my torch on him and saw his foot was bare. The machine-gunner beside him said: 'No good talking to him, sir.' I asked: 'What's wrong? What's he taken his boot and sock off for?' I was ready for anything odd in the trenches. 'Look for yourself, sir,' he said. I shook the man by the arm and noticed suddenly that the back of his head was blown out. The first corpse that I saw in France was this suicide. He had taken off his boot and sock to pull the trigger of his rifle with his toe; the muzzle was in his mouth. 'Why did he do it?' I said. 'He was in the last push, sir, and that sent him a bit queer, and on top of that he got bad news from Limerick about his girl and another chap.' He was not a Welshman, but belonged to the Munsters; their machine-guns were at the extreme left of our company. The suicide had already been reported and two Irish officers came up. 'We've had two or three of these lately,' one of them told me. Then he said to the other: 'While I remember, Callaghan, don't forget to write to his next-of-kin. Usual sort of letter, cheer them up, tell them he died a soldier's death, anything you like. I'm not going to report it as suicide.' . . .

. . . I had worked it out like this. The best way of lasting the war out was to get wounded. The best time to get wounded was at night and in the open, because a wound in a vital spot was less likely. Fire was more or less unaimed at night and the whole body was exposed. It was also convenient to be wounded when there was no rush on the dressing-station services, and when the back areas were not being heavily shelled. It was most convenient to be wounded, therefore, on a night patrol in a quiet sector. You could usually manage to crawl into a shell-hole until somebody came to the rescue. Still, patrolling had its peculiar risks. If you were wounded and a German patrol got you, they were as likely as not to cut your throat. The bowie-knife was a favourite German patrol weapon; it was silent. (At this time the British inclined more to the 'cosh,' a loaded stick.) The most important information that a patrol could bring back was to what regiment and division the troops opposite belonged. So if a wounded man was found and it was impossible to get him back without danger to oneself, the thing to be done was to strip him of his badges. To do that quickly and silently it might be necessary first to cut his throat or beat in his skull.

Sir P. Mostyn, a lieutenant who was often out patrolling at Laventie, had a feud on with a German patrol on the left of the battalion frontage. (Our patrols usually consisted of an officer and one or, at the most, two men. German patrols were usually six or seven men under an N.C.O. German officers left as much as they decently could to their N.C.O.'s. They did not, as one of our sergeant-majors put it, believe in 'keeping a dog and barking themselves.') One night Mostyn caught sight of his opponents; he had raised himself on one knee to throw a percussion bomb at them when they fired and wounded him in the arm, which immediately went numb. He caught the bomb before it hit the ground and threw it with his left hand, and in the confusion that followed managed to return to the trench.

Like every one else I had a carefully worked out formula for taking risks. We would all take any risk, even the certainty of death, to save life or to maintain an important position. To take life we would run, say, a one-in-five risk, particularly if there was some wider object than merely reducing the enemy's man-power;

for instance, picking off a well-known sniper, or getting fire ascendancy in trenches where the lines were dangerously close. I only once refrained from shooting a German I saw, and that was at Cuinchy about three weeks after this. When sniping from a knoll in the support line where we had a concealed loop-hole I saw a German, about seven hundred yards away, through my telescopic sights. He was having a bath in the German third line. I somehow did not like the idea of shooting a naked man, so I handed the rifle to the sergeant who was with me and said: 'Here, take this. You're a better shot than me.' He got him, he said; but I had not stayed to watch.

About saving the lives of enemy wounded there was disagreement; the convention varied with the division. Some divisions, like the Canadians and a division of Lowland territorials, who had, they claimed, atrocities to avenge, would not only take no risks to rescue enemy wounded, but would go out of their way to finish them off. The Royal Welch Fusiliers were gentlemanly: perhaps a one-in-twenty risk to get a wounded German to safety would be considered justifiable. An important factor in taking risks was our own physical condition. When exhausted and wanting to get quickly from one point in the trenches to another without collapse, and if the enemy were not nearer than four or five hundred yards, we would sometimes take a short cut over the top. In a hurry we would take a one-in-two-hundred risk, when dead tired a one-in-fifty risk. In some battalions where the *morale* was not high, one-in-fifty risks were often taken in mere laziness or despair. The Munsters in the First Division were said by the Welsh to 'waste men wicked' by not keeping properly under cover when in the reserve lines. In the Royal Welch there was no wastage of this sort. At no time in the war did any of us allow ourselves to believe that hostilities could possibly continue more than nine months or a year more, so it seemed almost worth while taking care; there even seemed a chance of lasting until the end absolutely unhurt.

The Second Royal Welch, unlike the Second Welsh, believed themselves better trench fighters than the Germans. With the Second Welsh it was not cowardice but modesty. With the Second Royal Welch it was not vainglory but courage: as soon as they arrived in a new sector they insisted on getting fire ascendancy. Having found out from the troops they relieved all possible information as to enemy snipers, machine-guns, and patrols, they set themselves to deal with them one by one. They began with machine-guns firing at night. As soon as one started traversing down a trench the whole platoon farthest removed from its fire would open five rounds rapid at it. The machine-gun would usually stop suddenly but start again after a minute or two. Again five rounds rapid. Then it usually gave up.

The Welsh seldom answered a machine-gun. If they did, it was not with local organized fire, beginning and ending in unison, but in ragged confused protest all along the line. There was almost no firing at night in the Royal Welch, except organized fire at a machine-gun or a persistent enemy sentry, or fire at a patrol close enough to be distinguished as a German one. With all other battalions I met in France there was random popping off all the time; the sentries wanted to show their spite against the war. Flares were rarely used in the Royal Welch; most often as signals to our patrols that it was time to come back.

As soon as enemy machine-guns had been discouraged, our patrols would go out with bombs to claim possession of No Man's Land. At dawn next morning came the struggle for sniping ascendancy. The Germans, we were told, had special regimental snipers, trained in camouflaging themselves. I saw one killed once at Cuinchy who had been firing all day from a shell-hole between the lines. He had a sort of cape over his shoulders of imitation grass, his face was painted green and brown, and his rifle was also green fringed. A number of empty cartridges were found by him, and his cap with the special oak-leaf badge. Few battalions attempted to get control of the sniping situation. The Germans had the advantage of having many times more telescopic sights than we did, and steel loopholes that our bullets could not pierce. Also a system by which the snipers were kept for months in the same sector until they knew all the loopholes and shallow places in our trenches, and the tracks that our ration-parties used above-ground by night. . . .

In the instructors' mess the chief subjects of conversation besides local and technical talk were *morale*, the reliability of various divisions in battle, the value of different training methods, and war-morality, with particular reference to atrocities. We talked more freely there than would have been possible either in England or in the trenches. We decided that about a third of the troops in the British Expeditionary Force were dependable on all occasions; these were the divisions that were always called on for the most important tasks. About a third were variable, that is, where a division contained one or two bad battalions, but could be more or less trusted. The remainder were more or less untrustworthy; being put in positions of comparative safety they had about a quarter of the casualties that the best divisions had. It was a matter of pride to belong to one of the recognized best divisions—the Seventh, the Twenty-ninth, Guards', First Canadian, for instance. They were not pampered when in reserve as the German storm-troops were, but promotion, leave, and the chance of a wound came quicker in them. The mess agreed that the most dependable British troops were the Midland county regiments, industrial Yorkshire and Lancashire troops, and the Londoners. The Ulster-man, Lowland Scots and Northern English were pretty good. The Catholic Irish and the Highland Scots were not considered so good—they took unnecessary risks in trenches and had unneces-sary casualties, and in battle, through they usually made their objective, they too often lost it in the counter-attack; without of-ficers they were no good. English southern county regiments varied from good to very bad. All overseas troops were good. The depend-ability of divisions also varied with their seniority in date of pro-motion. The latest formed regular divisions and the second-line territorial divisions, whatever their recruiting area, were usually inferior. Their senior officers and warrant-officers were not good enough.

We once discussed which were the cleanest troops in trenches, taken in nationalities. We agreed on a list like this, in descending order: English and German Protestants; Northern Irish, Welsh and Canadians; Irish and German Catholics; Scottish; Moham-medan Indians; Algerians; Portuguese; Belgians; French. The Bel-gians and French were put there for spite; they were not really dirtier than the Algerians or Portuguese.

Atrocities. Propaganda reports of atrocities were, we agreed, ridiculous. Atrocities against civilians were surely few. We remem-bered that while the Germans were in a position to commit atroc-ities against enemy civilians, Germany itself, except for the early Russian cavalry raid, had never had the enemy on her soil. We no longer believed accounts of unjustified German atrocities in Bel-gium; knowing the Belgians now at first-hand. By atrocities we meant, specifically, rape, mutilation and torture, not summary shootings of suspected spies, harbourers of spies, *francs-tireurs*, or disobedient local officials. If the atrocity list was to include the accidental-on-purpose bombing or machine-gunning of civilians from the air, the Allies were now committing as many atrocities as the Germans. French and Belgian civilians had often tried to win our sympathy and presents by exhibiting mutilations of children—stumps of hands and feet, for instance—representing them as deliberate, fiendish atrocities when they were merely the result of shell-fire, British or French shell-fire as likely as not. We did not believe that rape was any more common on the German side of the line than on the Allied side. It was unnecessary. Of course, a bully-beef diet, fear of death, and absence of wives made ample provision of women necessary in the occupied areas. No doubt the German army authorities provided brothels in the principal French towns behind the line, as did the French on the Allied side. But the voluntary system would suffice. We did not believe stories of forcible enlistment of women.

As for atrocities against soldiers. The difficulty was to say where to draw the line. For instance, the British soldier at first regarded as atrocious the use of bowie-knives by German patrols. After a time he learned to use them himself; they were cleaner killing weapons than revolvers or bombs. The Germans regarded as atrocious the British Mark VII rifle bullet, which was more apt to turn on striking than the German bullet. For true atrocities, that is, personal rather than military violations of the code of war, there were few opportunities. The most obvious opportunity was in the interval between surrender of prisoners and their arrival (or non-arrival) at headquarters. And it was an opportunity of which advantage was only too often taken. Nearly every instructor in the mess knew of specific cases when prisoners had been murdered on the way back. The commonest motives were, it seems, revenge for the death of friends or relations, jealousy of the prisoner's pleasant trip to a comfortable prison camp in England, military enthusiasm, fear of being suddenly overpowered by the prisoners or, more simply, not wanting to be bothered with the escorting job. In any of these cases the conductors would report on arrival at headquarters that a German shell had killed the prisoners; no questions would be asked. We had every reason to believe that the same thing happened on the German side, where prisoners, as useless mouths to feed in a country already on short rations, were even less welcome. We had none of us heard of prisoners being more than threatened at headquarters to get military information from them; the sort of information that trench-prisoners could give was not of sufficient importance to make torture worth while; in any case it was found that when treated kindly prisoners were anxious, in gratitude, to tell as much as they knew.

The troops that had the worst reputation for acts of violence against prisoners were the Canadians (and later the Australians). With the Canadians the motive was said to be revenge for a Canadian found crucified with bayonets through his hands and feet in a German trench; this atrocity was never substantiated, nor did we believe the story freely circulated that the Canadians crucified a German officer in revenge shortly afterwards. (Of the Australians the only thing to be said was that they were only two generations removed from the days of Ralph Rashleigh and Marcus Clarke.) How far this reputation for atrocities was deserved, and how far it was due to the overseas habit of bragging and leg-pulling, we could not decide. We only knew that to have committed atrocities against prisoners was, among the overseas men, and even among some British troops, a boast, not a confession.

I heard two first-hand accounts later in the war.

A Canadian-Scot: 'I was sent back with three bloody prisoners, you see, and one was limping and groaning, so I had to keep on kicking the sod down the trench. He was an officer. It was getting dark and I was getting fed up, so I thought: "I'll have a bit of a game." I had them covered with the officer's revolver and I made 'em open their pockets. Then I dropped a Mills' bomb in each, with the pin out, and ducked behind a traverse. Bang, bang, bang! No more bloody prisoners. No good Fritzes but dead 'uns.'

An Australian: 'Well, the biggest lark I had was at Morlancourt when we took it the first time. There were a lot of Jerries in a cellar and I said to 'em: "Come out, you Camarades." So out they came, a dozen of 'em, with their hands up. "Turn out your pockets," I told 'em. They turned 'em out. Watches and gold and stuff, all dinkum. Then I said: "Now back into your cellar, you sons of bitches." For I couldn't be bothered with 'em. When they were all down I threw half a dozen Mills' bombs in after 'em. I'd got the stuff all right, and we weren't taking prisoners that day.'

The only first-hand account I heard of large-scale atrocities was from an old woman at Cardonette on the Somme, with whom I was billeted in July 1916. It was at Cardonette that a battalion of French Turcos overtook the rear guard of a German division retreating from the Marne in September 1914. The Turcos surprised the dead-weary Germans while they were still marching in column. The old woman went, with gestures, through a pantomime of slaughter, ending: 'Et enfin, ces animaux leur ont arraché les oreilles et les ont mis à la poche.' The presence of coloured troops in Europe was, from the German point of view, we knew, one of the chief Allied atrocities. We sympathized. Recently, at Flixé-

court, one of the instructors told us, the cook of a corps head-
quarter-mess used to be visited at the château every morning by a
Turco; he was orderly to a French liaison officer. The Turco used
to say: 'Tommy, give Johnny pozzy,' and a tin of plum and apple
jam used to be given him. One afternoon the corps was due to
shift, so that morning the cook said to the Turco, giving him his
farewell tin: 'Oh, la, la, Johnny, napoo pozzy to-morrow.' The
Turco would not believe it. 'Yes, Tommy, mate,' he said, 'pozzy
for Johnny to-morrow, to-morrow, to-morrow.' To get rid of him
the cook said: 'Fetch me the head of a Fritz, Johnny, to-night. I'll
ask the general to give you pozzy to-morrow, to-morrow, to-
morrow.' 'All right, mate,' said the Turco, 'me get Fritz head to-
night, general give me pozzy to-morrow.' That evening the mess
cook of the new corps that had taken over the château was surprised to find a Turco asking for him and swinging a bloody head
in a sandbag. 'Here's Fritz head, mate,' said the Turco, 'general
give me pozzy to-morrow, to-morrow, to-morrow.' As Flixécourt
was twenty miles or more behind the line . . . He did not need to
end the story, but swore it was true, because he had seen the head.

We discussed the continuity of regimental *morale*. A captain in
a line battalion of one of the Surrey regiments said: 'It all depends
on the reserve battalion at home.' He had had a year's service when
the war broke out; the battalion, which had been good, had never
recovered from the first battle of Ypres. He said: 'What's wrong
with us is that we have a rotten depot. The drafts are bad and so
we get a constant re-infection.' He told me one night in our sleeping hut: 'In both the last two attacks that we made I had to shoot
a man of my company to get the rest out of the trench. It was so
bloody awful that I couldn't stand it. It's the reason why I applied
to be sent down here.' This was not the usual loose talk that one
heard at the base. He was a good fellow and he was speaking the
truth. I was sorrier for Phillips—that was not his name—than for
any other man I met in France. He deserved a better regiment.
There was never any trouble with the Royal Welch like that. The
boast of every good battalion in France was that it had never lost
a trench; both our battalions made it. This boast had to be understood broadly; it meant never having been forced out of a trench
by an enemy attack without recapturing it before the action ended.
Capturing a German trench and being unable to hold it for lack
of reinforcements did not count, nor did retirement from a trench
by order or when the battalion of the left or right had broken and
left a flank in the air. And in the final stages of the war trenches

could be honourably abandoned as being entirely obliterated by bombardment, or because not really trenches at all, but a line of selected shell-craters.

We all agreed on the value of arms-drill as a factor in *morale*. 'Arms-drill as it should be done,' someone said, 'is beautiful, especially when the company feels itself as a single being and each movement is not a movement of every man together, but a single movement of one large creature.' I used to have big bunches of Canadians to drill four or five hundred at a time. Spokesmen came forward once and asked what sense there was in sloping and ordering arms and fixing and unfixing bayonets. They said they had come to France to fight and not to guard Buckingham Palace. I told them that in every division of the four in which I had served there had been three different kinds of troops. Those that had guts but were no good at drill; those that were good at drill but had no guts; and those that had guts and were good at drill. These last fellows were, for some reason or other, much the best men in a show. I didn't know why and I didn't care. I told them that when they were better at fighting than the Guards' Division they could perhaps afford to neglect their arms-drill.

We often theorized in the mess about drill. We knew that the best drill never came from being bawled at by a sergeant-major, that there must be perfect respect between the man who gives the order and the men that carry it through. The test of drill came, I said, when the officer gave an incorrect word of command. If the company could carry through the order intended without hesitation, or, suppose the order happened to be impossible, could stand absolutely still or continue marching without any disorder in the ranks, that was good drill. The corporate spirit that came from drilling together was regarded by some instructors as leading to loss of initiative in the men drilled. Others denied this and said it acted just the other way round. 'Suppose there is a section of men with rifles, and they are isolated from the rest of the company and have no N.C.O. in charge and meet a machine-gun. Under the stress of danger that section will have that all-one-body feeling of drill and will obey an imaginary word of command. There will be no communication between its members, but there will be a drill movement. Two men will quite naturally open fire on the machine-gun while the remainder will work round, part on the left flank and part on the right, and the final rush will be simultaneous. Leadership is supposed to be the perfection for which drill has been instituted. That is wrong. Leadership is only the first stage.

Perfection of drill is communal action. Drill may seem to be antiquated parade-ground stuff, but it is the foundation of tactics and musketry. It was parade-ground musketry that won all the battles in our regimental histories; this war will be won by parade-ground tactics. The simple drill tactics of small units fighting in limited spaces—fighting in noise and confusion so great that leadership is quite impossible.' In spite of variance on this point we all agreed that regimental pride was the greatest moral force that kept a battalion going as an effective fighting unit, contrasting it particularly with patriotism and religion.

Patriotism. There was no patriotism in the trenches. It was too remote a sentiment, and rejected as fit only for civilians. A new arrival who talked patriotism would soon be told to cut it out. As Blighty, Great Britain was a quiet, easy place to get back to out of the present foreign misery, but as a nation it was nothing. The nation included not only the trench-soldiers themselves and those who had gone home wounded, but the staff, Army Service Corps, lines of communication troops, base units, home-service units, and then civilians down to the detested grades of journalists, profiteers, 'starred' men exempted from enlistment, conscientious objectors, members of the Government. The trench-soldier, with this carefully graded caste-system of honour, did not consider that the German trench-soldier might have exactly the same system himself. He thought of Germany as a nation in arms, a unified nation inspired with the sort of patriotism that he despised himself. He believed most newspaper reports of conditions and sentiments in Germany, though believing little or nothing of what he read about conditions and sentiments in England. His cynicism, in fact, was not confined to his own country. But he never underrated the German as a soldier. Newspaper libels on Fritz's courage and efficiency were resented by all trench-soldiers of experience.

Religion. It was said that not one soldier in a hundred was inspired by religious feeling of even the crudest kind. It would have been difficult to remain religious in the trenches though one had survived the irreligion of the training battalion at home. A regular sergeant at Montagne, a Second Battalion man, had recently told me that he did not hold with religion in time of war. He said that the niggers (meaning the Indians) were right in officially relaxing their religious rules when they were fighting. 'And all this damn nonsense, sir—excuse me, sir—that we read in the papers, sir, about how miraculous it is that the wayside crucifixes are always getting shot at but the figure of our Lord Jesus somehow don't get hurt, it fairly makes me sick, sir.' This was to explain why in giving practice fire-orders from the hill-top he had shouted out: 'Seven hundred, half left, bloke on cross, five rounds consecrate, FIRE!' His platoon, even the two men whose letters home always had the same formal beginning: 'Dear Sister in Christ,' or 'Dear Brother in Christ,' blazed away.

The troops, while ready to believe in the Kaiser as a comic personal devil, were aware that the German soldier was, on the whole, more devout than himself in the worship of God. In the instructors' mess we spoke freely of God and Gott as opposed tribal deities. For the regimental chaplains as a body we had no respect. If the regimental chaplains had shown one tenth the courage, endurance, and other human qualities that the regimental doctors showed, we agreed, the British Expeditionary Force might well have started a religious revival. But they had not. The fact is that they were under orders not to get mixed up with the fighting, to stay behind with the transport and not to risk their lives. No soldier could have any respect for a chaplain who obeyed these orders, and yet there was not in our experience one chaplain in fifty who was not glad to obey them. Occasionally on a quiet day in a quiet sector the chaplain would make a daring afternoon visit to the support line and distribute a few cigarettes, and that was all. But he was always in evidence back in rest-billets. Sometimes the colonel would summon him to come up with the rations and bury the day's dead, and he would arrive, speak his lines, and hastily retire. The position was made difficult by the respect that most of the commanding officers had for the cloth, but it was a respect that they soon outwore. The colonel in one battalion I served with got rid of four new chaplains in as many months. Finally he applied for a Roman Catholic chaplain, alleging a change of faith in the men under his command. For, as I should have said before, the Roman Catholics were not only permitted in posts of danger, but definitely enjoined to be wherever fighting was so that they could give extreme unction to the dying. And we had never heard of an R.C. chaplain who was unwilling to do all that was expected of him and more. It was recalled that Father Gleeson of the Munsters, when all the officers were put out of action at the first battle of Ypres, stripped off his black badges and, taking command of the survivors, held the line.

Anglican chaplains were remarkably out of touch with their troops. I told how the Second Battalion chaplain just before the

Loos fighting had preached a violent sermon on the battle against
sin, and how one old soldier behind me had grumbled: 'Christ,
as if one bloody push wasn't enough to worry about at a time.'
The Catholic padre, on the other hand, had given his men his
blessing and told them that if they died fighting for the good cause
they would go straight to Heaven, or at any rate would be excused
a great many years in Purgatory. Someone told us of the chaplain of his battalion when he was in Mesopotamia, how on the
eve of a big battle he had preached a sermon on the commutation
of tithes. This was much more sensible than the battle against sin,
he said; it was quite up in the air, and took the men's minds off
the fighting. . . .

SIEGFRIED SASSOON,
COLLECTED POEMS, 1908–1956

At Carnoy
Down in the hollow there's the whole Brigade
Camped in four groups: through twilight falling slow
I hear a sound of mouth-organs, ill-played,
And murmur of voices, gruff, confused, and low.
Crouched among thistle-tufts I've watched the glow
Of a blurred orange sunset flare and fade;
And I'm content. To-morrow we must go
To take some cursèd Wood . . . O world God made!

July 3rd, 1916.

Stand-to: Good Friday Morning
I'd been on duty from two till four.
I went and stared at the dug-out door.
Down in the frowst I heard them snore.
'Stand to!' Somebody grunted and swore.
  Dawn was misty; the skies were still;
  Larks were singing, discordant, shrill;
  They seemed happy; but *I* felt ill.
Deep in water I splashed my way
Up the trench to our bogged front line.

Source: From *Collected Poems, 1908–1956* (London: Faber &
  Faber Ltd.), pp. 22, 24, 68–71, 90, 91. Reprinted by permission
  of George Sassoon.

Rain had fallen the whole damned night.
O Jesus, send me a wound to-day,
And I'll believe in Your bread and wine,
And get my bloody old sins washed white!

Counter-Attack

We'd gained our first objective hours before
While dawn broke like a face with blinking eyes,
Pallid, unshaved and thirsty, blind with smoke.
Things seemed all right at first. We held their line,
With bombers posted, Lewis guns well placed,
And clink of shovels deepening the shallow trench.
   The place was rotten with dead; green clumsy legs
   High-booted, sprawled and grovelled along the saps
   And trunks, face downward, in the sucking mud,
   Wallowed like trodden sand-bags loosely filled;
   And naked sodden buttocks, mats of hair,
   Bulged, clotted heads slept in the plastering slime.
   And then the rain began,—the jolly old rain!

A yawning soldier knelt against the bank,
Staring across the morning blear with fog;
He wondered when the Allemands would get busy;
And then, of course, they started with five-nines
Traversing, sure as fate, and never a dud.
Mute in the clamour of shells he watched them burst
Spouting dark earth and wire with gusts from hell,
While posturing giants dissolved in drifts of smoke.
He crouched and flinched, dizzy with galloping fear,
Sick for escape,—loathing the strangled horror
And butchered, frantic gestures of the dead.

An officer came blundering down the trench:
'Stand-to and man the fire-step!' On he went . . .
Gasping and bawling, 'Fire-step . . . counter-attack!'
   Then the haze lifted. Bombing on the right
   Down the old sap: machine-guns on the left;
   And stumbling figures looming out in front.
   'O Christ, they're coming at us!' Bullets spat,
And he remembered his rifle . . . rapid fire . . .
And started blazing wildly . . . then a bang

Crumpled and spun him sideways, knocked him out
To grunt and wriggle: none heeded him; he choked
And fought the flapping veils of smothering gloom,
Lost in a blurred confusion of yells and groans . . .
Down, and down, and down, he sank and drowned,
Bleeding to death. The counter-attack had failed.

The Rear-Guard
(HINDENBURG LINE, APRIL 1917)

Groping along the tunnel, step by step,
He winked his prying torch with patching glare
From side to side, and sniffed the unwholesome air.

Tins, boxes, bottles, shapes too vague to know;
A mirror smashed, the mattress from a bed;
And he, exploring fifty feet below
The rosy gloom of battle overhead.

Tripping, he grabbed the wall; saw some one lie
Humped at his feet, half-hidden by a rug,
And stooped to give the sleeper's arm a tug.
'I'm looking for headquarters.' No reply.
'God blast your neck!' (For days he'd had no sleep,)
'Get up and guide me through this stinking place.'
Savage, he kicked a soft, unanswering heap,
And flashed his beam across the livid face
Terribly glaring up, whose eyes yet wore
Agony dying hard ten days before;
And fists of fingers clutched a blackening wound.

Alone he staggered on until he found
Dawn's ghost that filtered down a shafted stair ·
To the dazed, muttering creatures underground
Who hear the boom of shells in muffled sound.
At last, with sweat of horror in his hair,
He climbed through darkness to the twilight air,
Unloading hell behind him step by step.

Wirers

'Pass it along, the wiring party's going out'—
And yawning sentries mumble, 'Wirers going out.'

Unravelling; twisting; hammering stakes with muffled
    thud,
They toil with stealthy haste and anger in their blood.

The Boche sends up a flare. Black forms stand rigid there,
Stock-still like posts; then darkness, and the clumsy
    ghosts
Stride hither and thither, whispering, tripped by
    clutching snare
Of snags and tangles.
                      Ghastly dawn with vaporous coasts
Gleams desolate along the sky, night's misery ended.
Young Hughes was badly hit; I heard him carried away,
Moaning at every lurch; no doubt he'll die to-day.
But *we* can say the front-line wire's been safely mended.

Attack

At dawn the ridge emerges massed and dun
In the wild purple of the glow'ring sun,
Smouldering through spouts of drifting smoke that
    shroud
The menacing scarred slope; and,
    one by one,
Tanks creep and topple forward to the wire.
The barrage roars and lifts. Then, clumsily bowed
With bombs and guns and shovels and battle-gear,
Men jostle and climb to meet the bristling fire.
Lines of grey, muttering faces, masked with fear,
They leave their trenches, going over the top,
While time ticks blank and busy on their wrists,
And hope, with furtive eyes and grappling fists,
Flounders in mud. O Jesus, make it stop!

Survivors

No doubt they'll soon get well; the shock and strain
    Have caused their stammering, disconnected talk.
Of course they're 'longing to go out again,'—
    These boys with old, scared faces, learning to walk.
They'll soon forget their haunted nights; their cowed
    Subjection to the ghosts of friends who died,—
Their dreams that drip with murder; and they'll be
    proud

Of glorious war that shatter'd all their pride . . .
Men who went out to battle, grim and glad;
Children, with eyes that hate you, broken and made.

Craiglockart. October, 1917.

Remorse

Lost in the swamp and welter of the pit,
He flounders off the duck-boards; only he knows
Each flash and spouting crash,—each instant lit
When gloom reveals the streaming rain. He goes
Heavily, blindly on. And, while he blunders,
'Could anything be worse than this?'—he wonders,
Remembering how he saw those Germans run,
Screaming for mercy among the stumps of trees:
Green-faced, they dodged and darted: there was one
Livid with terror, clutching at his knees . . .
Our chaps were sticking 'em like pigs . . . 'O hell!'
He thought—'there's things in war one dare not tell
Poor father sitting safe at home, who reads
Of dying heroes and their deathless deeds.'

THE COLLECTED POEMS OF WILFRED OWEN

Dulce Et Decorum Est

Bent double, like old beggars under sacks,
Knocked-kneed, coughing like hags, we cursed through sludge,
Till on the haunting flares we turned our backs
And towards our distant rest began to trudge.
Men marched asleep. Many had lost their boots
But limped on, blood-shod. All went lame; all blind;
Drunk with fatigue; deaf even to the hoots
Of tired, outstripped Five-Nines that dropped behind.

Gas! Gas! Quick, boys!—An ecstasy of fumbling,
Fitting the clumsy helmets just in time;
But someone still was yelling out and stumbling

Source: From *The Collected Poems of Wilfred Owen* (London: Chatto & Windus, Ltd.), pp. 55–61, 74–75, 84–85. Copyright 1945, © 1963 by Chatto & Windus, Ltd. Reprinted by permission of Chatto & Windus and New Directions Publishing Corp.

And flound'ring like a man in fire or lime . . .
Dim, through the misty panes and thick green light,
As under a green sea, I saw him drowning.
In all my dreams, before my helpless sight,
He plunges at me, guttering, choking, drowning.

If in some smothering dreams you too could pace
Behind the wagon that we flung him in,
And watch the white eyes writhing in his face,
His hanging face, like a devil's sick of sin;
If you could hear, at every jolt, the blood
Come gargling from the froth-corrupted lungs,
Obscene as cancer, bitter as the cud
Of vile, incurable sores on innocent tongues,—
My friend, you would not tell with such high zest
To children ardent for some desperate glory,
The old Lie: Dulce et decorum est
Pro patria mori.

Asleep

Under his helmet, up against his pack,
After the many days of work and waking,
Sleep took him by the brow and laid him back.
And in the happy no-time of his sleeping,
Death took him by the heart. There was a quaking
Of the aborted life within him leaping . . .
Then chest and sleepy arms once more fell slack.
And soon the slow, stray blood came creeping
From the intrusive lead, like ants on track.

*   *   *

Whether his deeper sleep lie shaded by the shaking
Of great wings, and the thoughts that hung the stars,
High pillowed on calm pillows of God's making
Above these clouds, these rains, these sleets of lead,
And these winds' scimitars;
—Or whether yet his thin and sodden head
Confuses more and more with the low mould,

His hair being one with the grey grass
And finished fields of autumns that are old . . .
Who knows? Who hopes? Who troubles? Let it pass!
He sleeps. He sleeps less tremulous, less cold
Than we who must awake, and waking, say Alas!

The Letter

With B.E.F. June 10. Dear Wife,
(O blast this pencil. 'Ere, Bill, lend's a knife.)
I'm in the pink at present, dear.
I think the war will end this year.
We don't see much of them square-'eaded 'Uns.
We're out of harm's way, not bad fed.
I'm longing for a taste of your old buns.
(Say, Jimmie, spare's a bite of bread.)
There don't seem much to say just now.
(Yer what? Then don't, yer ruddy cow!
And give us back me cigarette!)
I'll soon be 'ome. You mustn't fret.
My feet's improvin', as I told you of.
We're out in rest now. Never fear.
(VRACH! By crumbs, but that was near.)
Mother might spare you half a sov.
Kiss Nell and Bert. When me and you—
(Eh? What the 'ell! Stand to? Stand to!
Jim, give's a hand with pack on, lad.
Guh! Christ! I'm hit. Take 'old. Aye, bad.
No, damn your iodine. Jim? 'Ere!
Write my old girl, Jim, there's a dear.)

The Sentry

We'd found an old Boche dug-out, and he knew,
And gave us hell, for shell on frantic shell
Hammered on top, but never quite burst through.
Rain, guttering down in waterfalls of slime,
Kept slush waist-high and rising hour by hour,
And choked the steps too thick with clay to climb.
What murk of air remained stank old, and sour
With fumes of whizz-bangs, and the smell of men

Who'd lived there years, and left their curse in the den,
If not their corpses. . . .
　　　　　　　　　　　　There we herded from the blast
Of whizz-bangs, but one found our door at last,—
Buffeting eyes and breath, snuffing the candles,
And thud! flump! thud! down the steep steps came thumping
And sploshing in the flood, deluging muck—
The sentry's body; then, his rifle, handles
Of old Boche bombs, and mud in ruck on ruck.
We dredged him up, for killed, until he whined
"O sir, my eyes—I'm blind—I'm blind, I'm blind!"
Coaxing, I held a flame against his lids
And said if he could see the least blurred light
He was not blind; in time he'd get all right.
"I can't," he sobbed. Eyeballs, huge-bulged like squids',
Watch my dreams still; but I forgot him there
In posting Next for duty, and sending a scout
To beg a stretcher somewhere, and flound'ring about
To other posts under the shrieking air.

　　　　　　　　*　　　　*　　　　*

Those other wretches, how they bled and spewed,
And one who would have drowned himself for good,—
I try not to remember these things now.
Let dread hark back for one word only: how
Half listening to that sentry's moans and jumps,
And the wild chattering of his broken teeth,
Renewed most horribly whenever crumps
Pummelled the roof and slogged the air beneath—
Through the dense din, I say, we heard him shout
"I see your lights!" But ours had long died out.

S.I.W.

　　　I will to the King,
　　　And offer him consolation in his trouble,
　　　For that man there has set his teeth to die,
　　　And being one that hates obedience,
　　　Discipline, and orderliness of life,
　　　I cannot mourn him.

　　　　　　　　　　　　　　W. B. YEATS

I. THE PROLOGUE

Patting good-bye, doubtless they told the lad
He'd always show the Hun a brave man's face;
Father would sooner him dead than in disgrace,—
Was proud to see him going, aye, and glad.
Perhaps his mother whimpered how she'd fret
Until he got a nice safe wound to nurse.
Sister would wish girls too could shoot, charge, curse;
Brothers—would send his favourite cigarette.
Each week, month after month, they wrote the same,
Thinking him sheltered in some Y. M. Hut,
Because he said so, writing on his butt
Where once an hour a bullet missed its aim
And misses teased the hunger of his brain.
His eyes grew old with wincing, and his hand
Reckless with ague. Courage leaked, as sand
From the best sand-bags after years of rain.
But never leave, wound, fever, trench-foot, shock,
Untrapped the wretch. And death seemed still withheld
For torture of lying machinally shelled,
At the pleasure of this world's Powers who'd run amok.

He'd seen men shoot their hands, on night patrol.
Their people never knew. Yet they were vile.
"Death sooner than dishonour, that's the style!"
So Father said.

II. THE ACTION

One dawn, our wire patrol
Carried him. This time, Death had not missed.
We could do nothing but wipe his bleeding cough.
Could it be accident?—Rifles go off . . .
Not sniped? No. (Later they found the English ball.)

III. THE POEM

It was the reasoned crisis of his soul
Against more days of inescapable thrall,
Against infrangibly wired and blind trench wall
Curtained with fire, roofed in with creeping fire,
Slow grazing fire, that would not burn him whole

But kept him for death's promises and scoff,
And life's half-promising, and both their riling.

IV. THE EPILOGUE

With him they buried the muzzle his teeth had kissed,
And truthfully wrote the Mother, "Tim died smiling".

[S.I.W. is an abbreviation for Self-Inflicted Wound.]

Soldier's Dream

I dreamed kind Jesus fouled the big-gun gears;
And caused a permanent stoppage in all bolts;
And buckled with a smile Mausers and Colts;
And rusted every bayonet with His tears.

And there were no more bombs, of ours or Theirs,
Not even an old flint-lock, nor even a pikel.
But God was vexed, and gave all power to Michael;
And when I woke he'd seen to our repairs.

Sonnet
ON SEEING A PIECE OF OUR ARTILLERY
BROUGHT INTO ACTION

Be slowly lifted up, thou long black arm,
Great gun towering towards Heaven, about to curse;
Sway steep against them, and for years rehearse
Huge imprecations like a blasting charm!
Reach at that Arrogance which needs thy harm,
And beat it down before its sins grow worse;
Spend our resentment, cannon,—yea, disburse
Our gold in shapes of flame, our breaths in storm.

Yet, for men's sakes whom thy vast malison
Must wither innocent of enmity,
Be not withdrawn, dark arm, thy spoilure done,
Safe to the bosom of our prosperity.
But when thy spell be cast complete and whole,
May God curse thee, and cut thee from our soul!

GERMAN STUDENTS' WAR LETTERS,
TRANSLATED AND ARRANGED FROM THE ORIGINAL EDITION
OF DR. PHILIPP WITKOP BY A. F. WEDD

FRITZ FRANKE, Student of Medicine, Berlin
Born December 31st, 1892, at Munich.
Killed May 29th, 1915, near Kelmy on the Dubissa.

Louve, November 5th, 1914.
Yesterday we didn't feel sure that a single one of us would come
through alive. You can't possibly picture to yourselves what such a
battle-field looks like. It is impossible to describe it, and even now,
when it is a day behind us, I myself can hardly believe that such
bestial barbarity and unspeakable suffering are possible. Every foot
of ground contested; every hundred yards another trench; and
everywhere bodies—rows of them! All the trees shot to pieces; the
whole ground churned up a yard deep by the heaviest shells; dead
animals; houses and churches so utterly destroyed by shell-fire that
they can never be of the least use again. And every troop that
advances in support must pass through a mile of this chaos,
through this gigantic burial-ground and the reek of corpses.

In this way we advanced on Tuesday, marching for three hours,
a silent column, in the moonlight, towards the Front and into a
trench as Reserve, two to three hundred yards from the English,
close behind our own infantry.

There we lay the whole day, a yard and a half to two yards below the level of the ground, crouching in the narrow trench on a
thin layer of straw, in an overpowering din which never ceased all
day or the greater part of the night—the whole ground trembling
and shaking! There is every variety of sound—whistling, whining,
ringing, crashing, rolling . . . the beastly things pitch right above
one and burst and the fragments buzz in all directions, and the
only question one asks is: 'Why doesn't one get me?' Often the
things land within a hand's breadth and one just looks on. One
gets so hardened to it that at the most one ducks one's head a little

Source: From *German Students' War Letters*, translated and arranged from the original edition of Dr. Philipp Witkop by A. F.
Wedd (New York: E. P. Dutton & Co., Inc.), pp. 123–125,
141–142, 208–209, 315–316. Reprinted by permission of E. P.
Dutton & Co., Inc. and Methuen & Co. Ltd.

if a great, big naval-gun shell comes a bit too near and its grey-green stink is a bit too thick. Otherwise one soon just lies there and thinks of other things. And then one pulls out the Field Regulations or an old letter from home, and all at once one has fallen asleep in spite of the row.

Then suddenly comes the order: 'Back to the horses. You are relieved!' And one runs for a mile or so, mounts, and is a gay trooper once more; hola, away, through night and mist, in gallop and in trot!

One just lives from one hour to the next. For instance, if one starts to prepare some food, one never knows if one mayn't have to leave it behind within an hour. If you lie down to sleep, you must always be 'in Alarm Order'. On the road, you have just to ride behind the man in front of you without knowing where you are going, or at the most only the direction for half a day.

All the same, there is a lot that is pleasant in it all. We often go careering through lovely country in beautiful weather. And above all one acquires a knowledge of human nature! We all live so naturally and unconventionally here, every one according to his own instincts. That brings much that is good and much that is ugly to the surface, but in every one there is a large amount of truth, and above all strength—strength developed almost to a mania!

Gorze, March 26th, 1915.

. . . It will be a big undertaking for our whole nation—and especially for our Parliamentary Parties after peace is restored to draw practical results from our spiritual experience, and success will be only partial.

HANS MARTENS, Technical Student, Charlottenburg
Born September 23, 1892.
Killed July 14th, 1915, near Rudnicki, on the Szlota Lipa.

February 4th, 1915.
It won't be long now before I am at the Front again, thank God! I'd rather be in the filthiest trench than here—one doesn't notice all the suffering so much out there. My one and only wish is that I may at last really *do* something in a battle! For when you simply stand in a trench and mayn't move, while shells and trench-mortars keep coming over, well, that may be fighting but far from *doing anything*: it is the exact and horrible opposite. And that is the disgusting part of this war: it's all so mechanical; one might call it

the trade of systematic manslaughter. One takes part in it out of enthusiasm for the object, while hating and despising the means one is forced to employ to attain that object.

The trench-mortars which both sides have recently introduced are the most abominable things of all. They fire noiselessly and a single one often kills as many as 30 men. One stands in the trench, and at any moment a thing like that may burst. The only consolation when one sees the awful explosion made by ours, which is so terrific that sometimes fragments fly back as far as our own parapet, is that in this case too our productions are more effective than those of the French.

Very few people have the chance of doing anything active out here, and I regret that so far I have not been one of them.

RICHARD SCHMIEDER, Student of Philosophy, Leipzig
Born January 24th, 1888.
Killed July 14th, 1916, near Béthenville.

In the Trenches near Vaudesincourt, March 13th, 1915.
The crucial point in the battle-area has long since ceased to be the right wing (Flanders), having been transferred to the neighbour-hood of Souain-Perthes, in Champagne.

Anybody who, like myself, has been through the awful days near Penthy since the 6th of February, will agree with me that a more appalling struggle could not be imagined. It has been a case of soldier against soldier, equally matched and both mad with hate and rage, fighting for days on end over a single square of ground, till the whole tract of country is one blood-soaked, corpse-strewn field. . . .

On February 27th, tired out and utterly exhausted in body and mind, we were suddenly called up to reinforce the VIIIth Reserve Corps, had to reoccupy our old position at Ripont, and were immediately attacked by the French with extraordinary strength and violence. It was a gigantic murder, by means of bullets, shells, axes, and bombs, and there was such a thundering, crashing, bellowing and screaming as might have heralded the Day of Judgment.

In three days, on a front of about 200 yards, we lost 909 men, and the enemy casualties must have amounted to thousands. The blue French cloth mingled with the German grey upon the ground, and in some places the bodies were piled so high that one could take cover from shell-fire behind them. The noise was so terrific that orders had to be shouted by each man into the ear of the next. And whenever there was a momentary lull in the tumult of battle and the groans of the wounded, one heard, high up in the blue sky, the joyful song of birds! Birds singing just as they do at home in spring-time! It was enough to tear the heart out of one's body!

Don't ask about the fate of the wounded! Anybody who was incapable of walking to the doctor had to die a miserable death; some lingered in agony for hours, some for days, and even for a week. And the combatants stormed regardlessly to and fro over them: 'I can't give you a hand,—You're for the Promised Land,—My Comrade good and true.' A dog, dying in the poorest hovel at home, is enviable in comparison.

There are moments when even the bravest soldier is so utterly sick of the whole thing that he could cry like a child. When I heard the birds singing at Ripont, I could have crushed the whole world to death in my wrath and fury. If only those gentlemen—Grey, Asquith, and Poincaré—could be transported to this spot, instead of the war lasting ten years, there would be peace tomorrow!

WALTER SCHMIDT, Student of Natural History, Tübingen
Born October 12th, 1892, at Tuttlingen.
Killed April 16th, 1917, near Laon.

Bivouac, August 30th, 1916.
I received your nice letter of July 29th here on the Somme, where we have been since the 1st of August, in the Guinchy-Guillemont sector. What I have been through during this time surpasses in horror all my previous experiences during the second year of the war. As a gunner I don't wish to complain, and I willingly admit that the infantry in this salient have had a far worse time, but the sort of thing that has been happening in our firing-position is quite sufficient even for anybody who had been through a good deal.

You will no doubt have learned from the newspapers and other sources about how the English, with the aid of their airmen, who are often 1,500 ft. above the position, and their captive-balloons, have exactly located every one of our batteries and have so smashed them up with long-distance guns of every calibre that the artillery here has had unusually heavy losses both of men and material. Our dug-outs, in which we shelter day and night, are not

even adequate, for though they are cut out of the chalk they are
not so strong but that a 'heavy' was able a few days ago to blow
one in and bury the whole lot of men inside. The gun-emplace-
ments are surrounded by a ring of shell-craters and every day
some heaps of 50 to 100 shells are blown up by a direct hit. When
we are firing a barrage the men have to cross a stretch of open to
get to their gun and then, without taking any notice of falling
shells, we have to fire as hard as we possibly can. A few days ago
the whole detachment of an N.C.O. and three men were killed by
a direct hit during the barrage. As nobody else wanted to fire a
gun covered with corpses, the Fähnrich and I took on the job, and
there, in the midst of dead bodies and blood and in full view of
death, I was filled with a feeling of profound happiness because
the attack had been frustrated. We have carried out our task if the
enemy fails to break through, even if thousands of us have been
killed. What does an individual life matter on such occasions, and
can one spend it to greater advantage than in offering it up as
part of the general sacrifice? These are perhaps banalities and
platitudes, but one often realizes their truth and value when
one is put to the test. Death may be bitter, but we can conquer it
in advance, and then the object of it—the salvation of the Fatherland—shines through all the blood and horror and one no longer
dreads it.

VIII. The Home Front: Women and the War

THE CLASH and thunder of combat in the First World War all too
easily diverted attention from the "home front." No one would contend that in a pre-atomic age, while air power was still in its infancy,
women, children, the aged, and the incapacitated were exposed to as
much danger as the troops at the front. But nevertheless the home
front suffered, especially from food shortages and diseases caused by
malnutrition. Particularly vulnerable were the inhabitants of occupied
Belgium and the Central Powers who were subjected to the slow con-
striction of distant blockade. Even during the first part of the Peace
Conference hunger continued unabated in Germany and Austria because German ship owners would not donate their ships for humanitarian service since they thought the Allies might confiscate them.
Only in April, 1919, did relief shipments begin to arrive. Britain's
food supply was never affected to such a dangerous degree, but nevertheless rations were short during part of the U-boat campaign. In
time of war armies always have an overriding priority in access to the
food supply. Women, children, and the aged—especially among the

families of the poor—are the most likely victims of malnutrition in countries overrun by enemy armies or weakened by blockade. Whatever the rationing system, the wealthy always seem to fare better in war as they do in peace.

A partial compensation for the hardships which women endured was the sudden availability of a wide variety of so-called men's jobs in heavy industry, the metal trades, engineering, as well as in farm work. The labor shortages caused by conscription had to be filled at once. At a stroke many of the antifeminist myths about women's capacity and physical strength had to be re-examined as women took jobs in munitions plants. Women were thus placed in a rare position of bargaining strength, and various governments felt compelled at least to go through the motions of issuing edicts embodying the principle of equal payment for equal work. But in British and American practice there were so many flagrant violations of equality of wages that governmental commissions had to be set up to correct abuses. The commissions recommended enforcement of the principle of equal payment and the shortening of working hours in the interests of the health of the women as well as increased efficiency of production. Women, who have always constituted what has been called "the world's largest minority group," were given a degree of self-reliance which was reflected in their successful demands for the vote in postwar Britain, America, Germany, Russia, Austria, Hungary, Poland, Czechoslovakia, Sweden, and Denmark.

To illustrate the hardships and anxieties of the home front, we publish accounts of the wartime experiences of a celebrated British suffragette and one-time pacifist, and an obscure Austrian housewife.

Estelle Sylvia Pankhurst, a prolific writer (from whose *Home Front* we publish excerpts) and tireless activist in humanitarian causes, was born in Manchester in 1882. She was educated at the Royal College of Art, Kensington, and at the Academia in Venice. As a suffragette leader she became the honorable secretary of the Women's Social and Political Union. For her ardent pacifism she was imprisoned several times, and she engaged in thirteen hunger strikes in the course of her public life. Loathing the war, she tried to lessen its hardships for English working-class families by organizing the Mothers' Arms clinic and day nursery, a Montessori school, and several nonprofit restaurants. She founded the League of Rights for Soldiers' and Sailors' Wives and Relatives, and the National Labor Council for Adult Suffrage. When she was fined for speeches against the war, Derbyshire miners paid her fine. She championed the Russian Revolution, and as a militant antifascist she organized the Womens International Matteotti Committee to combat Mussolini's regime and his bellicose policies. As a by-product of her antifascism she developed a lasting interest in Ethiopia, being a founding member of the Abyssinia Association. Her former pacifism was abandoned in the face of fascist aggression in the 1930's and, as dynamic as ever, she strongly supported the war against the Axis. At the end of hostilities she went to live in Ethiopia, writing a dozen books about the country, and dying in Addis Ababa on September 27, 1960.

Far different was the obscure life of Frau Anna Eisenmenger, the widow of a Viennese physician who had died in 1917 the victim of overwork and malnutrition. Frau Eisenmenger's book *Blockade: The Diary of an Austrian Middleclass Woman, 1914–1924* (from which we publish excerpts) is a simple, unadorned recital of the corrosive effects of the wartime food and fuel shortages upon her family, and of the humiliating trials she had to undergo in trying, by hook or crook, to obtain food and warmth for them. If a middle-class Viennese family experienced such privations as the ones she describes, one can easily imagine the sufferings of the poor who seldom record their tribulations in diaries.

E. SYLVIA PANKHURST,
THE HOME FRONT

The Munitions Act was being rigorously applied. A fitter was fined £3 and costs at Wood Green Police Court for leaving his employment. In Glasgow, where industrial rebels were supposed to be plentiful as gooseberries, the Central Munitions Tribunal fined 17 workmen, who dared to strike, £10 each with the alternative of 30 days' imprisonment. An apprentice plater failed to obtain from the Munitions Tribunal permission to transfer to new employment, though his previous employers, James Fullerton & Co., of Paisley, had refused to restart him. He had left them and obtained work elsewhere because they were paying him less than the standard rate, but they had followed him up and procured his dismissal by another firm because he had left them without permission. Though Fullerton's would not take him back, the Munitions Act enabled them to punish the apprentice by keeping him unemployed for six weeks. It was all for the War, of course; but the interests of the employing class were by no means forgotten! At Armstrong Whitworth's in Manchester 151 men were discharged from the armour plate department, whilst the leaving certificates enabling them to accept work offered to them elsewhere were withheld. They appealed to the Munitions Tribunal for certificates permitting them to work elsewhere, but their case was shelved, lest the employer might possibly require them later.

At Cammell Laird's in Liverpool excessively long hours were being worked. It was common for a man to begin at 6 or 8 a.m. on

Source: From *The Home Front* (London: Hutchinson Publishing Group Ltd., 1932), pp. 206–213. Reprinted by permission of the publisher.

Saturday, work through the day and after a couple of hours off go on night duty. Then after another short rest he would be expected to go on day duty till 8 p.m. on Sunday. If these exhausted workers were late on Monday morning, they were "docked a quarter," and reported for loss of time. The firm complained to the Munitions Tribunal that their 10,000 men had lost 1,500,000 hours in twenty weeks. The offenders were permitted not a word in their defence, but fined from 5s. to 60s. each. They cried out in their indignation that there would be a revolution in the country, and were ordered to leave the court; they went with defiant cheers.

The Munitions Act was being used to prevent workers from changing their employment in order to secure higher wages, or positions of greater responsibility, or to obtain work nearer home, or in another district in view of family responsibilities. Leaving certificates were refused when the work was proving prejudicial to the health of the worker and where the character of the work had been changed and the worker found the new machinery unmanageable or injurious.

Shell-making had become the latest Society craze; a ghastly sport indeed! The Hillman Motor Company opened a factory for teaching "ladies with a few hours leisure." One hundred and twenty of them were to be accommodated, and it was hoped by their united efforts the weekly output would reach one shell per lady!

A band of leisured women were being trained at Erith to give weekend relief to the ordinary workers at Vickers who were toiling away continuously for 8s. to 14s. a week. For the well-to-do trainees a charming house had been lent by war enthusiasts, where board and service were provided for 15s. 6d. a week, their stipend during training being 15s. 6d. to 19s. 6d. Presently such well-to-do women were put in as overlookers at superior wages to supervise the ordinary worker.

The *Manchester Guardian* recorded the story of a lady of title who, having become a munitionette, gave a dinner-party to celebrate her first month of productive work. The guests were a duchess, the wife of a Cabinet Minister, and a working woman, introduced as "Mabel, my mate in the shop." The hostess and her "mate" wore print dresses with handkerchiefs swathed about their heads, their working uniform. The table was covered with oilcloth. The dinner was brought in by a maid, the hostess carved, the guests helped themselves to the vegetables. "The simple life," said the hostess. "Mabel and I only get fifteen bob a week and it won't

run to more." The butler, as she gaily explained later, had been
sent to the theatre "to get him out of the way." What fun indeed
for the titled few—and behind it the trenches. What ghoulish
sport!

In the cotton trade the employers had refused the workers a 5
per cent. increase in wages, to aid them in meeting the enhanced
cost of living. Yet Lloyd George was appealing to the cotton
operatives to agree to come under the compulsion of the Munitions Act on account of the huge quantities of cotton goods the
Government was requiring for the War. The great majority of the
operatives had always been women; the withdrawal of men for
the Army thus affected the cotton industry less than others. To
secure more cheap labour, the employers were demanding that
children should begin work as half-timers at eleven years, instead
of at twelve; and as full-timers at twelve years, instead of at
thirteen.

As the War progressed trade after trade was put under the
Munitions Act. Employers were eager to seize the powers it gave
them. In 1916 a woman came to me who had been making military
tents at Groom's, in Limehouse, and earned 23s. to 24s. a week.
She was transferred to the making of garments for men civilians,
on which she could earn only 11s. or 12s. Unwilling to accept such
a pittance, she left the factory and applied for work to the Gov-
erment-appointed Metropolitan Munitions Committee at Park
Royal, Acton, set up to facilitate the recruitment of women for
munition work. There she was told that she could not be given
employment unless her late employer would release her. Groom's
refused to consent. There seemed no alternative for the woman,
save to return to Groom's, or remain unemployed for six weeks.
She came to me for advice. I telephoned to the Munitions Office,
giving all particulars and urging that discharge certificates were not
required by women employed in the clothing trade. The official to
whom I spoke, admitted that Groom's was not a controlled factory, but declared the question of discharge certificates so complicated that no opinion could be expressed in this case. By dint of
persistence, I secured an interview between the officials at the
Munitions Office and the woman concerned. They sent her back to
me, with an involved communication, stating that if the woman
found it difficult to get work without a discharge certificate, she
might apply to a Tribunal; but that it was doubtful whether a
Tribunal had jurisdiction "in cases where the applicant is not employed in an establishment falling within the Minister's orders."

The Minister's own headquarters, the Munitions Office, was not prepared to say. A memorandum enumerating the classes of work in which leaving certificates were required was enclosed, in order that I might decide for myself whether the applicant belonged to any such class. The Munitions Office refused to take the responsibility of deciding. If the woman found further difficulty in getting employment, however, permission was given for her to show this most evasive communication to any prospective employer. For that purpose it might be regarded as an official letter.

Thus they were winning the war to end war!

"EAT LESS MEAT"

McKenna, the new Chancellor of the Exchequer, announced that the War was costing more than £3,000,000 a day, which must be met by "our own domestic economies." War propaganda increased and grew more costly. Ladies of title took pledges to abstain from luxuries, "as far as possible." Rich men were tempted to patriotism by expensive dinners with which war loan vouchers were given away. Even in the East End, patriotic meetings were held to urge the working classes to self-denial.

The Board of Trade called on the public to eat less meat. Runciman circularised the secretaries of women's societies, asking us to impress this appeal upon our members, and offering to pay the cost of summoning meetings for this purpose. A general meeting of our East End members replied to him that the average working woman house-keeper could not introduce further economics without injury to the physique of her family, and that the majority of our members were only able to purchase meat for their families once a week.

The Coal Committee appointed by the Government declared that the price of coal was unjustifiably high. We demanded the national control of coal under the supervision of a committee, composed in one third of working women housewives, one third experts, and one third organised workers in the trade, and the establishment of similar committees to safeguard the supplies of food and milk.

The Parliamentary reports made sordid reading, crammed as they were with stories of hardship and corruption brought to light by the questions of Members, who told of soldiers' camps understocked, of other camps overstocked; of bread, biscuits and bully beef thrown into the sea, used for kindling fires and mending roads, sold by pilfering officials; of boots and clothing stolen and thrown away, and rifles burnt for firewood; of fuses costing 15s. each, though French fuses of superior pattern cost only 7s. 6d. Members declared that the business men of the country were "sick" of the laxity and incompetence of War Office methods. A Member reported the lordly insistence of some official upon paying an account "in gross," though the manufacturer had sent in a reduced account giving credit for returned empties. One Member even went so far as to declare it necessary that two or three of the principal War Office incompetents should be hung in Whitehall as a warning to the rest.

Revelations in regard to meat, wheat, freight and munitions constantly appeared. We called for people's auditors, to investigate Government war expenditure, popularly elected, like the citizens' auditors of some of the great towns. At all times such auditors would exercise a valuable check on official probity.

The rise in prices was accelerated by huge Government purchases for the Army and Navy. On the fact being disclosed, the Government admitted that it had bought thousands of tons of Australian corned beef at 8¼d. per lb., though the average price in the London meat market per dozen 6-lb. tins was only 5¾d. per lb. Dr. Macnamara, however, declared the price paid by the Government "not unreasonable." Government buyers expected to pay high prices, and patriotic vendors were eager that they should. Patriotic farmers, foreseeing a shortage of low-priced labour, reduced their crops. Patriotic stock raisers, seeing the cost of fodder rise and anxious to profit to-day by the boom in the price of meat, killed off their stock, not scrupling to slaughter large numbers of cows in calf. It was reported that many poor beasts gave birth in the slaughter-house and that calves were taken alive from their mothers just killed.

Immediately after the declaration of war, Acts designed to safeguard the purity of the milk supply were passed into law. On June 22nd, 1915, an Act was passed postponing these safeguards. A committee of enquiry under Lord Milner and Lord Inchcape was now appointed to safeguard home food production. It contained but one representative of Labour and not a single woman.

Runciman told the Commons that he had made a very hard bargain for the carriage of frozen meat from the Argentine, and expressed the hope that he might be "exculpated from any moral guilt" since he had acted in the public interest. It transpired that the rates secured by Runciman under this "hard bargain" were actually higher than the contract prices private firms were arranging for themselves. A committee, mainly composed of shipowners, with Lord Inchcape, the chairman of the P. and O. Shipping Company, had been appointed to advise the Government what compensation it should pay to the owners whose ships were taken over by the Government. With Runciman of the great shipping family as President of the Board of Trade, their interests were in safe custody!

Dr. Macnamara told a meeting of East End munition workers that there was "no room for the man who desires more to make his bit than to do his bit!" Yet that very week the *Manchester Guardian* published the fact that whilst the freight charge for wheat across the Atlantic was 1d. per bushel before the War, it was now 1s. 8d. The cost of carrying wheat from the Argentine had risen 500 per cent.

In the early months of the War the Government had given financial aid to assist in promoting British dyes; it later acquired the greater part of the indigo crop to aid this venture; yet it refused to take adequate steps to protect the people against extortionate charges for food and fuel.

Whenever one touched war work Scandal poked out her ugly head; there was abundant food for her, but she was swiftly thrust back into her kennel. Whilst compulsion was applied to spur exhausted workers in the privately owned munition factories, the thirty and forty ton hammers were idle at Woolwich Arsenal. The 4,000 ton press had only been worked on odd jobs since war began. On June 14th, 1915, the men working on it were told there would be no more work for them unless unexpected orders came in. The new field-gun annex was only half used and work on 18-pounder field guns—the very guns which were supposed to be lacking at the Front—had entirely ceased. The total orders for these large guns since the beginning of the War had amounted to but 12 to 14 weeks' work. On July 1st Members complained that 97 per cent. of the large work was given out to contractors and only 3 per cent. to the Arsenal. Will Crooks, the Labour M.P. for Woolwich, declared that steel and other material bought for the Arsenal had been sent by the Arsenal for use by private firms. In the huge inability to see the truth affecting every belligerent nation men cried out for life to be saved by sending more munitions to the trenches. Even those who believed themselves Pacifists, like Lansbury, were of this mind. He wrote:

"The women of East London have sent their men to fight. Those of us who hate and detest war know that these men must be

armed and fed, and while the War lasts we shall all do our best to
see that this is done."

Poor women, they did not so; I never knew one of them who
did not see her man go with weeping and bitter regret, who did
not strive and hope for him to remain at home.

Strikes began to break out. The L.C.C. tramway men struck for
a war bonus, which was denied them, although receipts had risen
by £8,500 a week, and owing to enlistments, 2,000 fewer men were
handling the increased traffic. The strike caused tremendous excitement in London and an outcrop of volunteer strike breakers.
When the men returned on promise of arbitration, they found that
no men between 21 and 40 were to be reinstated. That was the
war-time way of dealing with strikers; an effective means of pro-
curing the docility of Labour.

In the burst of artificial war prosperity, in which anything
would sell, scamping, adulteration and profiteering ran rife. A
young Jew, dodging war service, who used to hang about our
offices, disclosed to me casually that he was using our telephone to
discover where certain commodities could be bought, then offering them for sale at an increased figure, and if his offer were accepted, instructing the vendor to deliver the goods to his customer.
Thus without risk or expenditure, he was making a profit from
the prevailing eagerness to obtain materials. On every hand one
saw small firms becoming large ones; their owners moving from
mean little houses into spacious ones, discarding omnibuses and
buying motors, their way of life expanding in all directions into
luxury.

Patriotism was fashionable, and patriotism at other people's expense most fashionable of all. A poor woman whose husband had
just been killed at the Front was informed that the Royal Patriotic Fund had granted her £7, and that she must apply for it to
the local S.S.F.A. Then a certain lady called from the Association
and told the widow that she had put the money in the bank for her
and that if she wanted "to hear any more about it" she must call on
this lady next week. Crushed by her grief, the widow heard of this
"blood money," as poor women called it, scarcely caring what
might happen to it; but a week later her two-year-old child was
taken seriously ill, and the doctor ordered special nourishment
which she could not afford to buy. She hastened to the S.S.F.A.
and pleaded for the money due to her; for some of it; even for 10s.
The lady she had previously seen refused to hand over one penny,
insisting that £5 of it must be put into War Loan, and the rest

held in the bank. A woman brought the poor widow to me. I put the case in the hands of one of our solicitors, who eventually secured the widow her money.

Poverty and overstrain were evidenced by the increase in the death rate of women from consumption, which had been falling steadily during the preceding ten years, and which mounted higher with every year of war. The general death rate for civilians, which had been falling, also rose.

The Minister of Education now gave instructions that the school feeding of necessitous children must cease. From one school near us nearly fifty children, whose need had been recognised by the School Managers, were thus left to go hungry. The number of children attending our "Penny Carltons," as the Press termed what we had named "Cost Price Restaurants," leapt up by 100 per cent. Though on the part of voluntary enthusiasts there was a concentration of effort to save the babies never previously made, the then appallingly high infant death rate rose, especially in London, where from 103 per 1,000 births in 1914, it became 112 per 1,000 births in 1915.

As the summer advanced diarrhœa and enteritis attacked huge numbers of tiny victims. Poor mothers came flocking to our clinics with their wasting infants, wizened and fleshless from wasting, twisted and misshapen by rickets. Rickets, impetigo, scabies— which the soldiers brought home with them—poverty diseases; I learnt to know them sorely.

We made no pretence of confining ourselves to preventive medicine, as the Minister of Health now advises. We did what we could for the sufferers, only referring them elsewhere for treatment we were unable to give. To have done otherwise would greatly have limited our usefulness; indeed the majority of our patients would have gone untreated. The hospitals were too much taken up with soldiers to give adequate attention to ailing babies. Our patients were generally too poor to pay for attention from the local private practitioners, who in any case were less able to advise in relation to pregnancy and infant nurture than our own doctors, who specialised in such work.

I believe that if professional interests were put on one side it would be found best for the present maternity and infant welfare centres to treat the bulk of the ailments they now refer to private general practitioners.

A lady came to me from the Beit clinic for sea water plasma injections, urging me to use this treatment for infantile diarrhœa.

In a few days we had it working, and obtained from it remarkable
results under Dr. Alice Johnson, who attended our cases at the
Mothers' Arms. Numbers of infants brought to us in a state of
collapse, despaired of by the general practitioners, were restored. I
realised how handicapped is the doctor attending poor people
when circumstances permit him to order nothing for his patients
beyond a bottle of medicine. Many sick babies we took into the
nursery by night, as well as by day. They were the special charge
of Nurse Hebbes, who nursed them with patient tenderness, spending herself unsparingly. "I believe you love them better than the
healthy babies," I said to her, watching her fondling a piteous little
morsel, who crinkled his shrivelled face to smile as her finger gently
stroked his cheek. She answered with wan brightness: "I think
I do."

It seemed a miracle to witness the tiny creatures recovered from
the collapse of imminent death, the listless, flaccid limbs gradually
regaining vigour. Yet the process of recovery was slow indeed as
compared with their swift failing. Several times it happened that
after a baby had been nursed patiently to apparent health, and had
been sent away to the country to assure its stability, it would return home, catch a chill or some childish ailment, collapse and die,
quite suddenly, as though the physical well-being we had built for
the little body had been merely a house of cards. It was the sad
loss of infants for whom she had laboured with beautiful devotion,
and the tragic state of overburdened mothers in crowded homes,
which sent Nurse Hebbes to be the first nurse in the birth control
clinic of Dr. Marie Stopes. . . .

The Ministry of Munitions was issuing notices calling for from
800 to 1,000 new women munition workers each week. A man-
power board was in being; a woman-power board was added. Industrial compulsion was made more complete. Men not medically
fit for the Army were to be enrolled at the Labour Exchange,
where, though passed as physically unfit for the Army, they were
nevertheless given the alternative of munition work or the Army.
It was assumed that of course they would choose the former alternative. As a condition of getting the work which would thus
save him from the trenches, each unfit man must "voluntarily" sign
a form binding him to work wherever the Ministry of Munitions
might direct at 7d. per hour, and an additional 2s. 6d. a week if he
had four or five children, or 5s. if he had six or more. A subsistence

allowance of 2s. 6d. a day was added, if the work obliged him to live away from his home. He remained liable to recall to the Army at any time. Military representatives assured employers that if there were any "hanky panky" on the part of any man thus supplied to them, the man could be taken for the Army and another man sent to work in his place.

The Orient steamship line threatened to hand over to the military authorities any employee who refused to accept a wage reduction of £1 8s. a month. Few men could resist such pressure. Remember that for the unfit man taken into the Army there was no pension if his health broke down under training; no pension for his family if he died. Overtime was exacted, and accepted with avidity under pressure of rising prices which the low wage could not meet without grievous privations.

So the War spread its huge tentacles to all sections of the people, breaking them at the Front, bleeding them of energy and the joy of life in the munition factories. Larger and larger numbers were subjected to the poisonous dust and fumes of the high explosives. The "yellow girls" working in T.N.T. were a common sight. They were kept out of view as far as might be. Restaurant proprietors issued orders to their managers not to serve munition workers. Olive Beamish, a Suffragette hunger-striker, and one of our East End organisers, went to lunch at Fleming's, in Oxford Street. The manageress came to her sternly: "You know you cannot be served!" Beamish retired indignant and wrote a letter of protest to the firm. She received a courteous reply, regretting that she had been mistaken for a munition worker. She had been wearing a khaki-coloured raincoat.

In the general relaxation of the Factory Acts the protection of children was being swept away. It was made permissible to work children of 14 years a 6o-hour week, exclusive of meal intervals, and since they might be employed up to 13½ hours in a single day, it was virtually impossible for inspectors to detect violations of the regulations. Girls under 16 years were employed on night shifts even in Woolwich Arsenal.

There were now 60,000 fewer children in the schools, the number of infants under five had been reduced from 55,000 to 25,000, and the number of children of 13 to 14 years was nearly 20,000 less than in 1914. 13,750 children of school age were employed by farmers, 516 of them under 12 years of age. 20,000 teachers had enlisted. W. C. Anderson complained that 100,000 children had been disturbed in their schooling on account of military arrangements, and that such alternative accommodation as had been provided was often overcrowded and unsuitable.

Yet many of diverse views believed that war-time conditions were preparing a more efficient civilisation after the War. Conservatives of militarist mind cherished the hope that the employers were rising to what they considered their proper position as generals of industry, and the masses becoming more disciplined to their essential function: the supply of such labour as cannot be provided by machinery, for reasons either of economy or capacity. State Socialists, and foremost amongst them Beatrice and Sidney Webb, saw in this era the coming of the system they had long looked for. Already Sidney Webb and Arnold Freeman had published a textbook of the desired developments to follow from this beginning. They declared that whilst "a century ago the servile State was no comic figment, but a reality, it is no longer true that the mass of the people are at the mercy of Capitalism." The question was amazingly put:

"Will Great Britain in 1936 be a finer country to live in than it would have been had not the sharp prick of war aroused us from our slothful acquiescence in the social iniquities that persist around us?"

This read as a grim joke to those of us who toiled amongst the miseries of the people ground in the mills of warfare.

Conferences on industrial organisation and the demands the workers should make, both during and after the War, were held by numerous organisations in the hope of influencing the Trade Unions. Our W.S.F. probably started this fashion in London.

Arriving early for one such conference, organised by the Fabian Research Department, in Tothill Street, I found Bernard Shaw in lively discussion with a group of his Fabian colleagues, declaring, in his challenging, jaunty way: "I have not the slightest objection to the servile State, provided I can get my oar in."

Beatrice Webb took the chair, black-gowned and circumscribed, a carefully reared indoor nineteenth-century product who had missed the enlargement of motherhood. She defended the unequal payment of men and women on the trivial ground that women were more costly than men to their employers, who must provide separate lavatories and other amenities for them. It was with difficulty I compelled her to permit my entry into the discussion to put the opposing view. I was not the desired Trade Union official, with mind open for indoctrination by Fabian argument, but a competing theorist, eager to convert him to other policies. I should probably have failed to overcome her determination to wave me into silence, save that a cue was given which enabled me to strike in with: "When Lloyd George wrote me the letter on women's wages which Mr. Cole has mentioned . . ."

Miles Malleson, who had been invalided out of the Army in January 1915, now published, through Henderson's at the "Bomb Shop" in Charing Cross Road, two anti-war plays entitled "D Company" and "Black 'Ell." These plays were banned and Malleson obtained on this account a popularity which remained with him after the War. He came down to us at Old Ford with his mother to rehearse his children's play, "Paddly Pools," which Patricia Lynch was teaching some of our children.

With the official admission that food prices had risen 65 per cent. and the total cost of living 45 per cent., the Government agreed to grant a war bonus to all its full-time employees, except those who had already received war increases, or had been newly engaged during the War. This tardily granted privilege amounted to 4s. a week for those whose wages were less than 40s. a week, 3s. for those paid 40s. to 60s. a week. Women and persons under eighteen years were to get half the bonus.

The old-age pensioners still vainly awaited the 2s. 6d. a week increase promised for those who suffered exceptional hardship.

Stanton, the victor of Merthyr, cried out in Parliament: "Why do you not choke these Pacifists down?" Colonel Norton Griffiths demanded African labour for this country, declaring that France was already importing thousands of Kaffirs and Chinese, to make good the shortage of "white labour," and that the "fight to a finish" would demand more of this. Black troops had long been used at the Front. Outhwaite replied that those who supported the "fight to a finish" should carry it out, as they declared they would, "to the last shilling," but not by lending it to the Government at 6 per cent. interest. Prophetically he declared that after the War the forces of revolution would sweep over Europe to determine who should pay for "this wild debauch of blood." No one in this country believed him, but in Russia the Conservative Party was already asking for peace with Germany, because the continuance of warfare would mean the collapse of the monarchical systems of Europe.

ANNA EISENMENGER,
BLOCKADE: THE DIARY OF AN AUSTRIAN MIDDLE-CLASS WOMAN,
1914–1924

OCTOBER 25TH, 1918
ALARMING NEWS FROM THE FRONT. FOOD
SITUATION INCREASINGLY DIFFICULT

At last a letter from Karl, delivered to us by one of his comrades on the journey to the Western Front. This man told me that Karl had been transferred to the trenches as the result of a dispute with his superior officer. He also brought a pamphlet, which has been dropped in large quantities over our positions by enemy aeroplanes. The Entente are trying to incite our troops to rebellion. They promise a favourable peace if our soldiers will go home. Does the Entente need yet more weapons with which to fight against us? Karl's letter breathes the deepest depression. He is stationed near Sette Communi. They are standing up to their knees in water. He asks for shoes, as his own have rotted through being incessantly damp.

"The life here is unworthy of any human being. I ask myself again and again how the motley collection of older men and young boys in these front positions endure this life. Insufficient food, tattered shoes and uniforms. No possibility of keeping one's self clean. Are our human sensibilities already utterly stupefied?"

Poor Karl. If I had any say in the matter, I should be in favour of concluding peace immediately. Wilson, with his Fourteen Points, offered us a good, honourable peace. Why didn't we grasp at it?

In a postscript Karl writes:

"I feel convinced that we can't go on like this. The War will end soon, one way or another. See that you get in food supplies, for Vienna will be eaten out of house and home by the soldiers when they come back. I too suffer from chronic hunger."

I talked it over with Liesbeth. She thinks that Karl's letter is exaggerated. But Liesbeth's catarrh is worse, and Wolfi is begging for milk; it is now a week since we had the ¼-pint of milk due to

Source: From *Blockade: The Diary of an Austrian Middle-Class Woman, 1914–1924* (London: Constable Publishers, 1932), pp. 16–28, 39–42, 187–191. Reprinted by permission of the publisher.

us on our ration cards. I resolve to *"hamster."** During my husband's lifetime, I dared not do this. When he was seriously ill, I did it without his knowledge. I did not feel that I was becoming demoralised—on the contrary, I might almost say: Have I not the right to guard and protect the life of my family? For all its rigorous organisation, the State could not feed its citizens, and it cannot do so to-day. For a long time we have only been getting a part of the food due to us on our ration cards. The doctors have discovered that, even if we got the whole of our ration, this would only be sufficient to meet one-fourth of the food requirements of an adult person weighing 11 stone. Aunt Bertha, out of an excessive and misguided conscientiousness, has insisted on living exclusively on the official food rations; in consequence she is now ill with softening of the bones—a striking proof that to obey the food laws is equivalent to suicide. Karl's letter proved to me that, in spite of our privations in the Hinterland, we are no longer in a position to feed our armies. If the War is to end soon, as Karl declares and as I pray to God it may, I shall have to provide for another three hungry stomachs in addition to Wolfi and his ailing mother. Although I had now and then had recourse to one of the much abused *"Schleichhändler"*† in order to procure the necessary foodstuffs for our household, such as milk, eggs, butter or fat, I was far from having accumulated any surplus stores. The foodstuffs distributed by the Government were very dear, but the prices charged by the Schleichhändler were often five or six times as high. Below are the official prices of some of the principal rationed foodstuffs, together with the prices of the same articles in the year 1914, before the War:

The prices are, unless otherwise stated, the official wholesale prices per 100 kilogrammes.‡ To get the retail prices 20 to 25 per cent. should be added in each case.

It will be seen from the following table that the wholesale prices of the most important foodstuffs had tripled or quadrupled during the four war years. At the present time these foodstuffs are distributed by the Food Control authorities according to ration cards, but so irregularly and in such small quantities that, in order not to starve, one is forced to have recourse to the flourishing Schleichhändler, whose extortionate charges are a good two hun-

* Hoard food.
† Smugglers.
‡ 100 kilogrammes = about 2 cwt.

	PEACE PRICES, 1914.		WAR PRICES, 1918.	
	KRONEN.	HELLER.*	KRONEN.	HELLER.
Wheat	22	—	62	—
Rye	19	50	65	—
Oats	19	—	60	—
Barley	16	84	60	—
Cooking peas	28	74	120	—
Lentils	43	88	150	—
Beans	30	44	100	—
Potatoes	6	89	20	—
Sugar beet	2	30	12	—
Cabbage	4	—	56	—
Raw sugar	26	67	112	—
Refined sugar	34	67	186	—
Molasses	6	—	40	—
Cattle	93	—	380	—
Beef, per kilogramme	1	80	20	—
Lard, per 100 kg.	163	40	1140	—
Eggs, each	—	9	—	50
Butter, fat	2	50	27	—

dred or three hundred per cent. above the official prices, and are increased in proportion to the increased necessity of the buyer.

So I decided to hamster. The little fortune which I had inherited from my father brings me in now, with cautious investment, about 5,000 kronen† per annum. When my husband was still alive and our dear Austria was undisturbed by war, I used this money for the purpose of improving my children's education and for little excursions and summer holidays. The idea that I could be of some pecuniary assistance to my husband had always afforded me immense satisfaction. Since my husband's death, or rather, perhaps, since the outbreak of this unhappy war, intellectual interests have been forced into the background. Already in the year 1914 we housewives began to suffer from measures of economy, which were not improved when the military authorities took over the control of supplies. We submitted uncomplainingly, because we received news of victories both on the Western and the Eastern Fronts and of hundreds of thousands of prisoners. And each of these victories must be bringing blessed peace nearer to us. Now, at the end of the fourth year of war, when the Central Powers and their whole civilian population are like a besieged fortress

* 1 Austrian (pre-War) Krone = Heller = 10d.
† About £200.

cut off from all external supplies and without any hope of breaking through the hunger blockade, I am no longer disposed to sacrifice any more members of my family to the Moloch of war.

OCTOBER 26TH, 1918
I INFRINGE THE FOOD LAWS BY A SUCCESSFUL "HAMSTERING" EXPEDITION

Some farmers living on the outskirts of Vienna, whose families have been professionally attended by my husband, had already during my husband's lifetime wanted to prove their affection and gratitude by little presents of foodstuffs. My husband had flatly refused these tokens of appreciation. I now resolved to visit these people. Liesbeth was coughing a great deal, and in her condition nourishing food was a vital necessity. I drew from my bank 20,000 kronen* in cash. The bank clerk, who had attended to me and advised me for years, recommended me to convert my money into Swiss francs. When I objected that private dealings in foreign currencies were not allowed, he whispered to me that he would manage it for me if I would authorise him to do so. The transaction must, of course, be effected secretly, since it was forbidden by law. I had already resolved that day to infringe one law by the illicit purchase of supplies, but now I nervously rejected my adviser's offer. "You will regret it, gnädige Frau. Only Switzerland and Holland will keep their currencies stable." "No, no, I prefer not; financial transactions are beyond me."

To-day I travelled outside the boundaries of Vienna for the first time after a long interval. On the trams there were only women conductors, who did their work quietly and efficiently. I took a train on the Südbahn which had a connection with a train to Laxenburg. Apart from a few men on leave, my companions were mostly women, armed with rucksacks or handbags. Hamstering is forbidden, but after all it is only the primitive instinct of self-preservation. The second-class carriage in which I was seated had a strangely dilapidated appearance. The leather covers had great holes where pieces had obviously been hurriedly cut off or torn off. The leather straps for letting down the windows were also missing. Leather has become a rarity for civilians and inhabitants of the Hinterland. New shoes are practically unobtainable. One sees fantastic substitutes for shoes, with wooden soles and any sort of upper. People seize upon leather, none the less, wherever

* About £833.

they can find it. Our carriage had no window panes; one side of
the openings was nailed up with boards. Only women were working in the fields, except for a boy or an old man here and there
and sometimes a few Russian prisoners of war. A man home on
leave was leading the conversation in our compartment. At the
Front, he said, things were even worse than in the Hinterland.
No one had enough to eat there. The Hungarians were to blame
for it all; they had abundance of everything and fattened their
pigs with maize, but they refused to give anything to us. . . .
"No, no," said a woman, who was carrying two empty rucksacks.
"It's the Food Controllers who are to blame for everything and
the Schleichhändler, who are all becoming millionaires. But if
there were no Food Controllers, there would be no Schleichhändler. . . ."

At Laxenburg the scene was already more animated. Although
Emperor Karl and his family had transferred the Court from
Laxenburg to the military headquarters at Baden, a few officers of
the Royal Household had remained behind and a regiment of
Hungarian artillery was quartered there. In order to reach my
farmer acquaintances I had to cross the vast Laxenburg Park,
famous for its magnificent stretches of forest and meadow
land. . . .

My watch pointed to eleven. I should have to hurry. At noon I
found the farmer's wife at home. She was very kind and friendly,
though she herself has plenty of troubles. Her husband has for
weeks been lying wounded in a hospital at the Front. Her eldest
child is ten years old, there are three younger ones, and another is
on the way. She cannot cope with the work, the fields are untilled.
There are no farm labourers, and the girls are all running off to
the munition factories. "If only my husband were at home." She
sympathised with my troubles and pitied me, for, after all, she has
more to eat than I have. She packed bread, flour, beans, bacon
and honey into my hand-basket, as much as I could carry. The
prices which she charged me were moderate. She advised me not to
go through the town, but to take the path across the fields to the
station in order to avoid the police. "They are very down on the
hamsterers." Although I kept on repeating to myself all the way
to the station that there was no harm in what I was doing, I
stumbled anxiously and guiltily to the station across turnip fields
and ploughed land. Unmolested, but exhausted by the weight of
my load and the fear of being discovered, I reached home. The
food I have secured to-day at the cost of a fairly large amount of

money and a still larger amount of nervous strain has a peace value of not quite 10 kronen!

OCTOBER 27TH, 1918
ERNI WOUNDED

To-day a letter arrived signed by Erni but written in an unfamiliar hand. Erni is lying wounded at Innsbruck. His life is in no danger. An injury to the eyes, which they hope is not serious. As soon as he is fit to be moved he will come to Vienna. "An injury to the eyes, which they hope is not serious." I felt a vague, terrible anxiety—for Erni's big, blue, childlike eyes. Liesbeth soothed me. We persuaded ourselves that we ought to be glad and grateful when a slight wound brought our men into a hospital and so for the time being into safety. "How glad I was," said Liesbeth, "when Rudi came to Vienna with his arm wound. And now we shall soon have Erni here and be able to nurse and spoil him." A Surgeon-Major-General, who is a friend of ours, has promised me to expedite Erni's transference to Vienna, so I have given up for the time being my plan of going to Innsbruck.

NOVEMBER 1ST, 1918
WRETCHED MEALS. EXTRA EDITION.
ERNI COMES BACK

Liesbeth, Wolfi and I were seated at our wartime breakfast table. From a "hamstered" tin of milk I was spooning out the scanty rations for Liesbeth and Wolfi into bowls filled with hot water. After the spoon had been used, it was carefully scraped, so that not a drop of milk should be lost. Wolfi was then allowed to lick the spoon, which he did with great thoroughness and obvious enjoyment. Fortunately the milk was sweetened. For months we have been getting only saccharine on our ration-cards, or very small portions of sticky, yellow, unpalatable raw sugar. The rations, if one gets them at all, are so small that it is impossible to meet one's sugar requirements with them for a week, allowing one cup of tea a day. Tea and coffee I have in fact long since banished from our menu as luxurious stimulants without any nutritive value. Strangely enough, it was our old cook, now my only remaining help with the housework and otherwise not at all given to complaining, who objected most strongly to this rule. She is a Viennese, and even in prosperous times many Viennese lived mainly on coffee and milk with the famous and excellent Viennese bread and rolls. Both now belong to history, and Wolfi only knows Kipfel* and Semmel† from the enthusiastic descriptions of Kathi, who keeps on sighing: "If I could only have my coffee and my roll again!" The portion of the loaf which we draw on our ration cards I divide up very carefully by means of scratches on the crust. I use a very sharp knife for cutting the loaf, for any crumbling would mean waste. The bread is pale yellow and moist as long as it is fresh. Although it is kept in the bread pan, it gets dry very quickly. When it is bitten, it grates against the teeth as though it contained sand. It is made of a mixture of maize flour, horsechestnut flour and a little rye. Liesbeth can hardly digest it, and I have difficulty in persuading her to eat a part of her ration. A so-called plum jam is supposed to make the bread more palatable. It looks like cart grease and has an indefinable but, at any rate, a sweetish taste. It is my unpleasant duty as housewife to find all these dubious foodstuffs excellent and tasty in order not to rob my three table companions of their appetite, which at any rate in Wolfi's case is still approximately normal. He tolerates the bad and insufficient fare comparatively well, whereas we adults frequently suffer from digestive troubles which take away all our appetite. . . .

Karl has come back. Owing to a slight attack of diarrhœa, he was taken to a military hospital and then by train through Trieste to Vienna. Since the Hungarians have withdrawn from the field, the War is ended for our soldiers too.

Karl looked very ill. He had no underlinen or socks. His uniform was dirty and in rags. "Mother, I am famished!" he said, and walking straight into the kitchen without waiting for me to bring him something he began to devour our rations of bread and jam. "Forgive me, Mother, but we have got into the habit of taking what we can find." He only greeted us very casually and did not notice until much later that Erni, who had come in to welcome him on Liesbeth's arm, was wounded. "Hullo! So it's caught you too!" and then, still hurriedly chewing and swallowing: "Well, just wait! We'll pay them out yet, the war profiteers and parasites. We've grown wiser out there in the trenches, far wiser than we were. Everything must be changed, utterly changed."

I got ready the bath and clean underlinen. After his bath Karl went straight to bed, but he was too excited to sleep, although it was almost 11 o'clock at night. He telephoned to Edith, and then

* Small loaves.
† White rolls.

he made us all come to his bedside, for he wanted to tell us about himself. He told us that he had been lucky to get the attack of diarrhœa, and that the others who had to remain at the Front were all dead or taken prisoners. The Italians had gone on attacking in spite of the Armistice. For another whole day they had fired on our retreating columns in the Fellathal and had captured several divisions. That, however, was the only victory they had won. It was contemptible, but war made every one base and contemptible. He had become so too. Karl also told us that in his section near Sette Communi, Americans and English were fighting against us and that the Americans and English had already occupied Trieste. For the first time in the history of the world Americans and English had landed as enemies on our coast. After the proclamation of the Armistice all military discipline went to pieces. Everyone was intent only on getting home and made for home by the way that seemed to him quickest and surest. The men trampled down whatever stood in their way, even if the obstacle were their own officers. Woe to the officers who were unpopular with their men! The soldiers besieged the transport trains and plundered the stores to supply themselves with food for the journey. Karl told us that he was crowded with almost a hundred other men in a goods truck intended for forty men or ten horses. Wounded, nurses, generals, soldiers were jumbled together anyhow. Soldiers who could not get into the carriages sat on the steps, the buffers or the roofs. Many of them fell off from sheer exhaustion and were run over. The Südbahn tunnels were full of seriously wounded and dead, who had been pushed down from the roofs of the carriages. But after all what did it matter? A few hundred dead more or less among the millions of war victims. . . . But in the next war there would be no one foolish enough to risk his life, they would see to that. . . . Karl was evidently in a nervous, over-excited state, but he went on talking, and only after I had entreated him several times did he consent to try to get to sleep.

"We are all tired, Karl, and it is already past midnight. . . ."

"Do you know, Mother, how I feel here? In a clean bed, washed and fed? As if I were in heaven. . . . Oh no, there is no heaven so beautiful. . . . As if I were in a beautiful dream . . . and in that dream I shall try to find sleep."

We left Karl's room in order to go to bed ourselves. As I was helping Erni undress, he said: "Mother, Karl seems to me like a

complete stranger. Perhaps it is only because I can't see him. But
that I hope I shall be able to do again soon."

Although I was nervously and physically exhausted, sleep refused to close my eyelids. For a long, long time I lay awake,
agitated by the horrors of the War. I found myself marvelling that
civilised human beings could live through all the brutalities which
war entailed for themselves and others without going utterly to
pieces. . . .

MARCH 15TH, 1919

STILL NO PEACE

Five months after the Armistice we housewives are suffering
more acutely than in the worst war years. The peace negotiations, in which only the representatives of the victorious powers
and of the newly-founded states of Czechoslovakia, Poland,
Lithuania and Latvia take part, are constantly adjourned and protracted. In the Entente camp more and more voices proclaim that
the murderous blockade is at length to be discontinued. France,
who apparently predominates in all these discussions, again and
again puts forward objections and demands more conferences.

Meanwhile thousands of invalids, women, children and infants,
are perishing of hunger and cold. There are no longer any swad-
dling bands in which to wrap the newly-born. People use paper, if
they have any, or old scraps of material. Meat is no longer ob-
tainable through the regulation channels, only dried cod, of which
the Viennese have a horror despite their hunger. The Entente
have too little meat themselves to be able to spare us any, and
American frozen meat is too expensive by the time it has crossed
the ocean and reached Vienna. I have joined in an appeal from
the women of Vienna for the abolition of the Meat Centres. The
only result of the Government control of meat seems to be that
meat has become quite unobtainable. The farmers are clearly opposed to Government control, and the whole population suffers
from this fact. I believe that meat will be easier to obtain if the
sale of our meagre supplies of it is unrestricted. Perhaps I and the
many other housewives are wrong, but nothing could be worse
than the conditions under Government control. So away with
the Centres. The following is an announcement of the Food
Centres, which I give word for word:—

"As meat and other foodstuffs are not at present available, in
the 90th week only pickled cabbage at the reduced price of 30
heller per kilo, can be supplied to the most destitute. The Gov-

ernment dining rooms, public war kitchens and welfare institutions will be allotted 20 dekagrammes* per head."

Thus the Government now has nothing but pickled cabbage to distribute on its food cards.

We only exist thanks to charitable gifts from abroad, and the American food parcels in particular have saved the lives of many of us Viennese. To-day I read in the newspaper: "The President of the Salzburg Provincial Government has been arrested for illicit trading in the Government property entrusted to him, such as foodstuffs, leather, clothes, etc." These are the enemies in our own camp, but how few of them are detected!

I have received a letter from my sister in Berlin, from which I quote a few passages: "Berlin is in a state of uproar. Civil war is raging in all parts of the city, so that I can no longer venture out of doors. The general strike and civil war in Berlin are not German but French. The war indemnity which the victors, seated round their green table, have decided to impose upon Germany, is fixed with the intention of loading the coming generation too with an overwhelming burden of debt. When a nation, like the German nation to-day, has lost faith in its own salvation, when it has swallowed its pride in the hope of being able to appease its hunger after the Armistice, when all hopes of a better future have been dispersed by an inhuman peace without regard to promises, then that nation does away with order and tries to achieve by force what can really only be achieved by systematic planning. If the Entente hatches further disaster instead of restoring normal conditions by a reasonable peace, then not only Germany but all the European countries will be threatened with incalculable internal dangers. Munich has indeed, with the aid of General Hoffmann, rid itself of its Bolshevist adventurers; we are still struggling against the Spartacists, who exploit the despair of the masses for the purpose of their political machinations. I believe that the bulk of the German people have too much sound sense to rush into such adventures, but they could hardly be blamed if they did succumb to the allurements of the Bolsheviks." This is what my sister writes.

Meanwhile not only the crown lands but all the parishes outside Vienna have issued decrees forbidding people from other parts to enter their territories. Now, if I journey to Laxenburg, I am a smuggler and liable to arrest. The Volkswehr is now the supreme

* About 7 ounces.

authority in connection with the supervision of food-distribution. Through the Volkswehr one can obtain transport permits for rucksacks, which are otherwise forbidden for everyday transport. Naturally a bourgeois cannot get a permit. But as business is done in these permits too, I have secured one through Schani. As long as my stock of cigars holds out, I shall have Schani's help, but I am filled with horror and alarm when I see how this precious possession is melting away.

We heard that Germany, though she herself is suffering acute distress, has voluntarily cut down her flour ration in order to be able to help us starving Viennese. The Entente, at the instigation of the French, forbids the union of Germany with Austria, which was decreed at Weimar. Moreover, the Germans are suffering more and more violence and oppression in the territories occupied by the enemy.

IX. Mutiny

THE BEST-KEPT secret of the First World War was the mutiny which flared in the French army in May and June, 1917. The seemingly endless prolongation of the war threatened to turn France into a charnel house. The foolhardy and disastrous campaign of Chemin des Dames, which was undertaken in April, 1917, by General Robert Nivelle, Joffre's successor, at last pushed the heroic but jaded army to the brink of revolt. Enormous casualties suffered by the Second Colonial Infantry Division in its attacks upon prepared positions at Heurtebise goaded the survivors into insurrection on May 3. Signs were posted on the walls of their billets proclaiming: "Down with the war! Death to those who are responsible!"

Within several weeks mutiny had tainted seventy-five regiments of infantry, twenty-three battalions of chasseurs, and twelve regiments of artillery. Especially susceptible to disaffection were divisions scattered through the four armies which had been the most brutally repulsed in Nivelle's offensive. Demoralized troops openly defied their officers, drunkenly sang the "Internationale," chanted demands for furloughs, discharged their rifles into the air, and committed acts of vandalism. By June no less than fifty-four divisions—half the divisions of the French army—were openly insubordinate. The mutiny spread until only two of twelve divisions in Champagne were considered reliable, and no division between Soisson and Paris could be trusted to obey orders. The outbreaks generally occurred when troops on leave were ordered back to the trenches; when troops were forced to go through tiresome, pointless "busy work" in repetitious training maneuvers; when furloughs were delayed; or when billets were intolerable or the food inedible. Under such provocations the mutineers gathered around their spokesmen, who were generally noncommissioned officers who harangued them. The troops were not entirely lacking in respect for their lieutenants, but they ignored their orders.

Astonishingly, the extent of the mutinies was so effectively suppressed by the French command that, according to General Erich Ludendorff, the Germans "heard but little about the mutinies and that only by degrees. Only later on did we learn the whole truth." It was too late for the Germans when they did learn the magnitude of the insurrection, for by then remedial measures had already been taken by General Henri Philippe Pétain. The quelling of the mutinies was one of the greatest services which the controversial General Pétain rendered to France. He called a halt to further massive offensives until the Americans could arrive; he ordered the strict policing of railway stations and their environs, and the punishment of released soldiers who took part in pacifist agitation in war plants where they were allowed to work. He commanded the officers to show concern for their enlisted men by improving their mess and billets, by curtailing unnecessary exercises, and by regularizing furloughs, especially for troops in the front lines. The exact degree of punishment meted out to the ringleaders of the mutinies has never been officially revealed. The French government acknowledged only twenty-three executions, but Field Marshal Sir Douglas Haig noted in his diaries of November, 1917, that he was told that "there were 30,000 'rebels' who had to be dealt with." Unconfirmed rumors persisted that whole units of mutinous *poilus* were marched off to isolated areas where they were deliberately shelled by French artillery.

Fortunately we have the testimony of an eye-witness to many incidents in the mutinies, Major General Sir Edward L. Spears, who was a British liaison officer at the headquarters of the French Fifth Army. Born August 7, 1886, Spears was privately educated and in 1903 entered the Kildare Militia. He was gazetted to the Hussars in 1906, and was serving as a temporary captain upon the war's outbreak, when he was called for liaison duty with the French Fifth Army. Winston Churchill wrote of him: "It was his duty to gain and hold the confidence and good will of the French Army Command and to preserve so far as possible in frightful circumstances their physical contact and moral relationship. The difficulties were enormous. . . . That a young officer should have acquitted himself so effectively in the white heat of this crisis explains his rise from the rank of a Subaltern to that of a General Officer." Spears was wounded four times and showered with honors. He served in the House of Commons from 1922 until 1924, and was again M.P. from 1931 until 1945. During the Second World War he was Churchill's personal representative to the French prime minister in the chaotic days of May–June, 1940, and he later headed the British mission to General De Gaulle. He was head of the Spears mission to Syria and Lebanon in 1941, and was first minister to those republics when they gained independence in 1942. He is author of *Prelude to Victory, Assignment to Catastrophe, Liaison, 1914,* and *Two Men Who Saved France: Pétain and De Gaulle,* from which we publish our excerpt.

Major General Sir Edward Spears,
Two Men Who Saved France: Pétain and De Gaulle

Towards the end of April 1917, the fortune of war appeared
to turn against the Allied armies after having smiled on them for
a brief moment. The dazzling hopes of the early spring, which the
German withdrawal to the Hindenburg Line, America's entry
into the war, and the anticipated impact of the Franco-British
offensives had caused the leaders of the Coalition to hold out,
were dashed to the ground. *The grand strategic triumph on which
so much had been staked turned into a series of dearly-bought
minor successes in a prolonged campaign of merciless attrition.*
Russia defaulted and her army began to disintegrate. The newspapers reported, often with approval, the early revolutionary
measures—the setting up of workers' and soldiers' committees, the
abolition of saluting and of military ranks. The enemy Command,
its confidence restored, directed with dogged determination the
battles in Artois, the Chemin-des-Dames, and Champagne, and
after holding up our progress, banked on renewing their successes.

The French army was exhausted. Hopelessness and *pessimism
spread to it* from the interior, *swamping as it did so the mood of
superficial enthusiasm, whipped up from above,* which had never
really taken root.

The fighting troops were at the end of their tether. Those in
authority must have seen this quite well, yet they continued to
count on them, so often in the past three years had they witnessed
their capacity for performing the impossible. This time, however,
*there were men in the ranks who not only could not but would
not answer the call. This was the crisis.* It struck, like a bolt from
the blue, among the units due to be sent up the line to the two
deadliest of the danger-spots, the Chemin-des-Dames and the
Monts-de-Champagne.

*First incidents between 29th April and 17th May. Reorganisa-
tion of the French High Command. Gravity and rapid extension
of the crisis.*

Source: From *Two Men Who Saved France: Pétain and De
Gaulle* (London: Eyre & Spottiswoode, Ltd.), pp. 86-98. Reprinted by permission of Eyre & Spottiswoode, Ltd. and Stein
and Day Publishers.

On 29th April an infantry regiment stationed at Mourmelon was ordered up the line to the sector of the Moronvilliers Heights, where it had carried out attacks on the 17th April and subsequent days and from which it had been withdrawn for a short period of rest only five days before. It was known to the men that they would be employed in a new offensive. They also knew that their division was being sent back into action when other major formations which had also taken part in the attack of 17th April were still resting far from the front. Two or three hundred men, almost all from the battalion chosen to lead the new offensive, failed to appear when their unit was leaving for the front and then announced that they would not march. The unit's officers and NCOs proved incapable of quelling the outbreak, which, however, was put down by the divisional commander within twenty-four hours.

News of this incident soon got round and other mutinous outbreaks followed. On 4th May a number of sudden desertions occurred among members of an infantry regiment in action in the Chemin-des-Dames area. In the quarters of a colonial regiment due to take part in an attack in the same sector *the men noisily refused to fight*, an action clearly provoked by the circulation of leaflets on which were blazoned such inflammatory slogans as "Down with the War!", "Death to the Warmongers!", etc. On 16th and 17th May serious trouble of a similar nature broke out in a battalion of Chasseurs, and in an infantry regiment in a reserve position on the Aisne. These unhappy incidents multiplied to a point where *the safety and cohesion of the whole army were in jeopardy*.

It was precisely on this same date, the 17th, that the French High Command was reorganised. Its first duty was to assess objectively the seriousness of the trouble so as to weigh the gravity of its task. It saw the deadly virus of indiscipline spreading. It received alarming reports from all sides. They poured in—almost uninterruptedly, alas!

19th May: In a Chasseur battalion south of the Aisne three armed companies staged *noisy demonstrations* in cantonments.

20th May: Two complete infantry regiments in the Chemin-des-Dames sector refused to obey orders. Individual *acts of insubordination* were reported in an infantry regiment in the same area.

21st and 22nd May: In an infantry regiment resting in the Tardenois district an attempt was made by agitators to stir up trouble among the men. *Delegates were elected to present at headquarters a protest against a continuation of the offensives;* a group of trouble-makers marched to the divisional depot and created a disturbance. Nearby, in another infantry regiment in the same division, *groups of soldiers turned on their officers, sang the Internationale and threw stones at them.*

25th May: In the Vosges, up to that time completely untroubled by the outbreaks, one section of an infantry regiment refused to embus for the front. They were incited to this act of defiance by their own sergeant.

26th May: Three infantry regiments of a division recalled to the front after a rest period in the Aisne sent representatives to join *in discussions at which plans for an attempted general mutiny were being hatched.*

27th May: Demonstrations and disturbances occurred in an infantry regiment out of the line in Lorraine. In the Tardenois district the men of an infantry regiment *shouted seditious slogans, sang the Internationale, and insulted and molested their officers while the regiment was embussing.*

28th May: A *serious extension of indiscipline and mutiny* was reported from six infantry regiments, a battalion of Chasseurs, and a regiment of dragoons stationed on the Aisne and farther south.

29th, 30th and 31st May: The situation deteriorated and indiscipline spread to the majority of the regiments of eight divisions and to a colonial artillery regiment, all of which had been in action in the Chemin-des-Dames sector or were about to be sent back there.

1st, 2nd and 3rd June: *Zenith of the crisis.* In fifteen to twenty units belonging to sixteen divisions, either in action or resting in the same area, men of all arms were involved for three days in the most violent outbreaks of disorder.

This catalogue of disturbances, shocking though it is, still gives an inadequate picture of the plight of the French army as the intoxicating madness spread. A detailed examination of some of the most typical cases will help us to understand better the anguish of the High Command under the threat of this appalling danger.

Example of a premeditated and methodically planned mutiny in a regiment: 28th–30th May

This was an example of a type of mutiny *conceived in cold blood, systematically organised and obstinately conducted* in an infantry regiment which up to that moment had been regarded as quite first class. Planned over a long period, it developed without a hitch, and in an atmosphere of total assurance.

This unit had taken part in May 1916 in the first attempt to re-capture Fort Douaumont, where it showed great courage and sustained heavy losses. From June 1916 to February 1917 it was almost continuously in the line in the tough Eparges sector, ex-posed to constant shelling, surprise attacks and enemy mines. At this point *symptoms of serious physical and moral exhaustion* be-came noticeable in its ranks—symptoms which affected the junior officers as well, and to which their superiors, up to the regimental and brigade commanders themselves, appeared to pay too little re-gard, whereas it should have made them doubly watchful and active, doubly willing to show themselves and take personal risks, to give encouragement and set an example. Action had been taken against certain of these officers whose grip on the situation had been notoriously feeble, and in February 1917 the unit was with-drawn for a rest. By the spring, there were grounds for hoping that when it returned to the fighting line it would once more justify its former reputation. But this moment was delayed, since the grand plan for a strategic exploitation of the attack of 16th April failed to materialise, and *the regiment was left in inglorious inactivity near Paris.* There the men, too closely in touch with the rear, were affected by the bad spirit in the interior. They listened to the *complaints of a multitude of camp-followers whose attitude re-flected the labour unrest and strikes spreading throughout the country.* They settled down all too well to their prolonged inactiv-ity, to the absence of danger, and to the enjoyment of the com-forts which came their way as a result. And when, on Whit Sunday, the lorries arrived to bring this agreeable and restful ex-istence to an end, and trundle them off to the dreaded destination of Laffaux, the harrowing farewells overcame their sense of duty. It was then that *they began to be influenced by the propaganda directed at them at the departure point, and to believe—what they were always being told—that they would be fools indeed to go and get themselves killed when so many others had apparently refused to march.*

On 28th May, at the end of its journey, the regiment installed itself in three small villages in a sector to the south of Soissons.

After the midday meal, 'la Soupe,' between 150 and 180 men attended a meeting in one of the hamlets, listened to a number of inflammatory speeches, fell in on the road in marching order, and coolly informed their company officers, when these arrived to disperse them, *that they refused to go up to the line. They had,* they said, *had enough of the war. They wanted a cease-fire immediately* and thought the Deputies had been wrong in December not to negotiate on the German proposals. They claimed that as Russia crumbled, leaving the German war-machine free to re-mass on the French front, the Government were simply pulling the wool over people's eyes, and that in fact everyone knew that the Americans would not be able to come into the war in time to be of any use. The fighting soldiers, they complained, were not getting proper leave; their rations were inadequate, their wives and children were "starving to death." *They were no longer willing to sacrifice their lives when shirkers at home were earning all the money, taking the women around in cars, cornering all the best jobs, and while so many profiteers were waxing rich.*

The mood of these demonstrators was calm and resolute. They were not drunk. They wanted their protest reported to the Government. They still respected their officers and dispersed when these told them to do so.

Misled by the ease with which they appeared to have won this round, the officers, from the divisional commander down to the most junior second lieutenants, spent the night of the 28th/29th advising each other that the best line to adopt *was one of patience and accommodation.* They moved around talking to each other when each officer should instead have returned immediately to exert his authority in his unit. They looked on the mutineers, naïvely, as mere strikers whom words would certainly soon restore to a better way of thinking. Then at dawn on the 29th they all returned to their units, with instructions to put the men to light fatigues around the camp, to give them a few pep talks, but to make no reference to the outbreak of the day before, and, most important, in no circumstances to resort to force, even if individual soldiers or groups of men tried to go off on their own.

This made it possible for the demonstrators of the day before to assemble again on the morning of the 29th and form themselves into a column—this time some 400 strong. Most of these had got themselves up to look like *strikers,* and appeared with walking sticks, flowers in their button-holes, and unbuttoned jackets. They marched in turn to the quarters of each of the two other battalions. There they were joined in the course of the morning by several hundred more supporters. By the end of the midday meal there were more than 800 of them, from every unit in the regiment. They answered to a bugle, and in due course moved off to rally support from the regiment next in line. Their discipline was excellent. They had been told by their leaders to do nothing which might provoke violence and to confine themselves to signifying *their fixed and unalterable determination to take no part in any further costly attacks.* They made this point firmly to the Divisional Commander. "You have nothing to fear, we are prepared to man the trenches, we will do our duty and the Boche will not get through. But we will not take part in attacks which result in nothing but useless casualties. . . ." They maintained the same position when harangued by the Corps Commander, who upbraided them, offered them fatherly advice, and threatened dire punishments in his various attempts to move them. All to no avail. With unshakeable politeness they repeated their complaints against the Government and what was happening in the interior, adding that *they would hold the line but would refuse to take part in any new offensive and demanded immediate peace.* About midafternoon they reached the quarters of the neighbouring regiment. Here the mutineers were fewer in number but much wilder. They urged them to be calm and to maintain respect for their officers. Then, *led on as usual by some extremely skilful organisers,* who seem from the evidence to have acted like true mob leaders throughout, they decided to continue their impressive march round the other units of the division and then to go on and capture some trains in which to set off for Paris with their own crews in the drivers' cabs. But, if necessary, they were prepared to march on the capital by stages in order to bring their demands before the Chamber of Deputies. Meanwhile they returned to their own cantonments for the night.

At dawn on the 30th, under orders from the High Command, motor convoys arrived at the camps to act as transport for the three battalions. This time all the officers were at their posts, and with tougher instructions. They shouted louder than the agitators and made their men obey them. The mutineers put up some resistance but did board the lorries. On the journey they continued their attempts at incitement, and tried to stir up the troops they met on the way. They made "hands up" and "thumbs down" signs. They whistled. They sang the Internationale. They waved bits of red cloth. They distributed leaflets containing the text of their refusal to fight and encouraged others to follow their example.

On the evening of the 30th and on the following days the regiment was halted in isolation from other units, then moved to the Verdun sector by train. The rebellious spirit persisted, but the demonstrations became less frequent. The High Command split up the battalions, and during the month of June *Courts Martial were held*. A corporal and three privates were sentenced to death for "deserting their post and refusing to obey orders in the presence of the enemy". The regiment itself supplied the firing squads and several detachments for the expiatory ceremony, which took place without incident on 28th June. *On 29th June, the regiment was stripped of its colours.* The battalion to which the leading spirits of the mutiny had belonged was disbanded on 16th July, and the necessary new postings among the officers took place.

That was the end of it. In July the two remaining battalions gave an honourable account of themselves at Verdun. In 1918 the regiment was reconstituted. It was twice mentioned in dispatches, received back its colours, and was decorated with the lanyard of the Croix de Guerre on the very spot where the 1917 mutinies had taken place.

Example of a violent outbreak in a regiment of the line: 1st–3rd June

Another type of *outbreak was violent in character and the spirit animating it was revolutionary*.

Here again our example is an infantry regiment with a first-class record and reputation and forming part of a crack division. After much hard fighting during the battle of the Somme, it was not sent back to rest as it had been led to hope that it would be. Instead, it was moved to the Argonne sector, where it suffered heavy casualties during the winter of 1916–17. It took part in the April offensive, achieving an appreciable but exceedingly costly success. It was then kept for five weeks in the line, although nearly all the neighbouring units were sent back to be reconstituted. Finally, it was sent to rest in the Tardenois area and was looking forward to catching up on its arrears of leave, when, after only a few days, on the afternoon of 1st June, the order came to return to the trenches.

At 1 pm on that day, angry protest broke out in the camp. The Colonel and the other officers rushed to the scene, but their attempts to control the disorder had little or no result. At 5 pm a procession was formed and moved off to the strains of the Internationale. *The Brigade Commander, who acted with energy, was given a violently hostile reception and greeted with cries of "Kill him!" Insults were hurled at him. He was pushed and jostled. The stars on his cuffs and his epaulettes were ripped off, as was the flag on his car.* The Divisional Commander succeeded with difficulty in forcing his way to the town hall, in front of which the mutineers were assembled. He was unable to make himself heard above the shouts and was forced by threats to postpone the regiment's departure for the front. Meanwhile, *some of the mutineers had armed themselves with wire cutters and cut the barbed wire round the punishment centre.* The prisoners were released and one of them, a lawyer, and editor of a trench newspaper, became the guiding spirit of the revolt. "Friends," he told his rescuers, "I am delighted that our movement has met with such success. We shall not be alone. I have channels of information which enable me to tell you as a fact that this evening twelve divisions have taken the same action as ourselves. Cars from Paris have set out for every sector with the mission of bringing this good news to all our comrades." The mutineers, still shouting murderous threats against their Brigadier, broke the windows and doors of the town hall with paving stones, overturned the lorries in the streets, broke the windows of houses and forced the occupants to join them.

The morning of the 2nd June began rather more calmly, though crowds of drunken soldiers were still milling about in disorderly mobs, singing the Internationale and sporting red flowers in their jackets. *The organisers of the outbreak had had numerous posters stuck up on the walls bearing the words*: *"Vive la Paix au nom de toute l'Armée!"* (*"Long live Peace, in the name of the whole Army!"*) with the result that, that evening, a new mob of demonstrators, about 2,000 strong, were repeating the exploits of the evening before, *with red flags flying* and shouts of "Long live the Revolution! Down with the war! Long live Peace! Down with tyrants!"

On 3rd June and during the next few days the regiment was moved in lorries to another camp, and the trouble subsided—far more quickly than could have been hoped—as the principal trouble-makers lost their hold over the men. Very soon the agitation had died down altogether and the men had returned, without exception, to the path of duty.

Further examples of violent outbreaks among fighting units and on the trains: 2nd–8th June

Other scenes of violent mutiny. On the evening of 2nd June, in the same area, there were rumblings of unrest in the cantonment of a battalion of Chasseurs. The commanding officer and a captain who stepped in vigorously were repulsed with stones and sticks and forced to take refuge in the CO's lodgings. *The front of the house was sprayed with bullets from the mutineers' automatic rifles*, and the Adjutant and another officer who attempted to come to the rescue of their superior officer were chased across the neighbouring gardens. *The insurgents set fire to the huts of a company which attempted to oppose the revolt, and engaged in a veritable running battle, in which several NCOs and Chasseurs were wounded.* As night ended, they retired exhausted to their huts, and no repetition of this outbreak occurred next day.

On the evening of 7th June, an incident took place at Château-Thierry station, where men *off a leave-train returning from Paris threw stones at the lamps in the entrance, sang the Internationale and shouted anti-war slogans.* A railway official, a man in his fifties, was savagely struck. A posse of policemen hurried to the scene and found themselves involved in a real battle. Their chief was wounded and had to be rushed to hospital. When an effort was made to get the train on its way, *the men jammed the brakes on, then charged onto the platforms and rushed the station manager's office* to demand the release of two of their number who had been placed under arrest. They did not return to their carriages until a company of armed troops had arrived to restore order, and then not before they had successfully demanded that the latter sheathe their bayonets. *And when the train did move, it was with the shouted threat: "We'll be back soon—with grenades!"*

The same thing happened at Esternay on 8th June. *The men of the leave draft, shouting noisily, rushed at the RTO, who attempted to arrest two of them and get them back on to their train. They beat him with sticks, punched him in the face, knocked him down, and only let him go when he was no longer physically in any condition to exert his authority.* They manhandled another officer in the outer entrance of the station. They invaded the station master's office after breaking the windows, shouted and hurled insults at the station master when he tried to interfere, then gradually dispersed and got back into the trains bound for their various destinations.

General character of the crisis from June to September

The mutinies took many forms, of which examples of the most typical have been given above, and reached their peak on 2nd June, when seventeen outbreaks were reported. The situation remained serious up to 10th June, with an average of seven incidents a day. During the rest of the month the daily average was one. In July the total fell to seven incidents altogether, in August to four, and in September to one.

Altogether, *151 incidents were recorded and examined, of which 110 were concerted outbreaks of genuine gravity.* Out of the total of 151, 112 took place in the Aisne area behind the Chemin-des-Dames sector of the front (plus five on the other parts of the front but among units which had come from the Chemin-des-Dames sector). Eight occurred in the Monts-de-Champagne district (plus two which took place in other parts of the front but involved troops from Champagne), and twenty-two occurred in various other parts of the army zone.

A total of 110 units were affected. Sixty-eight of them were present (in the line or in reserve) on the Aisne on 16th April, and six were before Monts-de-Champagne. Between them they consisted of:

> 76 Infantry Regiments
> 2 Colonial Infantry Regiments
> 21 Chasseur Battalions
> 1 Territorial Infantry Regiment
> 8 Artillery Regiments
> 1 Regiment of Dragoons
> 1 Senegalese Battalion

These units belonged to fifty-four different divisions—that is, more than half the total number of divisions in the French army at that time.

Disturbances also occurred on 110 trains and had repercussions in 130 stations due to repeated acts of indiscipline along the whole length of the lines. These disorders were an extension of those in the interior of the country, and all converged to reach their point of greatest intensity in the areas just behind the line. Angoulême, Bordeaux, Nantes, Toulouse, St. Pierre-des-Corps, St. Etienne and Limoges had all been centres of serious unrest. This spread along the lines of communication towards the army zone until it reached the main lines, of which the principal was the line Paris–Châlons–Nancy.

Such was the storm of madness which for several weeks swept a harassed and distracted France, threatening to blind her both to her objectives and to her duties.

PART III

The War's Diplomacy

X. America Enters the War

IF GERMANY had not resorted to unrestricted submarine warfare as a counterstrategy to British efforts at economic strangulation, it is unlikely that America would have become a belligerent in the First World War. Possessing vast resources within its remote boundaries, isolationist by tradition, diverse in its ethnic composition, antimilitarist in spirit, America was nevertheless drawn into the war's vortex because German submarines (in contrast to the British surface fleet) killed 240 of its citizens and destroyed its property on the high seas. Counterbalancing much of the German U-boat provocation was the fact that England also flagrantly violated America's neutral rights, but by less deadly means.

On August 4, 1914, President Woodrow Wilson issued a formal proclamation of neutrality; two weeks later he urged his fellow Americans to remain neutral "not only in act but in word and thought." This soon proved to be a counsel of perfection, but at the outbreak of the war any course other than neutrality would have been regarded as mad, considering the nation's history. The American government could predict the onset of the "tribal syndrome"—the ethnocentric identification of the average citizen with the country of his ancestral extraction. Professor Ernest R. May wrote in his authoritative book, *The World War and American Isolation*, "Owing to the large English and German elements in the population, government leaders assumed that the nation could never take part on either side without bringing on a civil war at home." In addition to the large numbers of German-Americans, settled especially in the Midwest, were citizens of Irish extraction whose rancor toward England was as deep seated as the antipathy of American Jews against tsarist Russia, the land of the pogroms. But "moral support," or a "predilection" for one belligerent as opposed to another was only velleity; it did not signify any compelling desire for America to take an active part.

Events, however, were to work against America's "sitting out" the war. The German invasion of neutral Belgium, the sack of Louvain, and the bombing of the open city of Antwerp inflamed American opinion to such an extent that President Wilson estimated that 90 percent of the citizens were at heart pro-Ally, as were, in fact, the president himself and his cabinet. But as Professor May explained, "It was thought possible to be sympathetic yet completely neutral. Although resentment could be stirred by decisions harmful to the Allies, even stronger emotions might be called up by actions that seemed partisan or unneutral." Apart from a few fire breathers such as Theodore Roosevelt, most American spectators felt only the urge to cheer or curse from the sidelines; they certainly did not want to enter the lists.

The expectation of a short war soon proved illusory, and the American government had to make a number of decisions affecting its neutrality. President Wilson's government announced that no armed ships of the belligerents would be allowed to leave American ports. This immobilized a number of German merchant vessels equipped with gun mountings and high-speed engines which could have been used as auxiliary cruisers. However, the British Admiralty successfully persuaded America to release from its harbors British vessels "armed for defense." The counselor of the State Department, Robert Lansing, accepted the distinction between the offensive and defensive armament. At the outbreak of the war the British cabinet issued an order-in-council expressing its intention of abiding by the Declaration of the London Maritime Conference of 1908–9, an unratified code of sea warfare which exempted from the contraband list certain commodities such as copper ore and cotton, which were important American exports. Washington thereupon urged all the belligerents to accept the Declaration. But on August 20, 1914, the British cabinet reversed itself with the equivocal announcement that it would comply with the Declaration "subject to certain modifications and additions . . . , indispensable to the efficient conduct of . . . naval operations." For several months the British navy was so preoccupied with transporting troops to France and guarding its ocean commerce that it could do little to clamp a blockade upon Germany, although it did drive German commerce from the seas. On September 26, 1914, the United States asked the British to accept the Declaration of London *in toto*, which, if agreed upon, would have obligated the British to allow neutral vessels unimpeded access to German ports or to such neutral ports as Rotterdam (whence there could be transshipment to Germany), and to retain on the noncontraband list such strategic materials as cotton, copper, raw textiles, rubber, leather, nitrates and paper—all of which were convertible to military use. As a conciliatory expedient, Britain offered "to buy" suspected contraband which it was determined to seize. If Britain had fully complied with the Declaration, it would have been seriously hampered in its successive efforts to strangle Germany economically.

A grave issue was posed for America and other neutrals in October, 1914, when the British Admiralty proclaimed an extensive mine zone in the North Sea. London asked that neutral ships use only the easily patrolled Straits of Dover instead of the sea lanes between the Hebrides and the Faroe Islands, to the north of Scotland. Neutral vessels would be given safe passage by being assigned Admiralty pilots to guide them through the mine fields. In practice, the neutral ships first had to put in British ports, where they were subjected to leisurely search for contraband before they took on the Admiralty pilots to guide them through the mine fields to their Scandinavian, Dutch, or German destinations. The Scandinavian shipping companies, which carried most of the American cargo and passengers in North Sea waters, docilely complied with the Admiralty's demands. During the first six months of the war President Wilson's government offered no protest to the mining; its vessels submitted to search and took aboard Admiralty pilots, with the result that no American ships were sunk by the British. This complaisant attitude provoked the supporters of Germany to denounce America's unneutral acquiescence in Britain's violation of international law by its brazen mining of the open sea.

With the increasing realization that the war would be long and the supplies of ammunition soon exhausted, the prospects seemed excellent for an American war boom which could reverse the business recession which the nation had been experiencing in 1914. The United States government revoked its initial ban on commercial loans to the belligerents, which made it easier for the Allies, with their superior fleets, to obtain munitions, food, draft animals, and clothing. France applied to the banking house of J. P. Morgan and Company for the first of a succession of loans. The National City Bank of New York lent money to the German government. But as the war dragged on, long-term commercial credit extended to France, Great Britain, and Russia greatly exceeded what was offered Germany. Pro-Germans complained that American banks had thereby accumulated a vested interest in an Entente victory for the guaranteed recovery of their loans. The American policy of allowing unlimited manufacture and sale of munitions evoked no protests until after the Battle of the Marne, when German agents in America began organizing a publicity campaign for an arms embargo. Bills to embargo arms were introduced in Congress but were successfully opposed by President Wilson's administration. The domination of the Atlantic sea lanes by the Allied fleets permitted arms shipments to reach Entente ports but not those of the Central Powers, which the German supporters considered to be an unfair traffic, even if there were no legal grounds for calling it unneutral.

Following the British victory over a German squadron in the Battle of Dogger Bank on January 24, 1915, Berlin and London began vying with one another in successive efforts to strangle each other economically. The outcome was to be Germany's undoing, for its U-boat campaign was eventually to trigger America's entry into the war. During the first six months of the war, the German navy had generally followed the accepted usages of international law in commerce raiding. The cruiser *Emden*, for example, provided for the safety of the passengers and crews of the enemy ships which it sank in the Indian Ocean. It could not conduct the ships into prize courts or German ports, since nearly all the German colonial harbors were seized early in the war. Even the U-boat commanders were expected to ignore the great risk to their thin-skinned, cockle-shell crafts by surfacing, challenging suspected enemy vessels, and allowing the crews to take to their life boats before sinking the intercepted ships. But after the land fighting had settled into the stalemate of trench warfare, a new U-boat strategy—nothing less than a ruthless submarine "blockade" of the British Isles—was threatened in an interview which Grand Admiral von Tirpitz gave to the American journalist Karl von Wiegand on December 23, 1914. "England wants to starve us," Tirpitz said. "We can play the same game. We can bottle her up and destroy every ship that endeavors to break the blockade. . . . We are superior to England in submarines of the larger types."

On January 26, 1915, two days after the Dogger Bank defeat, the German Federal Council announced that on February 1 it was taking under its control all the stocks of grain and flour in the country. This implied that food was to be considered a military commodity to which the armed forces would have first claim. The action at once boomeranged, for until then the British had allowed neutral ships carrying foodstuffs to proceed to German as well as to neutral ports. The British promptly seized the American freighter *Wilhelmina*, lying at anchor in Falmouth harbor, laden with foodstuffs consigned to Germany. Thus began a starvation campaign which Germany was destined to lose. On February 2, 1915, Great Britain abandoned what was left of the Declaration of London by placing *all* goods on its contraband list. The British government tried to defend its action by claiming that the decision of the German Federal Council to take all foodstuffs under its exclusive control created, in effect, a total war economy, and this justified the Allies in declaring as contraband all goods consigned to Germany.

Admiral von Tirpitz's threat of impending blockade was confirmed by a proclamation on February 4 which stated that "the waters around Great Britain and Ireland, including the English Channel, are hereby proclaimed a war region. On and after February 18 every enemy merchant vessel found in this region will be destroyed, without its always being possible to warn the crews or passengers of the dangers threatening. Neutral ships will also incur danger in the war region, where, in view of the misuse of neutral flags ordered by the British Government, and incidents inevitable in sea warfare, attacks intended for hostile ships may affect neutral ships also."

The American government became increasingly apprehensive over the blockade threat, and on February 20, 1915, Secretary of State William Jennings Bryan issued a communication urging "Germany and Great Britain to agree: (1) That neither will sow any floating mines, whether upon the high seas or in territorial waters; that neither will plant on the high seas anchored mines except within cannon range of harbors for defensive purposes only; and that all mines shall bear the stamp of the Government planting them and be so constructed as to become harmless if separated from their moorings. (2) That neither will use submarines to attack merchant vessels of any nationality except to enforce the right of visit and search. (3) That each will require their respective merchant vessels not to use neutral flags for the purpose of disguise or *ruse de guerre*." Bryan proposed further that Germany should allow American food imported into Germany to "be consigned to agencies to be designated by the United States Government." Great Britain was asked not to place foodstuffs on the contraband list, nor to interfere with food shipments to the noncombatant population in Germany "if consigned to agencies designated by the United States Government in Germany."

Secretary of State Bryan's proposal was disregarded by both Britain and Germany. On March 2, British Prime Minister Asquith announced a virtual blockade of the German coast, warning that no neutral vessel would be allowed to enter or to leave any German port. U-boat warfare now had its opportunity, although it began in 1915 largely as a bluff of *Schrecklichkeit*. When Admiral Hugo von Pohl, the militant advocate of a submarine offensive, replaced Admiral Friedrich Ingenohl as the commander of the German High Seas Fleet, the German navy had only 21 U-boats available for North Sea operations, and of this number only 9 were diesel powered and had a radius of operations that could reach Britain's west coast. A prewar German naval study had estimated that it would require 220 U-boats to destroy British shipping. But sporadic acts of terror could produce a dramatic impact. The U-boat sinking of the British passenger steamer *Falaba* on March 28, 1915, took 1 American life. On April 28 a German plane attacked the American ship *Cushing*. A U-boat torpedoed the American vessel *Gulflight* on May 1, taking 2 American lives. This was followed by a submarine attack which had vast repercussions—the torpedoing of the Cunard liner *Lusitania* off Kinsale, Ireland, on May 7, 1915, by the *U-20* at the order of Commander Walter Schwieger. One thousand one hundred and ninety-eight passengers and crewmen were killed, including 139 Americans, mostly women and children.

The reaction of most Americans was a paroxysm of indignation, and any determination to maintain peace at any price diminished steadily from that day. On May 13 President Wilson sent the first of several grim notes to Berlin demanding reparations for the loss of the American lives on the *Lusitania*, and insisting on Germany's "strict accountability" in taking "the usual precaution of visit and search to ascertain whether a suspected merchantman [was] in fact carrying contraband of war under a neutral flag." It was difficult for Germany to comply with Wilson's demand since many enemy merchantmen were armed, and some of the British "cargo" vessels were in reality disguised, heavily armed Q-ships. And in naval warfare U-boats on the surface were notoriously sitting-duck targets. President Wilson's demands were tantamount to an insistence upon the abandonment of submarine warfare. His pacifistic Secretary of State William Jennings Bryan was so disturbed by the implications of the President's stern protests that he resigned, being replaced by Robert Lansing. The new secretary was in full agreement with Wilson, and German equivocations over just what was meant by "freedom of the seas" were firmly rejected by Washington until October, 1915, when Berlin finally agreed that merchant ships would not be sunk without warning or without safeguarding noncombatant lives. Germany's compliance with Wilson's demands represented the sobering influence of Chancellor

Bethmann-Hollweg, who clearly understood that unrestricted submarine warfare would "inevitably cause America to join our enemies."
His perspicacity was shared by the German ambassador to Washington, Count Johann-Heinrich von Bernstorff, who had convinced Foreign Minister von Jagow of the disastrous consequences of drawing
America into the war.

There followed a lull in German-American relations. One reason
that Germany seemed conciliatory was because its submarine fleet was
still too small to clamp an effective blockade around Great Britain.
But during the course of 1915 and the spring of 1916, the shipyards at
Kiel worked night and day constructing new U-boats of advanced design. By the spring of 1916 Germany was falling under the ascendancy
of General von Hindenburg and General Ludendorff, who shared
Grand Admiral Tirpitz's conviction that the U-boat, used without
squeamish restrictions, was Germany's last hope for victory.

German-American relations were threatened with rupture again on
March 24, 1916, when Commander Herbert Pustkuchen of the U-29
torpedoed the Channel steamer *Sussex*, British owned but leased to
France. The commander mistook the *Sussex* for a mine layer and
ordered it sunk. The blast only damaged the ship, but of the 325 passengers aboard, of whom 25 were Americans, 80 were killed or injured, 4 Americans being among the latter. President Wilson, after
waiting for an investigation which convinced him that the ship had
been torpedoed and not damaged by a mine, sent an ultimatum to
Berlin on April 10. Wilson warned that "unless the Imperial Government should now declare its intention to abandon its present practices
of submarine warfare and return to a scrupulous observance of the
practices clearly prescribed by the law of nations, the Government of the United States can have no choice but to sever diplomatic
relations with the German Empire altogether." Germany backed down
partially. Although public opinion in Germany clamored for a massive
U-boat campaign, Emperor William yielded to the wise counsel of
Theobald von Bethmann-Hollweg and Gottlieb von Jagow, and on
May 3 he gave American Ambassador Gerard a mild reply. The note
stated that although Germany had not been sinking ships indiscrimi-
nately, its government was nevertheless ordering its naval authorities
to conduct submarine operations everywhere according to the general
rules of international law as regards visit and search. The note added
the proviso that Germany would expect America to compel England
likewise to observe international law in its naval warfare; otherwise
Germany would reserve complete freedom of action. This was the last
triumph of restraint in the kaiser's war policy. Admiral Tirpitz resigned in despair over what looked like the final renunciation of unrestricted use of the submarine—the sovereign weapon.

All of the German forces of the Right—the pan-Germanists, the
military faction, the Conservatives—wanted to be rid of the quixotic
influence of Bethmann, Bernstorff, and von Jagow. They eventually
prevailed over the unstable kaiser. Emperor William acceded to the
implacable Ludendorff and on November 22, 1916, he replaced von
Jagow at the foreign ministry with Arthur Zimmermann. Von Jagow

wrote of his successor: "With Zimmermann the fanatical U-boat warriors thought they had a free hand. He was in his heart always pro-U-boat." A more plausible case for the risky U-boat strategy could now be made, for by January, 1917, Germany had built 111 seagoing submarines, and scores of others were under construction. The U-boat fanatics scorned the idea of a serious "war" with an America which had under arms so trifling a force as 87,000 in August, 1914, and which, two years later, could not even bring the Mexican "bandit" Pancho Villa to heel.

The U-boat proponents were given a pretext for employing their strategy when the Allied statement of war aims was made public on January 10, 1917, in response to President Wilson's inquiry addressed to all the belligerents. The Allies demanded the restoration of Belgium, Serbia, and Montenegro; the evacuation of the invaded territories in France, Russia, and Rumania; the restitution of "provinces formerly torn from the Allies by force"; the "liberation" of Italians, Slavs, and Rumanians. The German Supreme High Command regarded these aims as no less than the intention to dismember and dishonor Germany and its allies. Germany had been deliberately vague in its response to Wilson's inquiry as to its war aims. But the way was now clear to rally Reichstag and public support for the retention of the territories already won by the German armies, and for starving England into submission.

At a conference called by the kaiser in the castle of Pless on January 10, 1917, Field Marshal von Hindenburg, General Ludendorff, and Admiral Henering von Holtzendorff brushed aside the prophetic warnings of Chancellor Bethmann-Hollweg that unrestricted U-boat warfare would inevitably add America to the list of Germany's enemies, reviving their confidence; that German-American citizens would not revolt; that American ships and troops would actually reach Europe. Disdaining the pessimism of Bethmann the Cassandra, Admiral Holtzendorff assured the kaiser: "I guarantee on my word as a naval officer that no American will set foot on the continent!" This convinced the kaiser and on January 31, 1917, the German government announced that beginning on February 1, its submarines would sink without warning *all* ships, including neutrals after a brief period of grace, which were sighted within a broad zone around Great Britain, France, Italy, and the eastern Mediterranean. One American vessel a week would be allowed to sail to and from England by a specified route.

President Wilson's response was to sever diplomatic relations with Germany on February 3. Since the kaiser's government had already discounted the probability of America's entry into the war, the new foreign minister, Zimmermann, wanted to distract and pin down the United States by embroiling it in further conflict with Mexico (with whom it had already been skirmishing in an ineffectual "punitive campaign" to capture the bandit and border raider, Pancho Villa), and by making America fear a possible Japanese *volte face* and attack. On March 1 Americans were outraged by the publication of the notorious Zimmermann Telegram, which had been intercepted by British naval intelligence and divulged to President Wilson. In his cable Zimmermann had instructed the German minister in Mexico City, Heinrich von Eckhardt, to propose to the president of Mexico a German-Mexican alliance, and to promise German support in a Mexican reconquest of Texas, New Mexico, and Arizona. Mexico was to persuade Japan to change sides in the war from the Allies to the Central Powers. After the provocation of the Zimmermann Telegram, war with Germany was all but inevitable.

The unrestricted submarine campaign was now waged with deadly efficiency against British and neutral shipping. By the end of the war, the U-boats sank 5,708 Allied and neutral ships, including about half of the United Kingdom's total cargo fleet. Until it became a belligerent and adopted the convoy system to which England belatedly resorted, America had its share of ship losses. The American vessels *Housatonic, Lyman M. Law, Algonquin, City of Memphis, Illinois, Vigilancia,* and *Healdton* were sunk by German submarines in the months of February and March, 1917. By now most Americans felt provoked beyond endurance. On April 2 President Wilson read a war message to a joint session of Congress. After impassioned and often bitter debate, the American declaration of war on Germany was adopted on April 6 by a vote of 82 to 6 in the Senate, and 373 to 50 in the House of Representatives. Contrary to the contemptuous predictions of the kaiser's military advisors, two million American troops and vast quantities of supplies were transported in vigilantly guarded convoys to Europe, and Germany's fate was thereby sealed by November 11, 1918.

To illustrate America's mixed feelings towards the war, we publish the pro-Allied speech of Congressman Joe H. Eagle of Texas, and the anti-British address of Congressman Willaim L. La Follette of Washington (not to be confused with the equally isolationist Senator Robert M. La Follette of Wisconsin).

Joe Henry Eagle,
Representative from Texas, U.S. Congress, House, *Congressional Record*, 65th Congress, 1st Session, April 5, 1917, LV, Part 1, 357.

Mr. Chairman, without any mental reservation whatsoever, I give my voice and my vote to this resolution. It states the truth in plain, simple words. The Imperial German Government, without formally declaring, has nevertheless made and still is making, war upon the United States. While professing to obey international law, her submarines have sunk American ships upon the high seas without search or warning, and while professing friendship for our people and Nation, she has thus murdered our men, women, and children. While herself professing to desire a free sea and "a place in the sun" she has without authority of international law announced to us that from February 1, 1917, one American ship will each week be allowed by her to enter and one to leave a port of her enemies, provided we paint that ship such color as she may prescribe and carry such cargo as she may designate and enter such port as she may permit, and that otherwise, without any warning, search, or seizure, her submarines will sink American ships and send American citizens to instant death. And she has made good her decree to this time. Thus she has as completely blockaded our ports and shores as if her fleet rode triumphant in our waters.

At every American port great steamships, laden with the cotton of the South, the corn and wheat and cattle of the West, the multiplied products of the North, and the manufactures of the East, lie at anchor afraid to move toward their destination because the German submarine lurks beneath the sea to sink ship and cargo and murder every soul on board without warning. And at each American port each warehouse is filled with American merchandise of both the raw and finished product which can not be discharged because the steamships thus lie at anchor, although a ready foreign market awaits such legitimate products of American farms, fields, mines, and factories, and although under unbroken international law for centuries it is lawful for such commerce to move. As a result tens of thousands of freight cars are similarly loaded and at the various ports of the country, ready to discharge, but used only as warehouses, thus entailing congestion and the paralysis of the Nation's transportation business. If this situation is not relieved, the normal and proper processes of the domestic peace and prosperity of the United States must shortly cease, and endless loss, confusion, and distress must ensue. As a result factories must close down, throwing hundreds of thousands of men out of employment; strikes and riots will prevail; the prices of wheat, cattle, corn, cotton, and all other raw products must fall, to the injury, if not the ruin, of the farmers; and an indescribable list of calamities must befall our people. And hence it is true that Germany has in effect blockaded our ports and shores.

It is more distressing that a great nation should, in violation of the accepted principles of international law, for which she has herself always heretofore stood, dictate to the neutral nations of the world where their ships, cargoes, and citizens may or may not go.

But more appalling still is the fact that Germany should, in the conduct of her submarine operations, lose all regard both for neutral rights under international law and for human life itself; for, notwithstanding her note to the United States less than a year ago that she would no longer sink merchant ships of neutrals

without conforming to that provision of international law requiring first warning and search and the safety of passengers and
crews, she has broken that solemn promise by her decree of January 31, 1917, and since then has sunk American ships at will
without warning and has thus murdered American citizens. Thus
the Imperial German Government has made and is making war
upon the United States. The situation is intolerable. Any other but
a calm, friendly, and peace-loving nation would promptly have declared war on Germany when, by order of her Government, her
merciless submarine sank the *Lusitania*, carrying over a thousand
human beings to instant death, of whom more than 100 were
American citizens. But, in friendship, we employed diplomacy
to induce Germany to forego such barbarity, and she gave her
solemn word thereafter to conform to international law. When, by
her decree of January 31, she broke her plighted faith with us,
ignoring our rights and the dictates of humanity, and trampled
under foot our most sacred sovereign rights, there is no alternate
left to us but abject debasement or resort to armed force. As for
me, there is no room left for argument. They have broken faith
and friendship and denied our rights, without which our national
sovereignty itself would be dishonored. To me the issue appears as
plain as the light of day. The cave man has once again broken
loose upon the world. He is mad and crazy. He knows not the im-
pulses of humanity; he respects neither his own treaties and agreements nor the rights of others; he feels not the sentiments of
truth or sympathy or justice; he is bent on the unwavering course
of brute force, pillage, and murder. That cave man is the crazy
German Emperor, and the heartless Prussian military caste and
oligarchy of autocratic power which surrounds, urges, and sup-
ports him.

They have uniformly perverted the truth, broken the faith of
their treaties, persistently violated the law of nations, trampled
under foot the highest rights of humanity, filled the world with
conscienceless spies, debased the consciences of their countrymen,
enslaved free peoples, violated their sacred promises to the United
States, plotted to array other nations with the Imperial German
Government and nation against us, violated our friendship and
hospitality by constituting their Washington embassy a nest of
spies and plotters against our industries, our institutions, and our
sovereignty, murdered 240 of our men, women, and children upon
the high seas, and persistently made war for many months upon
the United States, her property, her citizens, her rights, and her

sovereignty by ruthless submarine warfare upon the free high seas in admitted violation of her plighted word.

Our patient and peace-loving President, answering the united prayers of our peace-loving Nation, has uniformly pursued the methods of peace and diplomacy, making representations of our acknowledged rights, and, in the name of the ancient and unbroken friendship between the two great countries, appealed for justice, law, and the right to pursue undisturbed our acknowledged national rights. His representations have been evaded, denied, or spurned, and the sacred promises made by the Imperial German Government have been broken in an hour without warning. Further argument is in vain. The cave man with murder in his heart can not reason, will not reason. He has appealed to the elemental brute force. He must be put down or the free democracies of this world are doomed.

I am profoundly sorry for the kind and honest German people, who have been and are yet under the iron heel of the Prussian military oligarchy. It has been forced to use the keenest development yet known of the human brain for the most diabolical purposes yet conceived in the human heart.

The issue thus forced upon the United States is whether we shall abjectly crawl before organized hostile power or whether this Nation shall preserve its interests, its self-respect, its honor, its national existence. If the allies who are fighting the battle of the free democracies of the world shall fall before the mailed fist of Prussian militarism, the United States must be the next victim.

The same Prussian military caste still controls the German Nation which pounced on little Holland [actually it was Denmark] in 1864 and appropriated the two States of Schleswig and Holstein; which in 1866 pounced on Austria, its neighbor and of its own blood; which in 1870, for conquest, pounced like a tiger upon France and appropriated the two States of Alsace and Lorraine and $1,000,000,000 in gold to constitute its present war chest; and which, while pretending that a grasping, barbaric Russia, a vain, revengeful France, and a selfish, plotting England brought about the present European war to dismember the German Empire, thrust itself with the thoroughness of a machine and the fury of a volcano upon an unsuspecting Europe for conquest, glory, and indemnity; and that same Prussian military caste has taught each citizen of the German Empire that but for American money and supplies victorious Germany would long since have celebrated her victory, her conquest, and her huge indemnities. They would stiffen their German people against Americans as predicate to the day of reckoning the Government is sure to plan and force if it shall continue in power, especially as half the gold of all the world is within our vaults and we are least prepared to defend our rights against the most puissant nation in all the world. I am not deluded in the task we are about to undertake nor in the burden thus thrust upon us if we are to preserve this matchless Republic from destruction.

In girding up our loins as a Nation for the serious burden cast upon us we shall need every ounce of strength of a united people. For one I am weary of hearing of antagonisms and bitterness in the United States between the North and the South, between city and country, between capital and labor, between Jew and Gentile, between Catholic and Protestant, between prohibitionist and antiprohibitionist, between railroads and employees, between the producer and the manufacturer, between borrower and banker, between different races, creeds, and interests, as if each were not desirable and necessary to the other in the free economic, intellectual, and spiritual life of our Nation. And I am weary of constantly hearing of differentiations such as Irish-Americans, Jewish-Americans, Italian-Americans, English-Americans, and German-Americans, as if any foreign-born citizen, heartily welcome to our hospitable shores, yet bore allegiance in law or heart to any other land than free America; and I fervently pray, as I devoutly believe, that one compensation for our sacrifices and sufferings will be that hereafter all hyphens will disappear and that the chief and only boast of all men beneath the Stars and Stripes will be that he is an American citizen.

Therefore, in final analysis, it is a war unto death between autocracy and democracy, and autocracy has brought the challenge to our doors.

But for the cave man the German people would resume their normal peaceful relations of friendship and honor with all the world. One of the hopes of the awful catastrophe of European war is that the cave man may be conquered and the noble German people set free.

The United States should do a man's part in this crisis—not a craven's part of pretended defense only. If money is needed, it should be supplied without stint; if food and clothing, then our fields and mines and factories should supply it; if ships, then the valor of the line of John Paul Jones, Farragut, Semmes, and Dewey will respond; if men, then the best blood of all the world, acting in freedom's holy cause, will respond with enthusiasm wherever duty calls.

Now that the American people must take their firm and final stand for their acknowledged rights, let timidity and diplomacy and foreign sentiment and cowardly pacifism be engulfed at once in the mighty tide of American patriotic enthusiasm to defend our national rights, to uphold international law, to preserve civilization against autocratic brute force, to overthrow the last vestige of absolutism on earth, and to maintain our national sovereignty as the last and best hope of mankind.

WILLIAM L. LA FOLLETTE,
REPRESENTATIVE FROM WASHINGTON, U.S. CONGRESS, HOUSE,
Congressional Record, 65TH CONGRESS, 1ST SESSION,
APRIL 5, 1917, LV, PART 1, 371

Mr. Chairman, when history records the truth about this awful act we are about to commit here, which means the maiming and dismembering of thousands of our noble boys and the deaths of thousands more, it will record that the Congress of the United States made this declaration of war under a misapprehension of the facts inexcusable in itself and that the people at large acquiesced in it on the theory that the Congress should have the facts, and would not make a declaration of war not justified by every rule of equity and fair dealing between nations, impartially applied by this country to all belligerents, and that after our following that course one of these contesting nations, despite our impartial action, had wantonly destroyed our legitimate commerce and destroyed the lives of some of our people.

I say the people acquiesce in our actions here to-day on exactly that false assumption of the facts. We have not treated, as a Government, these belligerents with any degree of impartiality; but, on the contrary, have demanded of one of them absolute obedience to our ideas and interpretations of international law, and have allowed at least one of the other belligerents to override at will the established rules and practice of all the civilized nations of the world for a hundred years with but feeble protest, and, in many cases, with no protest at all.

We surrendered to Great Britain practically all we contested for in the War of 1812. It is true, as far as we know, that she has not impressed our seamen, but she has seized and appropriated to her own use entire cargoes and the ships that carried them. Not carriers in European trade, but carriers to South America.

One of the underlying causes of the awful holocaust in Europe was because Germany had by her systematized reductions in cost of manufacturing, by subsidization of transportation lines and methods of credits made such serious inroads on Great Britain's trade in South America as to seriously disturb her equanimity and threaten her prestige as well as attendant profits.

Mr. Chairman, this war now devastating Europe so ruthlessly is not a war of humanity, but a war of commercialism, and there is not a student of economic conditions within the sound of my voice but knows that to be the fundamental cause of that war, although there are many primary and intermediate questions entering into it. But I digress, Mr. Chairman. I have said that Great Britain has seized our ships engaged in peaceful commerce on the Western Hemisphere, surrounded by all the hallowed shades of the Monroe doctrine, which we are about to abrogate; has taken them to England and impressed them into her own service, and apparently without protest from our Government now demanding a strict accounting by Germany.

Mr. Chairman, there is no doubt in my mind but that Germany's action in regard to her submarine warfare is reprehensible, is wrong, and would merit punishment; but, Mr. Chairman, can we consistently declare war on Germany and enter into an alliance with "perfidious Albion," who, without regard to international law, laid down a prescribed zone in the Atlantic Ocean and the North Sea sowing those waters with deadly contact mines. Three of our vessels were sunk in this prescribed zone with attendant loss of life; many other vessels were likewise destroyed without protest by our Government, which by indisputable evidence has, to some extent at least, suppressed the facts in regard to the matter.

Mr. Chairman, is a life lost by the destruction of a vessel coming in contact with a floating mine less dear than one lost on a vessel sunk by a torpedo fired by a submarine? Is the water less cold or wet?

Mr. Chairman, the highwayman who holds you up is less culpable than the coward who sends you a bomb by express or through the mail or sets a spring gun. The floating mine, in my judgment, is more despicable than the submarine, whose operators are at least taking some chances of losing their own lives. We are asked to go into partnership with the belligerent who prescribed a zone and sowed it full of mines to help it destroy the belligerent who prescribed a zone and in that zone uses submarines. Oh, consistency, thou art a jewel! . . .

Mr. Chairman, the President of the United States in his message to Congress intimated that Germany had maintained a spy system in the United States, even to the extent of having spies in some of our departments. Mr. Chairman, that declaration was made no doubt for what it was worth, as far as affecting the judgment of Congress was concerned, but it was really meant for the consumption of the people at large, who are mostly unaware that the State Department of the United States Government has a secret fund for paying our own secret spies throughout the world, maintained in time of peace as well as in war time. Are our boys to be sent to punish Germany for doing that which, to some extent at least, we practice ourselves?

Mr. Chairman, this is probably no time for recrimination nor for referring to past mistakes, in my judgment, of the administration; but, Mr. Chairman, an administration which can not stand fair and open criticism of its action as an administration is unworthy of the respect of a democracy, and an attempt to stifle in any way such criticism is an attempt to shackle the liberties for which our forefathers contended, and future generations will pass judgment, probably unerringly, on an Executive who classed as willfully expressing no opinion but their own 12 men in one of the branches of the American Congress who did not supinely agree with him in a course that he himself subsequently characterized as ineffective and futile. These men had taken the same oath of office to uphold the Constitution of the United States as had the President. Their prerogative was legislative, his was executive. He has under the Constitution a right to advise, but that does not carry with it the right to criticize because his advice is not acquiesced in by all the Members of the Congress. Such criticism is, in fact, an attempt at coercion and intimidation which augurs but illy for our liberty if supinely submitted to.

The President of the United States in his message of the 2d of April said that the European war was brought on by Germany's rulers without the sanction or will of the people. For God's sake, what are we doing now? Does the President of the United States feel that the will of the American people is being consulted in regard to this declaration of war? The people of Germany surely had as much consideration as he has given the people of the United States. He has heard the cry of the Shylocks calling for their pound of flesh; later on he will hear the cry of Rachel weeping for her children and mourning because they are not, sacrificed to make good the pound of flesh in the name of liberty. The exclamation

"O Liberty! Liberty! how many crimes are committed in thy name!" was well made.

Ours is the greatest Nation on the face of the globe. We have had a chance, if we had maintained a strict neutrality, to have bound up the wounds of the oppressed and to have upheld the tenets of the highest civilization throughout the world. But, no; we are asked to go into partnership with the country that has never allowed justice and right to have any weight with her when conquest and gold were placed in the balance. In India, which she held by right of conquest, as a punishment to those natives of that country who desired to be free of England's yoke and rebelled, even as did we in our Revolutionary period, she mercifully tied many of the rebels to the mouths of her cannon and humanely blew them to atoms as a sample of English Christianity. She destroyed the Boer Republic by intrigue and force of arms; she forced, for love of gold, the opium trade on China. Christian England, our would-be partner! In the Napoleonic wars she, by force of arms, confiscated the entire shipping of small but neutral nations to her own use, just as she has in a smaller degree appropriated ships of our citizens to her own use within the past two years. During the Civil War she fell over herself to recognize the Confederacy, and gave it every encouragement possible. Now we are asked to become her faithful ally against a country that, whatever her faults, surely has no blacker record than that of Christian England; to contribute our money and our people in the holy name of liberty to destroy one belligerent, which the President designates as Prussian militarism, a menace to the world; but English navalism, which is surely as great a menace, we enter into partnership with. George Washington said, "Avoid European entanglements," but we are recklessly entering a path to the end of which no man can foresee or comprehend, at the behest of, in many cases, a venal press and of a pacifist President.

God pity our country, gentlemen of the House of Representatives, if you desire that this cup be placed to our country's lips to quaff for crimes committed by a country for unneutral actions and that we enter into an alliance with another country which has been much less neutral. You may do so; I can not so vote at this time.

Mr. Chairman, I am of French extraction; my forefathers fled from France to escape the ax after the edict of Nantes. I hate oppression; I hate deceit; I love liberty as my life. My ancestor after fleeing from France came to this country and settled in New Jersey when it was a wilderness, and gave his life in trying to conquer it. He escaped the ax in France, but was burned at the stake by the Indians in the then wilderness west of the settlements in New Jersey. He left three boys, all of whom took part in the Revolutionary War, and the one from whom I descended has his name inscribed on a tablet in the courthouse of the county seat of Putnam County, Ind., as one of the Revolutionary soldiers residing and dying in that county.

Mr. Chairman, I have one uncle lying in a soldier's grave at Marietta, Ga., who was with Sherman on his march to the sea and who gave up his life that Old Glory and all she represents should not perish from the earth. Mr. Chairman, the man who says I am not as patriotic as he lies in his throat. Is it a gauge of patriotism to vote calamity, debt, death, and destruction on our country in the judgment of a man who is not himself infallible? Have not those who view it the other way the same right to consideration and respect as those who see relief only through a sea of blood? God forbid that in free America such an unjust discrimination can ever be made. Yet the press is holding up to ridicule and contempt those of our citizens who counsel against entering into this awful carnival of death. They are sowing the wind, and later on will reap the whirlwind in all probability. The American people, if they value their freedom, will not long tolerate such a spirit of nontoleration.

Mr. Chairman, throughout the country patriotic meetings are being held to encourage enlistments of our young men and boys into the Army to engage in this war in advance of our declaration.

Mr. Chairman, I suggest a resolution, which should be passed and adhered to by the young men of our country and by our soldiers who are asked to enter the trenches of Europe:

"I hereby pledge myself to the service of my country and will guarantee to go and uphold its honor and its flag as soon as the sons of all the newspaper editors who have stood out for our entering the war, and who are of age for enlistment, have enlisted for the cause and the proprietors and editors themselves have patriotically enlisted, on the theory that they should feel it their duty to do so as instigators of the act."

Likewise, Mr. Chairman, the sons of manufacturers of ammunition and war supplies, and all stockholders making profits from such trade. They should freely offer their sons on the altar of their country and, in case of their being under military age, go themselves. Likewise, Mr. Chairman, the J. Pierpont Morgans and their associates, who have floated war loans running into millions which they now want the United States to guarantee by entering the European war; after they and all the holders of such securities have offered their sons and themselves, when of military age, on the altar of their country, and, Mr. Chairman, when the above-mentioned persons have no sons and are too old themselves to accept military service, then they shall, to make good their desire for the upholding of American honor and American rights, donate in lieu of such service of selves or sons one-half of all their worldly goods to make good their patriotic desire for our entering the European war in the name of liberty and patriotism.

Mr. Chairman, it will be fitting for those who have really nothing at stake in this war but death to enter into it and give their lives in the name of liberty and patriotism, after the persons covered by the above resolution have done their part as above suggested and many thousands of our citizens will see it that way ere long.

Mr. Chairman, I have voted since I have been a Member of Congress at all times for the largest supply bills offered to take care of and build up our Army and Navy and put ourselves into a state of reasonable preparedness for any difficulties which may arise, and I shall, while I am a Member of the House, in case this cup is put to our country's lips, vote for everything which in my judgment is essential to her success, keeping in mind always the fundamentals of our liberties; but, Mr. Chairman, while I am a Member I shall claim the same right to free speech and expression I am willing to accord to my compeers.

May God guide us and keep us.

XI. The Treaty of Brest-Litovsk

ON SEPTEMBER 5, 1914, a Tripartite Agreement was signed by Great Britain, France, and Russia whereunder the three Allies bound themselves not to make a separate peace with the Central Powers. Nevertheless, on March 3, 1918, Russia signed the harsh Peace of Brest-Litovsk and withdrew from the war. The reasons for the Russian defection were substantially the same as the causes of the Russian Revolution of March 1917, but with the supervenient factor of Bolshevik strategic planning for ultimate world revolution. The hordes of Russian troops were mostly peasants who fully shared the muzhiks' chronic land hunger which had not been appeased by Premier Stolypin's ineffectual efforts to replace the communal proprietorship of the mir with a peasant proprietorship. Moreover, many of the troops were members of disaffected national, ethnic, or religious minorities which had been alienated by the Russification policies of the tsars Alexander III and Nicholas II.

In absolute figures, the Russians sustained more casualties in the First World War than any other belligerent—4,012,000 known dead or presumed dead. Their "human wave" infantry charges (sometimes with troops equipped with bayoneted rifles but with no cartridges) against the Germans and the Austro-Hungarians had taken a ghastly toll. The Russian shortages of shells, cartridges, field guns, rifles, and transport facilities prevented any successful exploitation of the Brusilov offensive in Galicia, Volhynia, and Bukovina in June and July, 1916. The offensive had helped the Western Allies by compelling the Germans to withdraw troops from Verdun to shore up the front in the East. Brusilov captured Bukovina and part of Eastern Galicia. The Russians took 350,000 prisoners—the disaffected Slavs in the Austro-Hungarian ranks deserted en masse in many engagements—but the offensive exacted the staggering toll of over 1,000,000 Russian casualties, which undermined morale and gravely impaired Russian fighting capacity. The result was to be revolution and collapse.

Nicholas II, the last of the tsars, tried to save the tottering regime by dismissing the Grand Duke Nicholas as commander in chief and assuming the supreme command himself. Ultimate disaster was at least postponed by the incompetent tsar's reliance upon General Alexeiev for all technical decisions. But General Michael Grigori Alexeiev was gravely handicapped by the fact that the neurotic tsarina, who dominated the tsar, was in turn dominated by the dissolute, semiliterate Siberian monk Grigori Rasputin, who would demand the battle plans that he might "pray over them," but following his orisons he would relay the orders of the battle to German intelligence agents—for a price. There was widespread Germanophilia in Petrograd court circles, not only because of the German extraction of the tsarina and the presence of many Balts in the administration, but also because many Russian conservatives feared that an Allied victory would compel Russia to "liberalize" the regime.

Food shortages in Petrograd in February, 1917, proved the final provocation for the long-suffering Russian masses, and the Duma (the parliament created in 1905 with only advisory powers) insisted upon the tsar's abdication. The weak-willed Nicholas acquiesced in this ultimatum on March 15, and a provisional government was established under the direction of Prince George Lvov, chairman of the Union of Zemstvos.

The March Revolution was received with delight in Allied capitals, for it was assumed that a new regime replacing the corrupt pro-Germans in court circles would prosecute the war with more vigor. The conversion of Europe's most reactionary autocracy into a democracy would also make it easier to entice America into the war. Prince Lvov encouraged false hopes in the Allies when he said on April 27: "The provisional Government considers it its right and duty to declare

that the purpose of free Russia is not domination over other peoples
. . . nor the violent occupation of foreign territories, but . . . carry-
[ing] out the will of the people and protect[ing] the rights of our
fatherland, at the same time fully observing all obligations made in
regard to our Allies." However, the provisional government spoke
only for itself and not for the Russian masses, who as yet did not know
of the imperialistic secret treaties, but who were already longing for
peace at any price by the summer of 1917.

Undercutting the authority of the provisional government was the
rival Petrograd Soviet, or council, a revival of the type of self-
constituted revolutionary pressure group which had first appeared during the Russian Revolution of 1905. Soon after its emergence on March
12, 1917, the Petrograd Soviet issued "Order Number 1," in which it
urged the war-weary soldiers to set up their own soviets, to obey
only the Petrograd Soviet, and to retain their weapons—with a hint
that their rifles might soon be more profitably used against their landowners than against the troops of the Central Powers.

Profiting by a political amnesty declared by the provisional government, thirty-two Russian Bolshevik revolutionaries traveled from their
Swiss exile in a guarded railway car (the misnamed "sealed car")
across Germany to Denmark and by a circuitous route on to Petrograd. German Chancellor Bethmann-Hollweg and the Foreign Office
readily granted safe passage, while the military diarchy of Ludendorff
and Hindenburg was downright enthusiastic over the opportunity to
sow revolutionary discord in Russia and thereby compel the moribund
nation to sue for peace on Germany's terms. In mid-April Lenin,
Zinoviev, Radek, Krupskaya, and other Bolsheviks were thus allowed
to return to Russia to agitate and propagandize. Lenin and the Bolshevik faction soon gained ascendancy over the Petrograd Soviet, out-
maneuvering the more moderate Menshevik members as well as the
Socialist Revolutionaries. On May 17 Leon Trotsky, the future organ-
izer of the Red Army, arrived in Petrograd from America. Trotsky
utilized his magnetic gifts of oratory to popularize the idea of "all
power to the Soviets" which redounded to the advantage of the Bolsheviks, whose party he belatedly joined. Lenin and Trotsky demanded the
end of the war by an assumption of power by the "proletariat" in *all*
countries—an utterly unrealistic counsel of perfection urged by the
revolutionary doctrinaires, as the events of 1918 and 1919 were to
disclose. Only defeated nations would be disposed to revolt, not the
victorious—a truth too elementary for the subtle Bolshevik ideologues
to take seriously.

The provisional government replaced General Alexeiev with General Alexis Brusilov, who launched a final sanguinary offensive on
July 1, 1917, in the region of Stanislav. The war-weary Russian troops
made initial headway against the Austrians, but they fought under
handicaps difficult even to comprehend. In many instances only one
Russian soldier in six or eight possessed a rifle, and the hapless troops
longed above all for peace, home, and land. Even so, on the first day
of the attack the Russians captured 36,000 prisoners. But General
Hoffmann, who had been in real control of the eastern front since

1916, directed a German and Austrian counterattack which by early August drove the Russians out of Galicia and Bukovina. The Russian army had become an inert mass which was completely receptive to tirelessly reiterated Bolshevik propaganda: "Why fight any more? Take your gun and go home and seize your parcel of land!" Such was the insidious refrain. In September, 1917, the Germans, under General von Hutier's command, captured Riga, thrusting aside the token opposition.

What remained of the provisional government's authority was virtually destroyed on September 9, 1917, when Alexander Kerensky, Prince Lvov's successor as premier, appointed General Kornilov commander in chief—only to have the general turn upon him and attempt a military *coup d'état*. The inept but voluble Kerensky had to ask the Petrograd Soviet to come to the aid of the troops loyal to the provisional government in suppressing Kornilov's *Putsch*. The specter of a military dictatorship caused great alarm among the peasant masses, who feared a possible return of the execrated old regime. The hour was propitious for a Bolshevik seizure of power. The Bolshevik minority had undertaken such a coup in Petrograd on July 16, but the provisional government had not by then had sufficient time to demonstrate its dilatoriness and ineptitude in coping with such urgent problems as the need for sweeping land reform, or the firm renunciation of the imperialistic claims upon Constantinople set forth in the secret treaty of March 4, 1915, signed by Britain, France, and Russia. With deceptive ease, the Bolshevik-dominated Petrograd Soviet seized power on November 7. The garrisons of Petrograd had been thoroughly imbued with Bolshevik propaganda. The crew of the *Aurora* sailed the cruiser up the Neva from the base at Kronstadt and shelled the Admiralty and the Winter Palace, the seat of the provisional government. Bolshevik-led troops and armed workers then stormed the Winter Palace and captured most of the ministers, but Premier Kerensky fled in disguise. There was fitful, unco-ordinated opposition from university students in Petrograd, from some troops loyal to Kerensky, from Don Cossacks, and some opposition in Moscow, but the resistance was soon defeated or scotched, and there ensued in Russia a brief interlude of the "peace" of exhaustion.

The seizure of power by the Bolsheviks (who moved resolutely into a vacuum) was perhaps the most momentous event in the First World War, if not the most resounding political occurrence of the twentieth century. But the full significance of the event became apparent only gradually, since Russia was in such a state of weakness on November 7, 1917, that it was regarded as having only a minor nuisance value both to its Allies and to the Central Powers.

Lenin and his cohorts set to work with a flourish, profiting by the dilatoriness and the half measures of their predecessors, Lvov and Kerensky, by immediately proclaiming an array of internal reforms such as nationalization of all land without compensation, separation of church and state, abolition of all hereditary ranks and titles, the repudiation of the national debt, and so forth.

As regards "external" changes, the Council of Peoples Commissars, on November 21, proposed immediate armistice negotiations to the Central Powers command. At the same time, Commissar for Foreign Affairs Leon Trotsky sent a note to all the Allied ambassadors in Petrograd in which he made "a formal proposal for an immediate armistice on all fronts and an immediate opening of peace negotiation." On November 27, the German High Command agreed to begin armistice negotiations on December 2, fully aware that it had moribund Russia at its mercy. Sensing Allied hostility to ending the war at a time when German armies stood astride Europe from the Aisne River to the Gulf of Riga, Trotsky issued an ultimatum in a radio broadcast:

> On [1 December] we shall begin peace negotiations. If the Allied nations do not send their representatives, we shall conduct negotiations alone with the Germans. We want a general peace, but if the bourgeois in the Allied countries force us to conclude a separate peace the entire responsibility will be theirs.

The Allies sent an evasive response to this summons. The Bolshevik government thereupon disregarded the Tripartite Agreement of September 5, 1914, which had renounced the idea of a separate peace, and it began armistice negotiations with the Central Powers at Brest-Litovsk, in Eastern Poland. A truce was concluded on December 15. Meanwhile, the Bolsheviks had begun broadcasting to the world the texts of all the Allied secret treaties, hoping thereby to promote the overthrow of the capitalistic, imperialistic governments of all the belligerents by the disillusioned masses. The Bolsheviks engaged in protracted peace negotiations (described in the excerpts which we publish from *The War of Lost Opportunities*, by General Von Hoffmann), culminating in the Carthaginian peace of Brest-Litovsk, signed under duress on March 3, 1918, after the German armies had resumed the offensive without Russia being able to offer even token opposition any longer. Only the Allied military victory on the western front in November, 1918, nullified the treaty, thereby justifying the observation of Seton-Watson that it was Marshal Foch who "saved" Russia, not Lenin or Trotsky.

Brest-Litovsk was a disaster for Russia. Under the crushing terms of the treaty the Soviet government had to acknowledge the loss of 40 percent of the industry and industrial population of the former Russian Empire, 70 percent of the iron and steel production, 90 percent of its sugar refining, 75 percent of its coal fields, 33 percent of its railroad mileage, 25 percent of the arable land in European Russia (including the Ukraine, detached from Russia by separate treaty), and 33 percent of its population (sixty-four million former subjects of the Tsar). Russia had to agree not to raise its tariffs against the Central Powers above the limits of the Russian tariff of 1903, and not to impose prohibitions or duties on the export of timber or ores. This guaranteed the Central Powers access to cheap Russian raw materials. Brest-Litovsk made the Treaty of Versailles appear moderate by comparison.

Lenin and Trotsky proved themselves to be victims of their rigid

Marxist ideology, which postulated that capitalistically "advanced" countries (such as Germany) were the ones which were ripe for proletarian revolution. The ideologues overlooked the elementary but decisive factor that defeated armies are the ones likely to revolt, not the victorious—and the German army was on the verge of a stupendous triumph—the domination of Europe. Only the perseverance and ultimate victory of the Western Allies, bolstered by the entry of America into the war, saved Russia and Europe from a German hegemony under the military dictators Ludendorff and Hindenburg.

The chief negotiator for the Central Powers at Brest-Litovsk was General Maximilian von Hoffmann, born in Hamburg, January 25, 1869. The son of a prosperous lawyer, Hoffmann attended the Kriegsakademie at Torgau, where his aversion to close-order drill, athletics, and horsemanship seemed to bode ill for a military career which paradoxically turned out brilliantly for him. His keen intelligence and phenomenal memory enabled him to graduate with honors.

Young Hoffmann was posted to a tour of duty in the German embassy in Saint Petersburg, where he perfected his knowledge of the Russian language and mentality, which proved invaluable for the remainder of his military career. In 1899 he was attached to the Russian section of the general staff. The Chief of Staff, Count von Schlieffen, appointed him as the German military observer at Japanese headquarters during the Russo-Japanese War. Hoffmann was among the first to perceive the importance of trench warfare and the machine gun, but his reports on the likelihood of their revolutionizing the art of battle were largely ignored by his superior officers. He was promoted major in 1907, and was given staff assignments in Posen and Berlin. In Berlin he shared quarters with a fellow officer destined for the greatest military distinction—Erich Ludendorff.

At the war's outbreak Hoffmann was a staff officer in charge of operations for the Eighth Army. He conceived the plan for the stunning German victory at Tannenberg, although Ludendorff received the lion's share of credit, which properly belonged to Hoffmann. Following the departure of Ludendorff and Hindenburg from the eastern front in 1916, Hoffmann was left in virtual control. His great ability and the German military strength largely offset Austrian weakness. At Brest-Litovsk Hoffmann easily outmaneuvered the Bolsheviks, whose military position was all but hopeless. Hoffmann prevented the Austrians (panic stricken because of their homefront crisis of food shortages and ethnic disaffection) from settling for half a loaf of imperialistic gain. After the Allied victory in France in November, 1918, Hoffmann supervised the return of the German forces from the East to the Fatherland. Back in Berlin he began drawing up a "master plan" for the destruction of Bolshevik Russia which was all but ignored until Adolph Hitler made use of some of Hoffmann's ideas in planning the Nazi invasion of June, 1941. Hoffmann dabbled in Freikorps activities until his retirement in 1920. He then directed his attention to writing until his death at Bad Reichenhall on July 8, 1927.

GENERAL MAXIMILIAN VON HOFFMANN,
THE WAR OF LOST OPPORTUNITIES

THE ARMISTICE IN THE EAST

. . . The destiny of Russia was pursuing its course. The officers were deprived of their rank and discharged. Soldier councils were organized. With this destruction of discipline the Army was done for; the regiments degenerated into armed hordes which no longer possessed any sort of military value. The ruin of the Army went hand in hand with the internal decomposition. After one unsuccessful attempt, the Bolsheviks succeeded in getting all the power into their own hands. One of the first measures of the new Government was the dispatch of a wireless message on the 26th of November, in which the Commissary Krylenko, who had been promoted from being a corporal to the rank of Commander-in-Chief of the Army, inquired if the German General Headquarters were willing to conclude an Armistice.

General Ludendorff telephoned to me and asked: "Is it possible to negotiate with these people?" I answered: "Yes, it is possible to negotiate with them. His Excellency requires troops and these are the first that can come."

I have often thought since that it might have been better if the leaders of the German State and Army had refused to have any sort of negotiations with the Bolshevik usurpers. By giving the Bolsheviks the possibility of concluding a peace, and thus satisfying the longing of the people, we also gave them the opportunity of fortifying themselves in power and of retaining it. If Germany had refused to negotiate with them and had demanded representatives of the Russian People and a Government that would have been formed by a free election, the Bolsheviks would not have been able to remain in power. Still, I think, no man of sense will reproach us for having accepted Krylenko's proposal for an armistice.

The General Headquarters accepted Krylenko's proposal and on

Source: From *The War of Lost Opportunities* (New York: International Publishers, 1925), pp. 195–229. Reprinted by permission of International Publishers and Routledge & Kegan Paul, Ltd.

the 2nd of December the Russian Armistice Delegation crossed our lines at Dvinsk and proceeded to Brest-Litovsk. The Commander-in-Chief in the East received an order to conclude an Armistice. H.R.H. the Commander-in-Chief entrusted me with the direction of the negotiations. A few days before, von Rosenberg, who afterwards became Ambassador, arrived in Brest-Litovsk to represent the German Foreign Office. He had instructions only to be present at the negotiations and to have certain wishes of the Foreign Office taken into consideration. The General Headquarters looked upon the conclusion of an armistice as an entirely military question. Representatives of the Allied Powers also arrived. They were Lieutenant-Colonel Pokorny, for Austria-Hungary; Adjutant-General Zekke represented Turkey, and Colonel Gantschew was sent by Bulgaria.

The conditions that were to be demanded had been settled in principle by the General Headquarters some time before, and they had been sent to the Commander-in-Chief in the East. They were in accordance with the desire to end the War on one front, and they contained no conditions that were unjust or insulting for the Russians. Hostilities were to cease and each side was to retain the positions they held.

On such a basis the conditions of an Armistice could have been settled in a few hours with any normal adversary. With the Russians it was not quite so simple. The Russian Delegation was composed of Joffé, who afterwards unfortunately became so well known to us, Kameneff (Trotsky's brother-in-law), Mme. Byzenko, who had already achieved a certain amount of fame through the murder of a Minister, a non-commissioned officer, a sailor, a workman and a peasant. These were the members of the Commission who were entitled to a vote.

Admiral Altvater and a certain number of staff officers were attached to the Commission. They had no vote and had only to act as experts. Karachan was the secretary of the Commission. It was not difficult to house this Commission in some of the huts that we occupied in the Citadel of Brest-Litovsk. With regard to their board, I asked the Commission whether they would prefer to take their meals in the Staff Officer's Mess-room or to have their food sent in to them. The Russians accepted the first proposal. I had one of the large huts arranged for the meetings of the Commission. It was here that we first met the Russian delegates. H.R.H. the Commander-in-Chief greeted them in a speech of welcome and informed them that he was empowered by the Allied Chief Commands to conclude the terms of an Armistice, and that he had appointed me to conduct the negotiations. Joffé replied in a few words.

Then the negotiations began. The first condition the Russians made was that of entire publicity. They demanded to have the right, at the conclusion of each consultation, to make known by telegraph or wireless the exact text of what each party had said. I had nothing against this; but in order to avoid the publication of erroneous interpretations on one side or the other, I suggested the appointment of an auxiliary Commission which would draw up the minutes of each meeting immediately after it had taken place, and when these minutes had received the approval of both sides this text would be used for publication. The Russians agreed to this. Then we had to listen to a long propagandistic speech similar to many others we had to hear afterwards from Trotsky. It concluded with a demand to all the powers engaged in the War to end the struggle, to conclude an Armistice, and then settle the terms of a general peace.

My reply to this consisted of the question whether the Russian delegation was authorized by their Allies to make such proposals to us. The military representatives of the quadruple Alliance were present and they were willing to enter into negotiations. The Russians had to confess that they had no such authority. I therefore proposed that they should keep within the limits of the authority they possessed, and that we should proceed to the negotiations of a separate Armistice with Russia.

Other Russian attempts to change the negotiations into propagandistic channels I was also able to check. A little difficulty arose when Admiral Altvater suddenly demanded the evacuation of Riga and of the islands in the Moon Bay. Considering the state of affairs, I felt that this demand was an incomprehensible piece of assurance, and therefore I refused curtly and energetically to consider it at all. In a pamphlet that one of the Russian experts published afterwards, I saw that all the officers of the General Staff were unanimously against Altvater's idea, as it could not be supposed that we would agree to such a proposal. It was therefore quickly suppressed after my refusal.

The Russians laid great stress on the condition that all the German troops stationed along the Eastern front should remain there, in order to prevent us from transporting them to the West. This demand was easy for us to agree to. Already before the negotiations had begun in Brest-Litovsk the order had been given to send the bulk of the Eastern Army to the Western front. Consequently I was easily able to concede to the Russians, that during the Armistice that was about to be signed, the Germans would not send away any troops from the Eastern front except those that were already being moved, or that had already received orders to go.

Certain difficulties were also caused by the question of the intercourse between the two Armies. With the object of propaganda in view, the Russians naturally laid great store on the most extensive and unhindered intercourse between the trenches, while for us just the contrary was to be desired. I therefore proposed, as it seemed quite impossible to prevent all intercourse, that it was to be limited to certain places. In this way it would be possible to exercise some control, and to intercept the greater part of the propaganda literature that might be expected.

The further demand for the free admission into Germany of all Bolshevik literature and works of enlightenment I was obliged to refuse, but I said I was quite willing to assist in the export of this literature to France and England.

After much negotiation we at last succeeded in making the draft-treaty for an Armistice which was made out much according to the German plan. Then during lunch Joffé explained, that in order to obtain a power of attorney to sign a definite treaty for an Armistice he must go back to Petrograd. Although this delay was unpleasant for me, I did not share the suspicion of some of the Allies that Joffé's demand was only a manœuvre to break off the negotiations, and that the delegation would probably not return at all. I was not mistaken; however, the delegation returned at the appointed time, and the suspension of hostilities that had been arranged for the time of their absence was changed into an Armistice by the signing of the treaty by both parties.

As the delegates took their meals with us in the mess-room we had the opportunity of getting to know what sort of men some of them were. I had, of course, placed those members of the Commission who had a vote higher than those who were merely experts, so that the workman, the sailor and the non-commissioned officer sat in higher places than the Admiral or the officers. I shall never forget the first dinner we had with the Russians. I sat between Joffé and Sokolnikov, who is now the Commissioner of Finance. Opposite me was the workman, who was evidently caused much trouble by the various implements that he found on the table. He tried to catch the food on his plate first with one thing and then with another; it was only the fork that he used exclusively as a tooth-pick. Almost opposite me sat Frau Byzenko next to Prince Hohenlohe who had on his other side the peasant, a typical Russian figure with long grey curls and an enormous untrimmed beard. He caused a smile to appear on the face of the orderly who was serving round the wine, and had asked him if he would take claret or hock, and he inquired which was the stronger, as he would prefer to have that sort.

Joffé, Kameneff and Sokolnikov all appeared to be extraordinarily intelligent, more especially Joffé. They all spoke enthusiastically of the task that lay before them, the task of leading the Russian proletariat to the heights of happiness and prosperity. They all three did not doubt for a moment that this must happen if the nation governed itself according to the teaching of Marx. The least, that appeared before Joffé's mind's eye, was that all men should be well off, and that a few, among whom, as I gathered, he himself would be numbered, would be a little more than prosperous. To be sure, they all made no secret of the fact that the Russian Revolution was only the first step towards the happiness of all the nations. It was naturally impossible for a State governed on Communistic principles to continue to exist when it was surrounded by States governed by capitalistic systems; therefore the object they were all striving for was a universal revolution.

It was during these conversations that the first doubts rose to my mind if it had been right for Germany to enter into negotiations with the Bolsheviks at all. They had promised their people peace and happiness. If they were able to take the first home with them, would not their position be greatly strengthened in the eyes of the masses who had longed for peace for many years? Other doubts came into my mind during the conversations I had with the officers, especially with Admiral Altvater. I talked much with him about the extraordinarily fine Russian Army, and wondered how the Revolution could have so completely corroded it. Altvater replied:

"The influence of Bolshevik propaganda on the masses is enormous. I have already often talked with you about it, and complained that at the time I was defending Osel the troops actually melted away before my eyes. It was the same with the whole Army, and I warn you the same thing will happen in your Army."

I only laughed at the unfortunate Admiral. He was murdered some time after that.

THE PEACE OF BREST-LITOVSK

The execution of the terms of the Armistice that had been signed at Brest-Litovsk met with opposition on most parts of the front. It was not that the Russian troops were unwilling to have an Armistice, but because both on the Southern front and in the Caucasus the Bolshevik Delegation was not recognized as possessing the authority to conclude an Armistice. Of all the Commissions that had been appointed to carry out the conditions of the Armistice only one was able to reach its appointed place, and that was in the Northern sector, where it was able to reach Dvinsk. All those that had to go South could not cross the frontier for the time.

The Armistice was concluded with the view of bringing about a peace between Russia on the one side, and the Quadruple Alliance on the other. In order to carry this intention into effect the representatives of the four Powers assembled in Brest-Litovsk. The Secretary of State von Kühlmann came as the representative of the German Empire. By an order of the General Headquarters, I was appointed as their representative to assist the Secretary of State. I was placed under his authority and I had only the right of bringing the wishes, or the opinions of the General Headquarters forward for discussion and, if necessary, to protest against any measures taken by the Secretary of State. I wish this to be well understood, because public opinion is inclined to make the General Headquarters and me, as their representative, responsible for all that took place in Brest-Litovsk and more especially for the Peace that was dictated there. That is wrong. It is Count Hertling, who was at the time Chancellor of the Empire, and the Secretary of State for Foreign Affairs, who are alone responsible for the negotiations and the signing of the Peace that took place.

Count Czernin, a clever, distinguished man, who unfortunately had entirely shattered nerves, came as the representative of the Dual Monarchy. He was firmly convinced that Austria-Hungary would crumble to pieces if they could not obtain Peace very soon. The one thought that completely mastered him was the wish at the very least to come to some arrangement with Russia and to be able to take a Treaty of Peace home with him.

The Bulgarian mission was headed by their minister Popoff, an unimportant personage, with a limited political horizon and, perhaps, just in consequence of this, great obstinacy. The clever Minister President Radoslavor and the Turkish Grand Vizier Talaat only appeared on the scenes later.

The representatives of Turkey were at first the Ambassador in Berlin, and former Grand Vizier, Hakki, an unusually clever and skilful diplomatist and the Secretary of State for Foreign Affairs, Messimy Bey.

The leaders of the Russian delegation were at first: Joffé, Kameneff and Professor Pokrovsky.

To house and feed these numerous missions (they numbered together about four hundred people) was naturally no easy matter. However, thanks to the ability of the Quartermaster-General and of the managers of the various officers' messes, these difficulties were mastered. In the former Russian theatre, which had almost escaped destruction, a hall of sufficiently large dimensions was prepared for the general meetings; while for the smaller assemblies the smaller room we had used for the negotiations of the Armistice was at our disposal.

Shortly after the arrival of Kühlmann and Czernin, I was called upon to be present at a consultation that took place between them for the settlement of the first steps that were to be taken. The first thing that had to be done was to send the Russians an answer to their Peace proposals, which, like the proposals they had sent about making an Armistice, were addressed to all the belligerents and suggested that all should meet at a round table to negotiate the terms for putting an end to the fighting. The Russian proposals spoke of a Peace without annexations.

Secretary of State von Kühlmann's standpoint was that Germany would accept this proposal if the Russians were able to induce the Entente States to agree to such negotiations. In his opinion the settlement of the question of the Border States: Poland, Lithuania, and Kurland, did not come into the category of annexations as the legally appointed representatives of these States had decided of their own free will, a long time previously, to separate themselves from Russia and to place the settlement of their future status in the hands of Germany or the Central Powers. Count Czernin was naturally anxious to accept the proposal of a Peace without annexations, and he certainly ought to have been pleased to enter into negotiations on such a basis with the enemy Powers, who had decided on the partition of Austria-Hungary.

The two statesmen had decided to send an answer that agreed without any restrictions to a Peace without annexations if "the Entente Powers would also agree to negotiate a Peace on similar terms." I did not like this answer. First, because by adopting the Russian style, it contained a number of expressions that went against my feelings; and secondly, because at bottom it was a lie. It was entirely based on the conditional phrase: "If the Entente," etc. I considered it would have been more correct to have kept strictly to facts by answering the Russians that the Central Powers were willing to enter on negotiations for a general Peace, as they had proved by several proposals they had already made, and by the resolutions of the German Reichstag, but as the Russian Peace Delegation had no legal right to speak for the other Powers of the Entente, and until the Russians were able to produce credentials that would entitle them to do so, it would only be possible for them to negotiate a separate Peace with the Quadruple Alliance.

I mentioned my scruples to the Secretary of State. He, however, stuck to his decision. As he had gone with the Chancellor of State to the General Headquarters before coming to Brest-Litovsk, I had to suppose that during the consultation of the Highest Leaders of the State with the Highest Leaders of the Army, a decision had been arrived at with regard to the *modus procedendi*, so I had to submit.

When it came to the signing of the answer to the Russians, the Bulgarians made difficulties. Minister Popoff declared that they—the Bulgarians—had been promised certain portions of Serbia and the Dobrudja, and they could not think of endangering these promised territories by putting their signature to such an answer. They had entered into the War with the object of annexations and they had no intentions of resigning them. It was in vain that Kühlmann and Czernin lavished their persuasive eloquence on Popoff; even when they had explained to him a hundred times that there was no danger, that it was only done to make a good impression at the very beginning of the negotiations, that it was impossible to suppose England and France would agree to enter into negotiations of Peace, and that all the explanations that the Central Powers were giving now would be invalid if the Entente were not ready to negotiate—still he obstinately stuck to his "No."

General Gantscheff, the second Bulgarian representative, showed himself more amenable and more sensitive to this diplomatic logic. He sent a detailed telegram to Tzar Ferdinand and he was able to obtain from him an order for Popoff to sign. Messimy Bey was also in doubt about signing, but he was more easily persuaded by Kühlmann and Czernin than the Bulgarian could be. On the 24th of December the answer was delivered to the

Russians. Some expressions in this note, that appeared to me too humiliating, I had succeeded in having deleted or altered.

The Russians were triumphant and telegraphed their satisfaction to Petrograd. By mutual consent we had now to wait ten days, to give the Entente time to notify if they wished to participate in the Peace Conference.

Secretary of State Kühlmann and Count Czernin suggested to the Russians not to remain inactive during these ten days, but to organize a number of Commissions and to proceed at once to the settlement of various secondary points of the Treaty of Peace. The Russians agreed to this. Joffé and some of the members of the Delegation had the intention of again returning to Petrograd during that time. He hinted that when he came back he would probably be accompanied by the Commissioner for Foreign Affairs, Trotsky.

From the conversations we had I received the impression that the Russians had misunderstood the offer of our diplomatists, and that they supposed a peace without annexations would give them back the Polish, Lithuanian and Kurland Governments. My impression was confirmed by a conversation Major Brinckmann had with the Russian Lieutenant-Colonel Fokke. Fokke said quite positively that immediately after Peace had been signed the German troops would retire beyond the old frontier of 1914. I told the Secretary of State that I considered it impossible to allow the Russians to go back to Petrograd under such misapprehensions. If in Petrograd they not only led their Government, but also large circles of the people, to believe that the Peace they were about to sign would guarantee to Russia the old frontiers of 1914, the admission that their comprehension of it had been a false one and that the Note of the Central Powers must be understood differently, in other words that they had been deceived, could only result in frantic indignation on the Russian side. I therefore considered it was quite time to undeceive them on this point and I offered to do so.

The Secretary of State saw that I was right, and agreed with me. Count Czernin agreed, too.

That morning during lunch I said to Joffé, who sat next to me, I perceived that the Russian Delegation had understood the meaning of a peace without forcible annexations differently to the meaning attached to it by the representatives of the Central Powers. The latter took up the standpoint that it was not a forcible annexation if portions of the former Russian Empire decided, of their own free will, and by a determination of their existing political representatives, on a separation from the Union of Russian States, and on being united to the German Empire or any other State. The Russian rulers themselves had given these rights to the different States by their declaration of the Self-determination of Nations. This applied to the positions of Poland, Lithuania and Kurland. The representatives of the three States had announced their withdrawal from the Union of Russian States. The Central Powers did not consider it an annexation if the future fate of these States were decided by a direct understanding with their representatives, and with the exclusion of the Russian State.

Joffé looked as if he had received a blow on the head. After lunch we had a conference that lasted several hours. The Russians were represented by Joffé, Kameneff and Pokrovsky—the Germans by the Secretary of State, Czernin and myself. In this conference the Russians gave free vent to their disappointment and indignation. Pokrovsky said, with tears in his eyes, it was impossible to speak of a peace without annexations when about eighteen Governments were torn from the Russian Empire. In the end the Russians threatened to break off the conference and depart. Count Czernin was beside himself. He had brought with him instructions from the Kaiser not to allow the Conference of Brest to fail on any account, and if the worst came to the worst, and the German demands endangered its continuation, he was even to make a separate peace with the Russians. His nerves completely gave way, and he not only spoke very excitedly with the Secretary of State of his intentions of making a separate peace, but he also sent his military adviser, Lieutenant Field-Marshal Csicsericz, to my office, to threaten me in the same manner, evidently hoping to make an impression on the German Headquarters in this way. I could not understand the Count's excitement. In my opinion there was no question of the negotiations being broken off by the Russians. The Russian masses were longing for peace, the Army had crumbled away, it consisted now of mere insubordinate armed hordes, and the only possibility for the Bolsheviks to remain in power was by signing a peace. They were obliged to accept the conditions of the Central Powers, however hard they might be.

I therefore answered Lieutenant Field-Marshal Csicsericz's threat of a separate peace very calmly; that I thought this a brilliant idea, as it would free for us the twenty-five Divisions that till then I had been obliged to keep on the Austrian-Hungarian front, for the support of their Army. By a separate peace the right

wing of the German Army would be automatically covered by
Austria-Hungary, so that the military position of the German
Eastern Army would derive special benefit by such a measure.

Secretary of State Kühlmann also received Czernin's threat of
a separate peace with great calmness. He told me that he had requested a written statement of the standpoint of the Austro-
Hungarian Government, and it appeared to me that he was not
loath to have in his hands such a proof if the wishes of the General
Headquarters went too far. The excited discussions, and the still
more excited exchange of telegrams of these days had at first no
results as we were obliged to wait quietly to see if the Russian
Delegation would return from Petrograd or if it would not return,
though only one of us all who feared this was Count Czernin.

During this pause Count Czernin went to Vienna and Secretary
of State Kühlmann to Berlin, and by his request I accompanied
him.

When I was announced to General Ludendorff I was received
very coldly and with the angry question:

"How could you allow such a Note to be dispatched?"

I explained that I had supposed, and I was bound to suppose,
that the general outline of the negotiations had been discussed
and settled between the General Headquarters and the Chancellor
of the Empire and the Secretary of State during their conferences
in Kreuznach. General Ludendorff denied this, but admitted that
I had the right to suppose this had been done.

Even now it is a mystery to me that the General Headquarters
and the leaders of the Government had not arrived at an understanding of such a nature during the conference they had had on
the 18th of December. It is impossible to settle the lines for so
difficult a task as a Treaty of Peace by making all sorts of general
conversation on both sides.

In connexion with my conversation with General Ludendorff I
had to report myself to the Kaiser in the Bellevue Palace. His Majesty took great interest, both in the Armistice, which had been
concluded, and in the negotiations that were in progress. I had to
describe to him minutely all that had occurred and the personali-
ties of all who had taken part in the negotiations, and as my report
was not finished when the lunch hour approached, I was bidden
to lunch. After the meal His Majesty continued the conversation
on the question of the Eastern front and alluded to the Polish
difficulties. He demanded my opinion on the Polish question. I
hesitated a little and begged His Majesty to excuse me from giving

it, as my opinion differed from the views of the General Head-quarters and I did not wish to put myself in opposition to them. His Majesty replied:

"When your Chief War Lord wishes to hear your opinions on any subject, it is your duty to communicate them to him quite irrespective of their coinciding with the opinions of the General Headquarters or not."

I was an enemy of any settlement of the Polish question which would increase in Germany the number of subjects of Polish nationality. Notwithstanding the measures that Prussia had taken during many decades, we had not been able to manage the Poles we have, and I could not see the advantage of any addition to the number of citizens of that nationality. To add to Germany a broad strip of border-land with a population of about two million Poles, as the General Headquarters demanded would, in my opinion, only be a disadvantage to the Empire. I considered the so-called Germano-Polish settlement as still worse. In my opinion, the new Polish frontier ought to be drawn in such a way that it should bring to the Empire the smallest possible number of Polish subjects and that there should be only a few unimportant corrections of the frontier. To the latter I reckoned a small strip of land near Berdzin and Thorn, so that in any subsequent war the enemy artillery would not be able to fire straight into the Upper Silesian coal mines or on to the chief railway station of Thorn. I also calculated on the heights of Mlawa for the better defence of the Soldau district, and lastly, the crossing of the Bobi, near Osovice, which had caused us so many headaches.

The increase in Polish inhabitants, which would amount to about 100,000, would have to be taken into the bargain. But beyond that not a man.

During this conversation His Majesty agreed with me.

On the 2nd of January there was a consultation between the Government and the General Headquarters in the General Staff and afterwards a Privy Council in the Bellevue Palace. I was ordered to attend both. I tried in vain to see General Ludendorff for a moment previously, to inform him of the report His Majesty had demanded of me.

At the Privy Council the first subject of discussion was the progress of the negotiations in Brest-Litovsk. Secretary of State von Kühlmann made a statement of what had been done as yet, and how he expected the further progress of the negotiations would be, to which His Majesty assented. Then the Kaiser began to speak

on the Polish question. He had had the new Polish frontier drawn
on a map in accordance with my report, and said that he considered this the right one. He could not refuse to take into consideration the serious objections there were to the settlement proposed
by the General Headquarters and which, on his demand, had been
laid before him by me, in consequence of which he must retract
the consent he had previously given to the project of the General
Headquarters. General Ludendorff contradicted these objections
in a somewhat vehement manner. His Majesty's decision could
not be definitely given at once and he earnestly entreated that the
General Headquarters might be permitted to lay the case again
before His Majesty. General Field-Marshal von Hindenburg sec-
onded this request. His Majesty brought the somewhat painful
scene to an end by saying:

"I therefore await a further report from the General Headquarters."

The Privy Council had not settled anything definitely or decid-
edly. The Secretary of State had not been told quite clearly what
position he was to take up at Brest, nor had the Polish question
been decided. His Majesty the Kaiser had only approved of what
Kühlmann had done so far, and he had authorized him to continue
on the same path. The difficult problem of the Border States remained unsettled. It is true the General Headquarters had advised
a more rapid and energetic manner of carrying on the negotiations
at Brest, by which the fate of the Border States that were already
in the possession of Germany would be settled by their being
definitely separated from Russia and awarded to the Central Powers. However, the Secretary of State Kühlmann had been successful
in carrying his point of trying to have the separation of the Border
States not made by the way of annexation but by the more amica-
ble way of the Right of Self-determination of the Peoples. After
this meeting, on the evening of the 2nd of January, we started
again for Brest-Litovsk.

It was quite clear to me that General Ludendorff would be very
much offended with me for differing so completely from them on
the Polish question, and I had not deceived myself. Already the
next day I was telephoned to from Berlin, and informed that Hindenburg and Ludendorff had made a cabinet question of the case.
They both threatened to resign and demanded that I should be
recalled. The Kaiser gave in on the Polish question but refused to
alter the personal one. He protected me, as might have been
expected.

Besides these facts which were only told me, I felt the resentment of the General Headquarters personally in a series of orders and questions that were sent me in a form which showed me great men can also be very small sometimes.

At the end of the first week in January the Russians returned from Petrograd. I had never doubted that they would do so. The former leader, Joffé, returned, but not as the head of the deputation; his place was taken by Trotsky. There were two versions of the reason for this change: one report said Trotsky had been furious that Joffé had not seen at once the craftiness of the Central Powers' answer and that this was the cause of his being superseded; he was only retained in the delegation on account of his local and personal knowledge of Brest-Litovsk and its inhabitants, which he had acquired during the weeks he had been there and which the delegation wanted to utilize. The other version said that Joffé had really been enraged at the hypocritical offer of Peace made by the Central Powers and that he had refused to continue the negotiations. It was against his will and only at Trotsky's request that he had given in, and had consented to accompany the delegation and assist it with his personal knowledge.

Trotsky was certainly the most interesting personality in the new Russian Government: clever, versatile, cultured, possessing great energy, power of work, and eloquence, he gave the impression of a man who knew exactly what he wanted and who would not be deterred from using any means for the attainment of his end. The question has been much discussed whether he came with the intention of concluding a peace, or if from the very beginning he only wanted to find the most visible platform from which to propagandize his Bolshevik theories. Although propaganda played such a prominent part in the whole of the negotiations of the following weeks, I still think that Trotsky at first wanted to try to make peace and that it was only afterwards, when he had been driven into a corner by Kühlmann's dialectics, for which he was no match, that he thought of bringing the conference to a spectacular finish by declaring that, though Russia could not accept the conditions of peace offered by the Central Powers, nor even fully discuss them, still, it declared the War to be finished.

Even before the negotiations had begun a new group of participants presented themselves in Brest-Litovsk. They were the representatives of the Ukrainian Peasant States, whom the Rada had sent in order to make a separate peace for the Ukraine, basing their demand on the declaration of the Petrograd Soviet Govern-

ment regarding the Self-Determination of the Peoples. Secretary
of State Kühlmann and I received the Ukrainians with pleasure, as
their appearance offered a possibility of playing them off against
the Petrograd delegation. To Count Czernin, however, their arrival only caused a new trouble, as it could be foreseen that
the representatives of the Ukraine would make demands about
the political rights of their fellow countrymen who were living
in the Bukovina and East Galicia.

With Trotsky's arrival the unconstrained intercourse that had
existed until then outside the meeting-hall came to an end.
Trotsky requested that the Delegation might have their meals in
their quarters, and prohibited all private intercourse and all
conversations.

At the very beginning of the negotiations there was a slight
collision. Mr. Trotsky seemed to consider the platform in Brest-
Litovsk not large enough for his propagandistic designs. He demanded that the scene of the negotiations should be removed to
Stockholm. His chief object in this demand was the wish to get
away from Brest-Litovsk, the Military Headquarters in the War
zone, where it would be impossible to get into direct contact with
the dissatisfied elements of the Central Powers, with whose help
the inflammatory portions of his speeches would be underlined
and carried to wide circles of the people for propaganda purposes.

Naturally the Central Powers refused this demand. Then the
battle of words began between Trotsky and Kühlmann that lasted
several weeks, and led to nothing. It was only gradually that it
became clear to all the parties concerned in the negotiations that
the chief object Trotsky was pursuing was to preach the Bolshevik
doctrines, that he was only speaking to the gallery and did not set
the slightest store by any practical work that was to be done. Simultaneously with his speeches wireless messages were sent to
"all," inciting to revolt, to disobedience, to the murder of the officers. I protested energetically against this; Trotsky promised to
desist, but the instigating wireless messages continued to be sent.
The negotiations went farther and farther from their real object
and turned into theoretical discussions. Trotsky's tone became
with each day more aggressive. One day I therefore pointed out
to Secretary of State Kühlmann and Count Czernin that it was impossible to attain our object in this way; that it was absolutely
necessary to bring the negotiations back to a basis of facts, and
offered at the next opportunity to represent to the Russians how
the position really was, and why we were assembled there. As al-

ways the Secretary of State was quite of my opinion. Count Czernin, whose nerves became worse every day, as he felt that he never came an inch nearer his object of returning to Vienna with a Treaty of Peace, had some objections to make, as he still hoped by amiability and diplomatic cleverness to get round the Bolshevik gentlemen. At last he also gave in. It was decided that at the next favourable opportunity Secretary of State Kühlmann would pass the word on to me, and I should say whatever I thought necessary.

The opportunity came sooner than we had expected. Already the next day Kameneff, Trotsky's brother-in-law, made a speech by Trotsky's order, which made the blood of all the officers who were present rise to their heads. It was wonderfully audacious; the Russians might have had a certain right to speak in that way if the positions had been reversed, that is to say, if the German Army had been defeated and lay defenceless on the ground, and the Russian Armies had been victoriously in possession of German territory.

A glance at the Secretary of State showed me that his patience was also exhausted. He desired me to speak, and I explained to the Russians on the one side the exact position, and on the other side, the difference there was between their words and their deeds, how they made great speeches about freedom of conscience and freedom of words, self-determination of the peoples, and other beautiful things, and how in fact they permitted no sort of freedom in the spheres under their power. How they had dispersed with bayonets the Constitutional Assemblies that went against them, how they had expelled by force of arms the National Assembly of the White Russians in Minsk, in the same way as they had now turned out the freely elected Rada of the Ukrainians. The question of the Border States was settled for the German General Headquarters. They took up the standpoint that the legal representatives of these States had decided on separating from Soviet Russia, and that no further vote was necessary. I spoke seated and absolutely quietly; I neither raised my voice in any way, nor did I thump with my fist on the table as reports had it.*

When I finished there was profound silence. Even Mr. Trotsky, at the first moment, could not find a word in reply. It was difficult to find anything to say against it, as all I had asserted was in strict accordance with facts. The meeting was quickly adjourned.

---

* Compare my description with the report given by Karl Friedrich Nowak in his book, *The Collapse of the Central Powers* (Chapter: "Brest-Litovsk") which was written from details given by those who were present and is quite truthful on every point.

The actual effects of my explanations were not as great as I had expected. At the next meeting Trotsky confined himself to saying a few meaningless words of defence and immolated my speech as a simple expression of military propaganda. After this he still avoided touching on any grounds that might have led to practical work, and continued his dialectic fireworks. Unfortunately the Secretary of State also failed to take advantage of the position created by my speech to force the meetings to begin practical work.

Through the Chief of the Operations Department I had had my motives in making that speech explained to General Ludendorff and I had begged him to give me his opinion on it. General Ludendorff approved of my action, and encouraged me to do all I could to shorten the negotiations and bring them down to realities. Not having been able to attain any real advance by my interruption of Trotsky's flow of eloquence, another way was open to me: this was the negotiations with the Ukrainian Delegation.

The Ukrainian representatives do not hold themselves aloof from us as Trotsky did. They had their meals with us in the officers' mess-room, and they conversed with us quietly about their objects and their wishes. I had the impression that we would soon be able to come to terms with them. I therefore offered Count Czernin, who was naturally the most important personage in these negotiations with the Ukrainians my services as intermediary. In this I acted in accordance with the opinion I held that the conclusion of a separate peace between the Central Powers and the Ukraine would naturally also force Trotsky to emerge from his reserve. The young representatives of the Kiev Central Rada were not sympathetic to Count Czernin and he did not like to negotiate with young Messrs. Liubinsky and Sevruk, who were scarcely past their student years, on a footing of equality. I proposed that the Count should authorize me, first to find out privately from the Ukrainians under what conditions they would be willing to conclude a separate peace with the Central Powers. Count Czernin gave me this authority. After a certain amount of persuasion on my part the two Ukrainian gentlemen at last divulged their wishes. They extended to the annexation by the Ukraine of the districts round Cholm, and also the Ruthenian portions of East Galicia and the Bukovina.

As I considered an independent Polish State to be a Utopia, and I still hold that opinion, I had no hesitation in promising the Ukrainians my support with regard to the Cholm lands. On the other hand, I looked upon the demand for Austrian-Hungarian territory as a piece of impudence and I gave the two young men to understand as much, in a somewhat rough manner. They had evidently expected my reply, as they assured me most amiably that they would require to obtain new instructions from Kiev to be able to continue negotiations on the basis produced by our conversation.

Count Czernin's position became very difficult about this time owing to a food catastrophe that broke out in Vienna in consequence of the want of foresight of the Austro-Hungarian Government. In order to prevent a state of famine Berlin had to be asked for aid. Notwithstanding its own want, Berlin assisted but in consequence Count Czernin naturally was deprived of the possibility of threatening to conclude a separate peace with Trotsky, or even to try to do so. On the other hand the separate peace with the Ukraine which I had looked upon as a measure that might force Trotsky to sign a peace, now became, as a means of obtaining bread, a vital necessity for Count Czernin. It was a bad thing for Austria that it was impossible to hide her desperate position from the Ukrainians.

In the meantime their new instructions had arrived from Kiev, and they were submitted to me at another consultation. The Cholm district was *conditio sine qua non*. It apparently had dawned upon the Rulers in Kiev that the defeated side could not demand the cession of territory from the other party. They therefore renounced all claim to any part of East Galicia and the Bukovina, but they demanded that these districts should be formed into independent Austro-Hungarian Crownlands under the Habsburgers. I had the impression that the Ukrainians would not recede from these conditions, and that the critical position of Count Czernin was well known to them. Czernin's difficulties were twofold: if he consented to the cession of the Cholm district to the Ukraine, he was threatened with the deadly hatred of the Poles; if he agreed to the creation of Ruthenian Crownlands he introduced the question of Self-determination into the mixed nationalities of the Austro-Hungarian Empire, while on the other hand, the cession of the Cholm district without consulting the population was in exact opposition to the principles of Self-determination.

Czernin's indisposition entailed a pause of two days, after which he authorized me to continue negotiations with the Ukrainians on the basis of their demands and, if possible, come to a settlement with them.

In the meantime the negotiations with Trotsky went on in the same aimless manner.

Apparently the Russian Commissar of the People realized the danger with which he was threatened by our negotiations for a separate peace with the Ukraine, for suddenly he asserted that the Ukrainian representatives, whom till then he had recognized, had not the right to carry on a separate negotiation in the name of the Ukraine, as the frontiers between Soviet Russia and the Ukraine had not been fixed as yet. On this question and some others he must consult the Petrograd Government. He proposed to have again an interruption of a few days in the negotiations, as he was obliged to go to Petrograd.

Of course this was not the reason for his journey to Petrograd. I concluded that he wanted to convince himself how far the Bolshevik rule had become stabilized in Petrograd, if in consideration of the wishes of the people he would have to conclude a real peace with the Central Powers, or if he could bring the negotiations to an end with the spectacular effect he afterwards had recourse to. Secretary of State Kühlmann went to Berlin to render an account of the negotiations to the Reichstag and Count Czernin went to Vienna in order to obtain sanction for the conditions of peace with the Ukraine.

After the return of all the delegates, in the early days of February, Trotsky tried to prevent the separate Peace with the Ukraine in another way. He brought two Ukrainians with him, Medvediev and Shakhrei, who were sent not by the Central Rada, but by a new Bolshevik opposition government that had been formed in Kharkov. The representatives from the Central Rada protested against this attempt at checkmate, and it came to lively encounters between the Ukrainian and the Russian delegates. In an excellent speech Liubinski laid before the Bolsheviks the whole list of their sins. In his answer Trotsky contented himself with hinting that the power of the Central Rada had vanished and that its representatives could look upon their room in Brest-Litovsk as the only space of which they had any right to dispose.

Judging by the reports from the Ukraine that I had before me, Trotsky's words seemed unfortunately not to be without foundation. Bolshevism was advancing victoriously, the Central Rada and the Ukrainian provisional government had fled. Secretary of State Kühlmann and Count Czernin decided, however, despite these transitory difficulties for the Ukrainian government to adhere to the arrangements. The difficulties were transitory in so far as at any time we could support the government with arms and establish it again. They therefore refused to recognize the Ukrainian representatives whom Trotsky presented on the grounds that in the beginning of January, Trotsky himself had recognized the Ukrainian delegation as the representatives of the people.

During those days I often admired the young Ukrainians. It is certain that they knew that the possible help from Germany was their last hope, that their government was but a fictitious conception; nevertheless, they held to the demands they had succeeded in obtaining and they did not give way a finger's breadth in all their negotiations with Count Czernin.

The Peace with the Ukraine was signed. It was a hard blow for Trotsky, as it was clear that now the negotiations with him must be brought to some sort of conclusion.

In the meantime, despite my protest and notwithstanding all Trotsky's assurances, the propagandistic appeals "to all" and more especially to the troops were despatched as usual. It was at this time that an appeal was addressed to the troops in which they were summoned to murder their officers. Until now only the General Headquarters had urged that a decision should be arrived at with Trotsky but after this the Secretary of State, von Kühlmann, received a telegram from His Majesty instructing him to send an ultimatum to Trotsky demanding a settlement within twenty-four hours. But just at that moment the Secretary of State, von Kühlmann, had the impression that it might be possible to bring Trotsky to a settlement of the negotiations, as Trotsky, probably under the impression that the Peace with the Ukraine had, for the first time, approached the question of peace from a practical point. He had sent to ask the Secretary of State if it would not be possible, by some means, to arrange that Riga and the Islands that lay before it should be retained by the Russian Empire.

The Secretary of State was in a difficult position. He did not hesitate for a moment to sacrifice himself for what he thought right; he telegraphed in reply that the moment was ill-chosen to send an Ultimatum of such short respite and that he earnestly advised that it should not be presented. If His Majesty insisted on its delivery, the Government would have to find another Secretary of State. He would await an answer until four-thirty that afternoon; if by that time no further orders about the Ultimatum were received, he would pass on to the order of the day. Nothing occurred until four-thirty and Kühlmann kept the order for an Ultimatum in his pocket. He had tried to nail Trotsky down with this

Riga proposal. He had sent the Ambassador von Rosenberg to Trotsky to tell him that if he sent in a written offer of peace on the condition of Riga and the Islands remaining Russian it would be possible to discuss the question. After some hesitation Trotsky refused to comply with this demand. On the other hand he perceived that he could no longer go on simply making speeches and proposals, and that the Central Powers would now demand acts. He evidently also thought that he had produced sufficient effect with his propaganda, and now sought for an opening which would enable him to bring the Brest negotiations to an end in a way that would produce the greatest possible effect. In the meeting of the 10th of February he announced, that although he would sign no Treaty of Peace, Russia would consider the War at an end from that time, she would send all her Armies to their homes and that she would proclaim the fact to all the Peoples and all the States.

The whole congress sat speechless when Trotsky had finished his declaration. We were all dumbfounded. That same evening the Austro-Hungarian and the German diplomatists had a meeting to consult on the new position at which I was also summoned to assist. The diplomatists of both countries were unanimous in asserting that they would accept this declaration. As although no Peace had been signed the conditions of peace were established between the two countries by this declaration. I was the only one against it. We had made an Armistice with the Russians with the object of arranging the terms of peace. If peace were not concluded the object of the armistice was not attained, and, therefore, the armistice came automatically to an end, and hostilities must recommence. Trotsky's declaration was, in my opinion, nothing more than a denouncement of the Armistice.

I was unable to bring the diplomatists round to my opinion. One of Czernin's assistants, the Ambassador von Wiesner, quite misunderstanding the situation in the manner this diplomatist was wont to distinguish himself, had already telegraphed to Vienna that Peace was concluded with Russia. I apprised the General Headquarters of the results of these conversations and received a reply that the High Command was quite of my opinion. It is well known that the High Command of the Army was also able to persuade the Government and the Foreign Office to accept their point of view.

On the eighth day after the negotiations had been broken off so abruptly by Trotsky, the Eastern Army resumed the offensive. The demoralized Russian troops offered no kind of resistance, if it were possible even to call them troops, as it was only the staffs that still remained; the bulk of the troops had already gone home. We simply swept over the whole of Livonia and Esthonia, and took possession of them. Our troops were greeted everywhere as deliverers from the Bolshevik terror, and not only by the Baltic Germans, but likewise by the Letts and Esthonians.

Two days after our advance had recommenced a wireless message was received from Petrograd announcing that the Russians were ready to renew the negotiations and conclude a Peace and also begging that the German advance might be stopped. It had very quickly been proved that Trotsky's theories could not resist facts. The German Army advanced only as far as Lake Peipus and Narva, in order to release at least all the Baltic members of our race from the Bolsheviks and all their crimes. Then the advance was stopped and the Bolsheviks were informed that they might send a delegation, authorized to sign a Peace, to Brest-Litovsk. Almost immediately the delegation under the leadership of Sokolnikov, arrived. The representatives of the Quadruple Alliance, who had dispersed to all the points of the compass, also hastened back. But in the same manner as on the Russian side, so also on our side there appeared, one may say, only the second fiddles. Kühlmann, Czernin, Talaat, Rodoslavov, had gone in the meantime to Bucharest for the opening of the Peace Conference with Rumania and did not return, but sent their representatives. The Ambassador, von Rosenberg, came as the representative of Germany.

This time also the negotiations were carried on in a very extraordinary manner. At the first meeting von Rosenberg proposed to discuss at once each of the paragraphs of the draft of a Treaty of Peace he had brought with him; Sokolnikov replied to this proposal with a request that the whole draft might be read out to him. When it had been read to him, he said that he did not demand the discussion of the single points, and that the Russians were willing to sign the draft that had been presented to them. The only reason such a proceeding could have had was the intention to prove more completely that they were forced into signing a peace that was dictated to them. As propaganda has often asserted that I was the author of this "Peace of Violence," I wish again to state emphatically that I had not the slightest influence on the drafting of this Treaty of Peace; I became acquainted with its contents, for the first time, when it was publicly read aloud in the presence of the Russian Delegation. The definite acceptance of it by Sokolno-kov took place at a private meeting of the diplomats at which I was not even present.

Of course the greatest propaganda with this "Peace of Violence" was made by the Entente. I would only ask the Entente why they did not change this treaty when they had won the War and com-pletely changed the political conditions of Europe by the peace they dictated? The Peace of Brest-Litovsk was declared as an-nulled, but its chief conditions remained unchanged. It never oc-curred to the Entente to return to their former Ally, Russia, Poland, Lithuania, Livonia, Esthonia and Bessarabia. The only thing that was changed was the condition of dependence of the provinces that had been taken away from Russia.

XII. The "Horrors" of Versailles

A CONFLICT which had taken a toll within four years of 8,538,315 military personnel killed or died, 21,219,452 wounded, and 12,618,-000 civilian deaths from military action, massacre, starvation, or exposure, and which had incurred direct monetary costs of $186,333,-637,000 and indirect costs of $151,646,942,560, could reasonably have been expected to wreck beyond repair the economy, political structure, and social institutions of the belligerents. The miracle of the First World War was that the damage to the fabric of European civilization was as relatively restricted as it proved to be, affecting primarily the defeated nations. Italy, a "victor," was an exception; not so Russia which, although a one-time "ally," was as defeated as any of the Cen-tral Powers. And the war turned Italy toward fascism and Russia to-ward communism. Only the most sanguine of persons could have assumed that a peace of "forgetting and forgiving" would have been likely to follow such devastation, especially when it was regarded as axiomatic in the Allied countries that German aggressiveness was the primary cause of the war, as was stated in Article 231 of the Treaty of Versailles.

Such an optimist was John Maynard Keynes, an eminent British economist, political essayist, financier, and Maecenas. Born at Cam-bridge on June 5, 1883, Keynes was first educated as a mathematician, but with a bent toward polymathy he decided to study under the classical economist Alfred Marshall, from whom he derived a deep conservatism which he was eventually to shed. In fact, during the latter part of his life Keynes was viewed by some traditionalists as a wild radical because of his advocacy of a "mixed economy" in which private ownership would be combined with limited general planning, and in which governments would be encouraged to engage in pump-priming expenditures during a depression to reverse a downward spiral in purchasing power.

Upon graduation from Cambridge young Keynes spent several years in the civil service in India. In 1908 he returned to Cambridge as a lecturer in economics, remaining an active fellow of King's College until his death on April 21, 1946. He left a lasting impress not only upon his students but upon the whole field of twentieth-century economics, for today most capitalist governments are Keynesian to some degree. He served in the British Treasury during both world wars. In 1919 he was the British delegation's chief economic specialist during the peace negotiations at Versailles.

A few months after the close of the Versailles Conference Keynes published a book which aroused a prolonged furor, *The Economic Consequences of the Peace*. The book was written with a brilliance rarely found in economic treatises. It was replete with memorable character sketches of such political figures as Clemenceau, Wilson, and Lloyd George. Keynes was as disposed to assess motives as he was ready to appraise actions, and he thought that nearly all the major decisions of the peace makers were wrong. He set out to demonstrate the economic infeasibility of the Treaty of Versailles, which apparently was drafted with the intent of squeezing war costs out of the German lemon "until the pips squeaked." According to Keynes, Germany's flourishing prewar economy was attributable in part to its foreign trade, which had been promoted by its merchant marine, its foreign investments, and its industrial exports drummed up by unusually resourceful traveling salesmen. Moreover, Germany had enjoyed a thriving metallurgical industry based upon Ruhr coal and Lorraine iron ore deposits. In addition, the German transport and tariff system had contributed to the nation's prewar prosperity.

Keynes predicted that the Treaty of Versailles would hamstring the German economy by its stipulation that the bulk of the German merchant fleet would be turned over to the Allies. The German overseas colonies and even the private assets held in them by German citizens were seized, yet Germany was held responsible for unpaid debts in the former colonies. Not only were Alsace and Lorraine (the latter rich in iron ore deposits) taken from Germany, but private German property in these provinces was subject to liquidation at Allied discretion. And to pile Ossa upon Pelion, the Reparations Commission was authorized by the Treaty to exact up to $5 billion in reparations from Germany before May 1, 1921, irrespective of what the total reparations sum might eventually be.

The Treaty further reduced Germany's ability to pay reparations by ceding to Poland Upper Silesia with its anthracite deposits, and by turning over the Saar basin to French exploitation for fifteen years. Nevertheless Germany would have to deliver 25 million tons of coal a year to compensate the Allies, which would leave only 78 million tons for German use, disregarding the fact that its prewar coal consumption had averaged 139 million tons a year. The result would be the crippling of German industry, especially since the cession of Lorraine to France had removed from German control 74 percent of its previous source of iron ore.

In the opinion of Keynes, it would have been reasonable for the Allies to have compelled Germany to indemnify the Allies for the direct damages caused by their armed forces. Such a compensation would have totaled about $8.85 billion, or less than a quarter of the reparations eventually demanded by the Allies. As for means of payment, Germany, in theory, could have paid in metal, but its gold stock was only $300 million; it could have surrendered the ships or foreign securities which it still retained; it could have exported in sufficient quantity to earn enough gold or foreign exchange to pay its victors. But Germany's gold stock was piddling; if it liquidated all of its assets in Latin America or elsewhere it would have impaired further its already diminished productive capacity; if Germany dumped its exports in the Allied countries it would have been seriously competitive, especially with their metallurgical and textile industries; if Germany limited its imports—which were mainly food and raw materials—it would have reduced the productivity of its labor, and it would have manufactured fewer commodities. So Versailles was a victor's peace of self-defeating vindictiveness.

The Economic Consequences of the Peace (which was translated into eleven languages by 1924) caused shock and outrage in Allied nations and jubilation in Germany. Keynes had incurred the suspicion of being pro-German, although there was no proof of this. The *Times* estimated that "his bias had been throughout akin to that of the conscientious objector"—a reference to Keynes's opposition to conscription during the war, and to the support which he had given friends who had been conscientious objectors. But the strongest rebuttal of Keynes's attack on Versailles was long delayed. The counter blast, *The Carthaginian Peace or The Economic Consequences of Mr. Keynes,* was written by Etienne Mantoux in 1942 and published posthumously in 1946 after the young author had been killed in action in the Fighting French Forces a week before the end of the Second World War. Writing twenty-two years after the publication of Keynes's epochal work, Mantoux was in a position to expose the fallacies of *The Economic Consequences of the Peace,* a book filled with dire predictions. Mantoux was convinced that the publication of Keynes's jeremiad in the United States in January, 1920, had contributed to America's repudiation of President Woodrow Wilson and the Treaty of Versailles. Keynes's book became a sort of Bible for American isolationists. "The horrors of Versailles became a veritable article of faith." And the book had helped prepare the way for the rise of the Third Reich, since it inculcated a spirit of "mea culpism" in America and Britain. Germany's "war guilt" was largely superseded by the alleged Allied "guilt" of Versailles.

Mantoux turned Keynes's economic arguments against the distinguished economist. "Do not some of Mr. Keynes's more recent theories," asked Mantoux, "lend unexpected but powerful support to the view that payment of Reparations would in itself have actually helped Germany to become the greatest industrial nation in Europe? One of the main tenets of his *General Theory* is that, as long as full employment is not reached, investment expenditure, even for unproductive purposes, will create employment and income, and thereby contribute finally to increase the wealth of the community. Productive investment would no doubt be preferable; but even unproductive expenditure is 'better than nothing. . . .' If it is contended that Rearmament helped to enrich the German people after 1933, Reparations would, for the same reason, have enriched them after 1919."

Mantoux cited Keynes's prediction that the Treaty of Versailles would threaten Europe with "a long, silent process of semi-starvation," yet within ten years of the war "European standards of living had never been higher." Europe's iron output in 1929, instead of declining as a result of the Treaty, as Keynes had prophesied, was 10 percent higher than in the record year 1913. German steel production in 1927 was 38 percent more than in 1913. The productivity of the German coal mining industry in 1929 was 30 percent higher than prewar, and the actual coal output was also higher. In 1926 Germany exported twice as much coal as "the average (1909–13) pre-war exports of *all* her pre-war territories." In 1913 the German merchant marine totaled 5 million tons. Allied seizures had reduced it to 673,000 tons in 1920, but by 1930 it was a modern fleet of more than 4 million tons. Mantoux pointed out that "the monthly increase in German savings bank deposits was 84 million in 1913 . . . and in 1928 it was nearly 310 million." Keynes "predicted that in the next thirty years, Germany could not possibly be expected to pay more than 2 milliard marks a year in Reparation. In the six years preceding September 1939, Germany, by Hitler's showing, had spent each year on rearmament about *seven times* as much. . . ." So much for the accuracy of Keynes's economic perceptions and prophecies in regard to the "Carthaginian Peace" of Versailles.

Mantoux thought the chief defect of the Treaty of Versailles was the "failure to establish a true balance of power. . . . The cardinal vice of the system [was] in the constitution of a Europe where a strong and centralized Germany of some 70 millions remained surrounded by a string of small states, who had to rely for the preservation of their independence upon the assistance of faraway Powers. . . ." And those faraway Powers were either accomplices in the destruction of small states as in the case of France and Britain in the Czechoslovakian crisis of 1938, or they rendered only token aid as in the Polish crisis of 1939. Machiavelli would probably have attributed the failure of the Treaty of Versailles to the fact that it ignored the wise rule that an intelligent victor does one of two things to the vanquished: he crushes or conciliates. The Treaty of Versailles did neither: it scotched and irritated Germany, but did not deprive the Germans of the means of retaliation.

JOHN MAYNARD KEYNES,
THE ECONOMIC
CONSEQUENCES OF
THE PEACE

EUROPE AFTER THE TREATY

This chapter must be one of pessimism. The Treaty includes no
provisions for the economic rehabilitation of Europe,—nothing to
make the defeated Central Empires into good neighbors, nothing
to stabilize the new States of Europe, nothing to reclaim Russia;
nor does it promote in any way a compact of economic solidarity
amongst the Allies themselves; no arrangement was reached at
Paris for restoring the disordered finances of France and Italy, or to
adjust the systems of the Old World and the New.

The Council of Four paid no attention to these issues, being
preoccupied with others,—Clemenceau to crush the economic life
of his enemy, Lloyd George to do a deal and bring home something which would pass muster for a week, the President to do
nothing that was not just and right. It is an extraordinary fact that
the fundamental economic problems of a Europe starving and dis-
integrating before their eyes, was the one question in which it was
impossible to arouse the interest of the Four. Reparation was their
main excursion into the economic field, and they settled it as a
problem of theology, of politics, of electoral chicane, from every
point of view except that of the economic future of the States
whose destiny they were handling. . . .

The essential facts of the situation, as I see them, are expressed
simply. Europe consists of the densest aggregation of population
in the history of the world. This population is accustomed to a relatively high standard of life, in which, even now, some sections of
it anticipate improvement rather than deterioration. In relation to
other continents Europe is not self-sufficient; in particular it can-

not feed itself. Internally the population is not evenly distributed, but much of it is crowded into a relatively small number of dense industrial centers. This population secured for itself a livelihood before the war, without much margin of surplus, by means of a delicate and immensely complicated organization, of which the foundations were supported by coal, iron, transport, and an unbroken supply of imported food and raw materials from other continents. By the destruction of this organization and the interruption of the stream of supplies, a part of this population is deprived of its means of livelihood. Emigration is not open to the redundant surplus. For it would take years to transport them overseas, even, which is not the case, if countries could be found which were ready to receive them. The danger confronting us, therefore, is the rapid depression of the standard of life of the European populations to a point which will mean actual starvation for some (a point already reached in Russia and approximately reached in Austria). Men will not always die quietly. For starvation, which brings to some lethargy and a helpless despair, drives other temperaments to the nervous instability of hysteria and to a mad despair. And these in their distress may overturn the remnants of organization, and submerge civilization itself in their attempts to satisfy desperately the overwhelming needs of the individual. This is the danger against which all our resources and courage and idealism must now co-operate.

On the 13th May, 1919, Count Brockdorff-Rantzau addressed to the Peace Conference of the Allied and Associated Powers the Report of the German Economic Commission charged with the study of the effect of the conditions of Peace on the situation of the German population. "In the course of the last two generations," they reported, "Germany has become transformed from an agricultural State to an industrial State. So long as she was an agricultural State, Germany could feed forty million inhabitants. As an industrial State she could insure the means of subsistence for a population of sixty-seven millions; and in 1913 the importation of foodstuffs amounted, in round figures, to twelve million tons. Before the war a total of fifteen million persons in Germany provided for their existence by foreign trade, navigation, and the use, directly or indirectly, of foreign raw material." After rehearsing the main relevant provisions of the Peace Treaty the report continues: "After this diminution of her products, after the economic depression resulting from the loss of her colonies, her merchant fleet and her foreign investments, Germany will not be in a position to import from abroad an adequate quantity of raw material. An enormous part of German industry will, therefore, be condemned inevitably to destruction. The need of importing foodstuffs will increase considerably at the same time that the possibility of satisfying this demand is as greatly diminished. In a very short time, therefore, Germany will not be in a position to give bread and work to her numerous millions of inhabitants, who are prevented from earning their livelihood by navigation and trade. These persons should emigrate, but this is a material impossibility, all the more because many countries and the most important ones will oppose any German immigration. To put the Peace conditions into execution would logically involve, therefore, the loss of several millions of persons in Germany. This catastrophe would not be long in coming about, seeing that the health of the population has been broken down during the War by the Blockade, and during the Armistice by the aggravation of the Blockade of famine. No help, however great, or over however long a period it were continued, could prevent these deaths *en masse.*" "We do not know, and indeed we doubt," the report concludes, "whether the Delegates of the Allied and Associated Powers realize the inevitable consequences which will take place if Germany, an industrial State, very thickly populated, closely bound up with the economic system of the world, and under the necessity of importing enormous quantities of raw material and foodstuffs, suddenly finds herself pushed back to the phase of her development, which corresponds to her economic condition and the numbers of her population as they were half a century ago. Those who sign this Treaty will sign the death sentence of many millions of German men, women and children."

I know of no adequate answer to these words. The indictment is at least as true of the Austrian, as of the German, settlement. This is the fundamental problem in front of us, before which questions of territorial adjustment and the balance of European power are insignificant. Some of the catastrophes of past history, which have thrown back human progress for centuries, have been due to the reactions following on the sudden termination, whether in the course of nature or by the act of man, of temporarily favorable conditions which have permitted the growth of population beyond what could be provided for when the favorable conditions were at an end.

The significant features of the immediate situation can be

grouped under three heads: first, the absolute falling off, for the time being, in Europe's internal productivity; second, the breakdown of transport and exchange by means of which its products could be conveyed where they were most wanted; and third, the inability of Europe to purchase its usual supplies from overseas.

The decrease of productivity cannot be easily estimated, and may be the subject of exaggeration. But the *prima facie* evidence of it is overwhelming, and this factor has been the main burden of Mr. Hoover's well-considered warnings. A variety of causes have produced it;—violent and prolonged internal disorder as in Russia and Hungary; the creation of new governments and their inexperience in the readjustment of economic relations, as in Poland and Czecho-Slovakia; the loss throughout the Continent of efficient labor, through the casualties of war or the continuance of mobilization; the falling-off in efficiency through continued underfeeding in the Central Empires; the exhaustion of the soil from lack of the usual applications of artificial manures throughout the course of the war; the unsettlement of the minds of the laboring classes. . . . (To quote Mr. Hoover), "these are the great fundamental economic issues of their lives. But relaxation of effort is the reflex of physical exhaustion of large sections of the population from privation and the mental and physical strain of the war." Many persons are for one reason or another out of employment altogether. According to Mr. Hoover, a summary of the unemployment bureaus in Europe in July, 1919, showed that 15,000,000 families were receiving unemployment allowances in one form or another, and were being paid in the main by a constant inflation of currency. In Germany there is the added deterrent to labor and to capital (in so far as the Reparation terms are taken literally), that anything, which they may produce beyond the barest level of subsistence, will for years to come be taken away from them.

Such definite data as we possess do not add much, perhaps, to the general picture of decay. But I will remind the reader of one or two of them. The coal production of Europe as a whole is estimated to have fallen off by 30 per cent; and upon coal the greater part of the industries of Europe and the whole of her transport system depend. Whereas before the war Germany produced 85 per cent of the total food consumed by her inhabitants, the productivity of the soil is now diminished by 40 per cent and the effective quality of the live-stock by 55 per cent. Of the European countries which formerly possessed a large exportable surplus, Russia, as much by reason of deficient transport as of diminished output, may herself starve. Hungary, apart from her other troubles, has been pillaged by the Roumanians immediately after harvest. Austria will have consumed the whole of her own harvest for 1919 before the end of the calendar year. The figures are almost too overwhelming to carry conviction to our minds; if they were not quite so bad, our effective belief in them might be stronger.

But even when coal can be got and grain harvested, the breakdown of the European railway system prevents their carriage; and even when goods can be manufactured, the breakdown of the European currency system prevents their sale. I have already described the losses, by war and under the Armistice surrenders, to the transport system of Germany. But even so, Germany's position, taking account of her power of replacement by manufacture, is probably not so serious as that of some of her neighbors. In Russia (about which, however, we have very little exact or accurate information) the condition of the rolling-stock is believed to be altogether desperate, and one of the most fundamental factors in her existing economic disorder. And in Poland, Roumania, and Hungary the position is not much better. Yet modern industrial life essentially depends on efficient transport facilities, and the population which secured its livelihood by these means cannot continue to live without them. The breakdown of currency, and the distrust in its purchasing value, is an aggravation of these evils which must be discussed in a little more detail in connection with foreign trade.

What then is our picture of Europe? A country population able to support life on the fruits of its own agricultural production but without the accustomed surplus for the towns, and also (as a result of the lack of imported materials and so of variety and amount in the saleable manufactures of the towns) without the usual incentives to market food in return for other wares; an industrial population unable to keep its strength for lack of food, unable to earn a livelihood for lack of materials, and so unable to make good by imports from abroad the failure of productivity at home. Yet, according to Mr. Hoover, "a rough estimate would indicate that the population of Europe is at least 100,000,000 greater than can be supported without imports, and must live by the production and distribution of exports."

The problem of the re-inauguration of the perpetual circle of production and exchange in foreign trade leads me to a necessary digression on the currency situation of Europe.

Lenin is said to have declared that the best way to destroy the Capitalist System was to debauch the currency. By a continuing process of inflation, governments can confiscate, secretly and unobserved, an important part of the wealth of their citizens. By this method they not only confiscate, but they confiscate *arbitrarily*; and, while the process impoverishes many, it actually enriches some. The sight of this arbitrary rearrangement of riches strikes not only at security, but at confidence in the equity of the existing distribution of wealth. Those to whom the system brings windfalls, beyond their deserts and even beyond their expectations or desires, become "profiteers," who are the object of the hatred of the bourgeoisie, whom the inflationism has impoverished, not less than of the proletariat. As the inflation proceeds and the real value of the currency fluctuates wildly from month to month, all permanent relations between debtors and creditors, which form the ultimate foundation of capitalism, become so utterly disordered as to be almost meaningless; and the process of wealth-getting degenerates into a gamble and a lottery.

Lenin was certainly right. There is no subtler, no surer means of overturning the existing basis of society than to debauch the currency. The process engages all the hidden forces of economic law on the side of destruction, and does it in a manner which not one man in a million is able to diagnose.

In the latter stages of the war all the belligerent governments practised, from necessity or incompetence, what a Bolshevist might have done from design. Even now, when the war is over, most of them continue out of weakness the same malpractices. But further, the Governments of Europe, being many of them at this moment reckless in their methods as well as weak, seek to direct on to a class known as "profiteers" the popular indignation against the more obvious consequences of their vicious methods. These "profiteers" are, broadly speaking, the entrepreneur class of capitalists, that is to say, the active and constructive element in the whole capitalist society, who in a period of rapidly rising prices cannot help but get rich quick whether they wish it or desire it or not. If prices are continually rising, every trader who has purchased for stock or owns property and plant inevitably makes profits. By directing hatred against this class, therefore, the European Governments are carrying a step further the fatal process which the subtle mind of

Lenin had consciously conceived. The profiteers are a consequence
and not a cause of rising prices. . . .

The inflationism of the currency systems of Europe has proceeded to extraordinary lengths. The various belligerent Governments, unable, or too timid or too short-sighted to secure from
loans or taxes the resources they required, have printed notes for
the balance. In Russia and Austria-Hungary this process has
reached a point where for the purposes of foreign trade the currency is practically valueless. The Polish mark can be bought for
about three cents and the Austrian crown for less than two cents,
but they cannot be sold at all. The German mark is worth less than
four cents on the exchanges. In most of the other countries of
Eastern and South-Eastern Europe the real position is nearly as
bad. The currency of Italy has fallen to little more than a half of its
nominal value in spite of its being still subject to some degree of
regulation; French currency maintains an uncertain market; and
even sterling is seriously diminished in present value and impaired
in its future prospects. . . .

The countries of Europe fall into two distinct groups at the
present time as regards their manifestations of what is really the
same evil throughout, according as they have been cut off from
international intercourse by the Blockade, or have had their imports paid for out of the resources of their allies. I take Germany as
typical of the first, and France and Italy of the second.

The note circulation of Germany is about ten times what it was
before the war. The value of the mark in terms of gold is about one-
eighth of its former value. As world-prices in terms of gold are
more than double what they were, it follows that mark-prices inside Germany ought to be from sixteen to twenty times their pre-
war level if they are to be in adjustment and proper conformity
with prices outside Germany.* But this is not the case. In spite of
a very great rise in German prices, they probably do not yet average
much more than five times their former level, so far as staple commodities are concerned; and it is impossible that they should rise
further except with a simultaneous and not less violent adjustment
of the level of money wages. The existing maladjustment hinders
in two ways (apart from other obstacles) that revival of the import
trade which is the essential preliminary of the economic reconstruction of the country. In the first place, imported commodities

* Similarly in Austria prices ought to be between twenty and thirty times
their former level.

are beyond the purchasing power of the great mass of the population,* and the flood of imports which might have been expected to succeed the raising of the blockade was not in fact commercially possible.† In the second place, it is a hazardous enterprise for a merchant or a manufacturer to purchase with a foreign credit material for which, when he has imported it or manufactured it, he will receive mark currency of a quite uncertain and possibly unrealizable value. This latter obstacle to the revival of trade is one which easily escapes notice and deserves a little attention. It is impossible at the present time to say what the mark will be worth in terms of foreign currency three or six months or a year hence, and the exchange market can quote no reliable figure. It may be the case, therefore, that a German merchant, careful of his future credit and reputation, who is actually offered a short period credit in terms of sterling or dollars, may be reluctant and doubtful whether to accept it. He will owe sterling or dollars, but he will sell his product for marks, and his power, when the time comes, to turn these marks into the currency in which he has to repay his debt is entirely problematic. Business loses its genuine character and becomes no better than a speculation in the exchanges, the fluctuations which entirely obliterate the normal profits of commerce.

There are therefore three separate obstacles to the revival of trade: a maladjustment between internal prices and international prices, a lack of individual credit abroad wherewith to buy the raw materials needed to secure the working capital and to re-start the circle of exchange, and a disordered currency system which renders credit operations hazardous or impossible quite apart from the ordinary risks of commerce.

The note circulation of France is more than six times its pre-war level. The exchange value of the franc in terms of gold is a little less than two-thirds its former value; that is to say, the value of the franc has not fallen in proportion to the increased volume of the

---

* One of the most striking and symptomatic difficulties which faced the Allied authorities in their administration of the occupied areas of Germany during the Armistice arose out of the fact that even when they brought food into the country the inhabitants could not afford to pay its cost price.

† Theoretically an unduly low level of home prices should stimulate exports and so cure itself. But in Germany, and still more in Poland and Austria, there is little or nothing to export. There must be imports *before* there can be exports.

currency.* This apparently superior situation of France is due to the fact that until recently a very great part of her imports have not been paid for, but have been covered by loans from the Governments of Great Britain and the United States. This has allowed a want of equilibrium between exports and imports to be established, which is becoming a very serious factor, now that the outside assistance is being gradually discontinued. The internal economy of France and its price level in relation to the note circulation and the foreign exchanges is at present based on an excess of imports over exports which cannot possibly continue. Yet it is difficult to see how the position can be readjusted except by a lowering of the standard of consumption in France, which, even if it is only temporary, will provoke a great deal of discontent.†

The situation of Italy is not very different. There the note circulation is five or six times its pre-war level, and the exchange value of the lira in terms of gold about half its former value. Thus the adjustment of the exchange to the volume of the note circulation has proceeded further in Italy than in France. On the other hand, Italy's "invisible" receipts, from emigrant remittances and the expenditure of tourists, have been very injuriously affected; the disruption of Austria has deprived her of an important market; and her peculiar dependence on foreign shipping and on imported raw materials of every kind has laid her open to special injury from

* Allowing for the diminished value of gold, the exchange value of the franc should be less than 40 per cent of its previous value, instead of the actual figure of about 60 per cent, if the fall were proportional to the increase in the volume of the currency.

† How very far from equilibrium France's international exchange now is can be seen from the following table:

Monthly Average		Imports $1,000	Exports $1,000	Excess of Imports $1,000
	1913	140,000	114,670	25,685
	1914	106,705	81,145	25,560
	1918	331,915	69,055	262,860
Jan.–Mar.	1919	387,140	66,670	320,470
Apr.–June	1919	421,410	83,895	337,515
July	1919	467,565	123,675	343,890

These figures have been converted at approximately par rates, but this is roughly compensated by the fact that the trade of 1918 and 1919 has been valued at 1917 official rates. French imports cannot possibly continue at anything approaching these figures, and the semblance of prosperity based on such a state of affairs is spurious.

the increase of world prices. For all these reasons her position is grave, and her excess of imports as serious a symptom as in the case of France.*

The existing inflation and the maladjustment of international trade are aggravated, both in France and Italy, by the unfortunate budgetary position of the Governments of these countries.

In France the failure to impose taxation is notorious. Before the war the aggregate French and British budgets, and also the average taxation per head, were about equal; but in France no substantial effort has been made to cover the increased expenditure. "Taxes increased in Great Britain during the war," it has been estimated, "from 95 francs per head to 265 francs, whereas the increase in France was only from 90 to 103 francs." The taxation voted in France for the financial year ending June 30, 1919, was less than half the estimated normal *post-bellum* expenditure. The normal budget for the future cannot be put below $4,400,000,000 (22 milliard francs), and may exceed this figure; but even for the fiscal year 1919–20 the estimated receipts from taxation do not cover much more than half this amount. The French Ministry of Finance have no plan or policy whatever for meeting this prodigious deficit, except the expectation of receipts from Germany on a scale which the French officials themselves know to be baseless. In the meantime they are helped by sales of war material and surplus American stocks and do not scruple, even in the latter half of 1919, to meet the deficit by the yet further expansion of the note issue of the Bank of France.†

The budgetary position of Italy is perhaps a little superior to that of France. Italian finance throughout the war was more enterprising than the French, and far greater efforts were made to im-

---

* The figures for Italy are as follows:

Monthly Average		Imports $1,000	Exports $1,000	Excess of Imports $1,000
	1913	60,760	41,860	18,900
	1914	48,720	36,840	11,880
	1918	235,025	41,390	193,635
Jan.–Mar.	1919	229,240	38,085	191,155
Apr.–June	1919	331,035	69,250	261,785
July–Aug.	1919	223,535	84,515	139,020

† In the last two returns of the Bank of France available as I write (Oct. 2 and 9, 1919) the increases in the note issue on the week amounted to $93,750,000 and $94,125,000 respectively.

pose taxation and pay for the war. Nevertheless Signor Nitti, the
Prime Minister, in a letter addressed to the electorate on the eve of
the General Election (Oct., 1919), thought it necessary to make
public the following desperate analysis of the situation:—(1) The
State expenditure amounts to about three times the revenue. (2)
All the industrial undertakings of the State, including the railways,
telegraphs, and telephones, are being run at a loss. Although the
public is buying bread at a high price, that price represents a loss
to the Government of about a milliard a year. (3) Exports now
leaving the country are valued at only one-quarter or one-fifth of
the imports from abroad. (4) The National Debt is increasing by
about a milliard lire per month. (5) The military expenditure for
one month is still larger than that for the first year of the war.

But if this is the budgetary position of France and Italy, that of
the rest of belligerent Europe is yet more desperate. In Germany
the total expenditure of the Empire, the Federal States, and the
Communes in 1919–20 is estimated at 25 milliards of marks, of
which not above 10 milliards are covered by previously existing
taxation. This is without allowing anything for the payment of the
indemnity. In Russia, Poland, Hungary, or Austria such a thing as
a budget cannot be seriously considered to exist at all.*

Thus the menace of inflationism described above is not merely a
product of the war, of which peace begins the cure. It is a continuing phenomenon of which the end is not yet in sight.

All these influences combine not merely to prevent Europe from
supplying immediately a sufficient stream of exports to pay for the
goods she needs to import, but they impair her credit for securing
the working capital required to re-start the circle of exchange and
also, by swinging the forces of economic law yet further from equilibrium rather than towards it, they favor a continuance of the
present conditions instead of a recovery from them. An inefficient,
unemployed, disorganized Europe faces us, torn by internal strife
and international hate, fighting, starving, pillaging, and lying.
What warrant is there for a picture of less somber colors?

I have paid little heed in this book to Russia, Hungary, or Aus-

---

* On October 3, 1919, M. Bilinski made his financial statement to the Polish
Diet. He estimated his expenditure for the next nine months at rather more
than double his expenditure for the past nine months, and while during the
first period his revenue had amounted to one-fifth of his expenditure, for the
coming months he was budgeting for receipts equal to one-eighth of his
outgoings. The *Times* correspondent at Warsaw reported that "in general
M. Bilinski's tone was optimistic and appeared to satisfy his audience"!

tria.* There the miseries of life and the disintegration of society are too notorious to require analysis; and these countries are already experiencing the actuality of what for the rest of Europe is still in the realm of prediction. Yet they comprehend a vast territory and a great population, and are an extant example of how much man can suffer and how far society can decay. Above all, they are the signal to us of how in the final catastrophe the malady of the body passes over into malady of the mind. Economic privation proceeds by easy stages, and so long as men suffer it patiently the outside world cares little. Physical efficiency and resistance to disease slowly diminish,† but life proceeds somehow, until the limit

* The terms of the Peace Treaty imposed on the Austrian Republic bear no relation to the real facts of that State's desperate situation. The *Arbeiter Zeitung* of Vienna on June 4, 1919, commented on them as follows: "Never has the substance of a treaty of peace so grossly betrayed the intentions which were said to have guided its construction as is the case with this Treaty . . . in which every provision is permeated with ruthlessness and pitilessness, in which no breath of human sympathy can be detected, which flies in the face of everything which binds man to man, which is a crime against humanity itself, against a suffering and tortured people." I am acquainted in detail with the Austrian Treaty and I was present when some of its terms were being drafted, but I do not find it easy to rebut the justice of this outburst.

† For months past the reports of the health conditions in the Central Empires have been of such a character that the imagination is dulled, and one almost seems guilty of sentimentality in quoting them. But their general veracity is not disputed, and I quote the three following, that the reader may not be unmindful of them: "In the last years of the war, in Austria alone at least 35,000 people died of tuberculosis, in Vienna alone 12,000. To-day we have to reckon with a number of at least 350,000 to 400,000 people who require treatment for tuberculosis. . . . As the result of malnutrition a bloodless generation is growing up with undeveloped muscles, undeveloped joints, and undeveloped brain" (*Neue Freie Presse*, May 31, 1919). The Commission of Doctors appointed by the Medical Faculties of Holland, Sweden, and Norway to examine the conditions in Germany reported as follows in the Swedish Press in April, 1919: "Tuberculosis, especially in children, is increasing in an appalling way, and, generally speaking, is malignant. In the same way rickets is more serious and more widely prevalent. It is impossible to do anything for these diseases; there is no milk for the tuberculous, and no cod-liver oil for those suffering from rickets. . . . Tuberculosis is assuming almost unprecedented aspects, such as have hitherto only been known in exceptional cases. The whole body is attacked simultaneously, and the illness in this form is practically incurable. . . . Tuberculosis is nearly always fatal now among adults. It is the cause of 90 per cent of the hospital cases. Nothing can be done against it owing to lack of foodstuffs. . . . It appears in the most terrible forms, such as glandular tuberculosis, which turns into purulent dissolution." The following is by a writer in the *Vossische Zeitung*, June 5, 1919, who accompanied the Hoover Mission to the Erzgebirge: "I visited large

of human endurance is reached at last and counsels of despair and madness stir the sufferers from the lethargy which precedes the crisis. Then man shakes himself, and the bonds of custom are loosed. The power of ideas is sovereign, and he listens to whatever instruction of hope, illusion, or revenge is carried to him on the air. As I write, the flames of Russian Bolshevism seem, for the moment at least, to have burnt themselves out, and the peoples of Central and Eastern Europe are held in a dreadful torpor. The lately gathered harvest keeps off the worst privations, and Peace has been declared at Paris. But winter approaches. Men will have nothing to look forward to or to nourish hopes on. There will be little fuel to moderate the rigors of the season or to comfort the starved bodies of the town-dwellers.

But who can say how much is endurable, or in what direction men will seek at last to escape from their misfortunes?

---

country districts where 90 per cent of all the children were ricketty and where children of three years are only beginning to walk. . . . Accompany me to a school in the Erzgebirge. You think it is a kindergarten for the little ones. No, these are children of seven and eight years. Tiny faces, with large dull eyes, overshadowed by huge puffed, ricketty foreheads, their small arms just skin and bone, and above the crooked legs with their dislocated joints the swollen, pointed stomachs of the hunger œdema. . . . 'You see this child here,' the physician in charge explained; 'it consumed an incredible amount of bread, and yet did not get any stronger. I found out that it hid all the bread it received underneath its straw mattress. The fear of hunger was so deeply rooted in the child that it collected stores instead of eating the food: a misguided animal instinct made the dread of hunger worse than the actual pangs.' " Yet there are many persons apparently in whose opinion justice requires that such beings should pay tribute until they are forty or fifty years of age in relief of the British taxpayer.

Selected Bibliography

Origins

ALBERTINI, LUIGI, *The Origins of the War of 1914*, 3 vols. (New York, 1952–57).

BETHMANN-HOLLWEG, THEOBALD VON, *Reflections on the World War* (London, 1920).

CZERNIN, OTTOKAR, *In the World War*, English translation (New York, 1920).

FAY, SIDNEY B., *The Origins of the World War*, 2 vols. (New York, 1929).

FISCHER, FRITZ, *Germany's Aims in the First World War* (New York, 1967).

GEISS, IMANUEL (ed.), *July 1914: Selected Documents* (London, 1967).

Germany, Foreign Office, *Outbreak of the World War*, edited by Karl Kautsky, Max Montgelas, and Walther Schucking (New York, 1924).

GOOCH, G. P., and TEMPERLEY, H. V., *British Documents on the Origins of War*, 11 vols. (London, 1926–38).

MONTGELAS, MAX, *The Case for the Central Powers* (London, 1925).

RENOUVIN, PIERRE, *The Immediate Origins of the War* (New Haven, Conn., 1928).

SCHMITT, BERNADOTTE, *The Coming of the War*, 2 vols. (New York, 1930).

VON WEGERER, ALFRED, *A Refutation of the Versailles War Guilt Thesis* (New York, 1930).

General Works

ALBRECHT-CARRIÉ, RENÉ, *The Meaning of the First World War* (Englewood Cliffs, N.J., 1965).

BALDWIN, HANSON W., *World War I: An Outline History* (New York, 1962).

BARNETT, CORELLI, *The Swordbearers: Supreme Command in the First World War* (New York, 1964).

CHURCHILL, WINSTON S., *The World Crisis, 1911–1918*, 4 vols. (New York, 1927–30).

CRUTTWELL, C. R. M. F., *A History of the Great War* (Oxford, 1936).

EXPOSITO, V. J. (ed.), *A Concise History of World War I* (New York, 1964).

FALLS, CYRIL, *The Great War* (New York, 1959).

LIDDELL HART, B. H., *The Real War, 1914–1918* (Boston, 1930).

TAYLOR, A. J. P., *Illustrated History of the First World War* (New York, 1964).

TERRAINE, JOHN, *The Great War, 1914–1918* (New York, 1964).

The Western Front

BARBUSSE, HENRI, *Under Fire* (New York, 1917).

CLARK, ALAN, *The Donkeys* (New York, 1962).

CLEMENCEAU, GEORGES, *The Grandeur and Misery of Victory* (New York, 1930).

COOPER, DUFF, *Haig* (London, 1935).

CROWN PRINCE WILLIAM OF GERMANY, *My War Experiences* (New York, 1923).

FALKENHAYN, ERICH, *The German General Staff and Its Decisions, 1914–1916* (New York, 1920).

FOCH, FERDINAND, *The Memoirs of Marshal Foch* (Garden City, N.Y., 1931).

HARBORD, GENERAL JAMES G., *The American Army in France, 1917–1919* (Boston, 1936).

HORNE, ALISTAIR, *The Price of Glory: Verdun, 1916* (New York, 1962).

JOFFRE, MARSHAL JOSEPH, *The Personal Memoirs of Joffre* (New York, 1932).

KLUCK, GENERAL ALEXANDER VON, *The March on Paris* (New York, 1920).

RITTER, GERHARD, *The Schlieffen Plan* (London, 1958).

PERSHING, GENERAL JOHN J., *My Experiences in the World War*, 2 vols. (New York, 1931).

PÉTAIN, MARSHAL HENRI PHILIPPE, *Verdun* (New York, 1930).

SPEARS, GENERAL EDWARD L., *Liaison, 1914* (Garden City, N.Y., 1931).

SPEARS, GENERAL EDWARD L., *Prelude to Victory* (London, 1939).

TERRAINE, JOHN, *Haig: The Educated Soldier* (London, 1963).

TERRAINE, JOHN, *The Western Front, 1914–1918* (London, 1964).

THOMASON, JOHN W., *Fix Bayonets!* (New York, 1926).

TUCHMAN, BARBARA, *The Guns of August* (New York, 1962).

WILLIAMS, JOHN, *Mutiny, 1917* (London, 1962).

WOLFF, LEON, *In Flanders Fields* (New York, 1958).

The Eastern Front

BRUSILOV, GENERAL ALEKSEI A., *A Soldier's Notebook, 1914–1918* (London, 1930).

CHURCHILL, WINSTON S., *The Unknown War: The Eastern Front* (New York, 1931).

GOLOVIN, GENERAL NICHOLAS N., *The Russian Army in the World War* (New Haven, Conn., 1931).

GOURKO, GENERAL VASILII, *War and Revolution in Russia, 1914–17* (New York, 1919).

HINDENBURG, MARSHAL PAUL, *Out of My Life*, 2 vols. (New York, 1921).

HOFFMANN, GENERAL MAX, *The War of Lost Opportunities* (New York, 1925).

IRONSIDE, GENERAL SIR EDMUND, *Archangel, 1918–1919* (London, 1953).
IRONSIDE, GENERAL SIR EDMUND, *Tannenberg* (Edinburgh, 1928).
KNOX, MAJOR GENERAL SIR ALFRED, *With the Russian Army, 1914–1917* (London, 1921).
LUDENDORFF, GENERAL ERICH, *Ludendorff's Own Story*, 2 vols. (New York, 1919).
PARES, SIR BERNARD, *Day by Day with the Russian Army, 1914–1915* (Boston, 1915).
WASHBURN, STANLEY, *The Russian Campaign, April to August 1915* (New York, 1915).

The Italian Front

DALTON, HUGH, *With British Guns in Italy* (London, 1919).
FALLS, CYRIL, *Caporetto, 1917* (London, 1966).
MCENTEE, GIRARD L., *Italy's Part in Winning the World War* (New York, 1934).
MUSSOLINI, BENITO, *My Diary, 1915–17* (Boston, 1925).
SPERANZA, FLORENCE C. (ed.), *The Diary of Gino Speranza: Italy, 1915–1919*, 2 vols. (New York, 1941).

The Balkan Front

ABBOTT, GEORGE F., *Greece and the Allies, 1914–1922* (London, 1922).
ASHMEAD-BARTLETT, ELLIS, *The Uncensored Dardanelles* (London, 1928).
ASPINALL-OAOLANDER, C. F., *Military Operations, Gallipoli*, 2 vols. (London, 1928).
COBLENTZ, PAUL, *The Silence of Sarrail* (London, 1930).
Committee of Imperial Defence, *History of the Great War: Military Operations—Macedonia*, 2 vols. (London, 1933).
DAVIS, RICHARD HARDING, *With the French in France and Salonika* (New York, 1916).
HAMILTON, SIR IAN, *Gallipoli Diary*, 2 vols. (New York, 1920).
KANNENGIESSER, HANS, *The Campaign in Gallipoli* (London, 1928).
MOOREHEAD, ALAN, *Gallipoli* (London, 1956).
PALMER, ALAN W., *The Gardeners of Salonika* (New York, 1965).
SANDERS, LIMAN VON, *Five Years in Turkey* (Annapolis, Md., 1927).

The Near Eastern Fronts

BURNE, A. H., *Mesopotamia: The Last Phase* (London, 1937).
CANDLER, EDMUND, *The Long Road to Baghdad* (London, 1919).
DANE, E., *British Campaigns in the Nearer East, 1914–1918*, 2 vols. (London, 1919).
GRAVES, ROBERT, *Lawrence and the Arabs* (London, 1927).
HERBERT, AUBREY N., *Mons, Anzac, and Kut* (London, 1919).

LAWRENCE, T. E., *Seven Pillars of Wisdom* (Garden City, N.Y., 1935).
MacMUNN, GEORGE, and FALLS, CYRIL, *Military Operations, Egypt and Palestine*, 2 vols. (London, 1931).
WAVELL, ARCHIBALD P., *The Palestine Campaign* (London, 1931).

Naval Warfare

BENNETT, GEOFFREY, *The Battle of Jutland* (London, 1964).
BIRNBAUM, KARL E., *Peace Moves and U-Boat Warfare* (Stockholm, 1958).
CHATTERTON, E. K., *The Big Blockade* (London, 1932).
CORBETT, SIR JULIAN S., *History of the Great War: Naval Operations*, 3 vols. (London, 1920).
FROTHINGHAM, T. G., *The Naval History of the World War*, 3 vols. (Cambridge, Mass., 1924–26).
JELLICOE, LORD JOHN R., *The Grand Fleet, 1914–1916* (New York, 1919).
MARDER, ARTHUR J., *From Dreadnought to Scapa Flow*, 3 vols. (New York, 1961–66).
SIMS, ADMIRAL WILLIAM S., *The Victory at Sea* (London, 1920).
VON HASE, COMMANDER GEORG, *Kiel and Jutland* (London, 1921).

Air Warfare

ASHMORE, GENERAL EDWARD B., *Air Defence* (London, 1929).
CUNEO, JOHN R., *The Air Weapon, 1914–1916* (Harrisburg, Pa., 1947).
KIERNAN, R. H., *The First War in the Air* (London, 1934).
LEHMANN, CAPTAIN ERNST A. and MINGOS, H. L., *The Zeppelins* (New York, 1927).
OUGHTON, FREDERICK, *The Aces* (New York, 1960).
RALEIGH, SIR W. A., and JONES, H. A., *The War in the Air*, 6 vols. (Oxford, 1922–28).
RICKENBACKER, CAPTAIN EDWARD V., *Fighting the Flying Circus* (New York, 1919).
ROSS, ALBERT H., *War on Great Cities* (London, 1937).

Political and Diplomatic Works

BEAVERBROOK, LORD, *Politicians and the War, 1914–1916* (Garden City, N.Y., 1928).
CHAMBERS, FRANK P., *The War Behind the War* (New York, 1939).
GATZKE, HANS W., *Germany's Drive to the West* (Baltimore, Md., 1950).
GORLITZ, WALTER (ed.), *The Kaiser and His Court* (New York, 1964).
KENNAN, GEORGE, *Russia Leaves the War* (Princeton, N.J., 1956).

KING, JERE C., *Generals and Politicians* (Berkeley, Cal., 1951).
LLOYD GEORGE, DAVID, *The War Memoirs of David Lloyd George*, 6 vols. (Boston, 1933–37).
MAY, ERNEST R., *The World War and American Isolation* (Cambridge, Mass., 1959).
MAYER, ARNO J., *The Political Origins of the New Diplomacy, 1914–1917* (New Haven, Conn., 1959).
MEYER, HENRY C., *Mitteleuropa in German Thought and Action* (The Hague, 1955).
RUDIN, HARRY, *The Armistice, 1918* (New Haven, Conn., 1944).

Index